MERCHANT SHIPS: WORLD BUILT

1970 Volume XVIII

Frontispiece: 'MANHATTAN' *see under* 'M'

1970 Volume

Compiled by E. E. SIGWART

Merchant Ships: World Built

Vessels of 1,000 tons gross and over completed in 1969

ADLARD COLES LIMITED

3 Upper James Street, Golden Square, London, W.1

VOLUME XVIII
FIRST PUBLISHED 1970

PRINTED IN GREAT BRITAIN
BY EBENEZER BAYLIS AND SON, LIMITED
THE TRINITY PRESS, WORCESTER, AND LONDON
PUBLISHED IN GREAT BRITAIN BY ADLARD COLES LTD
3 UPPER JAMES STREET GOLDEN SQUARE LONDON W1
ISBN: 0 229 97496 1

PUBLISHER'S NOTE AND ACKNOWLEDGEMENTS

The register is composed mainly of large vessels over 1,000 tons gross, but as tonnage is misleading in giving a picture of the size of a ship (such as is the case with the *paragraph* vessels, which are up to 250 feet in length) a number of vessels of smaller tonnage (minimum overall length 200 feet) have been included. The technology of smaller ships is frequently original and advanced. One or two tugs have also been included, as noteworthy of their class. It will be noted that I have included in the illustrations a number of vessels reported in Volume XVII, of which photographs were not available at the time. Likewise this volume contains descriptions of some interesting ships, and it is hoped to include photographs of these in the next volume. As these volumes are intended to provide a continuous record, I feel that it is better to illustrate a noteworthy ship (such as *Antonio Lazaro*) late, than not at all. With the majority of ships these days being series built or very similar to each other, it is important to show the few being built to non-standard designs.

The publisher wishes to thank the secretary of Lloyd's Register, the editor of Lloyd's List, builders and steamship companies and editors of various shipping journals but in particular Mr W. D. Ewart, editor of *Fairplay* for his most generous and willing help with the illustrations, most of which appeared in his journal. The editor of *Shipping World* also generously assisted, as has Mr Laurence Dunn and Mr A. Duncan with several photographs.

Contents

Introduction

In the last volume it was recorded that over 1,100,000 tons of world shipping in excess of the previous year was launched. In 1969, the year under review, over 2,400,000 tons more than that year (1968) has been sent out on the oceans of the world, and as the majority of the world's shipyards have full order books for the next two or three years, it is likely that even this will be exceeded next year. As statistics at the end of the volume show, this is the fourth year in succession to break records. The four leading countries remain in the same order, but with France moving up to fifth place.

The year has been notable for three events, namely *Manhattan*'s adventurous journey through the North West Passage to Prudhoe Bay, the advent of the LASH ship, *Acadia Forest* with her new concept of transportation (not without labour troubles which were however, surmounted) and the proliferation of container services. *Queen Elizabeth 2* has proved a money spinner, though her first ventures in the cruising world have suggested one or two alterations in her decor, plus a small number of cabins affected by vibration to be rectified. This is in hand, and with normal luck, she should prove all that her owners and designers wish. The Austin & Pickersgill SD 14 (unfortunately misprinted as the SD 161 in the previous volume) goes from success to success, and with the IHI *Freedom* consistently changes places as the leaders in this field each having about 70 ships completed or on order. Ship designers are still producing drawings of revolutionary ships, the giant submarine tanker, super hydrofoils and hovercraft, articulated ships, etc., none of which have gone beyond the drawing board stage. Should *Manhattan*'s second trial voyage prove a success, a new generation of ice-breaking supertankers will emerge, followed possibly by other ice reinforced ships. Tankers of 400,000 tons are now on order, Globtik Tankers of London being the first with one on order from Ishikawajima Harima Heavy Industries in Japan. She is expected to be in service by 1973. Those in the region of 250,000—275,000 tons deadweight are becoming commonplace in the order books.

As regards the spate of mergers previously recorded, most of these are now consolidating and sorting themselves out. Some of the doomed yards have won a reprieve: Burntisland, having been taken over by the Robb-Caledon Group, are to produce parts for the Group ships; Blyth has been acquired by an industrial firm and is to start with a small ship; and Charles Hill's Albion yard at Bristol, again has two small ships under construction. Britain's newest yard, Campbeltown Shipyard Ltd, has launched its first ship, a 50 foot steel trawler. This yard is controlled by the Thames Launch Works Ltd, of Twickenham in association with Ferguson Bros of Port Glasgow, a member of the Scott Lithgow group. The Upper Clyde Shipbuilders have produced a new design of medium bulk carrier, the *Clyde* ship which has received a number of orders, and it seems that this financially-troubled consortium, may, with Government assistance, be moving into a viable concern. At the other end of the scale the well-known yard of James Pollock & Co Ltd, Faversham, builder of small ships, is closing down, being unable to cope with the increased costs of steel and labour. At the moment of going to press it seems that the Tilbury container handling ban may be lifted, with a new pay scheme for London dockers, and thus enable the long suffering UK-Australia container ships to return to their native land from Antwerp.

In addition to the steadily increasing size in bulk carriers of various types, together with the large number of container ships on order, plus a LASH ship for the Holland—America Line from Cockerill, a number of conventional cargo liners are coming off the stocks. British India Line has one more of the Amra class long-hatch ships, together with four 10,900 ton dw general purpose *Manora* class on order, and has just ordered two refrigerated pallet carriers. Strick line has a similar vessel to *Tabaristan* on the stocks, the Ellerman group has had the first of a new class, *City of Liverpool* launched at Dundee, while putting into service on the Liverpool-Lisbon run the container carriers *Minho*, *Tagus* and *Tormes*, all on long-term charter, after more than a century of break-bulk weekly liner service on the trade. But most break-bulk ships on order are designed to carry a number of containers as well as their general cargo. There appears to be a considerable demand for cruising liners. Both Cunard and P & O are reported to be considering ships to replace some of their older tonnage, while the Furness Withy group snapped up the CPSS *Empress of England* as soon as she became surplus to the latter's requirements and renaming her *Ocean Monarch* has placed her under the Shaw Savill flag on its round the world trade. The Norwegians are investing heavily in medium-size passenger cruising liners, mainly for operating in the US-Caribbean trade. Since 1965, they have invested £120,000,000 in 200,000 tons of cruising tonnage, built and building. OY Wartsila of Helsinki has contracted to build six, there are another four or five with German builders, and Swan Hunter is to build one. Three of the Wartsila ships are for the Royal Caribbean Cruise Lines (a consortium of the Gotaas-Larsen, I. M. Skaugen and Anders Wilhelmsen companies) and are of 17,500 tons approximately. Two more of the Wartsila ships are for Det Nordenfjeldske D/S and A. F. Klaveness, both of 22,000 tons, while a third is of 20,000 tons for the Bergen D/S. Another group, Norwegian Cruise Ships A/S (O. Lorentzen & Fearnley & Eger) has two 20,000 tonners under construction at Emden. The Swan Hunter ship is of 24,000 tons for the Norwegian-America Line, similar to the *Sagafjord*. Kloster has three cruise-ferryships of its *Starward* class under construction by A/G Weser, of about 15,000 tons. The latter ship is already in service, and is to be followed by *Skyward*, when they will join the 8,000 ton *Sunward* already operating in the Caribbean. F. Olsen is taking over the 10,000 ton *Blenheim* from Upper Clyde Shipbuilders, and is reported to be considering a second ship. The Danish Nord Line has a 12,500 tonner on order from Vickers, with options for three more ships. The American Overseas National Airways has a 15,000 ton ship building at Rotterdam, with options for two more. In Britain Furness Withy has received tenders as high as £6,000,000 for its proposed 6,000 ton 'Bed and Breakfast' ship, while the beautiful *Andes* is now reaching the economic end of her life, and will doubtless be replaced. American companies find it impossible to compete with all the foreign firms, and their foreign going passenger ships are mostly laid up. American Export has sold *Constitution* to Chandris Lines which has also acquired *President Roosevelt*. The two Moore-McCormack ships *Argentina* and *Brazil*, and *United States* and *Independence* are all laid up in reserve.

From ships to shipyards: in Tunisia, Messrs Lauritzen are examining the possibility of rehabilitating the major French Naval Dockyard at Bizerta, which is at present operating in only a very small way; in Italy, Italcantieri (the merger of Monfalcone, Genoa-Sestri & Castellamare di Stabia yards) can now build tankers of 320,000 tons, in addition to all types of merchant ships—the company has orders for six giants, including two of 251,000 tons; in Spain, Astilleros Espanoles has been formed by the merging of Cia Euskalduna de Construccion y Reparacion de Buques SA of Bilbao, Sociedad Espanola de Construccion Naval, Cadiz, and Astilleros de Cadiz. A further merger is that of Astilleros de Palma and Naviera Mallorquina y Ballester to open the new Mollet shipyards at Palma de Majorca. This is a repair and small-ship building yard. Spain is now a major force in giant tanker construction, having 320,000 tonners on order for the Gulf Oil Co, as well as a number of very large crude carriers completed. In Sweden, where the yards are experiencing financial difficulties, Eriksbergs M/V has acquired the A/B Lindholmens Varv. In Holland Mr Verolme's empire suddenly crashed in financial trouble, but with his resignation from the Board of Directors, the Dutch Government and other companies are contriving to keep the firm going, with various merger rumours circulating at present. The yard, modern and efficient, apparently suffered heavy losses by taking over the Netherlands Dock & Shipbuilding Co, with a labour shortage and insufficient reserves. Three famous Dutch liner companies are negotiating a merger. These are N. V. Stoomvaart Maatschappij Nederland, Koninlijke Rotterdam Lloyd and Koninlijke Java-China Paketvaart Lijnen. They are already connected through the Nederlandsche Scheepvaart Unie, a holding company with the majority of their shares, and a fourth line, the Vereenigde Nederlandsche Scheepsvaart Maatsschappij is expected to join. The result will be one of the world's major shipping firms. The first three have 196 ships with an aggregate of over 2,000,000 tons, while the latter has 36 ships of 410,000 gross register tons. The Swan Hunter subsidiary in Malta has received orders for two 420 ton dw coasters, the yard having already built a small amount of small specialized shipping. In Scandinavia, the eastern trade of the three countries has been centralized in Scanservice, jointly operated by the Wilhelmsen Line of Oslo, Swedish Asiatic Co, and the East Asiatic Co of Copenhagen. At present operating with conventional ships, four 1700 foot × 20 foot container ships are on order individually (E. Asiatic, two from Burmeister & Wain, Swedish East Asiatic one from Oresundsvarvet and Wilhelmsen, one from Tamano) at a total cost of £35,500,000. A similar container service is to be run in opposition to the pool of OCL, ACT and the other European lines by Scanaustral (Scandinavian Australia Carriers in which Wilhelmsen is the dominating partner to the extent of 50% participation, with Transatlantic SS Co (Gothenburg), and East Asiatic Co (Copenhagen) as its partners. It has ordered five 20,000 ton RoRo container ships carrying between 800/850 containers at a speed of 22 knots, and costing £26,500,000. After the loss of the two ore carriers *California Maru* and *Bolivar Maru* which broke in two and sank near the Japanese coast, the former recently and the latter a year ago, both in stormy seas, the Japanese Government has ordered an investigation into the structural strength of these plus 69 other ships all exceeding 656 feet in length and of over 50,000 tons deadweight. The ships are owned by sixteen different shipowners.

Among the Danube countries the Austrian yard of Korneuburg Schiffswerft A/S has orders for nine ships, four of 500 tons and five of 1000 tons gross for container carrying for the Dutch owner Johannes Bos, while Roumania, Bulgaria (building a 25,000 tons bulk carrier) and Hungary are building quite large ships.

Technical designs of the year include a revolutionary marine diesel engine from Burmeister & Wain, still on the drawing board with little disclosed, but which operates without crankshaft, and with pistons rotating the propeller shaft by means of hydraulic oil. When built, this engine will undergo long development tests. Mr J. A. Teasdale, a lecturer at Newcastle University Department of Naval Architecture has developed a coupling device, making the articulated ship possible. Vosper-Thornycroft has a minesweeper of 153 feet in length to build for the Royal Navy with a glass reinforced plastic hull, which, as far as is known, is the largest hull in the world of this type. In Japan Mitubishi is planning to fit a 200,000 ton oil tanker with eight nylon parachutes to shorten the stopping distance (of nearly 2½ miles after emergency stopping procedures at full speed) as an experiment. Ocean Aids in Britain has established a service in assisting repairs to ships at sea by the use of helicopters. They fly out and pick up the defective piece of machinery, fly it back to the repairers, to be ready for installation when the ship docks. This was successfully accomplished with the tanker *Bamford*, the helicopter winching the defective motors from the deck, flying back to St Just to refuel, then on to Tilbury to the London Graving Docks Company landing pad. Wartsila O/Y, the world's leading expert on icy-water traffic and ice breakers, is exploring the possibility of building ice breaking tankers. At the same time Messrs Lambert Bros (Shipping) Ltd, has calculated that a 500,000 ton tanker would need to operate at 16·5 knots with a shaft horsepower of 70,000 to prove economic. The ship would be 1240 × 213·5 × 124·7 feet in dimensions, with a draught of 88·6 feet. Under the Liberian flag she could undertake a time charter at $1·15 per ton dw per month, giving the owner a return of 10%.

The year 1969 therefore ends with the British shipbuilding industry facing the next decade in a confident and buoyant mood, with an order book of 4,500,000 tons, the highest for ten years. Labour relations continue to improve with employers, but the internal troubles of the unions are not in as satisfactory a state. Demarcation stoppages are ending with new agreements signed. A cloud of serious proportions is the rising price of steel, British steel being more expensive than European.

As a footnote, it has been announced that the pioneer nuclear ship *Savannah* is to be laid up as uneconomic, presumably having served her purpose as a 'trials horse'.

Westcliff-on-Sea, 1970. E.E.S.

Abbreviations

bb	Bulbous bow	loa	Length overall
bhp	Brake horse power	m	Moulded breadth
cpp	Controllable pitch propeller	na	Information not available
btp	Bow thrust propeller	OSD/CSD	Open/closed shelter deck
cu ft	Cubic feet	Pass	Passenger
cyl	Cylinder	r	Registered length
dw	Deadweight	ref	Refrigerated
grd	Geared	rpm	Revolutions per minute
ihp	Indicated horse power	sc	Screw
LASH	Lighter aboard ship	shp	Shaft horse power
lbp	Length between perpendiculars	tw	Twin

NOTE: The dimensions and tonnages given for ships of this class are normally those for "OPEN" condition.

CONVERSION TABLES - FEET TO METRES

Feet	*Metres*	*Feet*	*Metres*	*Feet*	*Metres*	*Feet*	*Metres*	*Feet*	*Metres*	*Feet*	*Metres*	*Feet*	*Metres*
1 ...	**0·305**	40 ...	12·192	250 ...	76·2	370 ...	112·8	490 ...	149·3	610 ...	185·9	730 ...	222·5
2 ...	**0·610**	50 ...	15·240	260 ...	79·2	380 ...	115·8	500 ...	152·4	620 ...	189·0	740 ...	225·6
3 ...	**0·914**	60 ...	18·288	270 ...	82·3	390 ...	118·9	510 ...	155·5	630 ...	192·0	750 ...	228·6
4 ...	**1·219**	70 ...	21·336	280 ...	85·3	400 ...	121·9	520 ...	158·5	640 ...	195·1	760 ...	231·7
5 ...	**1·524**	80 ...	24·384	290 ...	88·4	410 ...	125·0	530 ...	161·5	650 ...	198·1	770 ...	234·7
6 ...	**1·829**	90 ...	27·432	300 ...	91·4	420 ...	128·0	540 ...	164·6	660 ...	201·2	780 ...	237·8
7 ...	**2·134**	100 ...	30·480	310 ...	94·5	430 ...	131·1	550 ...	167·6	670 ...	204·2	790 ...	240·9
8 ...	**2·438**	200 ...	60·9	320 ...	97·5	440 ...	134·1	560 ...	170·7	680 ...	207·3	800 ...	243·9
9 ...	**2·743**	210 ...	64·0	330 ...	100·6	450 ...	137·2	570 ...	173·7	690 ...	210·3	900 ...	274·5
10 ...	**3·048**	220 ...	67·1	340 ...	103·6	460 ...	140·2	580 ...	176·8	700 ...	213·4	1000 ...	305·0
20 ...	6·096	230 ...	70·1	350 ...	106·7	470 ...	143·2	590 ...	179·8	710 ...	216·4	1100 ...	335·5
30 ...	9·144	240 ...	73·2	360 ...	109·7	480 ...	146·3	600 ...	182·9	720 ...	219·5	1200 ...	366·0

Alphabetical Register of Merchant Ships
1,000 tons gross and over

It is stressed that gross tonnage may be misleading in estimating the size of a ship. The tonnages used in this volume are from the latest corrections to the current Lloyd's Register at the time of going to print. However, as the ships are all new their tonnages are subject to revision with final measurements. Again, the new Freeboard Rules allow tankers and bulkers and other ships with the necessary steel fittings to carry a larger deadweight, amounting in large bulk ships, to many thousand tons. Change to the Liberian register, with American tonnage exemptions, may considerably reduce a ship's gross tonnage. Full particulars are not always available, especially for ships built abroad. A number of Russian ships have been reported in the Press which have not yet appeared in Lloyd's Register, and of which details are not yet available. They are not included in this register.

A

AALBORGHUS. *Danish.* Passenger and car ferry. Built by Cant. Nav. del Tirreno e Riuniti, Riva Trigoso, for Det forenede D/S, Alborg (DFDS). 7,698 tons gross, 1,083 tons dw, 409·92ft. loa × 63·18ft breadth × 17·09ft draught, two 12-cyl CNTR-B & W diesel, 13,200bhp, 20 knots.

ABERAVON. *British.* Grab dredger (hopper). Built by Ferguson Bros, Port Glasgow, Ltd, Port Glasgow, for British Transport Docks Board, Cardiff. 2,200 tons gross, 2,600 tons dw, 251·09ft loa × 50·09ft breadth × 16·5ft draught, two 12-cyl Paxman diesel, 3,000bhp, 11 knots.

ACADIA FOREST. *Norwegian.* Carrier (LASH). Built by Uraga HI, Ltd, Yokosuka, for A/S Moslash Shipping Co (Torrey Mosvold), Kristiansand. 36,862 tons gross, 43,000 tons dw, 859·58ft loa (incl bb) × 106·58ft m breadth × 36·92ft draught, cyl na, Sulzer diesel, 26,000bhp knots na.

ACT 1. *British.* Container ship, ref. Built by Bremer Vulkan, Vegesack, for Associated Container Transportation Ltd, London. 24,821 tons gross, 26,400 tons dw, 715ft loa (incl bb) × 95·25ft breadth × 34·5ft draught, Bremer, Vulkan-Stal Laval turbs, 30,000shp, 22 knots.

ACT 2. *British.* Container ship (1,223 × 20ft containers) ref 4 pass. Built by Bremer Vulkan, Vegesack, for Associated Container Transportation Ltd, London. 24,821 tons gross, 26,400 tons dw, 712·75ft loa × 95·25ft breadth × 34·5ft draught, Bremer-Vulkan Stal Laval turbs, 30,000shp, 22 knots.

ACTIVITY (Sis ASPERITY). *British.* Tanker. Built by N. V. Nieuw Noord Ned. Schps, Groningen, for F. T. Everard & Sons Ltd, London. 698 tons gross, 1,300 tons dw, 242·58ft loa × 34·09ft breadth × 13ft draught, 6-cyl Deutz diesel (btp), 1,380bhp, 12 knots.

ADAMAS. *Greek.* Cargo. Built by Ishikawajima-Harima HI, Nagoya, for Elikon Shipping Co, SA, Piraeus. 10,121 tons gross, 14,700 tons dw, 466·75ft loa (incl bb) × 65·09ft breadth × 29·64ft draught, 12-cyl Ishikawajima-Pielstick diesel, 5,130bhp, knots na.

AEGIR. *Icelandic.* Coastguard/salvage ship. Built by Aalborg Vaerft A/S, Aalborg, 1968, for Government of Iceland, Reykjavik. 927 tons gross, 150 tons dw, 229·18ft loa × 33·18ft breadth × 15·41ft draught, two 4-cyl tw sc MAN diesel, cpp, 8,600bhp, 19 knots.

AEGIS BANNER. *Greek.* Cargo. Built by Hellenic Shipyards, Skaramanga, for Cia. Nav. Marogulo SA, Piraeus. 9,000 tons gross, 15,000 tons dw, 462·5ft loa × 67·41ft breadth × 29ft draught, 5-cyl Sulzer diesel, 5,000bhp knots na.

AEGIS FAITH. *Greek.* Cargo (Liberty replacement type). Built by Bremer Vulkan, Vegesack, for Speedwell Shpg Co, Piraeus. 9,355 tons gross, 14,800 tons dw, 457·84ft loa × 69·09ft breadth × 29·58ft draught, 6-cyl Bremer Vulkan-MAN diesel, 7,200bhp, 15·5 knots.

AEGIS FAME. *Greek (Cyprus).* Cargo. Built by Hellenic Shipyards, Skaramanga, for Fame Shipping Co, Famagusta. 9,241 tons gross, 15,000 tons dw, 462·5ft loa × 67·5ft breadth × 29ft draught, 5-cyl Sulzer diesel, 5,500bhp, knots na.

AEGIS PIONEER. *Greek.* Cargo. Built by Bremer Vulkan, Vegesack, for Speedwell Shpg Co, Piraeus. 9,355 tons gross, 14,800 tons dw, 457·84ft loa × 68·92ft m breadth × 29·6ft draught, 6-cyl Bremer Vulkan-MAN diesel, 7,200bhp, 15·7 knots.

AGAPI. *Greek.* Cargo (25th Freedom type). Built by Ishikawajima-Harima HI, Tokyo, for Agapi Shpg Co, Piraeus. 10,006 tons gross, 14,912 tons dw, 466·75ft loa (incl bb) × 65·18ft breadth × 29·7ft draught, 12-cyl IHI-Pielstick diesel, 5,130bhp, 14·25 knots.

AGIP ROMA (Sis AGIP MILANO). *Italian.* Tanker. Built by Cantieri Nav. del Tirreno e Rinuiti SpA, Palermo 1968, for 'SNAM' Soc. Nat. Metanodotti SpA, Palermo. 46,975 tons gross, 83,740 tons dw, 846·5ft loa (incl bb) × 123·25ft breadth × 43·77ft draught, 10-cyl Fiat diesel, 23,000bhp, 17 knots.

AIKO MARU. *Japanese.* Cargo. Built by Tohoku Zosen, Shiogama, 1968, for Nakajima Kyodo KK, Nakajima. 2,985 tons gross, 4,825 tons dw, 319·25ft loa × 49·92ft breadth × 20·84ft draught, 6-cyl Ito Tekkosho diesel, 3,400bhp, 12·75 knots.

AINO (Sis SKAUFAST). *Norwegian.* Bulk carrier (ore). Built by Harland & Wolff, Belfast, for C. H. Sorensen & Sonner, Arendal. 57,204 tons gross, 106,500 tons dw, 855ft loa (incl bb) × 133·66ft breadth × 45·7ft draught, 9-cyl H & W, B & W diesel, 18,900bhp, 16 knots.

Aalborghus (not illustrated). Similar in appearance to the Winston Churchill and England, this ship and her sister, the Trekronor are however designed for the Copenhagen-Halsingborg-Aarhus route in the summer, and direct between Copenhagen-Aarhus in the winter, leaving the former at 2315 and arriving at Aarhus at 0745 next day. Built in Italy, they were delivered three months late owing to labour trouble in that country, but the Italian prices were most competitive compared with the Danish, and the owners state the quality of the Italian ships is fully equal to Danish building. The ship has accommodation for 950 passengers in two classes, and cabin accommodation for 456 plus reclining seats for 221. Bow and stern doors, together with fore and aft side ports on the port side are provided for all drive on and off types of vehicles, with a total capacity of about 135. A cargo hold is situated below the vehicle deck. Lounges, night clubs and bars are provided in addition to the restaurants. Propulsion is by twin B & W 42-VT2BF-90 diesels with a total of 12,000ihp for 21 knots service speed. Sperry retractable stabilizer fins and a bow thrust are fitted.

Act 2. (For illustration see jacket). This description applies equally to the two sister ships, namely Act 1 and Australian Endeavour (ex Act 3). They are single screw steam turbine refrigerated and general cargo container ships, designed especially for the UK-Australia container service, and capable of carrying 1,223 standard ISO containers, of the 20ft × 8ft × 8ft size at a service speed of $22\frac{1}{2}$ knots. The Associated Container Transport Ltd (the owners of the ships), are running them in conjunction with the BAY ships of Overseas Container Lines, the third ship being taken over by the Australian Coastal Shipping Commission and renamed.

The main steam turbine engines produce 30,000shp at 137 maximum revolutions, continuous rating, or a service horse power of 28,000 at 134rpm. The crew accommodation is air conditioned, with individual cabins, with private shower and toilet facilities. Other amenities are an iced water supply, television, laundries, hobby rooms, built in swimming pool, games rooms, bar, etc.

Of the containers, 455 are carried on deck, with 768 distributed throughout the ship's ten cellular holds, of which $3\frac{1}{2}$ (8, 9, 10 and 7 port) are designed for refrigerated containers. 40ft containers may be carried on deck if required, and in general, the holds may be likewise converted for any size of container. In the holds they are stacked 6 high and 8 abreast, whilst on deck they are stacked 3 high and 10 abreast. The first layer of deck units are secured by studs incorporated in the hatch covers, with the other two tiers being lashed in place above. They are designed to load and discharge solely by shore based cranes at Tilbury (not yet being used owing to difficulties with the dockers), Fremantle, Melbourne and Sydney. The Navigational equipment is very comprehensive (radio, VHF telephony, echo sounder by Kelvin-Hughes, Arma Brown Mark II gyro compass and auto pilot, D/F, two independent Decca Transistor true motion radars with automatic relative plotter, Decca Navigator, SAL log, off course monitor, and rpm indicators). Two motor lifeboats with Lister engines, capable of accommodating 55 persons each, with various rafts are carried. Two stabilization tanks of NPL design which may be filled with sea water and used for roll damping are situated at the forward end of the engine room. To ensure that the ship remains upright whilst working cargo, an automatic sensing device, working within plus or minus 3 degrees, automatically controls all transfer ballast pumps. Various electric monitoring devices are fitted throughout the ship, and automation is employed to a high degree, with remote control from both bridge and engine room. Cargo holds and engine room are protected from fire by a CO_2 flooding installation, with additionally a Siemens fire protection system in the engine room.

The comprehensive refrigeration machinery is provided with a data logger, and is designed to cope with deep frozen, normal frozen, deciduous and other cargoes. The containers are maintained at the desired temperatures by air circulation, the air being cooled by the latest type of fin coolers in cooler rooms at the sides of the cell. Visual and audible alarms are fitted, and inspection of the holds is greatly assisted by the innovation of twin bulkheads at the ends of the cells, which form cofferdams athwartships. Catwalks are provided in these which form a useful access to the holds. The company have ordered a Ro-Ro container ship from Eriksbergs, to be operated jointly with the Transatlantic SS Co of Gothenburg, on the service from Australia to the West Coast of USA and Canada.

A

(a)

(b)

(*a*) Acadia Forest (*b*) *Her LASH barges*

Shipping LASH barge

Acadia Forest. *The first ship in an entirely new system of mercantile transport, designed to co-ordinate inland and ocean water transport, sailed in October 1969 from US Gulf ports to the UK and Rotterdam. She discharged her UK cargo at a buoy in the Medway entrance and loaded there also. The idea behind the LASH (Lighter aboard ship) system is to utilize the vast inland waterway and port network of the world to offer a 'door to door' delivery. The ship wastes little time in port, as she can load or discharge a loaded 500 ton barge every 15 minutes with her own crane, giving a total handling capacity of 27,000 long tons of cargo in a 24 hour period. This first ship, operating on a 30 day turn round cycle (on the above route) spends nearly all her time at sea carrying 73 loaded barges, whilst similar ones are being filled and emptied at her ports of call in readiness for her arrival. When her sister ship is in service, they will offer a 15 day service, with barges being loaded up rivers and canals far from the seaport, and towed there for onward dispatch. Operated by Central Gulf Lines based in New Orleans, she is under long-term time charter from A/S Mosvold Shipping Co, Kristiansand, who had her constructed in Japan.*

Of 43,000 tons deadweight, she carries 73 loaded barges, in her holds and on deck, at a speed of about 20 knots. Each barge, uniform in size and capacity, measures 61·5ft×31·2ft×13ft, weighing 82 tons light, and capable of carrying 370 tons weight or 19,000cu ft of cargo at a loaded draught of 8·5ft. They are handled by an enormous 510-ton capacity travelling gantry crane on board the ship, giving her one of the greatest lifting capacities afloat. The rails are 210 metres long to the end of her cantilevered stern. Barges are quickly secured to the crane hooks by hydraulic latching devices. Her eastbound voyages at the moment are under contract to the International Paper Company, carrying about 250,000 tons of pulp annually (with products), returning to the United States with general cargo. It was due to her strong commitment with the paper company that her name was chosen, as the first paper produced from ground wood in America was from Novia Scotia, then known as Acadia. The maximum advantages claimed for the system are those of avoiding congestion in port, eliminating large capital expenditure on terminals, serving small ports inaccessible to ocean ships, assuring a steady flow of goods, keeping the ocean vessel in port for a minimum time, and one bill through loading, facilitating clearance and entrance of cargo. The ship was built by the Sumitomo Shipbuilding & Machinery Co under license from LASH systems Inc, the ship and barges were designed by Friede and Goldman, Naval Architects, New Orleans, and barges built by Equitable-Higgins Shipyards, New Orleans. The 2 ships will require a fleet of 383 barges for their operations. The Holland-America line (NASM) have ordered a 43,000 ton LASH ship from the Cockerill yard.

Aino *is one of two 106,500 ton bulk carriers built by Harland & Wolff at Belfast for Norwegian owners. The other ship, the* Skaufast *was illustrated in Vol XVII. They are the largest bulk carriers so far built at Belfast, and are fitted with H & W-B & W 84VT2BF-180 diesel engines with an output of 20,700bhp at 114rpm.*

AIU-DAG. *Russian.* Stern trawler, fish factory (ATLANTIK class). Built by Volkswerft Stralsund, Stralsund, 1967, for USSR. 2,657 tons gross, tons dw na, 269·58ft loa × 44·58ft m breadth × 16·41ft draught, two 8-cyl Liebknecht diesels, s sc, 2,320bhp, 13·25 knots.

AJKAL. *Russian.* Tanker. Built by Rauma-Repola O/Y, Rauma, 1967, for USSR. 3,500 tons gross, 4,600 tons dw, 348·25ft loa × 50·66ft breadth × 21·33ft draught, 5-cyl Bryansk-B & W diesel, 2,900bhp, 14 knots.

AKADEMIK FILATOV. *Russian.* Cargo, 8 pass. Built by Warnowwerft, Warnemunde, for USSR. 9,727 tons gross, 12,882 tons dw, 496·92ft loa × 66·66ft breadth × 28·86ft draught, 8-cyl DMR (Dieselmotorenwerk) MAN diesel, 9,600bhp, knots na.

AKADEMIK RYKACHYEV. *Russian.* Cargo. Built by Warnowwerft, Warnemunde, for USSR. 9,727 tons gross, 12,882 tons dw, 496·92ft loa × 66·66ft breadth × 28·86ft draught, 8-cyl DMR-MAN diesel, 9,600bhp, knots na.

AKADEMIK VERNADSKY. *Russian.* Research ship. Built by Mathias Thesen Werft, Wismar, 1967, for USSR, Sevastopol. 5,460 tons gross, 1,986 tons dw, 407·41ft loa × breadth na × 19·5ft draught, two 6-cyl tw sc Halberstadt-MAN diesel, 8,000bhp knots na.

AKADEMIK YUREYEV. *Russian.* Cargo. Built by Warnowwerft, Warnemunde, for USSR. 9,227 tons gross, 12,882 tons dw, 496·92ft loa × 66·66ft breadth × 28·86ft draught, 8-cyl DMR-MAN diesel, 9,600bhp, knots na.

AKADEMIK ZHUKOV. *Russian.* Cargo. Built by Warnowwerft, Warnemunde, for USSR. 9,727 tons gross, 12,882 tons dw, 496·92ft loa × 66·66ft breadth × 28·86ft draught, 8-cyl DMR-MAN diesel, 9,600bhp, knots na.

AKAKURA MARU. *Japanese.* Cargo. Built by Imabari Zosen, Imabari, 1968, for Niigata Rinko Kairiku Unso KK, Niigata. 2,984 tons gross, 5,500 tons dw, 308·41ft lbp × 51·58ft breadth × 21·66ft draught, 6-cyl Mitsubishi-Sulzer diesel, 3,300bhp, 12 knots.

AKHALTSIKHE. *Russian.* Tanker. Built by Rauma Repola O/Y, Rauma, for USSR. 3,675 tons gross, 5,000 tons dw, 348·25ft loa × 50·66ft breadth × 21·33ft draught, 5-cyl Valmet diesel, 2,900bhp, knots na.

AKHTUBA. *Russian.* Stern trawler, fish factory (ATLANTIK class). Built by Volkswerft Stralsund, Stralsund, 1967, for USSR. 2,650 tons gross, 1,152 tons dw, 269·58ft loa × 44·75ft breadth × 16·92ft draught, two 8-cyl s sc Liebknecht diesel, cpp, 2,320bhp, 13·5 knots.

AKHTUBA. *Russian.* Fishing, ref. Built by Mathias Thesen Werft, Wismar, for USSR. 1,110 tons gross, tons dw na, 214·92ft loa × 36·41ft m breadth × 11·84ft draught, 8-cyl Liebknecht diesel, 825bhp, knots na.

AKHUN (originally reported as AHUN). *Russian.* Fish factory, stern trawler (ATLANTIK class). Built by Volkswerft Stralsund, Stralsund, 1967, for USSR, Kerch. 2,650 tons gross, 1,152 tons dw, 269·58ft loa × 44·75ft breadth × 17·09ft draught, two 8-cyl s sc Liebknecht diesel, cpp, 2,320bhp, 13·5 knots.

AKI MARU. *Japanese.* Cargo (timber). Built by Tsuneishi Zosen, Numakuma, 1968, for Bingo Kyodo KKK, Numakuma. 2,995 tons gross, 5,113 tons dw, 334·33ft loa × 49·33ft breadth × 20·84ft draught, 6-cyl Mitsubishi diesel, 3,500bhp, 13 knots.

AKISHIMA MARU. *Japanese.* Cargo. Built by Kurushima Dock Co Ltd, Imabari, for Chuyo Kyodo KK, Matsuyama. 10,033 tons gross, 15,849 tons dw, 446·25ft lbp × 71·58ft breadth × 28ft draught, 6-cyl Kawasaki-MAN diesel, 7,500bhp, 14·5 knots.

AKTAU. *Russian.* Tanker. Built by Rauma-Repola O/Y, Rauma, 1967, for USSR. 3,674 tons gross, 4,962 tons dw, 347·75ft loa × 50·66ft breadth × 22·15ft draught, 5-cyl Bryansk-B & W diesel, 2,900bhp, 13·5 knots.

AKUSTIK. *Russian.* Stern trawler, fish factory (ATLANTIK class). Built by Volkswerft Stralsund, Stralsund, 1967, for USSR, Nakhodka. 2,657 tons gross, 1,152 tons dw, 269·58ft loa × 44·75ft breadth × 16·92ft draught, two 8-cyl s sc Liebknecht diesels, 2,320bhp, knots na.

AL FUNTAS. *Kuwait.* Tanker. Built by Sasebo HI, Sasebo, for Kuwait Oil Tanker Co Ltd, Kuwait (Common Bros, Management, Ltd). 107,409 tons gross, 208,810 tons dw, 1,067·33ft loa (incl bb) × 158·25ft breadth × 62ft draught, Ishikawajima turbs, 30,000shp, knots na.

Alaskan (ex *hospital ship* Haven)

She was originally laid down as the C4-S-B2 freighter Marine Hawk *but converted whilst building to USN requirements. As a hospital ship she saw service during World War II in the Pacific, and again later, in the Korean conflict. She then served as a dispensary ship in Long Beach until laid up in Suisun Bay, San Francisco in 1967. She was then acquired by her present owners, towed to the Bethlehem Steel Co's yard at Beaumont where at a total cost of the project (conversion and jumboizing) of $6,000,000 she emerged as the* Alaskan. *As the* Haven *she was 520ft overall, but when jumboized with a new 330ft long central section she acquired a length of 665ft, the same breadth and depth as before, and with the original bow and stern. There are 28 cargo compartments, each with an independent loading and dischcrging line with 28 pumps. There are 3 stainless steel tanks on deck aft with independent stainless steel piping and pumps. She is intended for liquid chemical carrying, of many different types.*

AL GHAZAL. *British*. Tanker. Built by N. V. Nieuwe Noord Ned. Schps., Groningen, 1968, for Dilmun Navigation Co Ltd, London. 653 tons gross, 1,200 tons dw, 223·66ft loa × 33·66ft breadth × 12·6ft draught, 8-cyl Deutz diesel, 1,060bhp, 11·5 knots.

AL JABIRIAH. *Kuwait*. Cargo, ref. Built by Kherson Shipyard, Kherson, 1968, for Kuwait Shipping Co (SAK), Kuwait. 10,355 tons gross, 12,760 tons dw, 510·75ft loa × 67·66ft breadth × 29·75ft draught, 6-cyl Bryansk diesel, 9,000bhp, knots na.

AL-PETRI. *Russian*. Stern trawler, fish factory (ATLANTIK class). Built by Volkswerft Stralsund, Stralsund, 1967, for USSR. 2,657 tons gross, tons dw na, 269·58ft loa × 44·58ft m breadth × 16·41ft draught, two 8-cyl s sc Liebknecht diesel, 2,320bhp, 13·25 knots.

AL SHAMIAH. *Kuwait*. Cargo, ref. Built by Nosenko Shipyard, Nikolaev, 1968, for Kuwait Shipping Co (SAK), Kuwait. 11,670 tons gross, 16,584 tons dw, 556·5ft loa × 71·58ft breadth × 32·8ft draught, 6-cyl Bryansk-B & W diesel, 12,000bhp, knots na.

ALASKA MARU. *Japanese*. Cargo. Built by Sanoyasu Dkyd Co Ltd, Osaka, for Marounouchi KKK, Tokyo. 15,572 tons gross, 22,750 tons dw, 508·5ft loa × 76·84ft breadth × 34·75ft draught, 7-cyl Uraga-Sulzer diesel, 8,400bhp, knots na.

ALASKAN (ex CLENDENIN, ex hospital ship HAVEN, ex MARINE HAWK). *USA*. Chemical tanker. Built by Sun SB & DD Co, Chester, 1944 (bow and stern sections), Bethlehem Steel Corpn, Beaumont (cargo section), 1969, for Morgan Guarantee Trust Co, New York. 15,222 tons gross, 24,437 tons dw, 665ft loa × 71·66ft breadth × 34·21ft draught, GEC turbs, 9,000shp, 17 knots.

ALBA. *Russian*. Stern Trawler, fish factory (ATLANTIK class). Built by Volkswerft Stralsund, Stralsund, 1967, for USSR. 2,657 tons gross, tons dw na, 269·58ft loa × 44·75ft breadth × 16·66ft draught, 2 × 8-cyl s sc Liebknecht diesel, 2,320bhp, 13·25 knots.

ALBERT FRIESECKE (Sis BISMARCKSTEIN). *German*. Cargo (63 containers × 20ft). Built by J. J. Sietas Schiffsw, Hamburg, 1968, for P. Dohle, Hamburg. 499 tons gross, 1,320 tons dw, 243ft loa × 35·5ft breadth × 12·92ft draught, 8-cyl Deutz diesel, 1,000bhp, 12·5 knots.

ALBION. *Liberian*. Bulk carrier. Built by Nippon Kokan KK, Shimizu, for Davenport Maritime Panama SA (A. Onassis), Monrovia. 15,808 tons gross, 26,000 tons dw, 576·09ft loa × 75·18ft breadth × 35·97ft draught, 8-cyl IHI-Sulzer diesel, 12,000bhp, 16·25 knots.

ALDENBURG. *German*. Cargo ref OSD/CSD. Built by Howaldtswerke-Deutsche Werft, Kiel, for H. Schuldt, Hamburg. 3,844/5,753 tons gross, 4,508/7,450 tons dw, 485·58ft loa × 63·09ft breadth × 21·41/26·56ft draught, 10-cyl Howaldt-MAN diesel, 14,000bhp, 23 knots.

ALEKSANDR PANKRATOV. *Russian*. Cargo. Builder na, Vyborg, for USSR. 1,816 tons gross, 2,260 tons dw, 269ft loa × 41ft breadth × draught na, cyl na, diesel, bhp na, knots na.

ALEKSEY. *Russian*. Stern trawler, fish factory (ATLANTIK class). Built by Volkswerft Stralsund, Stralsund, 1967, for USSR. 2,657 tons gross, tons dw na, 269·58ft loa × 44·62ft m breadth × 16·41ft draught, two 8-cyl s sc Liebknecht diesel, 2,320 bhp, 13·25 knots.

ALFA. *Brazilian*. Cargo OSD/CSD. Built by EMAQ Eng. Maq. SA, Rio de Janeiro, 1968, for Navegacao Continental Ltda, Rio de Janeiro. 1,260/1,992 tons gross, 2,272/3,040 tons dw, 259·58ft loa × 41·09ft breadth × 16·23/20·25ft draught, 6-cyl Villares-B & W diesel, 1,680bhp, 11·75 knots.

ALIAKMON. *Liberian*. Bulk carrier (ore). Built by Hakodate Dock Co Ltd, Muroran, 1968, for S. Livanos, Monrovia. 16,475 tons gross, 28,679 tons dw, 593·18ft loa (incl bb) × 76ft breadth × 35·05ft draught, 7-cyl IHI-Sulzer diesel, 11,200bhp, 15 knots.

ALISHER NAVOI. *Russian*. Cargo. Built by Brodogradiliste 3rd Maj, Rijeka, for USSR, Vladivostok. 11,290 tons gross, 13,778 tons dw, 522·92ft loa × 69·84ft breadth × 31·56ft draught, 8-cyl 3rd Maj-Sulzer diesel, 12,000bhp, knots na.

ALSTER EXPRESS. *German*. Container ship (728 × 20ft containers). Built by Blohm & Voss AG, Hamburg, for Hamburg-Amerika Linie, Hamburg. 14,071 tons gross, 11,000 tons dw, 560·75ft loa (incl bb) × 80·84ft breadth × 25·88ft draught, 9-cyl B & V-MAN diesel, 15,750bhp, 19 knots.

Alba. *One of the very large series of Atlantik class refrigerated stern trawlers ordered by the USSR from Volkswerft Stralsund, Stralsund. They are frequently noted in the register of this volume, and 107 have been ordered, one or two of them being transferred to satellite countries of Russia. The series has been in production now for one or two years.*

ALVARO OBREGON. *Mexican*. Tanker. Built by Ishikawajima-Harima HI, Nagoya, 1968, for Petroleos Mexicanos, Salina Cruz. 12,753 tons gross, 20,463 tons dw, 560·18ft loa × 72·41ft breadth × 29·96ft draught, 7-cyl IHI-Sulzer diesel, 8,000bhp, 14·75 knots.

AMATINA CAMARA. *Brazilian*. Bulk carrier (ore). Built by Cia Com. e Nav. Estaleiro Maua, Rio de Janeiro, 1968, for Navegacao Mercantil, Rio de Janeiro. 13,080 tons gross, 18,170 tons dw, 555·09ft loa × 70·25ft breadth × 30·05ft draught, 7-cyl Pesada-MAN diesel, 8,400 bhp, 15·75 knots.

AMBER PACIFIC. *British*. Bulk carrier. Built by Doxford & Sunderland SB & E Co Ltd, Sunderland, for Fife Shipping Co Ltd, London. 31,409 tons gross, 57,150 tons dw, 723·92ft loa × 104·18ft breadth × 41·31ft draught, 6-cyl Doxford diesel, 15,000bhp knots na.

AMDERMA. *Russian*. Stern trawler, fish factory (ATLANTIK class). Built by Volkswerft Stralsund, Stralsund, 1967, for USSR. 2,657 tons gross, tons dw na, 269·41ft loa × 44·58ft m breadth × 16·41ft draught, two 8-cyl s sc Liebknecht diesel, 2,320shp, 13·5 knots.

AMERICAN ASTRONAUT (originally to be AMERICAN LEADER). *USA*. Container ship. Built by Sun SB & DD Co Inc, Chester, Pa, for United States Lines, Inc, New York. 18,876 tons gross, 20,574 tons dw, 700·5ft loa × 90·18ft breadth × 32·14ft draught, GEC turbs, 27,300shp, 22 knots.

AMERICAN LARK. *USA*. Container ship (1,210 × 20ft containers). Built by Sun SB & DD Co, Chester, Pa, for United States Lines Inc, New York. 18,876 tons gross, 20,574 tons dw, 700·5ft loa × 90·18ft breadth × 32·14ft draught, GEC turbs, 27,300shp, 22 knots.

AMERICAN MAIL. *USA*. Cargo ref. Built by Newport News SB & DD Co, Newport News, for American Mail Line Ltd, Portland, Ore. 15,500 tons gross, 20,978 tons dw, 605ft loa × 82·18ft breadth × 33·96ft draught, GEC turbs, 21,600shp, knots na.

AMOCO BALTIMORE. *Liberian*. Tanker. Built by Mitsui Zosen, Tamano, for Interhemisphere Transport Co, Monrovia. 38,715 tons gross, 78,061 tons dw, 789·18ft loa (incl bb) × 118·18ft breadth × 44·25ft draught, 8-cyl, Mitsui-B & W diesel, 18,400bhp, 15·75 knots.

AMOCO YORKTOWN. *Liberian*. Tanker. Built by Mitsui Zosen, Tamano, for Interhemisphere Transportation Co, Monrovia (American Oil Co, Chicago). 38,714 tons gross, 78,061 tons dw, 789·18ft loa (incl bb) × 118·18ft breadth × 44·25ft draught, 8-cyl Mitsui-B & W diesel, 18,400bhp, 15·75 knots.

AMRA. *British*. Cargo. Built by Swan Hunter Shipbuilders Ltd, Readhead Yard, South Shields, for British India Steam Nav. Co Ltd, London. 10,031 tons gross, 13,950 tons dw, 503·75ft loa × 70·18ft breadth × 31·5ft draught, 6-cyl H & W, B & W diesel, 11,600bhp, knots na.

AMURSKIY ZALIV. *Russian*. Fish carrier ref. Built by Dubigeon-Normandie SA, Nantes, for USSR, Sevastopol. 13,000 tons gross, tons dw na, 540ft loa × 72·33ft breadth × 26·25ft draught, two 12-cyl s sc Bretagne-Pielstick diesel, 11,160bhp, 17·5 knots.

ANA MARIA BARRERAS. *Spanish*. Cargo, ref. Built by Maritima del Musel SA, Gijon, for Navipesca SA, Gijon. 1,598 tons gross, 2,980 tons dw, 274·09ft loa × 41·09ft breadth × draught na, 8-cyl Naval-Stork-Werkspoor diesel, 2,000bhp, 13·5 knots.

ANAHUAC 11. *Mexican*. Cement carrier (self unloading). Built by Ast. de Cadiz, SA, Seville, for Transportacion Maritima Mexicana SA, Tampico. 5,309 tons gross, 9,834 tons dw, 394ft loa × 69·84ft breadth × 21·66ft draught, two 8-cyl s sc Bazan-Sulzer diesel, 4,160bhp, 12 knots.

ANAMILENA (Sis ADRIANA). *Colombian*. Cargo. Built by Soc. Espanola de Const. Navales, Cadiz, 1968, for Colombiana Internacional de Vapores, Santa Marta. 2,296 tons gross, 3,125 tons dw, 305·18ft loa × 47·66ft breadth × 17·58ft draught, 9-cyl SECN-B & W diesel, bhp na, knots na.

ANASTASIA V (Sis JOANA). *Greek*. Bulk carrier. Built by Mitsui Zosen, Fujinagata, 1968, for West End Shpg Co SA, Monrovia (J. Livanos). 15,869 tons gross, 27,044 tons dw, 584ft loa × 75·18ft breadth × 34·68ft draught, 6-cyl IHI-Sulzer diesel, 9,600bhp, 17 knots.

A

American Astronaut. *Originally to be named* American Leader, *the 6th of the 'L' class of United States Lines container ships, she was renamed in honour of the Americans second moon landing. She and her 5 sisters are replacing 23 conventional cargo ships on the transatlantic run. The class was comprehensively described in Volume XVII.*

American Mail. *The series of ships, costing $80,000,000 for the 5 from the Newport News SB Co, are the largest general cargo liners in the world. The first 2, the* Alaskan Mail *and* Indian Mail *opened the service by the new class between the US and Canadian West Coast and Japan, Okinawa, Taiwan, Korea, Hong Kong and the Philippines carrying break bulk, refrigerated and bulk grain cargoes. They have 7 holds, 4 forward and 3 aft of the engine room. They have single hatches, but cargo work is assisted by 20-ton 'air cushion' fork lift trucks working below the main deck on the ship's compressed air supply, with pallets. The hatch covers are Macgregor hydraulic type, and the upper deck ones can accept two rows high of containers. Between holds numbers 5 and 6 there is a 70-ton Stulcken type derrick, serving both holds. There are 4 refrigerated compartments, with a total capacity of 21,839cu ft. The ships can carry bulk grain in the lower holds without shifting boards, a significant advance in cargo liner design. The ship's Master is provided with a calculation method which can demonstrate that adequate righting movement is always available to compensate for grain shifting. The system has been proved in operation. The ships can carry 409×20ft containers on deck and in the holds, of which 60 can be refrigerated. With a full container load, they can still carry about 10,000 tons of break-bulk cargo, the whole being handled by 15 and 20-ton derricks. Bridge control of manoeuvring the main engines is fitted, with an 800hp bow thruster of KaMeWa design. Otherwise all main engine controls are grouped in an engine-control room. With a deadweight of 22,000 tons and a speed of 21 knots they are outstanding in the cargo liner field. Their basic design is designated C5-S-75a. Their complement is 45, and they carry 12 passengers, achieving a trial speed of 23 knots at 24,000 maximum shp.*

ANDALUSIA (ex VALLE DE IBAIZABAL). *Italian*. LPG carrier, ref. Built by Ast T. Ruiz de Velasco, Bilbao, 1968, for Vasco Madrilena de Nav. SA, and sold to Cia Internazionale Stoccaggi Prodotti Petroliferi SpA, (CISPA). 1,760 tons gross, 2,226 tons dw, 248·18ft loa×39·5ft breadth×18·04ft draught, 8-cyl Naval-Stork-Werkspoor diesel, 2,000bhp, 14 knots.

ANDREAS N HADJIKYRIAKOS. *Greek*. Cement carrier. Built by Soc. Fin. & Ind. des At & Ch de Bretagne, Nantes & Dubigeon-Normandie, Nantes, for General Cement Co SA, Piraeus. 3,826 tons gross, 6,582 tons dw, 364·33ft loa×53·92ft breadth×21·62ft draught, two 8-cyl s sc MAN diesel, 4,400bhp, 15·5 knots.

ANDROS CASTLE. *Greek*. Bulk carrier. Built by Ishikawajima-Harima HI, Nagoya, for Northwestern Sea Carriers Corp, Piraeus. 21,399 tons gross, 39,152 tons dw, 623·33ft loa (incl bb)×90·75ft breadth×36·84ft draught, 7-cyl IHI-Sulzer diesel, 10,500bhp, 14·5 knots.

ANDROS MARINER. *Greek*. Bulk carrier. Built by Ishikawajima-Harima HI, Nagoya, for Northwestern Sea Carriers Corp, Piraeus. 21,399 tons gross, 39,185 tons dw, 623·33ft loa (incl bb)×90·75ft breadth×37·29ft draught, 7-cyl IHI-Sulzer diesel, 10,500bhp, 14·5 knots.

ANDROS STAR. *Greek*. Tanker. Built by Mitsubishi HI Ltd, Nagaski, for Panoceanic Transport Corp, Piraeus. 99,849 tons gross, 211,423 tons dw, 1,056·5ft loa (incl bb)×158·33ft breadth×63ft draught, Mitsubishi turbs, 28,000shp, knots na.

ANDWI. *Norwegian*. Bulk carrier. Built by Haugesund M/V A/S, Haugesund, for Rolf Wigands Rederi A/S, Bergen. 21,321 tons gross, 35,510 tons dw, 709ft loa×75·41ft breadth×36·05ft draught, 6-cyl Sulzer diesel, btp, 15,000bhp, 16 knots.

ANINA. *Roumanian*. Bulk carrier. Built by Santierul Naval, Galatz, for NAVROM Roumanian Maritime & Fluvial Navigation, Constantza. 9,557 tons gross, 12,680 tons dw, 487·75ft lr×64·84ft breadth×25·97ft draught, 6-cyl Cegielski-Sulzer diesel, 7,200bhp, 15 knots.

ANNETTE BOS. *German*. Cargo OSD/CSD. Built by Martin Jansen, Leer, for Johannes Bos, Hamburg. 1,100/2,784 tons gross, tons dw na, 324·92ft loa×46·09ft breadth×13·92/20·5ft draught, two 6-cyl s sc Motorenwerke Mannheim diesel, 3,600bhp, knots na.

ANNIE JOHNSON. *Swedish*. Container ship, ref. Built by Wartsila A/B, Abo, for Rederiaktiebolaget Nordstjernan, Stockholm (A. A. Johnson). 18,000 tons gross, tons dw na, 572·25ft loa×84·75ft breadth×33·09ft draught, two 12- and two 16-cyl tw sc Wartsila-Pielstick diesel, 26,040bhp, knots na.

Amra. Specially designed to meet the needs of customers on the liner service between Japan and the Persian Gulf ports, BI's latest ship is equipped with a 300-ton Stulcken heavy lift derrick. With the notation at Lloyds 'Strengthened for Heavy Cargoes', her design includes a ram bow, transom stern, a semi balanced Simplex rudder and a Stone-KaMeWa controllable pitch propeller. The main engine is a Harland & Wolff-B & W 6K74EF unit with a maximum continuous rating of 11,600bhp at 124rpm, and a service speed of 17 knots. There are three main, and very long, cargo compartments, with hatches of between 64ft and 65·5ft in length, each compartment being capable of accommodating very long objects. Her derrick was welded in the UK, being the second 300-ton Stulcken fitted to a British ship. In addition there are four 10-ton derricks fitted on the Stulcken masts, and four 8-ton Clark-Chapman cranes. Macgregor hatch covers are fitted throughout the weather deck, with the tween deck covers being of the multi folding hydraulically operated folding leaf type. With air conditioned accommodation, she is designed to operate with a general purpose crew. A sister ship will follow from Swan Hunter Shipbuilders Ltd.

ANNUKA AARINO (Sis SAARA AARINO). *Finnish*. Bulk carrier (ore). Built by Brodogradiliste 3rd Maj, Rijeka, for Palkki O/Y, Helsinki. 25,990 tons gross, 43,770 tons dw, 704·58ft loa × 90·41ft breadth × 33·86ft draught, 9-cyl 3rd Maj-Sulzer diesel, 14,400bhp, 16 knots.

ANSGARITURM. *German*. ORSV (12 pass). Built by J. G. Hitzler, Lauenburg, for Deutsche Ges. D/S Hansa, Bremen. 498 tons gross, 726 tons dw, 176·09ft loa × 36·92ft breadth × 11ft draught, two 12-cyl tw sc MWM diesel, btp, 1,900bhp, 12·5 knots.

ANTJE SCHULTE. *German*. Cargo, CSD. Built by Orenstein Koppel & Lubecker Masch, Lubeck, for Bernhard Schulte, Hamburg. 4,800 tons gross, 7,325 tons dw, 380·84ft loa (incl bb) × 56·5ft breadth × 24·7ft draught, 8-cyl Atlas-MaK diesel, 4,000bhp, knots na.

ANTON BUYUKLI. *Russian*. Cargo. Builder na, Russia, for USSR. 3,171 tons gross, tons dw na, measurements na, cyl na, diesel, bhp na, knots na.

AOI MARU. *Japanese*. Vehicle carrier. Built by Mitsui Zosen, Fujinagata, 1968, for Yamashita-Kinkai KK, Tokyo. 2,609 tons gross, 2,134 tons, dw, 406·84ft loa × 53·25ft breadth × 16·41ft draught, two 12-cyl tw sc Mitsui-B & W diesel, 11,800bhp, 19·5 knots.

AOTEAROA (ex AUCKLAND MARU). *New Zealand*. Cargo, ref. Built by Shikoku Dkyd, Takamatsu, for New Zealand Eastern Line, Mount Maunganui. 4,675 tons gross, 6,000 tons dw, 443ft loa × 59·09ft breadth × 23·25ft draught, 6-cyl Mitsui-B & W diesel, 8,300bhp, knots na.

APSHERON. *Russian*. Stern trawler, fish factory (ATLANTIK class). Built by Volkswerft Stralsund, Stralsund, 1967, for USSR. 2,657 tons gross tons dw na, 269·41ft loa × 44·58ft m breadth × 16·41ft draught, two 8-cyl s sc Liebknecht diesel, 2,320bhp, 13·5 knots.

AQUILON. *French*. Cargo, ref. Built by At & Ch de France-Bordeaux (France-Gironde), Dunkerque, for Cie des Messageries Maritimes, Marseilles. 8,581 tons gross, 6,600 tons dw, 472·41ft loa (incl bb) × 65·66ft breadth × 24·58ft draught, 6-cyl Creusot, B & W diesel, 12,600bhp, 20·5 knots.

ARABIYAH. *Kuwait*. Tanker. Built by Sasebo HI, Sasebo, for Kuwait Oil Tanker Co, Kuwait (Common Bros, Newcastle, managers). 107,436 tons gross, 208,907 tons dw, 1,067·33ft loa (incl bb) × 158·41ft breadth × 62·25ft draught, IHI turbs, 30,000shp, 16·5 knots.

ARACENA. *Spanish*. Stern trawler, fish factory, ref. Built by Hijos de Barreras SA, Vigo, for Armadores Pesqueros Asociados del Suratlantico, Cadiz. 2,396 tons gross, 3,396 tons dw, 347·75ft loa × 47·66ft breadth × 18·05ft draught, 12-cyl Barreras-Deutz diesel, 4,000bhp, 14 knots.

ARARAT. *Russian*. Tanker. Built by Rauma-Repola O/Y, Rauma, for USSR. 3,675 tons gross, 5,000 tons dw, 348·25ft loa × 50·66ft breadth × 21·33ft draught, 5-cyl Valmet-B & W diesel, 2,900bhp, knots na.

Anastasia V. *This bulk carrier is built to the maximum dimensions for the St Lawrence Seaway, as is her sister ship the Joana. Her IHI-Sulzer diesel engine gave her a trial speed of 16 knots at 119rpm. She has six cargo holds with Macgregor steel hatch covers, all forward of the bridge. The side tanks in the cargo spaces can be used for either cargo or ballast, and the cargo handling equipment consists of twelve 10-ton derricks. She has similar freeboard to a tanker.*

ARCOS. *Spanish*. Stern trawler, ref. Built by Ast. Construcciones SA, Vigo, for Armadores Pesqueros Asoc. del Suratlantico, Vigo. 2,400 tons gross, tons dw na, 347·75ft loa × 47·66ft breadth × 18·05ft draught, 12-cyl Barreras-Deutz diesel, 4,000bhp, 14 knots.

ARCTIC. *German*. Tug. Built by Rickmers Werft, Bremerhaven, for Bugsier Reederei und Bergungs A/G, Hamburg. 2,046 tons gross, tons dw na, 286ft loa × 48·58ft breadth × 21·66ft draught, two 16-cyl s sc Deutz diesel, bhp na, knots na.

Antonio Lazaro. *Not unlike the larger* Ciudad de Compostela *class, the* Cia Trasmediterranea *ordered 4 somewhat similar but smaller ships to help the annual congestion caused by Spain's booming tourist industry. First of these is this ship, with her sister* Vicente Puchol *being exactly similar. Carrying 500 passengers, they accommodate 50 first class in double cabins, another 100 second class in double cabins, and seating for 100 in the saloon, with another 100 seats in the cafeteria, 60 ordinary cars can be carried, loading and leaving the ship by bow and stern side doors on each side. In addition to the vehicles 200 tons of general cargo and 100 tons of refrigerated cargo can be carried, vegetable oil 90 tons, fuel 300 tons, water 275 tons plus 50 tons for passengers and 75 for vehicles bring the deadweight to 1,200 tons. The ships are driven by* Maquinista-B & W *diesels of 1035VBF62 type of 6,240bhp powering twin screws, giving a range of 4,000 nautical miles at 17 knots. The gross tonnage is 5,200 and length overall 350·75ft. Both ships are included in the register of Volume XVII.*

Aoi Maru. *The YS Nearseas Line (a Yamashita-Shinnihon subsidiary), have taken delivery of the car carrier* Aoi Maru. *She is a well designed roll on and off ship, mainly for the Japanese coastal trade between Nagoya and Tomakomai, between which ports she has reduced the steaming time from 2½ to 1½ days. She has 4 car decks above the weather deck and 3 within the hull, enabling her to carry 737 cars of the size Toyopet Crown, but she can also accommodate medium sized buses and other commercial vehicles. To ensure her stability fixed ballast is provided, in addition to water ballast tanks. Her bridge controlled engines are Mitsui-B & W 2M42CF type, with a maximum output of 5,900bhp at 248rpm, giving a trial speed of 22·58 knots, whilst her fully loaded service speed is 19·5 knots. The engines are also controllable from the engine room control station.*

ARCTIC SHORE (Sis PACIFIC SHORE). *British*. ORSV (ice strengthened for Nova Scotia work). Built by Cochrane & Sons Ltd, Selby, for Offshore Marine Ltd, London (Cunard group). 670 tons gross, tons dw na, 176·41ft loa × 38·33ft breadth × 11·75ft draught, two 12-cyl tw sc Lister diesel, btp, 3,500bhp, 12·5 knots.

ARCTIC TOKYO. (Sis POLAR ALASKA). *Liberian*. Liquified gas carrier, ref. Built by Kockums M/V A/B, Malmo, for Polar LNG Shpg Corpn, Monrovia (Phillips Pet Co, Oklahoma & Marathon Oil Co). 44,089 tons gross, 32,359 tons dw, 799ft loa × 111·5ft m breadth × 32·75ft draught, Kockums-Laval turbs, 20,000shp, 18·5 knots.

ARDSHIEL. *British*. Tanker. Built by Mitsui Zosen, Chiba, for P & O SN Co Ltd (Trident Tankers Ltd), London. 119,678 tons gross, 214,000 tons dw, 1,042·41ft loa (incl bb) × 157·92ft breadth × 63·23ft draught, IHI turbs, 28,000shp, knots na.

ARDTARAIG. *British*. Tanker. Built by Mitsui Zosen, Chiba, for P & O SN Co Ltd (Trident Tankers Ltd), London. 119,616 tons gross, 214,128 tons dw, 1,063·92ft loa (incl bb) × 157·92ft breadth × 63·25ft draught, IHI turbs, 28,000shp, 16 knots.

AREMAR. *Argentinian*. Cargo, ref. Built by Ast. Argentino Astarsa, Tigre, for Aremar CIFSA, Buenos Aires. 3,095 tons gross, 2,350 tons dw, 326·75ft loa (incl bb) × 44·66ft breadth × 17·75ft draught, 12-cyl Grand Motores Diesel (Cordoba)-Fiat diesel, 5,4000bhp 16 knots.

Aotearoa
Built for the Mitsui-OSK Lines as the Auckland Maru, *this ship was sold to the Mount Maunganui firm for the Japan–New Zealand trade.*

A

ARIADNE. *Greek.* Cargo (SD14). Built by Austin & Pickersgill Ltd, Sunderland, for Libramar Corpn, SA, Piraeus. 9,038 tons gross, 15,050 tons dw, 462·58ft loa × 67·18ft breadth × 29·07ft draught, 5-cyl Clark-Sulzer diesel, 5,500bhp, 14 knots.

ARISTARCHOS. *Greek.* Cargo (FREEDOM class). Built by Ishikawajima-Harima HI, Tokyo, for Pindos Shipping Co SA, Piraeus. 10,016 tons gross, 14,907 tons dw, 466·75ft loa (incl bb) × 65·09ft breadth × 29·70ft draught, 12-cyl IHI-Pielstick diesel, 5,130bhp, 14·25 knots.

ARISTEE. *French.* Cargo (timber). Built by At & Ch de Bretagne, Nantes, for Soc. Navale Caennaise (Anct G. Lamy & Co). 7,291 tons gross, 10,389 tons dw, 465·41ft loa × 58·41ft m breadth × 26·84ft draught, two 8-cyl s sc Atlantique-Pielstick diesel, 7,440bhp, 18 knots.

ARISTEUS. *Greek.* Cargo (FREEDOM class). Built by Ishikawajima-Harima HI, Tokyo, for Pindaros Shipping Co SA, Piraeus. 10,009 tons gross, 14,935 tons dw, 466·75ft loa (incl bb) × 69·05ft breadth × 29·7ft draught, 12-cyl IHI-Pielstick diesel, 5,130bhp, knots na.

ARISTOTELIS. *Greek.* Bulk carrier. Built by Osaka Zosensho, Osaka, 1968, for Prospathia Cia Nav SA, Piraeus. 24,599 tons gross, 42,197 tons dw, 666ft loa (incl bb) × 95·18ft breadth × 36·61ft draught, 6-cyl IHI-Sulzer diesel, 13,800bhp, 16 knots.

ARKTOS. *German.* Cargo OSD (for carrying 280 Volkswagen Emden-Ramsgate). Built by Schulte & Bruns, Emden, 1968, for Reed: Ferdinand Muller, Bremen. 975 tons gross, 775 tons dw, 265·75ft loa × 42·92ft m breadth × 16·58 ft draught, 6-cyl Deutz diesel, 2,550bhp, 15·5 knots.

Ardtaraig. *On charter to BP Ltd, and owned by the P & O subsidiary Trident Tanker Ltd, this VLCC (very large crude carrier) arrived at Angle Bay, Milford Haven on her maiden voyage in June 1969, where she is shewn in the illustration. The* Ardshiel *is a sister ship, and a third, the* Ardlui *will enter service in 1970. They are fitted with one steam turbine set of 28,000shp, which at 82·5 maximum output achieved a speed of 16·52 knots on loaded trials.*

A

AROSIA. *German.* Cargo OSD/CSD (part container ship). Built by J. J. Sietas Schiffsw, Hamburg, for Peter Dohle, Hamburg. 1,600/3,300 tons gross, 2,665/4,385 tons dw, 346·33ft loa (incl bb) × breadth na × 17·21/22·11ft draught, 4-cyl Atlas-MaK diesel, directional propeller aft, 3,500bhp, 15 knots.

ARRISHA. *British.* Tanker. Built by Schps 'Waterhuizen' J. Pattje, Waterhuizen, for Dilmun Navigation Co Ltd, London. 822 tons gross, 1,300 tons dw, 236·18ft loa × 37ft breadth × 12·5ft draught, 8-cyl Deutz diesel, 1,320bhp, knots na.

ARSENIY MOSKVIN. *Russian.* Cargo. Builder na, Viborg, for USSR, Leningrad. 1,818 tons gross, 2,250 tons dw, 269ft loa × 41ft breadth × draught na, cyl na, Skoda diesel, bhp na, knots na.

ARTLENBURG. *German.* Cargo, ref. OSD/CSD. Built by Howaldtswerke-Deutschewerft, Kiel for Harald Schulte, Hamburg. 3,844/5,754 tons gross, 4,580/7,570 tons dw, 485·66ft loa × 63·09ft breadth × 21·41/26·48ft draught, 10-cyl Howaldt-MAN diesel, 14,000bhp, 23 knots.

ASAHI MARU No 33. *Japanese.* Cargo. Built by Tsuneishi Zosen, Numakuma, 1968, for Osaka Asahi Kaiun K, Osaka. 3,842 tons gross, 6,401 tons dw, 351·41ft loa × 53·84ft breadth × 22·18ft draught, 8-cyl Mitsubishi diesel, 4,200bhp, knots na.

ASAHI MARU No 38. *Japanese.* Cargo. Built by Mitsubishi HI Shimonoseki, for Mitsubishi Shoki KK, Osaka. 4,211 tons gross, 6,600 tons dw, 375·18ft loa × 54·5ft breadth × 22·66ft draught, 6-cyl Mitsubishi diesel, 3,500bhp, knots na.

ASAHI MARU No 39. *Japanese.* Cargo. Built by Tsenuishi Zosen, Numakuma, for Osaka Asahi Kaiun K, Osaka. 3,950 tons gross, 6,497 tons dw, 357·75ft loa × 53·84ft breadth × 22·5ft draught, 8-cyl Mitsubishi diesel, 4,200bhp, knots na.

ASIA BRIGHTNESS. *Liberian.* Bulk carrier. Built by Maizuru Jukogyo, Maizuru, for Lib. Dig. Trans., Monrovia (World Wide SL HK). 11,434 tons gross, 19,133 tons dw, 512·33ft loa × 74·33ft breadth × 31·3ft draught, 7-cyl Maizuru-B & W diesel, 8,400bhp, 15 knots.

ASKANIA. *Russian.* Stern trawler, fish factory, ref (ATLANTIK class). Built by Volkswerft Stralsund, Stralsund, for USSR. 2,657 tons gross, 1,152 tons dw, 269·58ft loa × 44·75ft breadth × 16·41ft draught, two 8-cyl s sc Liebknecht diesel, 2,320bhp, 13·5 knots.

ASTRONOM. *Russian.* Stern trawler, fish factory, ref (ATLANTIK class). Built by Volkswerft Stralsund, Stralsund, 1967, for USSR. 2,657 tons gross, tons dw na, 269·58ft loa × 44·58ft m breadth × 16·41ft draught, two 8-cyl s sc Liebknecht diesels, 2,320bhp, 13·25 knots.

ATHOS. *Greek.* Cargo (IHI FREEDOM type). Built by Ishikawajima Harima HI, Nagoya, for Athos Shipping Co SA, Piraeus. 10,008 tons gross, 14,700 tons dw, 466·75ft loa (incl bb) × 65·09ft breadth × 29·62ft draught, 12-cyl IHI-Pielstick diesel, 5,130bhp, 14·25 knots.

ATLANTIC CAUSEWAY (Sis ATLANTIC CONVEYOR). *British.* Container ship. Built by Swan Hunter SB Ltd, Walker on Tyne, for Cunard Brocklebank Ltd, Liverpool. 14,946 tons gross, 16,480 tons dw, 695·84ft loa × 92ft breadth × 30·33ft draught, tw sc AEI turbs, btp, 38,500shp, 23 knots.

ATLANTIC CHAMPAGNE (Sis ATLANTIC COGNAC). *French.* Container ship, stern door. Built by Ch. Nav. de La Ciotat, La Ciotat, for Cie Generale Transatlantique, Dunkerque. 15,351 tons gross, 18,549 tons dw, 695·33ft loa × 92ft breadth × 27·88ft draught, tw sc Atlantique-Stal Laval turb, 35,000shp, 24 knots.

ATLANTIC CROWN. *Dutch.* Container Ship. Built by At & Ch de Dunkerque & Bordeaux, France-Gironde, Dunkerque, for N. V. Nederland-America Stoomvaart Maats, Rotterdam. 15,469 tons gross, 18,000 tons dw, 695·58ft loa × 92ft breadth × 30·5ft draught, tw sc AEI turbs, bhp na 24 knots.

ATLANTIC HAWK. *Liberian.* Bulk carrier. Built by Hakodate Dock Co Ltd, Hakodate, for S. Livanos (Hawk Shipping Co Ltd), Monrovia (S. Livanos). 16,291 tons gross, 28,700 tons dw, 593·18ft loa × 76ft breadth × 35·07ft draught, 7-cyl IHI-Sulzer diesel, 11,200bhp, 15 knots.

Atlantic Crown

Atlantic Crown. The two British (Cunard) owned second generation of roll on/off vehicle carrying/container ships for the N Atlantic trade are the Atlantic Causeway *and* Conveyor; *the Netherland-America line ship is the* Atlantic Crown, *the French Compagnie Generale Transatlantique vessels the* Atlantic Champagne *and* Cognac, *whilst the Swedish Wallenius firm (who originated the whole concept) operates the* Atlantic Cinderella. *The first generation is the* Atlantic *'S' class, described in previous volumes. These all form the Atlantic Container Line operating from and to 7 terminals in Europe and N America. For them the Macgregor organization has evolved a complete outfit of automated equipment for the most arduous conditions. This includes flush weather deck hatch covers, stern ramp (weighing 100 tons in 2 hydraulically articulated sections about 151ft in length) side, stern and bulkhead doors, and a hatch cover/ramp. The stern ramp is hinged at C deck level, and can take 2-way traffic with axle loadings up to 30 tons (as also can the hatch cover/ramp). Additional access is provided by the roll on/off method through 2 side shell doors, aft of amidships, port and starboard, to C deck then on to A and B decks. Various interior fixed ramps enable vehicles to proceed to other decks. The car decks can accommodate 880 low height vehicles. A very long ramp leads to D deck (heavy vehicles) then to E and F decks. When D deck is loaded, a 46×6 metre hatch/ramp closes the opening in C deck. Remote control of these is fitted. Access to the forward tween deck spaces is provided by two bulkhead sliding doors in the aftermost bulkhead of the cellular portion of the ship.*

The 'C' class have 5 wide hatchways, 1 to each of 5 container holds, in lieu of the two twin hatch set of their predecessors. The 5 holds are cellular, and have each a capacity of 125 containers, of the 40ft×8ft×8ft class. On deck they can stow 172 40ft units in 2 tiers, and 128 empty of the same type in the third and fourth tiers. The actual end section of the stern ramp is 49ft long and 23ft wide, and can, with special wheel arrangements, take a 300 ton load on a 60 ton rolling load. The Clark Chapman windlass of the two Cunard ships is bridge controlled. The main AEI twin turbines, with a total continuous maximum output of 38,500shp are either bridge or engine control room controlled. To improve manoeuvrability a 10 ton thrust Stone-KaMeWa bow thrust is fitted, and Sperry activated fin stabilizers to counteract rolling.

ATLANTIC HELMSMAN. *Liberian.* Bulk carrier. Built by Hakodate Dock Co Ltd, Hakodate, for Helmsman Shipping Co Ltd, Monrovia (S. Livanos). 16,291 tons gross, 28,650 tons dw, 593·18ft loa (incl bb)×76ft breadth×35·07ft draught, 7-cyl IHI-Sulzer diesel, 11,200bhp, 15 knots.

ATLANTIC HERITAGE. *Liberian.* Bulk carrier. Built by Hakodate Dock Co Ltd, Hakodate, for S. Livanos (Heritage Shipping Co Ltd), Monrovia. 16,291 tons gross, 28,707 tons dw, 593·18ft loa (incl bb)×76ft breadth×35·07ft draught, 7-cyl IHI-Sulzer diesel, 11,200bhp, 15 knots.

ATLANTIC HERO. *Liberian.* Bulk carrier. Built by Hakodate Dock Co Ltd, Hakodate, for Hero Shipping Co Ltd, Monrovia (S. Livanos). 16,475 tons gross, 28,696 tons dw, 593·18ft loa (incl bb)×76ft breadth×35·07ft draught, 7-cyl IHI-Sulzer diesel, 11,200bhp, 15 knots.

ATLANTIC HORIZON. *Liberian.* Bulk carrier. Built by Hakodate Dock Co Ltd, Hakodate, for Horizon Shipping Co Ltd, Monrovia (S. Livanos). 16,475 tons gross, 28,696 tons dw, 593·18ft loa (incl bb)×76ft breadth×35·07ft draught, 7-cyl IHI-Sulzer diesel, 11,200bhp, 15 knots.

ATLANTIC MARCHIONESS (Sis ATLANTIC MARQUIS). *Liberian.* Tanker. Built by Mitsubishi HI, Hiroshima, 1968 for Marchioness Shipping Co Ltd, Monrovia (S. Livanos). 40,962 tons gross, 87,007 tons dw, 839·92ft loa (incl bb)×126·5ft breadth×43·96ft draught, 9-cyl Mitsubishi-Sulzer diesel, 20,700bhp, 16 knots.

ATLANTIC SHIPPER. *German.* Cargo, ref, OSD. Built by Gebr. Schurenstedt, Bardenfleth, for Bernhard Warrings, Elsfleth. 499 tons gross, 1,195 tons dw, 243·25ft loa×38ft breadth×12ft draught, 8-cyl Atlas-MaK diesel, 1,400bhp, 12 knots.

A

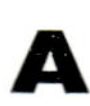

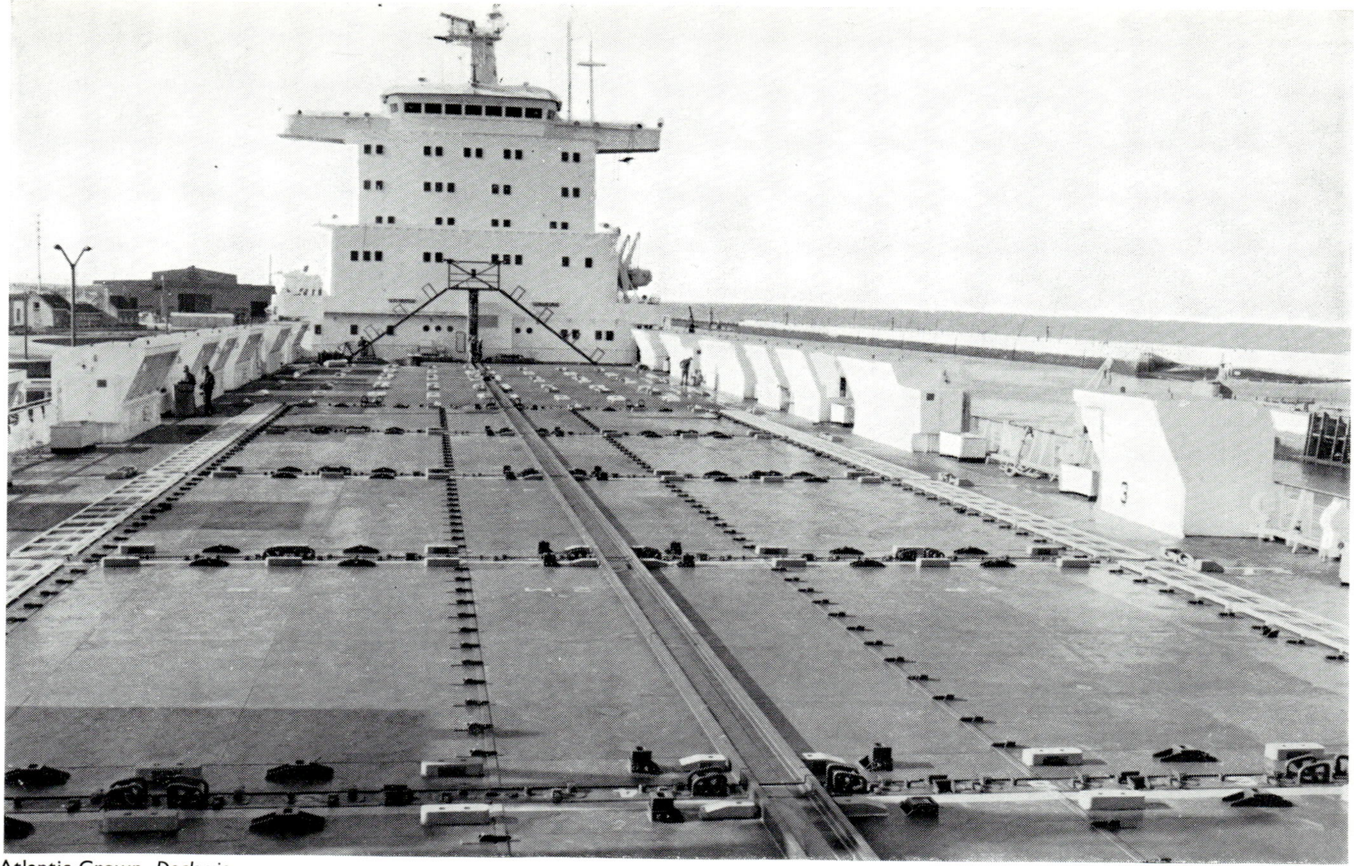

 Atlantic Crown. *Deck view.*

The bulk carrier August Pacific *belonging to Pacific Bulk Carriers of London and managed by the Fife Shipping Co (London) is powered by a 15,000bhp Doxford 76J 6-cylinder diesel engine.*

Australian Enterprise

AUGUST PACIFIC. *British*. Bulk carrier. Built by Doxford & Sunderland SB & E Co, North Sands Yard, Sunderland, for Pacific Bulk Carriers Ltd, London. 31,409 tons gross, 57,150 tons dw, 723·92ft loa × 104·18ft breadth × 41·3ft draught, 6-cyl Doxford diesel, 15,000bhp, 14·5 knots.

AUSTRALIA MARU. *Japanese*. Container ship. Built by Mitsui Zosen, Tamano, for Mitsui-OSK Lines KK, Osaka. 23,500 tons gross, 23,000 tons dw, 698·92ft loa (incl bb) × 95·25ft breadth × 34·41ft draught, 9-cyl Mitsui-B & W diesel, 34,200bhp, knots na.

AUSTRALIAN ENDEAVOUR (launched as ACT 3). *Australian*. Container ship, ref, 4 pass. Built by Bremer Vulkan, Vegesack, for Australian Coastal Shipping Commission, Melbourne. 25,144 tons gross, 26,420 tons dw, 712·75ft loa (incl bb) × 95·25ft breadth × 34·5ft draught, Bremer-Vulkan Stal Laval turbs, 30,000shp, 22 knots.

Australian Enterprise. *This ship is the first for a joint Australian-Japanese line between Australian and Japanese ports. The companies involved are, in Australia, the Australian National Line and Flinders Shipping Co, Pty Ltd, and in Japan, the Kawasaki Kisen Kaisha. She is the first roll on and off container ship built in Japan, and her sister run by the Kawasaki firm is the Australian Sea-Roader. A third vessel is building for Flinders. The ships will follow a 28-day regular schedule calling at Osaka, Yokkaichi, Nagoya and Yokohama and Brisbane, Sydney and Melbourne. Cargoes carried will be containers, pallets and flats as well as heavy vehicles, trailers and cars. There are 2 decks for loading roll on and off containers. Unitized cargo is carried on board up the stern ramp by fork lift trucks, trailers, etc., and the stern door can accommodate large fork lift 20-ton containers. The upper deck is loaded by wharf side crane as in ordinary container ships. The upper vehicle deck has 2 mezzanine decks forward for cars. The propelling power is a Kawasaki-MAN V8V 40/54 in 3 sets, each with a maximum continuous output of 8,690bhp at 400rpm, driving a Kawasaki-Escher-Wyss controllable pitch propeller, with a maximum trial speed of 25·6 knots, service speed being 21 knots. About 560 20ft containers can be carried, with about 110 medium sized cars.*

Leading Australian Enterprise

The Australian Trader *is shown at Bell Bay, Tasmania, on her maiden voyage from* Melbourne. *She can, with her roll on and off facilities handle 6,000 tons of cargo in less than 10 hours. She makes 3 round trips per week between Melbourne and Tasmania, carrying 200 passengers and 90 cars with a total cargo deadweight of 2,000 tons in addition. The lower hull is identical with that of the* Empress of Australia, *but above the shelterdeck she has been designed for the special requirements of the Searoad Service. The passengers are accommodated in either 1 or 2 berth cabins, of which about half have private bath and toilet facilities. The public rooms consist of a lounge, smokeroom and bar, dining room, cafeteria, milk bar and shop. Vehicles drive on board via the hinged stern door. Propulsion is by a twin set of 16-cylinder Atlantique-Pielstick diesels of PC 2V400 type developing 6,500bhp at 500rpm each, and driving twin screws through a 2·5:1 Renk gearbox. The engines are operated by remote control from either the bridge or the engine room control room. A Stone-KaMeWa variable pitch bow thrust propeller is fitted, and the ship has both Denny Brown fin type stabilizers and a Flume tank system.*

Axel Johnson. *The first of a class of 6 fast container ships carrying their own handling gear, that is, 2 movable ASEA portal type cranes capable of lifting any containers carried, together with two deck cranes of 25 and 10 lifting capacity. She inaugurated an express service between Europe and the West Coast of North America, the round voyage being made in 56 days between Sweden, Germany and Tilbury to WCNA ports between Los Angeles and Vancouver. The time from Tilbury to Los Angeles is 15 days, and to Vancouver 22 days. Some of these West Coast ports have no container handling equipment, hence it is carried on the ship. The class will operate with the semi-containerized and lengthened Rio de Janeiro class. Including the capacity of the containers carried on deck, the total hold capacity is, 1,200,000cu ft, of which 270,000 is refrigerated. This may be made up of 548 containers of 20ft type plus 62 of the 40ft type, plus 200,000cu ft of general cargo. Four Wartsila-SEMT-Pielstick diesels of the medium speed type are geared to twin KaMeWa controllable pitch propellers which gave a trial speed of 25 knots, but the service speed is about 22·5 knots. One 12-cylinder PC2V and one 16-cyl PC2V are coupled to each propeller, and the maximum power developed is 28,000bhp. The Johnson Line subsidiary data processing company Datema has developed a sophisticated system through which the company obtains constant information as to the location, contents and destination of every container, which with automatic planning programmes make certain that the right container is available to each shipper when and where he wants it. A wide selection of Johnson Line containers is available ranging from 126cu ft to 2,225cu ft.*

A

AUSTRALIAN ENTERPRISE. *Australian.* Container ship. Built by Kawasaki HI Ltd, Kobe, for Australian Coastal Shipping Commission, Melbourne. 16,580 tons gross, 11,000 tons dw, 596·09ft loa (incl bb)×82·25ft breadth×27ft draught, three 16-cyl s sc Kawasaki-MAN diesel, 26,070bhp, knots na.

AUSTRALIAN SEA ROADER. *Japanese.* Container ship. Built by Kawasaki HI, Ltd, Kobe, for Kawasaki KKK, Kobe. 9,271 tons gross, 11,400 tons dw, 596·09ft loa (incl bb)×82·18ft breadth×27ft draught, three 16-cyl Kawasaki-MAN diesel, s sc, 26,070bhp, knots na.

AUSTRALIAN TRADER. *Australian.* Pass/car ferry, stern doors (200 pass). Built by NSW Government SB & E Co, Newcastle, NSW, for Australian Coastal Shipping Commission, Melbourne. 7,005 tons gross, 3,160 tons dw, 445·09ft loa×70·58ft breadth×20ft draught, two 16-cyl tw sc Atlantique-Pielstick diesel, 14,800bhp, 17·5 knots.

AUTSE. *Russian.* Tanker. Built by Rauma-Repola O/Y, Rauma, for USSR. 3,674 tons gross, 5,000 tons dw, 348·25ft loa×50·66ft breadth×21·32ft draught, 5-cyl Valmet-B & W diesel, 2,900bhp, knots na.

AXEL JOHNSON. *Swedish.* Container ship. Built by O/Y Wartsila A/B, Abo, for Red. Nordstjernan, Stockholm (Johnson Line). 16,284 ton gross, 14,700 tons dw, 572·25ft loa×84·75ft breadth×32·84ft draught, two 12- and two 16-cyl tw sc Wartsila-Pielstick diesel cpp, 26,040bhp, 23 knots.

AYNAZHI. *Russian.* Tanker. Built by Rauma-Repola O/Y, Rauma, 1968, for USSR, Batumi. 3,674 tons gross, 5,000 tons dw, 348·25ft loa×50·66ft breadth×21·33ft draught, 5-cyl Valmet-B & W diesel, 2,900bhp, 14 knots.

AZTECA. *Mexican.* Bulk carrier. Built by Stocznia Szczecinska, Szczecin, for Transportacion Maritima Mexicana, SA, Vera Cruz. 16,039 tons gross, 25,660 tons dw, 610·25ft loa (incl bb)×75ft breadth×34·5ft draught, 6-cyl Cegielski-Sulzer diesel, 9,600shp, 15·5 knots.

B

BAHIA DE COCHINOS. *Cuban.* Cargo, ref. Built by Uddevallavarvet A/B, Uddevalla, for Empresa Navegacion Mambisa, Havana. 10,972 tons gross, 15,550 tons dw, 531·09ft loa×67·41ft breadth×32ft draught, 7-cyl Uddevalla-B & W diesel, 11,900bhp, 18 knots.

BAILUNDO (launched as ARTEMONAS). *Portuguese.* Cargo. Built by Stocznia Szczecznia, Szczecin, for Companhia Colonial de Navegacao S.a.r.l. Lisbon. 6,804/10,552 tons gross, 12,800/16,600 tons dw, 519·66ft loa (incl bb)×69·09ft breadth×27·58/32·8ft draught, 6-cyl Cegielski-Sulzer diesel, bhp na, knots na.

BAKAR. *Yugoslav.* Cargo, ref. Built by Italcantieri SpA, Monfalcone, for Jugoslavenska Linijska Plovidba, Rijeka. 6,275/8,555 tons gross, 8,439/— tons dw, 497·41ft loa (incl bb)×65·75ft breadth×draught na, 7-cyl CRDA-Fiat diesel, 10,500bhp, 18·75 knots.

BAKARITSA. *Russian.* Cargo. Builder na, Viborg, 1968, for USSR. 4,896 tons gross, tons dw na, 400·09ft loa×54·92ft breadth×22·22ft draught, 9-cyl Bryansk-B & W diesel, bhp na, knots na.

BAKHCHISARAY. *Russian.* Stern trawler, fish factory, ref (ATLANTIK class). Built by Volkswerft Stralsund, Stralsund, 1968, for USSR. 2,657 tons gross, 1,149 tons dw, 269·58ft loa×44·75ft breadth×16·41ft draught, two 8-cyl s sc Liebknecht diesel, 2,320bhp, 13·25 knots.

BAKNES. *British.* Bulk carrier. Built by Scotts SB & E Co Ltd, Greenock, for H. Clarkson & Co Ltd (Tenax SS Co Ltd), London. 13,400 tons gross, 21,206 tons dw, 520ft loa×75ft breadth×31·29ft draught, two 8-cyl s sc B & W diesel, 8,800bhp, knots na.

BALKHASH. *Russian.* Cargo. Builder na, Krasnoyarsk, for USSR, Archangel. 1,217 tons grcss, tons dw na, measurements na, cyl na, diesel, bhp na, knots na.

B

BALTIC. *German.* Tug. Built by F. Schichau GmbH, Bremerhaven, 1968, for Bugsier Reederei & Bergungs, Hamburg. 662 tons gross, tons dw na, 166·58ft loa × 38·41ft breadth × draught na, 12-cyl Deutz diesel, 4,200bhp, 15 knots.

BALTIC CONCORD (launched as ELKE KAHRS). *German.* Cargo/containers (63 × 20ft). Built by J. J. Sietas Schiffsw, Hamburg, for Johann Kahrs, Hamburg (J. Thode mgr). 500 tons gross, 1,227 tons dw, 242·84ft loa × 35·41ft m breadth × 12·97ft draught, 8-cyl Atlas-MaK diesel, 1,400bhp, 12·5 knots.

BALTIJSKIJ 68 and 69. *Russian.* Cargo. Builders na, Russia, 1967, for USSR. 1,865 tons gross, tons dw na, measurements na, cyl na, diesel, bhp na, knots na.

BANAGRANDE. *Liberian.* Cargo, ref. Built by Kawasaki Dkyd Co Ltd, Kobe, for Bana Navigation Co Ltd, Monrovia (Taiships, Hong Kong). 7,005 tons gross, 7,029 tons dw, 462·66ft loa (incl bb) × 60·84ft breadth × 26·58ft draught, 9-cyl Kawasaki-MAN diesel, 12,600bhp, 21 knots.

BANDIM. *Portuguese.* LPG carrier, ref. Built by Est Nav de Viana do Castelo, Viana do Castelo, 1968, for Sacor Maritima Ltda, Lisbon. 1,844 tons gross, 1,841 tons dw, 271·33ft loa × 43·58ft m breadth × 15·25ft draught, 8-cyl MAN diesel, 2,260bhp, 13 knots.

BARFONN. *Norwegian.* LPG carrier, ref. Built by Ch Naval de La Ciotat, La Ciotat, for Sigval Bergesen, Stavanger. 9,000 tons gross, 7,100 tons dw, 414·41ft loa × 60·41ft breadth × 23·96ft draught, 6-cyl CCMec-Sulzer diesel, 8,000bhp, 16 knots.

BARON DUNMORE (Sis BARON FORBES). *British.* Bulk carrier. Built by Haugesunds M/V A/S, Haugesund, 1968, for Scottish Ship Management Ltd, Ardrossan (H. Hogarth & Sons Ltd). 12,660 tons gross, 19,958 tons dw, 530ft loa (incl bb) × 71·25ft breadth × 31·81ft draught, 6-cyl Hoverdverft-Sulzer diesel, 9,600bhp, 16 knots.

BARRAD FOAM. *Lebanese.* Cargo, ref. Built by At & Ch de La Rochelle-Pallice, La Rochelle-Pallice, 1968, for Barrad Shipping Co, Beirut (managed by Ned.-Antilles Ship Corp). 1,909 tons gross, 3,300 tons dw, 318·25ft loa × 47·66ft breadth × 20·33ft draught, 12-cyl Deutz diesel, 4,000bhp, 16 knots.

BASTIAAN BROERE (Sis JACOBUS BROERE). *Dutch.* Oil/chemical tanker. Built by N. V. Nieuw Noord Ned. Scheeps, Groningen, 1968, for Gebr. Broere (Curacao) NV, Willemstad. 1,279 tons gross, 2,267 tons dw, 270ft loa × 40·18ft breadth × 16·41ft draught, 6-cyl Industrie diesel, 1,499bhp, 12·5 knots.

BAUGNES. *Norwegian.* Bulk carrier. Built by Lithgows East Yard, Port Glasgow, for A/S Kristian Jebsen's Rederi, Bergen. 13,400 tons gross, 21,130 tons dw, 520ft loa × 75ft breadth × 31·25ft draught, two 8-cyl s sc B & W diesel, 8,800bhp, knots na.

BEAVERMONDO. *German.* Cargo OSD/CSD (chartered to Canadian Pacific). Built by Atlas-MaK Masch, Bremerhaven, for D. Oltmann, Bremen. 1,599/2,700 tons gross, 3,420/4,250 tons dw, 325·5ft loa × 47·92ft breadth × 17·58/20·39ft draught, 8-cyl Atlas-MaK diesel, 3,200bhp, 14·5 knots.

BEAVERRANDO (launched as RANDO). *German.* Cargo OSD/CSD. Built by Atlas-MaK Masch, Bremen, for D. Oltmann, Bremen (chartered to Canadian Pacific). 1,575/2,800 tons gross, 3,420/4,355 tons dw, 325·5ft loa × 47·92ft breadth × 17·58/20·39ft draught, 8-cyl Altas-MaK diesel, 32,100bhp, 14·5 knots.

BEKAS. *Russian.* Stern trawler, fish factory, ref (ATLANTIK class). Built by Volkswerft Stralsund, Stralsund, for USSR. 2,657 tons gross, 1,152 tons dw, 269·58ft loa × 44·75ft breadth × 16·41ft draught, two 8-cyl s sc Liebknecht diesel, 2,320bhp, 13·5 knots.

BELATRIX. *Panamanian.* Cargo. Built by Brodogradiliste 3rd Maj, Rijeka, for Cross Seas Shipping Corpn, Panama. 10,000 tons gross, 15,000 tons dw, 476ft loa × 67·75ft breadth × 29·55ft draught, 5-cyl 3rd Maj-Sulzer diesel, 7,700bhp, knots na.

B

BELE. *German*. Cargo OSD. Built by Husumer Schiffsw, Husum, for Heinrich Freudenberg, Hamburg. 500 tons gross, 276 tons dw, 250·33ft loa × 39·18ft breadth × 12·92ft draught, 8-cyl Deutz diesel, bhp na, knots na.

BELLA MAERSK (Sis BRIGIT MAERSK). *Danish*. Bulk carrier/cars. Built by Kaldnes M/V A/S, Tonsberg, for A. P. Moller, Copenhagen. 15,850 tons gross, 24,500 tons dw, 591·58ft loa × 75·18ft breadth × 33·48ft draught, 6-cyl Akers/Nylands-B & W diesel, 11,600bhp, 15·75 knots.

BELLNES. *British*. Bulk carrier. Built by Lithgows Ltd, Port Glasgow, for H. Clarkson & Co Ltd, London (Tenax SS Co Ltd, Mgrs). 12,404 tons, gross, 19,710 tons dw, 521·84ft loa (incl bb) × 71·41ft breadth × 31·1ft draught, 6-cyl Kincaid-B & W diesel, 6,550bhp, 14·75 knots.

BELO MUNDO. *Liberian*. Bulk carrier. Built by Hitachi Zosen, Innoshima, for Liberian Intercontinental SS Co Ltd, Monrovia. 11,415 tons gross, 18,170 tons dw, 479ft lbp × 74·33ft breadth × 29·5ft draught, 7-cyl Hitachi-B & W diesel, 8,400bhp, 15·25 knots.

BELOUGA. *French*. Cargo, ref. Built by At & Ch de Dunkerque & Bordeaux (France-Gironde), Dunkerque, for Cie de Navigation Fruitiereg Dunkerque. 8,553 tons gross, 6,550 tons dw, 472·41ft loa (incl bb) × 65·66ft breadth × 24·58ft draught, 6-cyl Creusot-B & W diesel, 13,860bhp 20·75 knots.

BELVAL. *Belgian*. Bulk carrier. Built by N. V. Boelwerft, Tamise, for Union Belge d'Enterprises Maritimes UBEM, SA, Antwerp. 12,850 tons gross, 20,000 tons dw, 524·92ft loa × 75·25ft breadth × 32·47ft draught, 6-cyl ACEC-MAN diesel, 8,400bhp, knots na.

BERGE TASTA. *Norwegian*. Tanker. Built by A/S Rosenberg M/V, Stavanger, for Sigval Bergesen dy & Co, Stavanger. 79,969 tons gross, 156,400 tons dw, 956·09ft loa × 135·09ft breadth × 62·37ft draught, 7-cyl B & W diesel, 27,500bhp, 15 knots.

BERGEVIK. *Norwegian*. Tanker. Built by Hitachi Zosen, Innoshima, for Sigval Bergesen dy & Co, Stavanger. 54,282 tons gross, 86,000 tons dw, 864·5ft loa (incl bb) × 128ft breadth × 42ft draught, 9-cyl Hitachi-B & W diesel, 20,700bhp, 15·5 knots.

BERKELEY. *British*. Tanker. Built by N/V Scheeps v/h H. H. Bodewes, Millingen, for Bowker & King Ltd, London. 730 tons gross, 1,200 tons dw, 211·75ft loa × 31·25ft breadth × 12ft draught, 8-cyl Blackstone diesel, 660bhp, 10 knots.

BETA. *Brazilian*. Cargo OSD. Built by Emaq Eng. Maq. SA, Rio de Janeiro, for Navegacao Continental Ltda, Rio de Janeiro. 1,992 tons gross, 3,040 tons dw, 259·75ft loa × 41·09ft breadth × 16·25ft draught, 6-cyl Villares-B & W diesel, 1,680bhp, 11·75 knots.

BETELGEUSE. *Panamanian*. Cargo. Built by Brodogradiliste 3rd Maj, Rijeka, for Cross Seas Shp. Co, Panama. 10,000 tons gross, 15,000 tons dw, 475·75ft loa × 67·75ft breadth × 29·52ft draught, 5-cyl 3rd Maj-Sulzer diesel, 7,700bhp, knots na.

BIANCA. *Norwegian*. Bulk carrier. Built by Burmeister & Wain, Copenhagen, for Arthur h. Mathiesen, Oslo. 29,844 tons gross, 51,100 tons dw, 718ft loa × 100·09ft m breadth × 39·55ft draught, 8-cyl B & W diesel, 13,200bhp, 15·5 knots.

BIDEFORD. *British*. Tanker. Built by Kawasaki Dkyd Co Ltd, Sakkaide, for Blandford Shipping Co Ltd, London. 107,924 tons gross, 217,206 tons dw, 1,072ft loa (incl bb) × 158·33ft breadth × 54ft draught, Kawasaki turbs, 28,000shp, 16 knots.

BIESZCZADY. *Polish*. Bulk carrier, 8 pass (B 520-1 class). Built by Stocznia Szczecinska, Szczecin, for Polish SS Co, Szczecin. 10,847 tons gross, 15,432 tons dw, 513·18ft loa × 67·09ft breadth × 30·09ft draught, 6-cyl Cegielski-Sulzer diesel, 7,200bhp, 16 knots.

BIRKALAND. *Swedish*. Cargo OSD/CSD. Built by Eriksbergs M/V A/S, Gothenburg, for A/B Svenska Orient Linien, Gothenburg. 6,150/6,940 tons gross, 9,025/12,800 tons dw, 458ft loa × 80·75ft breadth × —/31ft draught, two 10-cyl s sc Eriksbergs-Pielstick diesel, 8,600bhp, 16·75 knots.

BISCAY MARU. *Japanese*. Ore/oil carrier. Built by Ishikawajima-Harima HI, Aioi, for Daiichi Chuo KK, Tokyo. 56,687 tons gross, 101,170 tons dw, 821·84ft loa (incl bb) × 127·75ft breadth × 49·84ft draught, 9-cyl IHI-Sulzer diesel, 21,600bhp, 16 knots.

B

BLAGOVESHCHENSK. *Russian*. Cargo. Built by Nystads Varv A/B, Nystads, for USSR. 2,920 tons gross, 3,400 tons dw, 335ft loa × 46·09ft breadth × 18·75ft draught, 5-cyl Bryansk-B & W diesel, 2,900bhp, knots na.

BLESSING. *Liberian*. Bulk carrier. Built by Maizuru Jukogyo Ltd, Maizuru, for Blessing Co Ltd, Monrovia (Taiships, Hong Kong). 30,695 tons gross, 60,542 tons dw, 738·18ft loa (incl bb) × 105·75ft breadth × 40·66ft draught, 6-cyl Maizuru-Sulzer diesel, 13,800bhp, knots na.

BODAIBO. *Russian*. Cargo. Built by Stocznia Gdanska, Gdansk, 1967, for USSR, Vladivostok. 4,689 tons gross, 6,132 tons dw, 406·41ft loa × 55·92ft breadth × 22·37ft draught, 5-cyl Cegielski-B & W diesel, 5,450bhp, knots na.

BONNY. *Finnish*. Tanker. Built by Uddevallavarvet A/B, Uddevalla, for Algot Johannson, Mariehamn. 51,485 tons gross, 96,200 tons dw, 837·41ft loa × 127·92ft breadth × 47·22ft draught, 9-cyl Eriksbergs-B & W diesel, 23,200bhp, 16·5 knots.

BORELAND. *Swedish*. Cargo OSD/CSD. Built by Eriksbergs M/V A/B, Gothenburg, for A/B Svenska Orient Linien, Gothenburg. 6,150/9,640 tons gross, 9,025/12,800 tons dw, 458ft loa × 70·75ft breadth × 31ft draught, two 10-cyl s sc Eriksbergs-Pielstick diesel, 8,800bhp, knots na.

BORGESTAD. *Norwegian*. Bulk carrier. Built by Brodogradiliste 'Uljanik', Pula, for Gunnar Knudsen, Porsgrunn. 18,524 tons gross, 26,000 tons dw, 534·84ft loa × 85·41ft breadth × 36·09ft draught, 6-cyl Uljanik-B & W diesel, 10,600bhp, knots na.

BORODINO. *Russian*. Tanker. Builder na, Leningrad, for USSR. 32,841 tons gross, tons dw na, 756·33ft loa × 101·75ft breadth × 38·05ft draught, turbine, 19,000shp, knots na.

BOSNA (ex PLEIADES). (Sis CASSIOPEIA). *Yugoslavian*. Cargo, ref. Built by Brodogradiliste 3rd Maj, Rijeka, for Jugoslavenska Linijska Plovidba, Rijeka. 6,963 tons gross, 10,845 tons dw, 508·58ft loa × 67·41ft breadth × 26·77ft draught, 6-cyl Stork diesel, 10,500bhp, knots na.

BOTANY BAY. *British*. Container ship, ref. Built by Howaldtswerke-Deutsche Werft, Hamburg, for Furness Withy & Co Ltd (Overseas Containers Ltd, Magrs). 26,876 tons gross, 29,100 tons dw, 752·41ft loa (incl bb) × 100·25ft breadth × 35·09ft draught, Stal-Laval turbs 32,400shp, 21·5 knots.

BOW CECIL. *Norwegian*. Chemical tanker. Built by Trosvik Verksted, A/S, Brevik, for Rederi Jacob Christensen, Bergen. 1,195 tons gross, 3,000 tons dw, 272·41ft loa × 44·09ft breadth × 18·22ft draught, two 8-cyl s sc Normo diesel, cpp, btp, 2,050bhp, 12·5 knots.

BOW CEDAR. *Norwegian*. Chemical tanker. Built by Akers Nylands Verksted, Oslo, for A/S Rederiet Odfjell, Bergen. 12,868 tons gross, 21,380 tons dw, 560ft loa × 72ft breadth × 33·07ft draught, 6-cyl Akers-Nylands diesel, cpp, 11,600bhp, knots na.

BOW LIND. *Norwegian*. Chemical tanker. Built by Moss Vaerft & Dokk A/S, Moss, for A/S Rederiet Odfjell, Bergen. 6,467 tons gross, 9,837 tons dw, 396·33ft loa × 60·75ft breadth × 29·66ft draught, 7-cyl Akers Nylands-B & W diesel, cpp, 5,400bhp, 15 knots.

BOW QUEEN. *Norwegian*. Chemical tanker. Built by Trosvik Verksted A/S, Brevik, for A/S Rederiet Odfjell, Bergen. 1,199 tons gross, 3,000 tons dw, 272ft loa × 45·5ft breadth × 18·22ft draught, two 8-cyl s sc Normo diesel, 2,080bhp, knots na.

BOWTRADER. *British*. Sand suction dredger. Built by Ailsa SB Co Ltd, Troon, for British Dredging (Sand and Gravel) Ltd, Cardiff. 1,400 tons gross, 2,450 tons dw, 282·84ft loa × 48·09ft breadth × 13·92ft draught, 8-cyl English Electric diesel, 2,100bhp, 12 knots.

BRACIGOVO. *Bulgarian*. Cargo OSD/CSD. Builders na, Bulgaria, for Navigation Maritime, Bulgare. 1,325/1,515 tons gross, tons dw na, measurements na, cyl na, diesel, bhp na, knots na.

BRIDGENESS (Sis BRISTOLIAN). *British*. Tanker. Built by Bayerische Schiffsb. GmbH, Erlenbach, for Bowker & King Ltd, London. 797 tons gross, 1,130 tons dw, 187·5ft loa × 36·41ft breadth × 11·47ft draught, 8-cyl Blackstone diesel, 660bhp, 10 knots.

B

B

The Belouga is the fifth in a series of 8 fast refrigerator cargo ships being built for various French liner companies. She has been delivered to Le Cie de Navigation Fruitiere and is shown here leaving Dunkerque on trials. The others of the class are: Narval*—Chargeurs Reunis;* Fribourg*—Countage & Transports;* Aquilon*—Messageries Maritimes;* Ivondro*—Havnaise;* Marsouin*—Courtage & Transports;* Favorita*—Maritime Financing (Panama);* Fort Ste Marie*—C. G. Transatlantique. The* Aquilon *is experimentally fitted with computerized navigation aids. This permits precise astronomical calculations for fixing the position of the ship, utilizing the ship's speed, wind, current, etc, and displays the information visually on a screen. Great circle and other routes can be calculated, and with weather information permits the best routes to be selected. It also, with the radar, works out collision avoidance, following up to 6 echoes at one time.*

Bel-Hudson. *Ordered by G. Vefling of Tonsberg from Kaldines M/V (vide volume XVII) she was taken over when new by John Hudson Fuel & Shipping Ltd (a Williams Hudson subsidiary), being their largest ship to date. She was then sent to Hamburg, to become the first British ship to be fitted with Blohm & Voss car decks. She has a deadweight of 24,340 tons and a 15·25 knot speed. She is here shown in Vefling colours, the prefix* 'Bel-' *being a characteristic of these owners, as well as being used by another Norwegian firm, Christen Smith.*

BRIDGESTONE MARU V. *Japanese.* LPG carrier. Built by Kawasaki HI Ltd, Kobe, for Showa Kaiun KK, Tokyo. 40,934 tons gross, 44,600 tons dw, 690·66ft loa (incl bb) × 106·84ft breadth × 37·84ft draught, 8-cyl Kawasaki-MAN diesel, 14,000bhp, knots na.

BRISBANE TRADER. *Australian.* Car ferry, stern doors, side ports. Built by Evans Deakin Pty Ltd, Brisbane, for Australian Coastal Shipping Commission, Melbourne. 9,000 tons gross, 4,000 tons dw, 448ft loa × 70·58ft breadth × 20·25ft draught, two 8-cyl tw sc MAN diesel, 10,650bhp 17·5 knots.

BRISTOLIAN. *British.* Tanker. Built by Bayerische Schiffsb. GmbH, Erlenbach, for Bowker & King Ltd, London. 797 tons gross, 1,155 tons dw, 187ft loa × 36·25ft breadth × 11·05ft draught, cyl na, Blackstone diesel, 660bhp, 10 knots.

B

The Betelgueuse *is a 15,000 ton* Liberty Replacement *type of the Treci Maj (3rd May) shipyard of Rijeka. Four sister ships are under construction for these owners at Rijeka. All are fitted with a 3rd Maj-Sulzer 5RD76 type developing 7,700bhp for 15½ knot speed.*

The tanker Bonny *is at present, and at 96,200 tons dw, the largest ship in the Finnish merchant fleet. Two sister ships are under construction (one for E. Saanum of Mandal, Norway). She is fitted with an Eriksberg-B & W 9K84EF diesel engine.*

B

B

Bowtrader. *The sixth vessel built for her owners, the Bowtrader has a low superstructure in order to enable her to pass under River Thames bridges, and is the largest of her type for this passage. The propelling and dredging machinery consists of a Ruston & Hornsby ATCM type engine capable of developing 2,100bhp at 600rpm, and driving the propeller at 250rpm through a MWD type M2WR reverse/reduction coaxial gearbox. Part loaded, the ship achieved 12 knots on trials, with the engine controlled from the wheelhouse console by a Chadburn telegraph transmitter. Sand and gravel are drawn into the ship by a 30in diameter steel pipe and a 30in dredge pump supplied by Simons-Lobnitz Ltd, driven by the main engine through a gearbox. The dredging pipe is of a length capable of dredging to a depth of 72ft below the keel, and is lowered by davits and electric winches. Swell compensators allow for an 8ft swell. The cargo can be grabbed by shore cranes, or discharged by the dredge pump.*

BRITISH FIDELITY. *British.* Tanker. Built by Brodogradiliste 'Split', Split, for BP Tanker Co Ltd, London. 15,260 tons gross, 22,500 tons dw, 558·84ft loa (incl bb) × 81·5ft breadth × 31·09ft draught, 7-cyl Uljanik-B & W diesel, 8,254bhp, knots na.

BRITISH SECURITY. *British.* Tanker. Built by Eriksbergs M/V A/S, Gothenburg, for BP Tanker Co Ltd, London. 15,095 tons gross, 24,000 tons dw, 557·75ft loa × 81·18ft breadth × 31·18ft draught, 6-cyl Eriksbergs-B & W diesel, 7,600bhp, knots na.

BRITISH TENACITY. *British.* Tanker. Built by Eriksbergs M/V A/S, Gothenburg, for BP Tanker Co Ltd, London. 15,095 tons gross, 24,000 tons dw, 556·5ft loa (incl bb) × 81·41ft breadth × 31·33ft draught, 6-cyl Eriksberg-B & W diesel, 7,600bhp, 15 knots.

BRITISH UNITY. *British.* Tanker. Built by Brodogradilste 'Split', Split, for BP Tanker Co Ltd, London. 15,000 tons gross, 22,500 tons dw, 559·09ft loa (incl bb) × 81·5ft breadth × 31·09ft draught, 6-cyl Uljanik-B & W diesel, 8,254bhp, 14·75 knots.

BRITTA KRUGER. *German.* Cargo OSD/CSD part container ship. Built by Elsflether Werft AG, Elsfleth, for Hans Kruger GmbH, Hamburg. 3,373/5,383 tons gross, 5,132/7,047 tons dw. 385ft loa × 59·5ft breadth × 21·92/23·18ft draught, 12-cyl Blohm & Voss diesel, 5,950bhp, knots na.

Brage. With her sister Aegir delivered earlier in 1968, they were then the largest bulk carriers of the German Merchant Fleet and brought the total deadweight capacity of the owners, the 'Frigga' concern, to 500,000 tons in 13 ships.

BRUNES. *Norwegian.* Bulk carrier. Built by Lithgows Ltd, East Yard, Port Glasgow, for A/S Kristian Jebsens Rederi Bergen. 13,124 tons gross. 21,130 tons dw, 520ft loa × 75ft breadth × 31·25ft draught, two 8-cyl s sc B & W diesel, 8,800bhp, 15 knots.

BRUNI. *Norwegian.* Cargo, part container ship. Built by Schiffsw Neptun, Rostock, for J. Brunvall, Bergen. 2,889 tons gross, 4,099 tons dw 316·25ft loa × 48ft breadth × 19·37ft draught, 8-cyl Atlas-MaK diesel, 3,000bhp, 14 knots.

BRUNNECK. *German.* Oil rig supply vessel. Built by T. van Duivendijk's Schps: Lekkerkerk, for Deutsche DS Gs 'Hansa', Bremen. 500 tons gross, tons dw na, 252·58ft loa × 42·92ft breadth × 9·33ft draught, two 16-cyl tw sc Caterpillar diesel, 1,140bhp, knots na.

BRUNSWICK (Sis BRUNSRODE). *German.* Cargo, ref 12 pass. Built by Lubecker Flenderwerke AG, Lubeck, for W. Bruns & Co, Hamburg. 3,275 tons gross, 4,135 tons dw, 443·58ft loa (incl bb) × 56·84ft breadth × 21·21ft draught, two 12-cyl s sc Blohm & Voss diesel, 12,000bhp, 22 knots.

BULK PROSPECTOR. *German.* Bulk carrier. Built by A/S Frederikstad M/V, Frederikstad, for Sigurd Herlofson Reederei Gmb H, Bremen 21,815 tons gross, 36,550 tons dw, 635·09ft loa × 86·18ft breadth × 37·64ft draught, 8-cyl Frederikstad-Gotaverken diesel, 10,700 bhp. knots na.

B

The Bridgestone Maru V *was in October 1969 the largest liquified petroleum gas carrier yet built. She is on long term BP contract to carry LPG for delivery in Japan from Mina-al-ahmadi. She can carry up to 42,300 metric tons of propane and butane.*

Brunneck *and* Mariaeck *(not illustrated). Designed to meet the needs of the heavy plant contractor/user in the European area, the Hansa Line have taken delivery of these two special small ships with exceptional loading facilities. Individual loads up to 600 tons can be accepted. Though basically similar, the* Mariaeck *has a much deeper hold than her sister ship. They are designed for the same type of work as the two British* Fisher *vessels. These German ships are different in that they can discharge and load from either end, and can carry loads weighing twice as much as the earlier British ships. They can operate from riverside jetties, or beaches, or from pontoons. They have a similar type of silhouette to London's late* Flatiron *colliers, with light dismountable masts for proceeding under river bridges. The upper deck is virtually obstructionless from fore to aft, with split superstructure; accommodation and engine rooms port and starboard. Loads up to 400 tons are normally handled over the bow, the ship having a portable ramp. Clam type bow doors are fitted, and aft a ramp type stern door capable of taking 600 ton loads. Both these ramps are handled by portable derrick posts. There is an uninterrupted driveway from bow to stern through the ship of not less than 8 metres width, and they carry two special loading trollies.*

Though basically similar, the foregoing applies in particular to the Mariaeck. *Both ships are propelled by twin Caterpillar D399TA diesels, each driving a Van Voorden propeller through a 1·4* Reintjes *reduction gear box. A Schottel bow thrust unit is fitted, and like the main engines, is bridge controlled.*

One example of their work was the transporting by the Brunneck *of two 238-ton reactor vessels from Marina di Carrara to the Seal Sands jetty of the Tees Monsanto plant now building. These were 101ft long and 23ft in diameter. The Spanish ship* Navipesa Uno *is somewhat similar in appearance.*

British Unity. *The first of two sister ships ordered from the Jugoslav yard at Split, she is extensively automated with remote control equipment. The main engine is a B & W 67-VT2BF-160 diesel from Uljanik at Pula, which gives a speed of 15 knots. She has 33 cargo tanks, with a pump and pipeline system capable of carrying many different types of cargo, as she is designed as a 'Products' carrier.*

BUOR KHAYA. *Russian.* Cargo. Builder na, Russia, for USSR. 3,777 tons gross, tons dw na, measurements na, cyl na, diesel, bhp na, knots na.

BUREVESTNIK. *Russian.* Stern trawler, fish factory (ATLANTIK class). Built by Volkswerft Stralsund, Stralsund, 1967, for USSR. 2,657 tons gross, tons dw na, 269·58ft loa × 44·75ft breadth × 16·66ft draught, two 8-cyl s sc Liebknecht diesel, 2,320bhp, 13·5 knots.

BURHAVERSAND. *German.* Cargo OSD/CSD part container ship. Built by Schiffsw Heinrich Brand KG, Oldenburg, for Helmut Meyer, Brake. 999/1,999 tons gross, 2,010/3,320 tons dw, 302·84ft loa × 44·92ft breadth × 15·25/20ft draught, 12-cyl Deutz diesel, 3,000bhp, 15 knots.

Brunes. *First of a new series of 8 specialized bulk carriers, valued together at £14,000,000, built and building at Scott-Lithgow on the lower reaches of the Clyde for the Kristian Jebsens Rederi, Bergen and their associates, with possibly three more to be ordered. These builders have since 1949 built 19 ships for these owners, all delivered on time. They are specially designed to enter many of the shallow draft Australian ports, whose mineral sands and ore trades are a Jebsen speciality. Titan ore and mineral sands are the main cargo from both Eastern and Western Australian ports and Canada, with sulphur and phosphates as return cargoes. These ships, fully automated and of shallow draught, and of (as bulk carriers go) relatively small size, can use the small inlets where the ore is found, and handle it in the relatively small quantities that the trade demands. Titan ore and mineral sand are so expensive, and rare, and have to be picked up a little here and a little there, that a large ship, even if she could reach the sources, would tie up too much*

capital. The series started with the 15,000 ton Brunes *and* Bernes *in 1962,* Brimnes *in 1963, with the sister* Binsnes *and the 18,500 ton* Bolnes *in 1966. In 1967 the 18,350 ton* Birknes *appeared, with 1968 producing the* Baynes, Borgnes *and* Bellnes. *Now the first of the 20,000 tonners is in service. The principal associates are H. C. Clarkson & Co Ltd of London and the Tenax SS Co who manage many of the ships. The present* Brunes *is capable of operation with a small crew and an unmanned engine room. There are 6 main cargo holds (also suitable for other cargoes such as cement, grain without shifting boards, iron ore, etc.) with hoppered sides formed by the double bottom tanks carried up the ship's sides. Nos 2 and 5 holds are capable of being filled with water. There are six 12-ton Cargospeed swinging derricks, with two 5-ton, and two 1½-ton derricks for ships purposes. The propelling plant consists of two medium speed B & W 8S45HU diesels, manufactured by the Burmeister & Wain Copenhagen establishment, and installed by J. G. Kincaid & Co Ltd at Greenock. Running at 450rpm the speed is reduced through a Renk gearbox to 135rpm for the Stone-KaMeWa controllable pitch propeller. The machinery is both bridge and engine room control panel controlled, and each engine can operate independently. The Jebson fleet now consists of 28 ships, and sailings from West Australian ports average more than 1 per week with cargoes of ilmenite, alumina, talcum, rutile and phosphate.*

B

BUTANUEVE. *Spanish.* LPG carrier, ref. Built by Ast. de Cadiz SA, Seville, for Butano SA, Seville. 11,083 tons gross, 11,461 tons dw, 502·66ft loa (incl bb)×69·84ft breadth×27·92ft draught, 6-cyl Ast de Cadiz Manises-Sulzer diesel, 9,600bhp, 17 knots.

BUXTEHUDE II. *German.* Cargo (78×20ft containers or wood pulp). Built by J. J. Sietas, Hamburg, for Partenreederei 'Buxtehude II', Hamburg. 499 tons gross, 1,380 tons dw, 255·41ft loa×42·66ft breadth×13·05ft draught, 6-cyl Deutz diesel, 1,600bhp, 13 knots.

BYAKUDAN MARU. *Japanese.* Bulk carrier. Built by Mitsubishi HI Ltd, Kobe, for Tokyo Kaiji KK, Tokyo. 10,169 tons gross, 16,641 tons dw, 479ft loa×70·92ft breadth×30ft draught, 6-cyl Mitsubishi-Sulzer diesel, 8,000bhp, 17 knots.

C

C. S. FORESTER. *British.* Stern trawler. Built by Charles D. Holmes & Co Ltd, Beverley, Yorks, for Newington Trawlers Ltd, Hull. 1,300 tons gross, tons dw na, 161ft lbp×36·09ft breadth×draught na, 8-cyl Stork diesel, cpp, 1,950bhp, 14 knots.

C. V. LIGHTNING. *USA.* Container ship (928×20ft containers). Built by Bath Iron Works Corpn, Bath, Maine, for American Export-Isbrandtsen Lines Inc, New York. 17,902 tons gross, 16,343 tons dw, 610·5ft loa (incl bb)×78·18ft breadth×31·59ft draught, GEC turbs, 17,500shp, 21 knots.

C. V. SEAWITCH. *USA.* Container ship (928×20ft containers) CSD. Built by Bath Iron Works Corpn, Bath, Maine, 1968, for American Export-Isbrandtsen Lines Inc, New York. 17,902 tons gross, 16,343 tons dw, 610ft loa (incl bb)×78·18ft breadth×31·59ft draught, GEC turbs, 17,500shp, 21 knots.

C. V. STAGHOUND. *USA.* Container ship (928×20ft containers). Built by Bath Iron Works Corpn, Bath, Maine, for American Export-Isbrandtsen Lines Inc, New York. 17,902 tons gross, 16,343 tons dw, 610ft loa (incl bb)×78·18ft breadth×31·59ft draught, GEC turbs, 17,500shp, 21 knots.

CABO TRES MONTES. *Liberian.* LPG carrier, ref. Built by Kristiansand M/V A/S, Kristiansand, for Cabo Tres Montes Inc, Monrovia. 2,994 tons gross, 3,000 tons dw, 328·09ft loa×47·25ft breadth×18·66ft draught, 9-cyl Sulzer diesel, 2,340bhp, 13·75 knots.

CABRIES. *French.* Cargo. Built by Busumer Werft GmbH, Busum, for Cie Fabre, Soc. Gen. de Transports Maritimes, Marseilles. 499 tons gross, 1,023 tons dw, 250·58ft loa×44ft breadth×13·7ft draught, 16-cyl MAN diesel, cpp, btp, 2,300bhp, 14·5 knots.

C

Caribou. *The first of European Unit Routes Ltd (General Steam Navigator Co, London) second generation of container ships, the* Deer *class, is still a chartered vessel. She runs regularly from Tilbury to the Continent carrying 160 ISO 20ft containers. Her cellular structure also allows for 30ft and 40ft units also.*

C. S. Forester. *This sophisticated trawler is the first distant water fresh fish stern trawler to be built in the UK. Due to her high service speed of 14 knots she can fish in far waters, and still bring back her fresh catch for the market. The crew work in sheltered conditions, carrying out gutting and washing of the catch on the lower deck, where a gutting machine is to be installed. She has a much higher standard of accommodation than most trawlers, with air conditioned cabins, furnished in fire resisting materials. Her fire detecting appliances are very advanced. In the event of a fire, with her Minerva combustion-detector system, a fire alarm sounds on the bridge, the doors in a thwartship fireproof bulkhead close, and ventilation is shut off. In addition a sprinkler network is also fitted, which operates if excess heating occurs. She is also fitted with anti-icing precautions.*

The midships gantry incorporates the boiler-flue and engine exhausts, the W/T transmitter aerials are stainless steel whips, and the main radar scanner is fitted with a pneumatic ice cracking sleeve. In addition to normal comprehensive electronic navigation aids, she also has a Kelvin Hughes Humber Gear and Marconi Fishgraph. She is strengthened for ice navigation, and her stability tested in the National Physical Laboratory. Power is provided by a Stork-Werkspoor/VMF TMABF398 diesel engine of 1,950bhp, driving a Stone-KaMeWa controllable pitch propeller.

C. V. Staghound. *AEIL (American Export Isbrandtsen Lines) have taken delivery of their first purpose built all cellular container ships. The first was* Container Vessel Seawitch *built in 1968, the other of the trio being the* C. V. Lightning, *all named after famous clippers built by Donald Mackay in the last century. Costing $14,000,000 each, they have a capacity for 928 standard 20ft containers, or 464×40ft units, or a mixture of each. The company commenced container services with the converted bulk carriers renamed* Container Dispatcher *and* Container Forwarder *running between New York, Felixstowe and Le Havre. The latest class were originally ordered as break-bulk/container ships, but owing to the success of the others, were, at an early stage re-designed as they are now. Unlike most of their competitors, the bridge house is foward, and there is no cargo handling equipment. There are 4 holds forward of, and 1 aft of the machinery space. The after hold is fitted out as a single 40 cell group, with the other 3 having two 40 cell groups of guides. All can of course take 20ft units, two-to-one 40ft. One of the reasons for the 40ft choice is the growing demand for this size of container, and also the new design of portainer carne spreader can handle two 20ft units together. They have a bulbous bow and transom stern. Of the containers 316×20ft are stowed on deck. Below decks they are stowed six tiers deep and seven abreast. The ships are deliberately designed with a certain amount of permanent ballast. Of the lightship weight of 10,327 tons, 3,517 tons is permanent ballast. At a maximum draught of 31·58ft, the displacement is 26,670 tons, with a deadweight of 16,343 tons. 4,941 tons of water ballast can be carried, with a fresh water load of 219 tons. Fuel bunkers take 3,474 tons of heavy fuel, with 23½ tons lubricating oil and 1·2 tons of diesel oil.*

C

CAIRNVENTURE. *British.* Cargo. Built by E. J. Smit & Zos Scheeps, Westerbroek, for Shaw Savill & Albion Ltd, London. 1,436 tons gross, 2,570 tons dw, 253·18ft loa × 39ft breadth × 18·84ft draught, 8-cyl Atlas-MaK diesel, 1,400bhp, knots na.

CALIFORNIA GETTY. *USA.* Tanker. Built by Mitsubishi HI, Yokohama, 1968, for Hemisphere Transportation Corpn, Monrovia. 58,994 tons gross, 129,328 tons dw, 886·18ft loa (incl bb) × 139·58ft breadth × 54·97ft draught, Mitsubishi turbs, 24,000shp, 16 knots.

CAMARINA. *British.* Cargo. Built by N. V. Bodewes Scheeps, Martenshoek, for Hadley Shipping Co Ltd, London. 800/1,473 tons gross, —/2,570 tons dw, 253·58ft loa × 39ft breadth × 18·84ft draught, 8-cyl Atlas-MaK diesel, 1,400bhp, 12·5 knots.

CAMPEADOR. *Spanish.* Tanker. Built by Soc. Espanola de Const. Naval, Cadiz, for Cia Arrendataria del Monopolio de Petroles SA, Barcelona. 21,000 tons gross, 35,200 tons dw, 685·75ft loa × 87·09ft breadth × 35·09ft draught, 6-cyl SECNA-B & W diesel, 13,800bhp, 16 knots.

CAMPONALON. *Spanish.* Tanker. Built by S. A. Juliana Const. Gijonesa, Gijon, for Cia Arr. del Mon. de Petroles, SA, Cadiz. 4,270 tons gross, 6,290 tons dw, 406·33ft loa × 54·25ft breadth × draught na, 5-cyl SECN-B & W diesel, 3,850bhp, 13·5 knots.

CANGURO GIALIO. *Italian.* Passenger/car ferry. Built by Cant. Nav. Apuania, Carrara, for Traghetti Sardi SpA, Palermo. 5,070 tons gross, 3,350 tons dw, 462·55ft loa × 62·41ft breadth × 19ft draught, four 6-cyl tw sc Fiat diesel electric, 10,800bhp, knots na.

CANGURO GRIGIO. *Italian.* Passenger/car ferry. Built by Cantieri Navale Apuania, Carrara, for Traghetti Sardi SpA, Cagliari. 5,070 tons gross, 3,350 tons dw, 462·92ft loa × 62·41ft breadth × 19ft draught, four 6-cyl tw sc diesel electric Fiat, bhp na, knots na.

CAPE SABLE. *British.* Bulk carrier. Built by Marinens Hovedverft, Horten, for Lyle Shipping Co Ltd (Scottish Ship Management Ltd), Glasgow. 13,532 tons gross, 21,980 tons dw, 527·75ft loa (incl bb) × 75·18ft breadth × 32·09ft draught, 6-cyl Hovedverft-Sulzer diesel, 9,600bhp, 15·5 knots.

CAPE YORK. *British.* Bulk carrier. Built by A/S Horten Werft, Horten, for Lyle Shipping Co Ltd (Scottish Ship Management Ltd), Glasgow. 13,543 tons gross, 21,900 tons dw, 527·75ft loa (incl bb) × 75·18ft breadth × 32·09ft draught, 6-cyl Hovedeverft-Sulzer diesel, 9,600bhp, 15·5 knots.

CAPETAN MANOLIS. *Greek.* Cargo (SD 14). Built by Bartram & Sons Ltd, Sunderland, for Sea Eagle Shipping Co, Piraeus (Glafki Cia SA. Piraeus). 9,044 tons gross, 15,050 tons dw, 462·75ft loa × 67·18ft breadth × 29·04ft draught, 5-cyl Clark-Sulzer diesel, 5,500bhp, 14 knots,

CARACAS MARU (Sis CRISTOBAL MARU). *Japanese.* Cargo. Built by Mitsubishi HI Ltd, Kobe, for Mitsui-OSK Lines KK, Osaka. 6,887 tons gross, 11,450 tons dw, 467·5ft lbp × 72·25ft breadth × 27·84ft draught, 6-cyl Mitsubishi-Sulzer diesel, 9,600bhp, 18(20) knots.

CARIBBEAN ENTERPRISE (Sis CARIBBEAN VENTURE). *British.* Cargo (vehicle carrier, 52 trailers). Built by J. J. Sietas Schiffsw, Hamburg, for Common Bros, Management Ltd, Newcastle. 1,547 tons gross, 2,237 tons dw, 311·66ft loa (incl bb) × 57·41ft breadth × 16·45ft draught, two 8-cyl tw sc Deutz diesel, 4,000bhp, 16 knots.

CARIBOU (launched as FUCJSBERG). *German.* Container ship. Built by Schiffsw Hugo Peters, Wewelsfleth, for G. Graebe, Lubeck. 499 tons gross, 1,500 tons dw, 253·5ft loa × 42ft m breadth × 12·2ft draught, 8-cyl Atlas-MaK diesel, 1,650bhp, 13·5 knots.

CARINA. *Liberian.* Cargo (SD 14). Built by Austin & Pickersgill Ltd, Sunderland, for Mavroleon Bros (Ship Management) Ltd, Monrovia. 9,072 tons gross, 15,040 tons dw, 462·58ft loa × 67·18ft breadth × 29·05ft draught, 5-cyl Hawthorn-Sulzer diesel, 5,500bhp, 14 knots.

CARINA. *Polish.* Stern trawler, fish factory, ref (First B22 class). Built by Stocznia Gdanska, Gdansk, 1967, for PPDiUR 'Dalmor', Gdynia. 3,169 tons gross, 1,756 tons dw, 288·75ft loa × 47·66ft breadth × 18·37ft draught, 12-cyl Cegielski-Fiat diesel, 2,500bhp, 13·75 knots.

CARLO PORR. *German.* Cargo CSD. Built by Orenstein Koppel & Lubecker Masch, Lubeck, for Franz Hagen, Hamburg. 4,825 tons gross, tons dw na, 380·84ft loa (incl bb) × 56·5ft breadth × 24·7ft draught, 8-cyl Atlas-MaK diesel, 4,000bhp, knots na.

C

CAROLINE (Sis NADINE). *Liberian*. Bulk carrier. Built by Maizuru Jukogyo Ltd, Maizuru, for Global Bulk Carriers Inc, Monrovia. 14,672 tons gross, 26,250 tons dw, 564·33ft loa × 74·92ft breadth × 36·26ft draught, 7-cyl Maizuru-Sulzer diesel, 11,200bhp, 17·5 knots.

CAROLINE OLDENDORFF. *German*. Cargo CSD. Built by Bremer Vulkan, Vegesack, for Egon Oldendorff, Lubeck. 9,327 tons gross, 15,300 tons dw, 457·58ft loa × 68·92ft m breadth × 30·09ft draught, 6-cyl B. Vulkan diesel, 8,400bhp, knots na.

CASIMIR LE QUELLEC *French*. Chemical tanker. Built by Const. Ind & Naval de Bordeaux, Bordeaux, for Cie Francaise Navinox, Havre. 1,447 tons gross, 2,145 tons dw, 259·18ft loa × 40·66ft breadth × 16·56ft draught, 6-cyl MaK diesel, 2,000bhp, 13·75 knots.

CASSIOPEE. (Sis BETELGUESE). *French*. Tanker. Built by Ch de l'Atlantique, St Nazaire, 1968, for Cie Navale des Petroles, Havre. 61,766 tons gross, 119,531 tons dw, 924ft loa × 127·84ft breadth × 52·18ft draught, 10-cyl Atlantique-B & W diesel, 23,100bhp, 16 knots.

CATHARINA WIARDS. *German*. Cargo (Weser Typ 36). Built by A. G. Weser Werk Seebeck, Bremerhaven, for Kauffahrtei Seereederei Adolf Wiards & Co, Bremen. 9,320 tons gross, 15,600 tons dw, 463·25ft loa × 69ft breadth × 30·2ft draught, cyl na, MAN diesel, 6,520bhp, 15·25 knots.

CELTIC PRINCE (ex ARBON). *Dutch*. Cargo OSD/CSD. Built by Scheeps v/h De Groot & v.Vliet, Slikkerveer, 1968, for W. F. Kampman's Bevrachtingsbedrif, Willemstad NA. 499/1,439 tons gross, 1,402/1,530 tons dw, 254·75ft loa × 39·66ft breadth × 12·92/13·58ft draught, 6-cyl Industrie diesel, 1,560bhp, 12·5 knots.

CENTAURUS. *Polish*. Stern trawler, fish factory, ref. Built by Stocznia Gdanska, Gdansk, 1967, for PPD 'Dalmor', Gdynia. 2,827 tons gross, 1,450 tons dw, 278·84ft loa × 45·33ft breadth × 17·03ft draught, 8-cyl Zgoda-Sulzer diesel, 2,400bhp, 12·5 knots.

CHANG CHUN. *Chinese (Taiwan)*. Cargo. Built by Kurushima Dock Co Ltd, Imabari, for Wan Hai SS Co Inc, Keelung. 2,999 tons gross, 5,125 tons dw, 318·92ft loa × 51·25ft breadth × 20·92ft draught, 6-cyl Akasaka-Tekkosho diesel, 3,000bhp, 14·5 knots.

CHEMICAL TRANSPORT (Sis INDUSTRIAL TRANSPORT). *Canadian*. Chemical tanker. Built by Davie SB Co Ltd, Lauzon, for Hall Corpn of Canada, Toronto. 4,980 tons gross, 8,000 tons dw, 391ft loa × 55·33ft breadth × 21·71ft draught, two 10-cyl tw sc Fairbanks-Morse diesel, 3,332bhp, 12·5 knots.

CHIGUSA MARU. *Japanese*. Bulk carrier. Built by Nippon Kokan, Tsurumi, for Nippon Yusen Kaisha & Showa KK, Tokyo. 24,115 tons gross, 43,003 tons dw, 634·84ft loa (incl bb) × 96·84ft breadth × 37·18ft draught, two 12-cyl s sc Nippon-Kokan diesel, 10,600bhp, knots na.

CHOAN MARU. *Japanese*. Cargo. Built by Imai Zosen, Kochi, for Yasuda Kaiun KK, Kochi. 2,520 tons gross, 4,200 tons dw, 278·84ft lbp × 47·33ft breadth × 19·66ft draught, 6-cyl Ito Tekkosho diesel, 3,000bhp, 12·5 knots.

CHOKYU MARU No 18. *Japanese*. Cargo. Built by Imabari Zosen, Imabari, for Seno KKK, Nakaminato. 2,970 tons gross, 5,500 tons dw, 308·41ft lbp × 51·58ft breadth × 21·92ft draught, 6-cyl Hanshin diesel, 3,500bhp, 12·5 knots.

CHRISTIANE BOLTEN. *German*. Cargo. Built by Burntisland SB Co Ltd, Burntisland, for Aug Bolten Wm Miller's Nachfolger, Hamburg. 3,207/5,143 tons gross, 5,613/7,560 tons dw, 399ft loa (incl bb) × 56·92ft breadth × 21·75/25·92ft draught, 5-cyl Borsig-Fiat diesel, 6,000bhp, 16 knots.

CHRISTINE ISLE (Sis GWENDOLEN ISLE). *Liberian*. Container feeder ship. Built by Gebr. Schurenstedt, Bardenfleth, for Midsea Containerships Inc, Monrovia. 472 tons gross, 1,200 tons dw, 239·84ft loa × 42·33ft breadth × 12·33ft draught, 7-cyl MAN diesel, 1,770bhp, 13 knots.

CHRISTITSA. *Greek*. Bulk carrier. Built by Nippon Kokan, Tsurumi, for Pacific Corpn, Piraeus (Soc Suisse-Atlantique, Lausanne). 28,006 tons gross, 57,650 tons dw, 742·84ft loa × 102·33ft breadth × 40·67ft draught, 8-cyl Uraga-Sulzer diesel, 17,600bhp, 16 knots.

Cervantes. *Not previously illustrated in this series, this ship, with her sister the* Churruca *are the latest of the MacAndrews designed and owned ships. They are in the register of Volume XVII. Both their names, with those of the chartered V's mentioned later on in this volume are traditional names for the Company. They are of 1,470 tons gross, 2,000 tons deadweight and have a speed of 16 knots.*

Challenger. *(Not in the register section.) Formerly the 27,000 ton ore/oil carrier* P. G. Thulin, *this ship has been converted at Boele's Scheepswerven en Machine-fabriek NV, Bolnes, into an offshore workshop, and handed over to the Heerema Engineering Service, The Hague. In order to place very heavy parts on the bottom of the sea-bed, an 800-ton crane was fitted on board by IHC Holland, and as a result, certain changes had to be made for stability purposes. This was achieved by installing for practically the whole length of the ship, stabilization tanks 19·7ft high by 6·6ft wide. In order to maintain her in position at sea, two 90-ton winches have been located on the main deck, each having 4 drums, so that the vessel can be secured by 8 anchors. A bow propeller of 1,000hp has been installed to improve manoeuvrability. In order to facilitate the transportation of large and cumbersome objects, the deck has been made as flush as possible, by removing tank hatches, etc. Her extended periods at sea have necessitated supplies by helicopter, and a landing platform has been built forward. The* P. G. Thulin *was built in 1956 for Messrs Wm Muller & Co, Rotterdam.*

The tanker Chemical Transport *of 8,300 tons dw is seen here passing through the St Lawrence Seaway on her maiden voyage.*

Christiane Bolten *is the final ship to be built by the Burntisland yard for foreign owners, and is powered by a Borsic-Fiat diesel engine of 6,000bhp.*

Colorado. *Easily distinguished from the previous* California *class by 4 sets of derrick posts against 3 on the fore deck, the new class (the others being* Idaho, Michigan, Montana *and* Wyoming) *have increased speed, greater cargo capacity, gyro controlled flume stabilizers, fully automated engine rooms, accentuated bulbous bow to minimize pitching and wave making resistance, triple hatches at Nos 3, 4 and 5 holds and other features. With a 23 knot service speed at 24,000shp, their cargo capacity is 855,000cu ft, of which 40,000cu ft is refrigerated. The heavy derrick lifts 60 tons. 12 passengers are carried in considerable luxury in 8 cabins. The class are employed on the San Francisco to Honolulu, Okinawa, Japan and Hong Kong route, making two voyages per month. The* California *class operate two routes, namely San Francisco to Manila, Saigon and Bangkok, returning via Hong Kong and Taiwan to the Pacific northwest (1 voyage per month) and San Francisco to Japan, Korea and/or Taiwan, returning via Japan to the Pacific northwest (1 voyage per month). The* Illinois *class of 2* Mariner *ships operate 1 voyage per month to Japan, Korea and/or Taiwan from the Pacific northwest. The company advertise their services as 'under the Banner of the Red Sea Horse', which forms the 'S' on their funnels. The fleet consists of 13 high speed and modern cargo liners.*

CHRISTOPHER MEEDER. *German.* Cargo. Built by Schiffsw Hugo Peters, Wewelsfleth, for George Petersen, Rendsburg. 499 tons gross, 1,200 tons dw, 250·33ft loa × 36·75ft m breadth × 12ft draught, 8-cyl Atlas-MaK diesel, 1,150bhp, 12 knots.

CIDIA. (Sis BANDIM). *Portuguese.* LPG carrier, ref. Built by Est Nav de Viana do Castelo, Viana do Castelo, 1968, for Sacor Maritima Ltda, Lisbon. 1,844 tons gross, 1,744 tons dw, 271·33ft loa × 43·61ft m breadth × 15·25ft draught, 8-cyl MAN diesel, 2,140bhp, 14 knots.

CIS BROVIG. *Norwegian.* Tanker. Built by Hitachi Zosen, Innoshima, for Th Brovig, Farsund. 56,636 tons gross, 106,100 tons dw, 912·18ft loa (incl bb) × 128·09ft breadth × 47·6ft draught, 9-cyl Hitachi-B & W diesel, 20,700bhp, 15·5 knots.

CLIFFORD MAERSK. *Danish.* Cargo, ref, 6 pass. Built by Akers A/S Bergens M/V, Bergen, for A. P. Moller, Copenhagen. 10,918 tons gross, 13,935 tons dw, 559·75ft loa (incl bb) × 81·18ft breadth × 34·07ft draught, 9-cyl B & W diesel, btp, 20,700bhp, 22·75 knots.

CLUTHA OCEANIC. *Australian.* Bulk carrier (to carry bauxite, estimated 5,000,000 tons per year between Weipa and Gladstone, N. Queensland). Built by Whyalla SB & E Works, Whyalla, for Clutha Development Pty Ltd, Sydney. 30,000 tons gross, 54,000 tons dw, 754ft loa × 102·25ft breadth × 39·33ft draught, IHI-GEC turbs, 13,750shp, 15 knots

Conon Forest. The first British built ship in the International Scanscot pool of packaged timber carriers. There are 3 Swedish, 1 Norwegian and 1 British companies operating initially a pool of 8 ships, of which the British ones are operated by J. & J. Denholm (Management) Ltd, Glasgow, whilst the Swedish firm of AB August Leffler operates the others. She is the largest packaged lumber carrier so far completed in the UK, but two sisters, Vancouver Forest and Kyoto Forest will shortly join her. They are suitable for all solid bulk trades also. Specially built with 6 cargo holds with one continuous deck above, each cargo hold has two very large hatches abreast, thus opening up the whole ship for loading vertically by means of 5 hydraulically operated Hagglund 10-ton deck cranes. A special cargo 'spotting' device, consists of a geared 1hp electric motor on the crane hook, so that the packaged lumber may be turned into any position for stowing. Two 8-ton derricks, and an 8-ton derrick crane with a 75ft derrick are also fitted. A KaMeWa controllable pitch propeller is driven by a Sulzer 7RD 76/155 2 stroke diesel engine. The ship has a transom stern, giving a spacious poop deck.

Cornish City is the second of two sister ships built at Govan for Sir William Reardon Smith & Sons Ltd of Cardiff, and like all their ships, is registered at Bideford. She is suitable for several trades—as a medium sized container carrier or for general and bulk cargoes. Her propulsion is a twin diesel arrangement of Ruston AO engines developing a total of 9,000bhp and with a single screw giving 16 knots in service.

CONON FOREST. *British.* Bulk carrier (timber, packaged). Built by Upper Clyde Shipbuilders (Scotstoun Div) Ltd, Scotstoun, 1968, for J. & J. Denholm (Management) Ltd, Glasgow. 17,659 tons gross, 24,900 tons dw, 575ft loa × 87·25ft breadth × 31·86ft draught, 7-cyl Barclay Curle-Sulzer diesel, 11,200bhp, 15·5 knots.

CONTINENTAL PIONEER. (Sis CONTINENTAL SHIPPER). *Liberian.* Bulk carrier. Built by Mitsui Zozen, Osaka, for United SS Corpn, Monrovia. 15,474 tons gross, 25,942 tons dw, 584·33ft loa × 75·18ft breadth × 33·68ft draught, 7-cyl Uraga-Sulzer diesel, 11,200bhp, 15 knots.

COOLER SCAN. *Danish.* Cargo, ref. Built by Schlichting Werft, Travemunde, for Blaesbjerg & Co, Aarhus. 996 tons gross, 2,300 tons dw, 307·41ft loa × 44·33ft m breadth × 18·07ft draught, 12-cyl Deutz diesel, 4,000bhp, 17·25 knots.

CORATO. *British.* Cargo. Built by Scheeps 'Vooruitgang', Foxhol, for Hadley Shipping Co Ltd, London. 803/1,436 tons gross, —/2,570 tons dw, 253·58ft loa × 39ft breadth × 18·84ft draught, 8-cyl Atlas-MaK diesel, 1,400bhp, 11·25 knots.

CORFU ISLAND. *Liberian.* Cargo (SD 14). Built by Bartram & Sons Ltd, Sunderland, for Naxos Shipping Corpn, Monrovia. 9,045 tons gross, 15,110 tons dw, 462·75ft loa × 67·18ft breadth × 29·05ft draught, 5-cyl Clark-Sulzer diesel, 5,500bhp, 14 knots.

Cuthred. *Costing £300,000 this is the latest British Rail car ferry on the Portsmouth-Fishbourne route, increasing its passenger capacity by 100%, and for cars by 70%. Seats are provided for 400 people, of whom 357 are accommodated in covered deck lounges, of which one, the upper deck lounge, seating 131, has panoramic views over the Solent scene. Vehicles can drive on either end to the car deck, which can accommodate 48 private cars, or a mixture of lorries, coaches and cars. Last year the Isle of Wight routes, served by 10 ships, carried 317,000 vehicles. Propulsion is at 10 knots by a Davey-Paxman 8 RPHCM 378bhp diesel engine through Voith Schneider propeller units mounted fore and aft.*

C

CORNISH CITY. *British*. Cargo. Built by Upper Clyde Shipbuilders Ltd (Govan Div), Govan, for Sir Wm Reardon Smith & Sons Ltd, Bideford. 10,799 tons gross, 16,223 tons dw, 499·5ft loa (incl bb) × 72ft m breadth × draught na, two 9-cyl s sc Ruston Hornsby diesel, bhp na, 16 knots.

CRISTOBAL MARU. *Japanese*. Cargo. Built by Mitsubishi HI Ltd, Kobe, for Mitsui-OSK Lines KK, Kobe. 6,881 tons gross, 11,450 tons dw, 505·33ft loa (incl bb) × 72·25ft breadth × 26·41ft draught, 6-cyl Mitsubishi-Sulzer diesel, 9,600bhp, 18 knots.

CRYSTAL SCAN (launched as ARCTIC SCAN). *Danish*. Cargo, ref. Built by Nystads Varv A/B, Nystad, for Blaesberg & Co, Aarhus. 499/1,161 tons gross, 936/1,556 tons dw, 242·18ft loa × 35·09ft breadth × 12/15·43ft draught, 8-cyl Atlas-MaK diesel, 2,000bhp, 14 knots.

CUNENE. *Portuguese*. Cargo. Built by Stocznia Szczecinska, Szczecin, for Soc Geral de Comercie, Industria e Transportes, Lisbon. 6,804/10,552 tons gross, 12,800/16,600 tons dw, 517·75ft loa × 69·09ft breadth × 27·62/32·81ft draught, 6-cyl Cegielski diesel, 7,200bhp, knots na.

CUTHRED. *British*. Ferry. Built by Richards (Shipbuilders) Ltd, Lowestoft, for British Railways Board, London. 704 tons gross, 150 tons dw, 190ft loa × 51·5ft breadth × 6·5ft draught, two 8-cyl tw sc English Electric Group (Paxman) diesels, directional propellers, 2 fwd, 2 aft, 756bhp, 10 knots.

CYPRESS. *Norwegian*. Chemical tanker. Built by Ch Nav de La Ciotat, La Ciotat, for A/S Rederiet Odfjell, Oslo. 16,563 tons gross, 16,522 tons dw, 561·25ft loa × 80·18ft breadth × 28·73ft draught, 6-cyl Fiat diesel, 13,800bhp, knots na.

D

DAGMAR MAERSK. *Danish*. Tanker. Built by Nederland Dok & Scheeps, Amsterdam, for A. P. Moller, Copenhagen. 104,681 tons gross, 208,000 tons dw, 1,067ft loa (incl bb) × 154·92ft breadth × 62·3ft draught, cyl na, Atlantique-Stal Laval turbs, 28,000shp, 15 knots.

DAIAN MARU. *Japanese*. Bulk carrier. Built by Kanazashi Zosensho, Shimizu, for Masumoto Kaiun Sangyo KK, Akashi. 16,563 tons gross, 18,000 tons dw, 506·25ft loa × 77·58ft breadth × 30·09ft draught, 6-cyl Mitsui-B & W diesel, 8,300bhp, knots na.

DAIGOH MARU. *Japanese*. Bulk carrier (coal). Built by Mitsui Zosen, Tamano, for Mistui-OSK Lines & Shin Yei Sempaku KK, Tokyo. 36,646 tons gross, 58,874 tons dw, 750ft loa (incl bb) × 105·84ft breadth × 39ft draught, 6-cyl Mitsui-B & W diesel, 15,500bhp, 16·5 knots.

DAMODAR TANABE. *Indian*. Bulk carrier (four 8-ton MAN grabbing cranes). Built by Brodogradiliste 'Split', Split, for Damodar Bulk Carriers Ltd, Bombay. 24,573 tons gross, 43,800 tons dw, 634·5ft loa (incl bb) × 95·33ft breadth × 38·7ft draught, 6-cyl MAN diesel, 13,800bhp, 16 knots.

DAMODAR TASAKA. *Indian*. Bulk carrier. Built by Brodogradiliste 'Split', Split, for Damodar Bulk Carriers Ltd, Bombay. 24,330 tons gross, 45,300 tons dw, 634·5ft loa (incl bb) × 95·33ft breadth × 38·75ft draught, 6-cyl MAN diesel, 13,800bhp, knots na.

DAMPIER MARU. *Japanese*. Ore carrier. Built by Uraga HI Ltd, Yokosuka, for Daiichi Chuo KKK, Tokyo. 50,451 tons gross, 95,083 tons dw, 816·92ft loa (incl bb) × 126·5ft breadth × 47·5ft draught, 9-ycl Uraga-Sulzer diesel, 20,300bhp, 14·75 knots.

DANGELD. *British*. Cargo, ref (2 side ports). Built by Cochrane & Sons, Selby, for London & Rochester Trading Co Ltd, Rochester. 699 tons gross, 1,000 tons dw, 247ft loa × 40·84ft breadth × draught na, two 8-cyl tw sc Lister-Blackstone diesel, 2,000bhp, 13 knots.

DANIELLA. *Dutch*. Cargo. Built by Zaanlandse Scheeps, Zaandam, for Jumbo Ships, Willemstad, Curacao. 1,583 tons gross, 2,400 tons dw, 254·75ft loa × 44·58ft breadth × 18·05ft draught, cyl na, 1,500bhp, knots na.

DARIAL. *Russian*. Stern trawler, fish factory, ref (ATLANTIK class). Built by Volkswerft Stralsund, Stralsund, 1968, for USSR. 2,657 tons gross, 1,152 tons dw, 269·58ft loa × 44·75ft breadth × 16·41ft draught, two 8-cyl s sc Liebknecht diesel, cpp, 2,320bhp, 13·5 knots.

DAVID P. REYNOLDS. *Liberian*. Bulk carrier. Built by Howaldtswerke-Deutsche Werft, Hamburg, for Caribbean SS Co, SA, Monrovia (Reynolds Metals, Richmond, Vg). 28,565 tons gross, 47,435 tons dw, 743·33ft loa (incl bb) × 102·18ft breadth × 40·98ft draught, cyl na, AEG turbs, 18,000shp, knots na.

DAWN OF KUWAIT. *Kuwait*. Cargo (FREEDOM class). Built by Ishikawajima-Harima HI, Tokyo, for Mediterranean Maritime Co SAL, Kuwait. 9,650 tons gross, 14,000 tons dw, 465ft loa (incl bb) × 65·18ft breadth × 28·66ft draught, 12-cyl IHI-Pielstick diesel, 5,130bhp, 14·25 knots.

DELTA DUNARII. *Roumanian*. Stern trawler, factory ship, ref (B22 class). Built by Stocznia Gdanska, Gdansk, for Ministerul Industriei Alimentare, Galatz. 2,715 tons gross, 1,959 tons dw, 288·75ft loa × 47·66ft breadth × 18·37ft draught, 12-cyl Cegielski-Fiat diesel, cpp, 2,500bhp, 13·75 knots.

DENEB. *Spanish*. LPG carrier, ref. Built by Soc Espanola de Constr Naval, Bilbao, for Maritima de Fertilizantes SA, Bilbao. 3,200 tons gross, 3,400 tons dw, 341·25ft loa × 48·66ft breadth × 20·52ft draught, 6-cyl SECN-B & W diesel, 3,850bhp, 13·5 knots.

DENEB. *Norwegian*. Cargo OSD. Built by M. Kleven M/V, Ulsteinvik, for Det Bergenske D/S, Bergen, 499 tons gross, tons dw na, 256·58ft loa × 41·09ft breadth × draught na, 6-cyl Deutz diesel, cpp, 2,200bhp, 14 knots.

DENEBOLA. *Panamanian*. Cargo. Built by Brodogradiliste 3rd Maj, Rijeka, for Cross Seas Shipping Corp, Panama. 10,000 tons gross, 15,000 tons dw, 475·75ft loa × 67·75ft breadth × 29·52ft draught, 5-cyl 3rd Maj-Sulzer diesel, 7,700bhp, knots na.

DICTO. *Norwegian*. Bulk carrier. Built by Rheinstal Nordseewerke, Emden, for E. E. Aaby's Rederi A/S, Oslo. 14,318 tons gross, 22,224 tons dw, 536·58ft loa × 75ft breadth × 32·84ft draught, 7-cyl Borsig-Fiat diesel, 10,500bhp, 16 knots.

DIEDERIKA WIARDS. *German*. Cargo CSD (Weser Typ 36). Built by A. G. 'Weser' Werke Seebeck, Bremerhaven, for Kauffahrtel Seereederei Adolf Wiards & Co, Bremen. 9,305 tons gross, 15,600 tons dw, 463·25ft loa × 69ft breadth × 29·5ft draught, cyl na, MAN diesel, 6,520bhp, 15·25 knots.

DIEKSAND. *German*. Tanker. Built by Busumer Werft GmbH, Busum, for A. F. Harmstorf & Co, Hamburg. 499 tons gross, 1,285 tons dw, 241·75ft loa × 39·33ft m breadth × 12ft draught, 4-cyl Atlas-MaK diesel, 1,000bhp, 12 knots.

DIMITRI MENDELEYEV. *USSR*. Research ship. Built by Mathias Thesen Werft, Wismar, 1968, for USSR, Vladivostok. 5,460 tons gross 1,986 tons dw, 407·5ft loa × 55·92ft breadth × 19·5ft draught, two 6-cyl tw sc Halberstadt-MAN diesel, 8,000bhp, 18·25 knots.

DIMONA. *Norwegian*. Cargo. Built by A/S Porsgrunds M/V, Porgrunn, for Chr. J. Reim, Porsgrunn. 6,228 tons gross, 10,130 tons dw, 420·84ft loa × 52·66ft breadth × 27·81ft draught, 10-cyl MAN diesel, 4,200bhp, 13 knots.

DINNA SKOU. *Danish*. Cargo, ref, OSD/CSD, 75-ton derrick. Built by Helsingor Skibs & Msk, Helsingor, for Ove Skou, Copenhagen. 9,684 tons gross, 10,600/14,000 tons dw, 513ft loa × 65·09ft breadth × 26·55/31·25ft draught, 9-cyl Helsingor-B & W diesel, 10,800bhp, 18 knots.

DIRECTEUR GENERAL MAAST. *Dutch*. Cable ship. Built by E. J. Smit & Zn's Scheeps, Westerbroek, for Staatsbed der Post Telegrafie & Telefonie, The Hague. 629 tons gross, 300 tons cable, 179·58ft loa × 31·09ft breadth × 10·48ft draught, two 5-cyl tw sc Bolnes diesel, 350bhp, 10·5 knots.

DISCOVERY BAY. *British*. Container ship (1,300 × 20ft containers), ref. Built by Howaldtswerke-Deutsche Werft, Hamburg, for P & O Steam Nav Co Ltd (Overseas Containers Ltd), London. 26,876 tons gross, tons dw na, 752·41ft loa (incl bb) × 100·25ft breadth × 35·09ft draught, Stal Laval turbs, 32,400shp, 22 knots.

DITTE SKOU. *Danish*. Cargo, ref, 8 pass, 75-ton derrick. Built by Helsingor Skibs & Mask, Helsingor, for Ove Skou, Copenhagen. 6,582/9,584 tons gross, 10,610/14,000 tons dw, 513ft loa × 65·18ft breadth × 26·55/31·18ft draught, 9-cyl Helsingor-B & W diesel, 10,800bhp, 18 knots.

DAMODAR TANABE

D

Damodar Tanabe *is the first of two ships ordered by Damodar Bulk Carriers Ltd, of Goa, India from the Jugoslav SPLIT yard. Her MAN K62 86/180E diesel engine gives a service speed of 15·7 knots at 13,800bhp. Her sister ship is the* Damodar Tasaka.

Dangeld (*not illustrated*). *Specially built by the London & Rochester Co for their liner service between Whitstable and Esbjerg, this ship has been designed to replace the* Resurgence *of somewhat similar appearance, now undergoing survey before taking up the company's Lowestoft-Esbjerg trade. Her name is a departure from the usual '-ence' termination of London & Rochester names, but was chosen as being appropriate. She will maintain a weekly service, arriving on Wednesday and sailing for Whitstable on the following evening. Arriving in Whitstable on Saturday, she will sail again on Tuesday evening, the longer period in the UK being to allow shore leave to her personnel. Most of the Danish cargo is refrigerated, i.e. cheese, butter, lard for distribution to Southern English supermarkets, and poultry for the West of England. The deep freeze cargo is distributed to various parts of the UK, edibles to sausage manufacturers, non edibles to a factory in Glamorgan for gelatine production. General cargo is also carried. From the UK, general cargo and machinery are carried. She is an open shelter decker to ice class 3, and strengthened for grounding when required at certain states of the tide at Whitstable. She berths port side to the quay at both ports, and her cargo handling gear is designed accordingly. Both side and hatch loading are employed, fork lift palletization is the method. There are two side doors on the port side. A 5-ton Atlas-MaK crane serves both side doors and the forward hatch. Insulated cargo is loaded through a hatch offset to port just forward of the bridge, and flush to enable 6×20ft containers to be carried on deck. The Macgregor-Lund Mohr side doors may be used as ramps when trucking palletized cargo, operated hydraulically. 4 special Hyster 10,500lb capacity fork lift trucks are carried on board, with two Yale pallet transporters. Two Lister-Blackstone EWSL 8 MGR turbocharged diesels each developing 1,000bhp (mcr) at 900rpm, giving a speed of 14 knots. Each engine drives a fixed pitch propeller. Bridge control is fitted of the Bloctube type, and the machinery was installed by the Drypool Engineering Co Ltd. Accommodation is provided for 8 passengers in 2 and 4 berth cabins. Officers and crew number 11.*

DNEPRODZERZHINSK. *Russian.* Stern trawler, fish factory, ref (ATLANTIK class.) Built by Volkswerft Stralsund, Stralsund, for USSR, Odessa. 2,657 tons gross, 1,152 tons dw, 269·58ft loa × 44·75ft breadth × 16·41ft draught, two 8-cyl s sc Liebknecht diesel, 2,320bhp, 13·5 knots.

DOMINICA MARU. *Japanese.* Cargo. Built by Hitachi Zosen, Mukaishima, for Kobe KKK, Kobe. 8,800 tons gross, 12,000 tons dw, 427·25ft lbp × 68·41ft breadth × draught na, 6-cyl Hitachi-B & W diesel, 8,300bhp, knots na.

DON AMBROSIO. *Philippine.* Cargo. Built by Setoda Shipbuilding Co Ltd, Setoda, for Transocean Transport Corp, Manila. 4,000 tons gross, 6,070 tons dw, 374·18ft loa × 53·18ft m breadth × 21·66ft draught, 6-cyl Hitachi-B & W diesel, 3,300bhp, 12·5 knots.

DON SALVADOR. *Philippine.* Bulk carrier. Built by Hakodate Dock Co Ltd, Hakodate, for Northern Lines Inc, Manila. 10,964 tons gross, 18,733 tons dw, 508·5ft loa × 74·33ft breadth × 30·09ft draught, 7-cyl Mitsui-B & W diesel, 8,400bhp, 14·5 knots.

DONAU MARU. *Japanese.* Ore/oil carrier. Built by Mitsubishi HI, Ltd, Yokohama, for Sanko KKK, Osaka. 45,237 tons gross, 76,400 tons dw, measurements na, cyl na, bhp na, knots na.

DONETS. *Russian.* Cable ship. Built by O/Y Wartsila A/B Abo, 1968, for USSR. 5,600 tons gross, 3,245 tons dw, 427·84ft loa × 52·66ft breadth × 17ft draught, 5-cyl tw sc Wartsila diesel-electric, 4,950bhp, 14 knots.

DONETSKIY KOMSOMOLETS. *Russian.* Cargo. Built by A. Zhdanov, Leningrad, for USSR. 6,630 tons gross, tons dw na, 426·5ft loa × 58·5ft breadth × draught na, 7-cyl Bryansk-B & W diesel, 5,400bhp, knots na.

Dora Papalios *is the second 'SD 14' (of Austin & Pickersgill design) to be built by Hellenic Shipyards at Skaramanga.*

D

DONETSKIY SHAKHTER. *Russian*. Cargo. Built by A. Zhdanov, Leningrad, for USSR. 6,630 tons gross, tons dw na, 426·5ft loa (incl bb) × 58·5ft breadth × draught na, 7-cyl Bryansk-B & W diesel, 5,400bhp, knots na.

DORA PAPALIOS. *Greek*. Cargo (SD14). Built by Hellenic Shipyards, Skaramanga, for Codros Shipping Co, Piraeus (G. Papalios). 9,072 tons gross, 14,200 tons dw, 462·5ft loa × 67·41ft breadth × 29ft draught, 5-cyl Sulzer diesel, 5,500bhp, 14 knots.

DOROTHEA BOLTEN. *German*. Cargo, CSD. Built by Orenstein Koppel & Lubecker Masch, Lubeck, for Aug. Bolten Wm Miller's Nachfolger, Hamburg. 4,795 tons gross, tons dw na, 382·92ft loa × 56·58ft breadth × 24·68ft draught, 8-cyl Atlas-MaK diesel, 4,000bhp, knots na.

DORTHE MAERSK. *Danish*. Tanker. Built by Odense Staalskibs A/S, Lindo, for A. P. Moller, Copenhagen. 103,148 tons gross, 205,700 tons dw, 1,079·75ft loa × 143·66ft breadth × 64·92ft draught, cyl na, Stal Laval turbs, 28,000shp, knots na.

DOWA MARU No. 5. *Japanese*. Cargo. Built by Maizuru Jukogyo Ltd, Maizuru, for Kyowa Sangyo KK, Osaka. 2,075 tons gross, 3,520 tons dw, 262·41ft lbp × 42·41ft m breadth × 19ft draught, 8-cyl Hatsudoki diesel, 2,000bhp, 11·75 knots.

DRUZHBA NARODA. *Russian*. Tanker. Built by Stocznia im Komuny Paryskiej, Gdynia, for USSR. 14,203 tons gross, 20,000 tons dw, 581·58ft loa, × 73·5ft breadth × 30·75ft draught, 6-cyl Cegielski-Sulzer diesel, 9,600bhp, knots na.

DUBLIN. *British*. Tanker. Built by Hall, Russell & Co Ltd, Aberdeen, for Shell-Mex & BP Ltd, London. 1,077 tons gross, 1,537 tons dw, 214·75ft loa × 37·18ft breadth × 14·6ft draught, 8-cyl British Polar diesel, 1,200bhp, 11 knots.

DUTCH FAITH (Sis DUTCH SPIRIT). *Dutch*. Chemical tanker. Built by Schps v/h De Groot & v Vliet, Slikkeveer, for N. V. Tankvaart 'Rotterdam', Rotterdam. 999 tons gross, 1,800 tons dw, 227·33ft loa × 38·09ft breadth × 16·33ft draught, 8-cyl Smit-Bolnes diesel, 1,760bhp, 12 knots.

E

E. L. BARTLETT. *USA*. Pass ferry. Built by Jeffboat Inc, Jeffersonville, for State of Alaska, Dept of Public Works, Juneau. 934 tons gross, tons dw na, 193ft loa × 53·18ft breadth × 12·75ft draught, two 10-cyl tw sc Fairbanks-Morse diesel, 3,400bhp, 15 knots.

E. R. SCALDIA. *Belgian*. Bulk carrier. Built by N. V. Boelwerf SA, Tamise, for H. G. Ahlers, SA, Antwerp. 22,350 tons gross, 39,465 tons dw, 668·66ft loa (incl bb) × 89·5ft breadth × 37·3ft draught, 6-cyl ACEC-MAN diesel, 13,800bhp, 16 knots.

EAGLE CHARGER. *USA*. Tanker. Built by Bethlehem Steel Corpn, Sparrow's Point, for Eagle Terminal Tanker Inc, Wilmington, Del (UMC). 20,877 tons gross, 37,807 tons dw, 660·18ft loa × 90·18ft breadth × 36·64ft draught, GEC turbs, 15,000shp, 16 knots.

EAGLE GLORY. *Panamanian*. Bulk carrier. Built by Ishikawajima-Harima HI, Nagoya, for Glory Shipping SA, Panama. 23,472 tons gross, 41,280 tons dw, 634·84ft loa (incl bb) × 96·66ft breadth × 37·23ft draught, 7-cyl IHI-Sulzer diesel, 11,200bhp, 15·75 knots.

EAGLE LEADER. *USA*. Tanker. Built by Bethlehem Steel Corpn, Sparrow's Point, for United Maritime Corpn, Wilmington, Del. 20,887 tons gross, 37,807 tons dw, 660·18ft loa × 90·18ft breadth × 36·64ft draught, GEC turbs, 15,000shp, 16 knots.

EASTERN ACE. *Liberian*. Cargo. Built by Ishikawajima-Harima HI, Nagoya, for Liberian Equity Transports Inc, Monrovia (World Wide Shpg, Hong Kong). 9,777 tons gross, 16,500 tons dw, 477·66ft loa × 71·66ft breadth × 29·83ft draught, 6-cyl IHI-Sulzer diesel, 7,200bhp, knots na.

EASTERN ANNA. *Panamanian*. Cargo. Built by Hayashikane Zosen, Shimonoseki, for Rex Shipping SA, Panama. 3,999 tons gross, 5,900 tons dw, 356·66ft loa × 53·92ft breadth × 21·66ft draught, 6-cyl Mitsui-B & W diesel, 3,300bhp, 12·75 knots.

EASTERN BEAUTY. *Panamanian*. Cargo. Built by Tohoku Zosen, Shiogama, for Mascot Shipping Co SA, Panama. 6,252 tons gross, 9,659 tons dw, 418ft loa × 62·66ft breadth × 23·77ft draught, 6-cyl Hitachi-B & W diesel, 4,400bhp, 12·75 knots.

E

EASTERN MARY. *Liberian.* Cargo (timber). Built by Hitachi Zosen, Mukaishima, for Liberian Distance Transports Inc, Monrovia (World Wide S Co, Hong Kong). 11,432 tons gross, 19,152 tons dw, 512·33ft loa × 74·33ft breadth × 31·29ft draught, 7-cyl Hitachi-B & W diesel, 8,400bhp, 15 knots.

EASTERN MERIT. *Liberian.* Bulk carrier. Built by Ishikawajima-Harima HI, Nagasaki, for Liberia Noble Transports Inc, Monrovia (World Wide S Co, Hong Kong). 23,300 tons gross, 38,440 tons dw, 607ft loa (incl bb) × 90·75ft breadth × 38·64ft draught, 7-cyl IHI-Sulzer diesel, 11,200bhp, knots na.

EASTERN STAR. *Liberian.* Tanker. Built by Ast de Cadagua, Bilbao, for Byblos Shipping Co, Monrovia. 1,110 tons gross, 1,600 tons dw, 232ft loa × 36·18ft breadth × 14·25ft draught, 6-cyl Atlas-MaK diesel, 1,550bhp, knots na.

EDE SOTTORF. *German.* Container ship (260 × 20ft, 110 on deck) OSD/CSD. Built by Schiffs Unterweser, Bremerhaven, for Erich Drescher Hamburg. 3,200/5,477 tons gross, 5,300/7,300 tons dw, 408·41ft loa × 58ft breadth × 20·66/24·77ft draught, 16-cyl Deutz diesel, 6,400bhp, 16·5 knots.

EIGAMOIYA. *Nauru.* Cargo (phosphate) 12 pass. Built by Robb-Caledon SB's, Leith, for Nauru Local Government Council, Nauru. 4,426 ton, gross, 5,862 tons dw, 367·84ft loa × 55·18ft breadth × 22·5ft draught, two 6-cyl s sc Mirrlees National diesel, 5,040bhp, 15 knots.

EIKAKU MARU. *Japanese.* Cargo. Built by Usuki Tekkosho, Saiki, 1968, for Eiwa Kaiun KK, Kobe. 5,836 tons gross, 9,325 tons dw, 417·84ft loa × 59·18ft breadth × 23·66ft draught, 12-cyl IHI-Pielstick diesel, 5,580bhp, knots na.

EIKI MARU. *Japanese.* Cargo. Built by Usuki Tekkosho, Saiki, 1968, for Japan Line & Japan Kinkai KK, Tokyo. 4,233 tons gross, 6,665 tons dw, 374·84ft loa × 54·5ft breadth × 22·41ft draught, 6-cyl Hatsudoki diesel, 3,500bhp, knots na.

EIKO MARU. *Japanese.* Tanker. Built by Shin Naniwa Dock Co Ltd, Osaka, for Koei KK, Kobe. 2,568 tons gross, 4,200 tons dw, 304·41ft loa × 43·41ft breadth × 20·18ft draught, 6-cyl Akasaka Tekkosho diesel, 2,500bhp, 12·25 knots.

EKHOLOT. *Russian.* Fish factory. Built by Burmeister & Wain, Copenhagen, for USSR, Kaliningrad. 3,813 tons gross, 2,710 tons dw, 337ft loa × 52·66ft breadth × 18·22ft draught, 6-cyl B & W diesel, cpp, 3,100bhp, 14 knots.

EL MANSOURA. *Egyptian (UAR).* Cargo. Built by Suez Canal Authority, Port Fuad, for The United Arab Maritime Co, Alexandria. 2,800 tons gross, 4,000 tons dw, 330·75ft loa × 48ft breadth × 20·58ft draught, cyl na, MAN diesel, 3,080bhp, 14·5 knots.

ELIANE. (Sis MARY ANNE). *Liberian.* Ore/oil. Built by Hitachi Zosen, Innoshima, for Global Bulk Carriers Inc, Monrovia (Maritime Overseas Corpn, NY). 35,684 tons gross, 71,060 tons dw, 792·33ft loa (incl bb) × 106·18ft breadth × 45·96ft draught, 8-cyl Hitachi-B & W diesel, 18,400bhp, 15·75 knots.

ELISABETH OLDENDORFF. *German.* Cargo (BV Liberty replacement). Built by Bremer Vulkan, Vegesack, for Egon Oldendorff, Lubeck. 9,328 tons gross, 15,200 tons dw, 457·84ft loa × 68·84ft m breadth × 30·22ft draught, 6-cyl BV-MAN diesel, 8,400 bhp, 16 knots.

ELLEN ISLE. *German.* Cargo OSD container ship. Built by Gebr. Schurenstedt, Bardenfleth, for H. Wurthmann, Elsfleth. 999 tons gross, 2,350 tons dw, 313·58ft loa × 52·84ft breadth × 13·79ft draught, 8-cyl Atlas-MaK diesel, 3,500bhp, knots na.

ELNJA. *Russian.* Tanker. Built by Rauma-Repola O/Y, Rauma, for USSR. 3,500 tons gross, 4,600 tons dw, 348·25ft loa × 50·66ft breadth × 21·33ft draught, 5-cyl Valmet-B & W diesel, 2,900bhp, 14 knots.

EMBA. *Russian.* Tanker. Built by G. Dimitrov Shipyard, Varna, 1967, for USSR, Baku. 3,821 tons gross, 4,094 tons dw, 405·25ft loa × 52·5ft breadth × 14·41ft draught, 8-cyl diesel, bhp na, 10·75 knots.

Eigamoiya. *The first ship built for the Government of the island of Nauru in the Pacific, she has been designed to carry phosphate and general cargo. As phosphate supplies are dwindling on the island, it is hoped that their revenue may be replaced by establishing a Central Pacific inter-island service. Apart from a crew of 34, there are 7 passenger cabins. She is driven by 2 Mirrlees KDMR 6 4-stroke diesel engines geared to a single screw, which gave a trial speed in ballast of 16·7 knots, the service speed being 15 knots. She has an elaborate mooring system, by which she can lift, overhaul and lay her own moorings by means of a special electric mooring winch on the forecastle head. The engines can be controlled from the bridge, as well as from the normal engine room control room. There are 4 holds, No 1 being suitable for cased petroleum, whilst part of No 4 is refrigerated. Fresh water is carried in part of the double bottom, tunnel side tanks and tanks over the after peak, Nos 2 and 3 double bottom tanks hold the heavy fuel oil, with water ballast in the remaining double bottom tank and fore peak tank. The forward deep tank carries light diesel oil or water ballast. Phosphate will be carried outwards from Nauru, and portable steel hopper sides are fitted in the holds with a 40° slope. There are two 10-ton ASEA cranes at Nos 2 and 3 holds, and two 5-ton derricks at Nos 1 and 4.*

Elbe Express. *Four ships of this class, of which the* Elbe *and* Alster Express *are operated by the Hamburg-Amerika Line, are run in a joint service with the Norddeutscher Lloyd's* Mosel Express *and* Weser Express, *from the Continent via Felixstowe to New York, Philadelphia, Baltimore and Norfolk, on a weekly service. The ships are equipped with fin stabilizers, designed to reduce rolling within 6° limits. The Hapag/Lloyd claim that 'containers travel with passenger comfort!' Each ship can carry 786 × 20ft ISO standard containers or 300 × 40ft and 136 × 20ft. They are equipped with an automatic list-equalizing system, consisting of two tanks on either side of the ship (double bottom and wing tanks). As soon as a container is loaded or discharged on one side of the ship, a pumping system compensates this weight within seconds with water. The installation allows a one side loading and discharging up to 300 tons. There are two special tanks which permit measuring the ship's stability within a few minutes by an inclining test. 3 mooring winches aft, and 3 forward, of the automatic tensioning type keep the vessels under the cranes ashore. Twenty-one 40ft refrigerated containers can be carried. No passengers are carried, and the crew number 33, including 2 stewardesses. Navigation instruments include a gyro compass with auto-pilot, 2 radar sets (range up to 60 miles), VHF telephony, D/F weather chart receiver, 300-mile range Decca Navigator and 2,500-mile range Loran. The 9-cyl MAN diesel engine maintains a service speed of 20 knots at 122rpm and 15,750bhp.*

EMBA. *Russian*. Tanker. Builder na, Kerch, 1967, for USSR. 1,773 tons gross, 1,660 tons dw, 274·18ft loa × 39·5ft breadth × 15·25ft draught, cyl na, diesel, bhp na, knots na.

EMIL REITH. *German*. Cargo (2 pass). Built by Schiffsb Unterweser, Bremerhaven, 1968, for Reith & Co, Hamburg. 1,834 tons gross, 2,805 tons dw, 290·18ft loa × 44·75ft breadth × 17·14ft draught, 8-cyl Deutz diesel, 2,140bhp, 13·75 knots.

EMINENCE. *British*. Cargo. Built by Goole SB & R Co Ltd, Goole, for London & Rochester Trading Co Ltd, Rochester. 999 tons gross, 1,630 tons dw, 222ft loa × 38·66ft breadth × 13·84ft draught, 8-cyl Lister-Blackstone diesel, 1,000bhp, 10·5 knots.

ENCOUNTER BAY *British*. Container ship, ref. Built by Howaldtswerke-Deutsche Werft AG, Hamburg, for Scottish Shire Line, Cayzer Irvine & Co Ltd (Container Fleets Ltd). 26,750 tons gross, 29,150 tons dw, 745·75ft loa (incl bb) × 100·18ft breadth × 35ft draught, Stal Laval turbs, 32,000shp, 22 knots.

ENERGY EVOLUTION. *Liberian*. Tanker. Built by Sasebo HI, Sasebo, for Island Navigation Co, Hong Kong, Monrovia. 98,930 tons gross, 213,373 tons dw, 1,069·58ft loa (incl bb) × 158·41ft breadth × 63·43ft draught, GEC turbs, 30,000shp, 16 knots.

ENERGY TRANSPORT (Sis ENERGY GENERATION, building). *Liberian*. Tanker. Built by Sasebo HI, Sasebo, for Island Navigation Co (C. Y. Tung, Hong Kong), Monrovia. 99,332 tons gross, 213,724 tons dw, 1,069·58ft loa (incl bb) × 158·33ft breadth × 63·43ft draught, GEC turbs, 30,000shp, 16 knots.

ENIWA MARU. *Japanese*. Cargo. Built by Ishikawajima Ship & Chemical Co, Tokyo, for Hakuyo KKK, Osaka. 989 tons gross, 1,581 tons dw, 196·33ft loa × 37·18ft breadth × 15·5ft draught, two 6-cyl tw sc Yanmar diesel, 400bhp, knots na.

EOLO. *Spanish*. Cargo (timber). Built by Cia Euskalduna, Bilbao, for Naviera Bilbaina SA, Bilbao. 4,259 tons gross, 6,350 tons dw, 387ft loa × 53·25ft breadth × 22·12ft draught, 10-cyl Euskalduna-MAN diesel, 4,300bhp, 14 knots.

ERATO. *Greek*. Bulk carrier. Built by Ishikawajima-Harima HI, Aioi, for M. A. Karageorgis (Helles) Ltd, Piraeus. 12,754 tons gross, 19,618 tons dw, 502ft loa × 78ft m breadth × 30·57ft draught, 7-cyl IHI diesel-electric, 8,700bhp, 15·5 knots.

ERISKAY. *British*. Bulk carrier. Built by Scotts SB & E Co Ltd, Greenock, for John Swire & Sons Ltd, London. 12,485 tons gross, 19,050 tons dw, 520ft loa (incl bb) × 71·41ft breadth × 30·38ft draught, 7-cyl Scotts-Sulzer diesel, 8,700bhp, 15 knots.

ESPRESSO PIEMONTE. *Italian*. Vehicle ferry. Built by Cant. Nav. 'Luigi Orlando', Leghorn, for Societa Traghetti del Mediterraneo SpA, Porto Torres. 1,599 tons gross, 2,800 tons dw, 345·5ft loa × 57·5ft breadth × 15·92ft draught, two 16-cyl tw sc Fiat diesel, 8,000bhp, knots na.

ESSO ANGLIA (Sis ESSO PARIS). *British*. Tanker. Built by Ch de l'Atlantique, St Nazaire, 1968, for Esso Petroleum Co Ltd, London. 97,082 tons gross, 170,800 tons dw, 1,066ft loa (incl bb) × 157·25ft breadth × 55·33ft draught, Atlantique-Stal Laval turbs, 30,000shp, 16 knots.

ESSO BREGA. *Italian*. LPG carrier. Built by Italcantieri SpA, Genoa, for 'La Prora' SpA Trasporti, La Spezia. 30,455 tons gross, 22,000 tons dw, 681·5ft loa (incl bb) × 96·09ft breadth × draught na, Ansaldo-Stal Laval turbs, 15,000shp, 16 knots.

ESSO CHITTAGONG. *Panamanian*. Tanker. Built by Ishikawajima-Harima HI, Kure, for Esso Transport Tanker Co Inc, Panama. 12,994 tons gross, 20,950 tons dw, 557·84ft loa (incl bb) × 77·18ft breadth × 30·75ft draught, 6-cyl IHI-Sulzer diesel, 7,200bhp, knots na.

ESSO CONNECTICUT. *USA*. Tanker. Built by Ingalls Iron Works, Decatur, for Humble Oil & Refining Co, Wilmington, Del. 1,729 tons gross, tons dw na, 276ft loa × 55·18ft breadth × 12·56ft draught, 2-cyl tw sc Caterpillar diesel, 1,700bhp, 11 knots.

E

Encounter Bay. *The first container ship delivered to Overseas Containers Ltd of London. To be followed by five sisters, she was at the time, the largest container ship afloat. OCL was founded in 1965 by 4 major British shipping groups to share the immense financial outlay required to inaugurate the new container ship service to Australia, with the ancilliary berths and containers. These 4 are the P & O, Ocean Steamship, Furness Withy, and British & Commonwealth Groups. Of the 1,300 containers to be carried in each ship, 526 general cargo units are carried above deck, 470 general cargo units below deck, and 304 refrigerated units below deck. The containers below deck are stowed in 6 cellular holds, the after two of which are insulated for the carriage of refrigerated containers at temperatures down to —29°C, cooled air being supplied to the bottom of each container, and exhausted at the top. Either 20ft or 40ft units can be accommodated. 4 passive Flume anti-rolling stabilizing tanks are fitted, designed by J. J. McMullen Associates Inc. The control of the main engines at sea is by one officer from a control room in the forward section of the machinery space. The machinery is designed to run unattended in port. The turbines were claimed to be, at the time, the largest single screw set in operation, of 32,000shp giving 22 knots at 140rpm, and of Stal-Laval AP32/140 type.*

In October it was announced that an international consortium will be formed to operate the Europe-Australia container trade consisting of 1 integrated fleet of 13 ships as follows: UK—OCL 6×1,300 container ships, ACT 2×1,233 container ships; France—Messageries Maritimes 1×1,223 container ship; Germany—HAPAG 1×1,300 container ship, NDL 1×1,300 container ship; Holland—VNS 1×1,300 container ship; Italy—Lloyd Triestino 1×1,233 container ship. Separate owners will manage the ships, but schedule and cargo will be centralized in London.

On March 12th, 1970 the "Encounter Bay" arrived at Antwerp from Australia, being the first ship to make five round trips between the continent and Australia in one year. During this period she has carried over 200,000 tons. A conventional cargo liner would make two and a half trips in this time.

ESSO EUROPA. *Panamanian.* Tanker. Built by AG 'Weser', Bremen, for Esso Transport Co, Panama. 127,000 tons gross, 250,000 tons dw, 1,141·09ft loa×170·18ft breadth×65·48ft draught, GEC turbs, 31,550shp, knots na.

ESSO GOA. *Panamanian.* Tanker. Built by Ishikawajima-Harima HI, Kure, for Esso Transport Co Inc, Panama. 12,000 tons gross, 20,989 tons dw, 558ft loa (incl bb)×77·18ft breadth×30·86ft draught, 6-cyl IHI diesel, 7,200bhp, 14·5 knots.

ESSO INTERAMERICA. *Panamanian.* Tanker. Built by Ishikawajima-Harima HI, Kure, for Esso Transport Co Inc, Panama. 12,994 tons gross, 20,950 tons dw, 558ft loa (incl bb)×77·18ft breadth×30·86ft draught, 6-cyl IHI-Sulzer diesel, 7,200bhp, 14·75 knots.

ESSO KARACHI. *Panamanian.* Tanker. Built by Ishikawajima-Harima HI, Kure, for Esso Transport Co Inc, Panama. 12,000 tons gross, 20,987 tons dw, 558ft loa (incl bb)×77·09ft breadth×30·86ft draught, 6-cyl IHI-Sulzer diesel, 7,200bhp, 14·75 knots.

ESSO MALACCA. *Panamanian.* Tanker. Built by Ishikawajima-Harima HI, Kure, for Esso Transport Tanker Co Inc, Panama. 12,000 tons gross, 20,950 tons dw, 560·85ft loa (incl bb)×77·09ft breadth×30·75ft draught, 6-cyl IHI-Sulzer diesel, 7,200bhp, 14·75 knots.

ESSO NAGASAKI. *Panamanian.* Tanker. Built by Ishikawajima-Harima HI, Kure, for Esso Transport Co Inc, Panama. 12,995 tons gross, 21,118 tons dw, 558ft loa (incl bb)×77·18ft breadth×30·86ft draught, 6-cyl IHI-Sulzer diesel, 7,200bhp, 14·75 knots.

ESSO NORWAY. *Panamanian.* Tanker. Built by Howaldtswerke-Deutsche Werft, Kiel, for Esso Transport Co Inc, Panama. 84,996 tons gross, 190,000 tons dw, 1,062·18ft loa (incl bb)×155ft breadth×60·46ft draught, GEC turbs, 30,000shp, 16·75 knots.

ESSO PARIS (Sis ESSO ANGLIA). *French.* Tanker. Built by Ch de l'Atlantique, St Nazaire, for Esso Standard Soc Anon Francaise, Le Havre. 96,226 tons gross, 193,900 tons dw, 1,066·33ft loa (incl bb)×157·25ft breadth×60·5ft draught, Atlantique-Stal Laval turbs, 30,400bhp, 16·5 knots.

ESSO PENANG. *Panamanian.* Tanker. Built by Ishikawajima-Harima HI, Kure, for Esso Transport & Tanker Co Inc, Panama. 12,994 tons gross 21,118 tons dw, 558ft loa (incl bb)×77·18ft breadth×30·86ft draught, 6-cyl IHI-Sulzer diesel, 7,200bhp, 14·5 knots.

ESSO PORT DICKSON. *Panamanian.* Tanker. Built by Ishikawajima-Harima HI, Kure, for Esso Transport & Tanker Co, Panama. 12,994 tons gross, 20,950 tons dw, 558ft loa (incl bb)×77·18ft breadth×30·75ft draught, 6-cyl IHI-Sulzer diesel, 7,200bhp, 14·5 knots.

ESSO PORTOVENERE. *Italian.* LPG carrier. Built by Italcantieri SpA, Genoa, for 'La Prora' SpA Trasporti, Palermo. 30,700 tons gross, 22,000 tons dw, 681·5ft loa (incl bb)×96·09ft breadth×27·58ft draught, cyl na, Stal Laval turbs, 15,000shp, knots na.

ESSO SCOTIA. *British.* Tanker (VLCC—very large crude carrier). Built by A. G. 'Weser', Bremen, for Esso (International) Petroleum Co Ltd, London. 127,158 tons gross, 250,300 tons dw, 1,141·09ft loa (incl bb)×170·18ft breadth×65·38ft draught, Weser-GEC turbs, 31,550shp 16 knots.

ESSO YOKOHAMA. *Panamanian.* Tanker. Built by Ishikawajima-Harima HI, Kure, for Esso Transport & Tanker Co Inc, Panama. 12,994 tons gross, 21,106 tons dw. 558ft loa (incl bb)×77·18ft breadth×30·86ft draught, 6-cyl IHI-Sulzer diesel, 7,200bhp, 14·5 knots.

EVER SUCCESS. *Liberian.* Bulk carrier. Built by Namura Zosensho, Osaka, for Reliance Marine Corpn, SA, Monrovia. 9,465 tons gross, 16,700 tons dw, 477·33ft loa×71ft breadth×30·5ft draught, 6-cyl Mitsubishi-Sulzer diesel, 8,000bhp, knots na.

EVGENIA CHANDRIS. *British.* Tanker. Built by Odense Staalskibs A/S, Lindo, for Chandris Shipping Co Ltd, London. 103,194 tons gross, 205,600 tons dw, 1,079·58ft loa (incl bb)×143·66ft breadth×64·98ft draught, Stal Laval turbs, 28,000shp, 16 knots.

EVGENIY NIKONOV. *Russian.* Cargo. Builder na, Vyborg, for USSR. 4,796 tons gross, tons dw na, 400·09ft loa×54·92ft breadth×draught na, cyl na, Bryansk-B & W diesel, bhp na, knots na.

E

Opposite.
Here discharging the largest cargo of crude oil yet received at Milford Haven is the VLCC Energy Evolution *on charter to BP (with her sister* Energy Transport*). They are of 212,000 ton deadweight capacity. 6 of these ships of this class (belonging to the C. Y. Tung group) of 8 are powered by GEC MST 14 turbines and develop (as in these two ships) 30,000shp with a propeller speed of 80rpm, giving a service speed of 15·8 knots on an oil consumption of 122 tons per day. Steam is provided by a Foster-Wheeler type ESRD re-heat boiler providing steam for all services at sea, with main machinery and cargo oil tank cleaning equipment in use.*

Esso Bernicia *was used by the Esso Petroleum Co, with the aid of the survey division of the Decca Navigator Co Ltd in a series of shallow water manoeuvring trials in Cardigan Bay. For particulars of this 190,000 ton DW ship see volume XVII. Similar trials are to be carried out with the 250,000 ton DW* Esso Scotia *off the north coast of Spain.*

F

F. WIBORG FEKETE. *Norwegian*. Tanker. Built by Smith's Dock Co Ltd, Middlesborough, for Thomas F. Fekete & Co, Oslo. 1,998 tons gross, 5,200 tons dw, 354ft loa × 50·92ft breadth × 21·33ft draught, 16-cyl Smit and Bolnes diesel, cpp, 3,200bhp, knots na.

FAUSTINA. *Liberian*. Bulk carrier. Built by Sanoyasu Dockyard Co Ltd, Osaka, 1968, for West Coast Shipping Co Ltd, Monrovia. 16,158 tons gross, 27,365 tons dw, 577·09ft loa (incl bb) × 75·18ft breadth × 32·5ft draught, 7-cyl Mitsui-B & W diesel, 11,500bhp, 15·5 knots.

FAVORITA. *Liberian*. Cargo, ref. Built by At & Ch de Dunkerque & Bordeaux (France-Gironde), Dunkerque, for Maritime Finance Co, Monrovia. 8,426 tons gross, tons dw na, measurements na, cyl na, bhp na, knots na.

FEDERAL LAKES (Sis SIMSMETAL). *Greek*. Bulk carrier. Built by Doxford & Sunderland SB & E Co Ltd, Deptford Shipyard, for Patras Navegacion SA, Piraeus (Chandris, London, Managers). 12,748 tons gross, 20,000 tons dw, 525ft loa × 74·92ft breadth × 30·03ft draught, 6-cyl Hawthorn-Sulzer diesel, 10,200bhp, 15 knots.

FERNHAVEN. *Norwegian*. Tanker. Built by Kawasaki Dkyd Co Ltd, Sakaide, for Fearnley & Eger, Oslo. 108,758 tons gross, 216,549 tons dw , 1,072·84ft loa (incl bb) × 158·33ft breadth × 64·3ft draught, Kawasaki turbs, 28,000shp, 16·5 knots.

50 LET OKTYABRYA (originally reported as 50 LAT PAZOZIERNIKA). *Russian*. Fish factory. Built by Stocznia Gdanska, Gdansk, 1968, for USSR. 13,571 tons gross, 10,000 tons dw, 537·33ft loa × 69·75ft breadth × 26·5ft draught, 6-cyl Cegielski-B & W diesel, 7,200bhp, 15·25 knots.

50 LET SOVETSKY UKRAINY. *Russian*. Cargo CSD. Built by Stocznia Gdanska, Gdansk, 1968, for USSR. 10,183 tons gross, 12,725 tons dw, 507·41ft loa × 67·66ft breadth × 29·5ft draught, 6-cyl Cegielski-Sulzer diesel, 9,600bhp, 18·25 knots.

50 LET SOVETSKY VLASTI. *Russian*. Type na. Builder na, Gorky, 1967, for USSR. 2,219 tons gross, tons dw na, measurements na, cyl na. diesel, bhp na, knots na.

50 LET VLKSM. *Russian*. Fishing, ref. Built by Mathias Thesen Werft, Wismar, for USSR. 1,119 tons gross, tons dw na, 214·92ft loa × 36·41ft m breadth × 11·84ft draught, 8-cyl Liebknecht diesel, 825bhp, knots na.

FINIX. *Greek*. Cargo CSD. Built by Doxford & Sunderland SB & E Co Ltd, Sunderland, for Cia Nav Santa Caterina SA, Chios (Fafalios, London). 11,300 tons gross, 16,350 tons dw, 539·5ft loa × 70·14ft breadth × 31·69ft draught, 7-cyl Clark-Sulzer diesel, 10,500bhp, knots na.

FINN HEIDE. *German*. Cargo OSD/CSD. Built by Flensgurger Schiffs-Ges, Flensburg, for Leonhardt & Blumberg, Hamburg. 6,500/9,406 tons gross, —/15,250 tons dw, 458·41ft loa × 69·09ft breadth × —/30·16ft draught, 6-cyl Bremer-Vulkan-MAN diesel, 7,200bhp, knots na.

FINN-LEONHARDT. *German*. Cargo OSD/CSD (Liberty replacement type). Built by Flensburger Schiffs-Ges, Flensburg, for Leonhardt & Blumberg, Hamburg. 9,406 tons gross, 15,300 tons dw, 458·41ft loa × 68·92ft m breadth × 30·23ft draught, 6-cyl Bremer Vulkan diesel, 7,200bhp, 16 knots.

FINNCARRIER. *Finnish*. Cargo (container/vehicles). Built by O/Y Wartsila A/B, Helsingfors, for O/Y Finnlines Ltd, Helsingfors/Helsinki, 5,900 tons gross, 5,118 tons dw, 450·58ft loa × 80·5ft breadth × 18·66ft draught, two 12-cyl tw sc Wartsila-Pielstick diesel, 11,160bhp, knots na.

FIODOR GLADKOV. *Russian*. Cargo (B44 type). Built by Stocznia Gdanska, Gdansk, 1967, for USSR. 10,107 tons gross, 12,500 tons dw, 479·41ft lr × 66·41ft breadth × 29·5ft draught, cyl na, Cegielski-Sulzer diesel, 9,600bhp, 17·25 knots.

FLAMINGO. *Russian*. Stern trawler, fish factory, ref (ATLANTIK class). Built by Volkswerft Stralsund, Stralsund, 1968, for USSR. 2,657 tons gross, 1,152 tons dw, 269·58ft loa × 44·75ft breadth × 16·41ft draught, two 8-cyl s sc Liebknecht diesel, 2,320bhp, 13·5 knots.

FLINDERS BAY. *British*. Container ship, ref. Built by Howaldtswerke-Deutsche Werfte, Hamburg, for Ocean SS Co Ltd (Managers Container Fleets Ltd, London). 26,756 tons gross, 29,150 tons dw, 752·41ft loa × 100·25ft breadth × 35·09ft draught, Stal Laval turbs, 32,400shp, 22 knots.

Federal Lakes. *This is the 11th ship built by the Doxford & Sunderland group for Chandris interests. Each hold is served by two 10-ton derricks, and she has unusually large hatches for her size, namely 45ft × 36ft. Her main engine is a Hawthorn-Sulzer 6RD76 diesel, with a maximum rating of 10,200bhp at 122rpm. She is designed to maintain 15½ knots in service.*

FLIPPER. *Swedish.* Tanker (chemicals). Built by A/B Falkenbergs Varv, Falkenberg, for Lennart Kihlberg, Gothenburg. 1,599 tons gross, 2,850 tons dw, 269·58ft loa × 37·84ft breadth × 17·77ft draught, 16-cyl Brons diesel, cpp, 1,490bhp, 12 knots.

FORT LA REINE. *French.* Cargo, ref, 5 pass. Built by Const Nav & Ind de la Mediteranee (CNIM) La Seyne, 1968, for Cie Generale Transatlantique, Dunkirk. 9,873 tons gross, 8,712 tons dw, 486·58ft loa × 67·09ft breadth × 27·58ft draught, two 18-cyl s sc Atlantique-Pielstick diesel, 16,740bhp, 20·5 knots.

F

F

Flinders Bay. *The second of Overseas Containers Ltd container ships to enter the UK-Australian run (at present based on Rotterdam owing to Tilbury dockers refusal to handle the ships from the new especially built berth there),* the Flinders Bay *shows unmistakable signs of her Blue Funnel ancestry in her bow. Ocean Fleets (as the firm Blue Funnel A. Holt & Co with their associates are now termed) were given the job, as partners in OCL of designing the vessels.*

Finn Carrier *(not illustrated). A novel trailer ship of very angular appearance, the ship is designed for all the year service between Helsinki, Lubeck and Copenhagen, operating in conjunction with the passenger carrying* Finnhansa. *She is fully ice-strengthened with an ice-breaker bow, capable of carrying about 284×20ft standard pallets, together with 160 private cars. She is designed to operate independently of ice-breakers, and is twin screw with a large semi-balanced rudder. The builders, Wartsila, have developed a friction reducing arrangement, astern of the bow, known as the Dual Mixed Flow system. On either side of the bow, well below the waterline there are 15 openings, 30 centimetres in diameter. Air is forced out of these openings at one atmosphere pressure, forming a cushion of air between the hull and the ice; trials showed skin friction considerably reduced by this method. This air may also be used for transverse thrust when docking. Heeling tanks are also provided. Two large doors are available for stern loading into the trailer deck, with a bow door each side forward. Vehicles are transferred by ramps and a scissor lift. There are 7 lifts for lowering the 20ft pallets from the lower vehicle deck to the hold, with 3-ton cranes also available in the hold, which is equipped with rails for the pallets to travel on from port to starboard. The hold can also accommodate 24 cargo refrigerated units. Inflatable fenders are used between the trailer loads to prevent movement at sea. The upper vehicle deck can accommodate 71ft×30ft vehicles, and the lower deck 68ft×30ft. Main machinery is a Wartsila-Pielstick 12PC2V twin diesel operating controllable pitch propellers, which can be controlled either from the bridge or the engine room control. A total of 36 passengers can be carried, these being mainly lorry drivers, though the 12 cabins comprise 6 luxury double cabins, and 6 single first class, all capable of taking an extra bed. Adjoining these are the public rcoms and a sauna.*

FORT PONCHARTRAIN. *French.* Cargo, ref, 5 pass. Built by Cons Nav & Ind de la Mediterranee (CNIM), La Seyne, 1968, for Cie General Transatlantique, Dunkirk. 9,873 tons gross, 8,596 tons dw, 486·58ft loa×67·09ft breadth×27·58ft draught, two 18-cyl s sc Atlantique-Pielstick diesel, 16,740bhp, 20·5 knots.

FOSFORICO. *Spanish.* Oil/chemical tanker. Built by Ast de T. Ruiz de Velasco SA, Bilbao, for Naviera Quimica SA, Bilbao. 1,215 tons gross, 1,909 tons dw, 253·66ft loa×40·09ft m breadth×15·75ft draught, 6-cyl Naval-Stork-Werkspoor diesel, 1,550bhp, 12 knots.

FOSSHEIM. *Norwegian.* Cargo. Built by P. Lindenau, Kiel, for Frederik Hoyer, Skien. 4,129 tons gross, 6,348 tons dw, 369·84ft loa×53·84ft m breadth×22·55ft draught, 8-cyl Sulzer diesel, 3,500bhp, 14 knots.

FOUNTAINHEAD. *Liberian.* Bulk carrier. Built by Usuki Tekkosho, Saiki, for Galaxy Shipping Ltd, Monrovia (Patt, Manfield & Co, Hong Kong). 9,426 tons gross, 15,714 tons dw, 482·25ft loa×69·66ft breadth×29·22ft draught, 16-cyl IHI-Pielstick diesel, 7,400bhp, 14·5 knots.

FRECCIA ROSSA. *Italian.* Ferry. Built by Cantieri Navale Breda, Venice, for Soc Grandi Traghetti di Navigazione SpA, Palermo. 3,800 tons gross, 4,000 tons dw, 437·09ft loa×69·58ft breadth×18·86ft draught, two 8-cyl tw sc Fiat diesel, 14,720bhp, knots na.

FREE ENTERPRISE IV. *British.* Pass/car ferry, ro-ro, bow and stern doors. Built by N. V. Werf Gusto, Schiedam, for Townsend Carferries Ltd, Dover. 5,250 tons gross, 1,100 tons dw, 385·5ft loa×63·84ft breadth×13·75ft draught, three 12-cyl tr sc Smit-MAN diesel, btp, stp, 12,240bhp, 20·75 knots.

F

F

Free Enterprise IV. *Claimed to be the largest operating on the UK-Continent short sea route, this ship carries 1,200 passengers and 280 cars. With bow and stern doors, loading can be carried out simultaneously at two levels, through the stern at Dover, and through the bow at Zeebrugge. From the passenger point of view, the ship is more comfortable than her predecessors. Passengers enter from the entrance hall on the shelter deck, where are Bureau de Change facilities, then on to the main lounge deck. Spacious lounges are separated by shopping centres, bars and buffets. At the after end of the lounge deck is a spacious dining saloon. There are 3 other 'quiet' lounges on the deck above, of which the aftermost provides a panoramic view astern; these are fitted with reclining seats. On the boat deck are 17 2/4 berth cabins, with a limited number of cabins on the lower deck. All accommodation is fully air-conditioned. When the portable wing car decks are fitted, 1,200 tons of freight with a headroom of 14·5ft, and an axle loading of 13 tons can be stowed on the main deck. A sister ship,* No V *is building at the same builders.* No II *is to be dispensed with owing to her design making her unsuitable for carrying the high headroom commercial traffic now in operation.* No I, *however, can take this. At present* Nos I *and* II *operate the Dover-Calais route, and* Nos III *and* IV *the Dover-Zeebrugge. They provide up to 12 services per day between the former ports, and 4 on the latter route. The total maximum capacity is, 5,720 cars and 29,200 passengers daily. The owners of Townsend Ferries, European Car Ferries, also own the Thoresen Ferries from Southampton, but which operate independently. The chairman is also chairman of the ex-owners, George Nott Industries. Townsend were the pioneer cross channel car ferries, starting in 1928 with the* Artificer, *and gradually replacing the existing ship with a new one until the late 1950s. The firm was started by Captain Stuart Townsend.* No IV *is propelled by 3 Smit-MAN RBL66 12-cyl diesels, operating 3 KaMeWa controllable pitch propellers. There are 2 KaMeWa bow thrust units.* Free Enterprise I *is of 2,606 tons gross, whilst the latest ship is of 5,250 tons gross. The company also operate various holiday schemes with the aim of attracting traffic.*

FREEPORT I and **FREEPORT II** (not in Lloyds Register). *USA*. Non-propelled self unloading phosphate barges. Built by Avondale Shipyards, La, for Ohio River Co, Cincinnati. 10,851 tons gross, 26,000 tons dw, 472·41ft loa × 80ft breadth × 30ft draught,

FREJA. *German*. Cargo (63 × 20ft containers). Built by J. J. Sietas Schiffsw, Hamburg, for Johannes Bos, Hamburg. 499 tons gross, 1,225 tons dw, 242·33ft loa × 35·41ft m breadth × 12·97ft draught, 8-cyl Atlas-MaK diesel, 1,400bhp, 12·5 knots.

FREYBURG. *East German*. Cargo, ref, OSD/CSD (XD class). Built by Warnowwerft, Warnemunde, for Deutsche Seereederei, Rostock. 5,578/8,812 tons gross, 8,210/10,080 tons dw, 492·58ft loa × 66·25ft m breadth × 23·88/26·95ft draught, 8-cyl Dieselmotorenwerke-MAN diesel,11, 200bhp, 19·25 knots.

FRIBOURG. *French*. Cargo, ref. Built by At & Ch de Dunkerque & Bordeaux (France-Gronde), Dunkerque, for Soc. Courtage & Transport, La Rochelle. 8,593 tons gross, 6,595 tons dw, 472·41ft loa (incl bb) × 65·66ft breadth × 24·57ft draught, 6-cyl Le Creusot-B & W diesel, 12,600bhp, 21·5 knots.

FRIGO TIETE. *Brazilian*. Cargo, ref. Built by Maua, Cia Com e Nav Estaleiro, Rio de Janeiro, 1968, for Emp de Nav Allianca SA & Navegacao Mercantil SA, Rio de Janeiro. 4,106 tons gross, 4,300 tons dw, 413·75ft loa × 51·25ft breadth × 23ft draught, 7-cyl Pesada-MAN diesel, 7,700bhp, 18 knots.

FRITHJOF. *German*. Weather/mother ship (fishery). Built by Schlichting Werft, Travemunde, 1968, for Bund. fur Ernahrung, Landwirtschaft & Forsten, Cuxhaven. 1,637 tons gross, 2,140 tons dw, 249·3ft loa (incl bb) × 38·55ft m breadth × 17·03ft draught, three 12-cyl s sc Maybach-Benz diesel electric, btp, 2,800shp, 16 knots.

F

Fosforico (vide register vol XVII). The first special liquid chemical carrier to be built in Spain is now in service. She is fitted with stainless steel cargo tanks, pipelines and pumps. This material, though expensive, gives greater versatility to the ship as a vast range of corrosive chemicals, solvents, oils (minerals and vegetable) and wine can be carried. Her first cargo was sulphuric acid. There are 8 cargo tanks, which may be heated, and the pumps are controlled from a central panel on the bridge. Fire precautions consist of independent systems of steam and nitrogen. Her sister ship is the Sulfurico. The bridge has extremely good visibility, with a very comprehensive range of electronic equipment including telecontrol of the main engine, pumps and temperature recorders.

FROTANORTE. (Sis FROTASUL). *Brazilian.* Bulk carrier. Built by Ishikawajima do Brazil, Rio de Janeiro, for Frota Oceanica Brazileira, Rio de Janeiro. 13,873 tons gross, 24,640 tons dw, 578·75ft loa × 75·5ft breadth × 33·1ft draught, 8-cyl Ishibras-Sulzer diesel, 10,000bhp, 14·75 knots.

FUJI MARU No 12. *Japanese.* Tanker. Built by Shin Yamamoto Zosen, Kochi, for Fuji Unyu KK, Osaka. 999 tons gross, 2,000 tons dw, 213·25ft lbp × 34·5ft breadth × 16·84ft draught, two 6-cyl tw sc Daihatsu diesel, 1,500bhp, 11 knots.

FUJI MARU No 15. *Japanese.* Tanker. Built by Shin Yamamoto Zosen, Kochi, for Fuji Unyu KK, Osaka. 1,495 tons gross, 3,000 tons dw, 247·75ft lbp × 38·09ft breadth × draught na, two 8-cyl s sc Daihatsu diesel, 4,000bhp, knots na.

FUOHSAN MARU. *Japanese.* Ore/oil carrier (Japan-Persian Gulf-Brazil trade). Built by Hitachi Zosen, Innoshima, for Mitsui-OSK Lines KK, Osaka. 62,459 tons gross, 109,000 tons dw, 856·33ft loa (incl bb) × 132ft breadth × 50·09ft draught, 9-cyl Hitachi-B & W diesel, 23,200bhp, 15·25 knots.

FUUKI MARU *Japanese.* Ore carrier. Built by Ishikawajima-Harima HI, Aioi, for Shinwa Kaiun KK, Tokyo. 60,455 tons gross, 102,822 tons dw, 849·75ft loa (incl bb) × 135·58ft breadth × 48·25ft draught, 9-cyl IHI-Sulzer diesel, 21,600bhp, 14·75 knots.

G

GALLURA. *Italian.* Passenger/car/rail ferry (583 pass). Built by Cantiere Nav del Tirreno e Riuniti, Ancona, for Italian State Railways, Civitavecchia. 4,939 tons gross, 1,200 tons dw, 403·5ft loa × 58ft breadth × 16ft draught, two 6-cyl tw sc Fiat diesel, cpps, 8,000bhp, 18 knots.

GALYA KOMLEVA. *Russian.* Cargo (typ 301). Built by Schiffsw Neptun Rostock, 1968, for USSR, Murmansk. 3,684 tons gross, 4,638 tons dw, 346·75ft loa × 51·33ft breadth × 22·18ft draught, 6-cyl Halberstadt-MAN diesel, 3,250bhp, 14·3 knots.

GANTIADI. *Russian.* Fish factory ref. Built by N. V. Kon Maats 'De Schelde', Flushing, for USSR, Kerch. 4,199 tons gross, 2,560 tons dw, 340·09ft loa × 54·58ft breadth × 18·05ft draught, 8-cyl Schelde-Sulzer diesel, cpp, 3,000bhp, 14·5 knots.

GARCILASO. *Peruvian.* Cargo (one 60-ton derrick, container facilities). Built by O/Y Wartsila A/B, Abo, for Corporacion Peruana de Vapores, Callao. 9,464 tons gross, 13,100 tons dw, 493·84ft loa × 64·75ft breadth × 31·18ft draught, 6-cyl Wartsila-Sulzer diesel, 9,600bhp, 17 knots.

GAUCHO. *Brazilian.* Cargo OSD/CSD. Built by Industrias Reuindas Caneco, Rio de Janeiro, for Navegcao Minuano SA, Porto Alegre. 1,260/1,992 tons gross, 2,272/3,273 tons dw, 259·58ft loa × 41·09ft breadth × —/20·25ft draught, 7-cyl Ishibras-Sulzer diesel, 1,680bhp, 11·5 knots.

GAVRIL DERZAVIN. *Russian.* Cargo. Built by Brodogradiliste 'Uljanik', Pula, 1968, for USSR, Vladivostok. 10,457 tons gross, 14,200 tons dw, 524·58ft loa × 69·58ft breadth × 31·75ft draught, 8-cyl Uljanik-B & W diesel, 12,000bhp, 18·5 knots.

GAY LUSSAC. *Panamanian.* LPG carrier, ref. Built by Ch Naval de La Ciotat, La Ciotat, for Transoceangas Shipping, Panama. 27,725 tons gross, 27,200 tons dw, 633·25ft loa × 95·25ft breadth × 32·5ft draught, 6-cyl Fiat diesel, 13,800bhp, 16·75 knots.

GEEST DUIN. *Dutch.* Container ship OSD, 3 pass. Built by Scheeps v/h de Groot & Van Vliet, Slikkerveer, for Waling Van Geest & Zonen. 's Gravensande. 499 tons gross, 994 tons dw, 231·5ft loa × 33·92ft breadth × 11·57ft draught, 10-cyl Bolnes diesel, 1,000bhp, 12·5 knots,

GEISE. *German.* Cargo OSD/CSD (for Emden-Sweden paper trade). Built by Schulte & Bruns, Emden, for Schulte & Bruns, Bremen. 498/1,444 tons gross, 408/2,600 tons dw, 247·33ft loa × 38·75ft breadth × draught na, 8-cyl Deutz diesel, 1,320bhp, 12 knots.

GERDT OLDENDORFF. *German.* Cargo CSD (one 60-ton derrick; 1st Weser Typ 36 L). Built by A. G. 'Weser' Werk, Seebeck, Bremerhaven. for Egon Oldendorff, Lubeck. 9,786 tons gross, 16,260 tons dw, 491·41ft loa × 68·92ft breadth × 30·41ft draught, 8-cyl MAN diesel, 8,690bhp, 16·5 knots.

GERVALLA. *Norwegian.* Bulk carrier, ice strengthened. Built by Uddevallavarvet A/B, Uddevalla, for Gerrards Rederi, Kristiansand. 10,745 tons gross, 16,000 tons dw, 484·09ft loa × 70·66ft breadth × 29·33ft draught, 6-cyl Uddevalla Gotaverken diesel, cpp, 7,200bhp, 15 knots.

GERMUNDO. *Finnish.* Cargo. Built by O/Y Wartsila A/B, Abo, for F:a Gustav Erikson, Mariehamn. 4,450 tons gross, 6,400 tons dw, 380·58ft loa × 51·84ft m breadth × 23·92ft draught, 6-cyl Wartsila-Sulzer diesel, 5,000bhp, knots na.

GETALDIC. *Yugoslavian.* Cargo (HISPANIA-FREEDOM Type). Built by Ast de Cadiz SA, Seville, for Atlantska Plovidba, Dubrovnik. 9,907 tons gross, 15,540 tons dw, 471·51ft loa (incl bb) × 67·84ft breadth × 30·35ft draught. 6-cyl Cadiz-Sulzer diesel, 8,000bhp, 15 knots.

GIMLELAND. *Norwegian.* Bulk carrier. Built by Oresundsvarvet A/B, Landskrona, for Kr Haanes & Lief M Haanes, Kristiansand. 17,450 tons gross, 25,800 tons dw, 576·33ft loa × 87·41ft breadth × 32·48ft draught, 6-cyl Gotaverken diesel, 11,400bhp, knots na.

GIMONE. *French.* Tanker. Built by At & Ch de La Rochelle-Pallice, La Rochelle, for Cie Europeenne d'Armement, Bordeaux. 3,899 tons gross, 5,270 tons dw, 328·18ft loa × 52·66ft breadth × 18·41ft draught, two 6-cyl tw sc Stork diesel, 2,800bhp, 12 knots.

GINO LOLLI GHETTI. *Italian.* Ore/oil carrier. Built by Cantieri Navale Breda, Venice, for Societa 'CARBONAVI' SpA, Palermo. 28,345 tons gross, 46,000 tons dw, 710ft loa × 94ft breadth × 38·18ft draught, 7-cyl Fiat diesel, 6,100shp, 15 knots.

G

Glen Avon. *A sophisticated sludge disposal ship for the City Corporation of Bristol. She can transport 900 tons of digested sludge to the dumping ground in the Bristol Channel, the cargo being discharged by a combination of gravity and low pressure air in about 15 minutes. It is loaded under hermetically sealed conditions. Propulsion is by 2 Ruston 6APCM diesel engines, each developing 755bhp at 750rpm, driving Ajax controllable pitch propellers. Each propeller is hydraulically controlled and has fixed pitch from 225-150rpm, and variable pitch below these revolutions. On trial she reached approximately 12 knots. The engines are controlled by English Electric automatic control and watch keeping installations, resulting in the saving of 5 crew members. Since no engineers are carried, all essential machinery is duplicated. The ship and her machinery are checked and cleared by Marine Engineers between each 10 hour voyage, before handing over to the Master. Maintenance is carried out in port in free time.*

GLARUS. *Bulgarian.* Stern trawler, fish factory, ref (ATLANTIK class). Built by Volkswerft Stralsund, Stralsund, for Okeansky Ribolov, Bourgas. 2,657 tons gross, 1,152 tons dw, 269·58ft loa × 44·75ft breadth × 16·41ft draught, two 8-cyl s sc Liebknecht diesel, 2,594bhp, 13·5 knots.

GLORIA SIDERUM (PORT HULL ex HADA II, STAR HULL ex HERMES), 1969. *Liberian.* Twin hull heavy lift ship, 300-ton derrick. Built by N.V. Schps V/h De Groot & Vliet, Slikkerveer 1957, 56, for Holscher Shipping NV, Monrovia. 1,141 tons gross, 1,652 tons dw, 185·84ft loa × 67·92ft breadth × 11·97ft draught, two 8-cyl tw sc Industrie diesel, 1,200bhp, knots na. (Bought by Holscher from previous owners and converted.

GOLAR RON. *Liberian.* Tanker. Built by Kawasaki Dkyd Co Ltd, Kobe, for Ocean Oil Enterprises Inc, Monrovia (Gotass-Larsen, New York). 51,696 tons gross, 106,239 tons dw, 853ft loa (incl bb) × 131·5ft breadth × 51·03ft draught, Kawasaki turbs, 24,000shp, 16 knots.

GOLDEN FLEECE. *Greek.* Cargo (Nippon Kokan Liberty replacement). Built by Nippon Kokan, Shimizu, for Apollo, Shipping Inc, Piraeus (Apollo Shipping Inc, New York). 11,148 tons gross, 16,493 tons dw, 477·25ft loa × 72·33ft breadth × 30·64ft draught, 6-cyl Uraga-Sulzer diesel, 7,200bhp, 16·5 knots.

Owned by Midsea Containership Inc, Monrovia, the Gwendolen Isle is operated by the Amerind Corporation between New York and Bermuda on a regular weekly run, carrying 86×20ft refrigerated and dry cargo containers.

GOLDEN LANCE. *Greek*. Cargo (NKK Liberty replacement). Built by Nippon Kokan, Shimizu, for Apollo Shipping Inc, Piraeus. 11,148 tons gross, 16,493 tons dw, 477·25ft loa×72·33ft breadth×30·64ft draught, 6-cyl Uraga-Sulzer diesel, 7,200bhp, 15 knots.

GOLFO DE TONKIN. *Cuban*. Trawler, ref. Built by Ast Construcciones SA, Vigo, for Republica de Cuba, Havana. 1,500 tons gross, tons dw na, 249·33ft loa×39·41ft breadth×15·58ft draught, 8-cyl Barreras-Deutz diesel, 2,670bhp, knots na.

GOOILAND. *Dutch*. Cargo. Built by NV Mch & Schps P. Smit Jnr, Rotterdam, 1968, for NV Tot Voortz. vd Koninlijke Hollandsche Lloyd, Amsterdam. 4,846 tons gross, 9,055 tons dw, 484·09ft loa×69·18ft breadth×24·58ft draught, four 12-cyl s sc Schelde-Sulzer diesel, 5,500bhp, 15 knots.

GORKY. *Russian*. Fishing trawler, ref (KASPI class). Built by Mathias Thesen Werft, Wismar, for USSR, Vladivostok. 1,100 tons gross, tons dw na, 214·92ft loa×36·41ft m breadth×11·92ft draught, 8-cyl Liebknecht diesel, 825bhp, 10·5 knots.

GOROHOVETS. *Russian*. Type na. Builder na, Built by Giurgiu, 1968, for USSR, Izmail. tonnage na, measurements na, cyl na, diesel, bhp na, knots na.

GRECIAN LEGEND. *Liberian*. Bulk carrier. Built by Scotts SB & E Co Ltd, Greenock, for Legend Maritime Corpn, Monrovia (Goulandris, London). 22,998 tons gross, 41,450 tons dw, 662ft loa×92·18ft breadth×38·13ft draught, 6-cyl Scott-Sulzer diesel, 13,800bhp, knots na.

GREEN ROVER. (Sis GREY ROVER and BLUE ROVER). *British*. Fleet replenishment tanker. Built by Swan Hunter Sbs Ltd, Hebburn, for Ministry of Defence, DGST, London. 7,503 tons gross, 7,060 tons dw, 461ft loa×63·09ft breadth×24ft draught, two 16-cyl s sc Ruston Hornsby diesel, 16,000bhp, 19 knots.

G

GREEN WALRUS. *British*. Cargo. Built by Mitsubishi HI Ltd, Shimonoseki, for Jebmei Shipping Management Co Ltd, Hong Kong. 9,443 tons gross, 14,730 tons dw, 452ft loa (incl bb) × 65·84ft breadth × 30·62ft draught, 6-cyl Mitsubishi-MAN diesel, 5,600bhp, 14 knots.

GRETCHEN ISLE (launched as JOHANN BLUMENTHAL). *German*. Cargo. Built by Schiffsb Unterweser Bremerhaven, for Johann K Blumenthal Reederei, Kiel. 2,150 tons gross, 3,650 tons dw, 311·41ft loa × 46·25ft breadth × 18·66ft draught, 8-cyl Deutz diesel, 3,000bhp, knots na.

GREY FISH. (Sis BLACK FISH). *Dutch*. Oil rig supply ship, 24 pass. Built by Ziegler Freres, Dunkerque, for Vroon NV, Breskens. 255 tons gross, 200 tons dw, 133·75ft loa × 25·58ft breadth × 10·5ft draught, two 8-cyl tw sc Nydqvist & Holm diesel, cpps, btp, 2,200bhp, 15 knots.

GREY ROVER. *British*. Fleet replenishment tanker. Built by Swan Hunter Sbs Ltd, Hebburn, for Ministry of Defence, DGST, London. 7,450 tons gross, 7,060 tons dw, 461ft loa × 63·09ft breadth × 24ft draught, two 16-cyl s sc Ruston Hornsby diesel, 16,000bhp, 19 knots.

GUAVACORE. *German*. Cargo, ref. Built by A/S Nylands Akers M/V, Oslo, for K. G. Core Schiffahrts GmbH & Co, Hamburg. 5,927/8,185 tons gross, 8,420/10,090 tons dw, 485ft loa × 65·75ft breadth × 28/30·07ft draught, 7-cyl Nylands-B & W diesel, 11,500bhp, 20 knots.

GUNDULIC. *Yugoslavian*. Cargo (1st Freedom-Hispana). Built by Ast de Cadiz SA, Seville, for Atlantska Plovidba, Dubrovnik. 9,907 tons gross, 15,540 tons dw, 471·41ft loa (incl bb) × 67·84ft breadth × 30·35ft draught, 6-cyl Cadiz-Sulzer diesel, 8,000bhp, 15 knots.

GWARDIA LUDOWA. *Polish*. Cargo CSD/OSD. Built by Stocznia im Komuny Pariskiej, Gdynia, 1968, for Polish Ocean Lines, Gdynia. 5,621/8,590 tons gross, 9,431/11,684 tons dw, 500·66ft loa × 63·75ft breadth × 25·33/28·79ft draught, 6-cyl Cegielski-Sulzer diesel, 7,200bhp, knots na.

GWENDOLEN ISLE. *Liberian*. Container ship. Built by Gebruder Schurenstedt, Bardenfleth, for Midsea Containership Inc, Monrovia. 473 tons gross, 1,162 tons dw, 239·84ft loa (incl bb) × 42·33ft breadth × 12·37ft draught, 7-cyl MAN diesel, 1,970bhp, 13·75 knots.

GYOKUYO MARU. *Japanese*. Cargo. Built by Nipponkai HI, Co Ltd Toyama, for Yasuda Shintaku Ginko KK, Tokyo. 10,251 tons gross, 16,322 tons dw, 491ft loa × 74·25ft breadth × 29·84ft draught, 16-cyl Nippon Kokan-Pielstick diesel, 7,440bhp, 14·5 knots.

H.A.M. 308. *Dutch*. Suction hopper dredger. Built by Smit-Kinderdijk VOF, Kinderdijk, 1968, for NV Hollandsche Aanneming Maats NV, Rotterdam. 6,024 tons gross, 10,013 tons dw, 373·33ft loa × 61·75ft breadth × 27·86ft draught, two 20-cyl tw sc Smit-Bolnes diesel, cpps 7,320bhp, 13·5 knots.

HAI KING. *Chinese* (*Taiwan*). Cargo, ref. Built by Mitsubishi HI Ltd, Kobe, for China Merchants S Nav Co Ltd, Taipei. 11,026 tons gross, 12,200 tons dw, 526·92ft loa × 75·58ft breadth × 30·84ft draught, cyl na, Mitsubishi-MAN diesel, 13,800 bhp, knots na.

HAI LI. *Chinese* (*Taiwan*). Cargo, ref. Built by Taiwan Shipbuilding Corpn, Keelung, for China Merchants SN Co Ltd, Keelung. 3,688 tons gross, 5,597 tons dw, 351·18ft loa × 54·25ft breadth × 23·25ft draught, cyl na, Kawasaki-MAN diesel, 4,200bhp, 15·75 knots.

HAIMEN. *Canton Peoples' Republic of China*. Cargo. Built by Warnowerft, Warnemunde, 1968, for Peoples' Republic of China. 9,455 tons gross 12,430 tons dw, 494·33ft loa × 65·75ft breadth × 29·25ft draught, 9-cyl DMR-MAN diesel, 8,160bhp, 16·5 knots.

HAINING. *Canton Peoples Republic of China*. Cargo OSD/CSD (one 50-ton derrick). Built by Stocznia im Komuny Paryskiej, Gdynia, for Peoples' Republic of China. 5,714/8,727 tons gross, 9,300/11,600 tons dw, 500·66ft loa × 63·92ft breadth × 25·33/28·79ft draught, 6-cyl Cegielski-Sulzer diesel, 7,200bhp, 16·5 knots.

Hamburg (*see over*).

HAKOZAKI MARU. *Japanese*. Container ship. Built by Mitsubishi HI, Kobe, for Nippon Yusen Kaisha, Tokyo. 23,669 tons gross, 20,000 tons dw, 697·25ft loa (incl bb) × 98·5ft breadth × 31·18ft draught, 9-cyl Mitsubishi-Sulzer diesel, 34,200bhp, knots na.

HALO. *Liberian*. Bulk carrier. Built by Hitachi Zosen, Innoshima, for Liberian Halo Transports Inc, Monrovia. 13,562 tons gross, 23,924 tons dw, 564·33ft loa × 81·5ft breadth × 31·33ft draught, 7-cyl Hitachi-B & W diesel, 8,400bhp, 17 knots.

HAMBURG. *German*. Passenger (790 pass). Built by Howaldtswerke Hamburg AG, Hamburg, 1968, for Deutsche Atlantik Linie, Hamburg. 25,022 tons gross, 6,102 tons dw, 638·41ft loa (incl bb) × 87·33ft breadth × 27·15ft draught, tw sc AEG turbs, 22,660shp, 23 knots.

HAMILTON LOPES. *Brazilian*. Tanker. Built by Odense Staalskibs A/S, Lindo, for Petrobras Frota Nacional de Petroleiros, Rio de Janeiro. 60,900 tons gross, 114,800 tons dw, 881·25ft loa × 138ft breadth × 49·23ft draught, 9-cyl B & W diesel, 25,200bhp, knots na.

Hamburg. *The first large passenger ship built in Germany for 30 years, was delivered on her contract delivery date. She is designed as a one class 'hotel' ship solely for cruising, and is constructed entirely of non-inflammable materials. 2 Denny Brown-AEG fin type stabilizers are fitted for her passengers' comfort, and of her 12 decks, 2 are occupied entirely by a range of public rooms, with the 3 next decks being devoted to cabins. Forward on the promenade deck is a full width ballroom with a stage and dancefloor, and above it the Atlantic Club, with widespread views. On these 2 decks (the lido deck being the other) are club rooms, a night club, an attractive shopping centre, beauty salon and boutique, sports centre, chapel and a 290 seat theatre. There are 3 restaurants, which together can seat her normal cruising complement of 652. The largest is the Hamburg restaurant, with the Munchen room and grill room on the deck below. There is an indoor swimming pool and sauna, with a large open deck pool forward of her rather unusual and remarkable funnel, the shape of which must indubitably be a 'talking point' with her complement. The fore and aft passages in the cabin area are all on the centre line. Each cabin has a private bath and/or shower, television, radio, and individually controlled air conditioning, 2 full size beds, which are convertible into couches for day-time use. There are 3 types of cabin, 20 de-luxe apartments, 188 outside rooms and 111 inside ones, the latter being equipped with closed circuit television to compensate for lack of direct view. 9,000sq ft of deck space is provided for recreation. If used on a direct run, such as transatlantic, 790 passengers can be accommodated. The crew numbers 403. 10 motorboats are carried, of which 3 are ferry launches for cruise passengers. Denny Brown-AEG stabilizers are fitted. The AEG steam turbines are locally and engine room control room controlled, the turbine revolutions being reduced to 137rpm at the 5 bladed propellers, normal service rpm being 130 for 23 knots.*

Hamburg *funnel*

H

Hedwin. *The first vessel delivered to the newly formed Port of Tyne Authority, and the last vessel ordered by the predecessor, the Tyne Improvement Commission. Capable of operating under heavy weather conditions, she is registered as 100 A1 grab hopper dredger (sea-going) at Lloyds. She has a Priestman No 750 grabbing crane sited to work round the bow, which can handle the heaviest material from a dredging depth of 55ft. The working radius is 35ft, and over 80 operations in the hour can be performed at 35ft depth, loading the ship in just over 2 hours. There are 4 pairs of bridge controlled hydraulically operated bottom doors, and the propelling machinery is a British Polar MN16 diesel engine developing 1,260bhp at 335rpm and operating through a reverse/reduction gearbox gives a fully loaded speed of 10 knots.*

HANSA NORD. *Norwegian*. Cargo. Built by Schiffsw Neptun, Rostock, for Strandheim & Stensaker, Bergen. 3,044 tons gross, 4,165 tons dw, 334·58ft loa × 47·92ft m breadth × 19·22ft draught, 8-cyl Atlas-MaK diesel, 3,000bhp, knots na.

HANSEL. *Norwegian*. Cargo. Built by Schiffswerft Neptun, Rostock, 1968, for Strandheim & Stensaker, Bergan. 2,889 tons gross, 4,165 tons dw, 316·25ft loa × 48ft breadth × 19·32ft draught, 8-cyl Atlas-MaK diesel, 3,000bhp, 13 knots.

HAYATOMO MARU. *Japanese*. Bulk carrier. Built by Mitsui Zosen, Tamano, for Mitsui-OSK Lines KK, Osaka. 26,356 tons gross, 44,300 tons dw, 623·33ft loa (incl bb) × 96·92ft breadth × 39·18ft draught, 7-cyl Mitsui-B & W diesel, 13,100bhp, knots na.

HELEN MILLER. *British*. Cargo. Built by Burntisland SB Co Ltd, Burntisland, for Monroe Bros, Liverpool. 5,222 tons gross, 7,393 tons dw, 399ft loa × 56·92ft breadth × 25·84ft draught, 5-cyl Borsig diesel, 6,000bhp, 16·5 knots.

HELENE ROTH. *German*. Cargo OSD/CSD. Built by Schiffsw: Unterweser, Bremerhaven, for Ernst Jacob, Flensburg. 3,400/5,750 tons gross, 6,000/8,000 tons dw, 408·41ft loa × 59·33ft breadth × 21/26·25ft draught, 16-cyl Deutz diesel, 6,400bhp, 17 knots.

HELICE. *Norwegian*. Tanker (chemical). Built by Clelands SB Co Ltd, Wallsend, for Helge R Myhre, Stavanger. 1,599 tons gross, 2,843 tons dw, 277·25ft loa × 42·84ft breadth × 16·09ft draught, 8-cyl MWM diesel, cpp, 2,200bhp, 12·5 knots.

Hillah. *This dredger (vide Register Vol XVII) is a combination of new and old designing. 2 steam reciprocating engines provide the main propulsion, with, on the bridge a large automatic data logger, a highly complex piece of electronic equipment providing data on the behaviour of the ship, the engines and the dredging operation. She is designed by Knud E. Hansen of Copenhagen, and is the first dredger to have this extensive equipment. She has twin suction tubes, and can discharge the spoil either overboard, into barges or via a floating pipeline to the shore, by means of twin dredge pumps mounted forward. Manoeuvrability is assured by means of twin controllable pitch propellers, twin rudders and a bow thrust unit. Air conditioned accommodation is for a total of 81 crew. She is designed for the Iraqi Ports Administration, and can dredge in a maximum depth of 21·5 metres. Her length is 394ft, and her main engines of IHC-Brouwer GB 11A type drive her at 14 knots.*

HENRIETTE HELLESKOV. *Danish.* Cargo. Built by N. V. Bodewes Schps, Martenshoek, 1968, for R. O. Danielsen, Copenhagen. 500 tons gross, 1,300 tons dw, 241·92ft loa × 38·84ft breadth × 12·18ft draught, 6-cyl Atlas-MaK diesel, 1,100bhp, 12 knots.

HIJIRI MARU. *Japanese.* Bulk carrier. Built by Sumitomo SB & Mchy Co Ltd, Yokosuka, for Itaya Shosen KK, Tokyo. 16,800 tons gross, 22,062 tons dw, 516·41ft loa (incl bb) × 79·84ft breadth × 31·84ft draught, 7-cyl Sumitomo-Sulzer diesel, 8,400bhp, knots na.

HIKO MARU. *Japanese.* Cargo. Built by Mitsui Zosen, Tamanao, for Sanko KKK, Tokyo. 11,600 tons gross, 19,390 tons dw, 508·66ft loa (incl bb) × 74·92ft breadth × 30·47ft draught, 7-cyl Mitsui-B & W diesel, 9,400bhp, 15 knots.

HINRICH WITT. *German.* Cargo CSD. Built by Orenstein Koppel & Lbcr, Lubeck, for Gebr Rademacher, Hamburg. 4,825 tons gross, 7,200 tons dw, 382·58ft loa (incl bb) × 56·84ft breadth × 24·71ft draught, 8-cyl Atlas-MaK diesel, 4,000bhp, knots na.

Hiryu. *(Not in the register section.) Delivered in March 1968 to the Japanese Maritime Safety Agency for operation in the Tokyo Bay area, by Nippon Kokan Kabushiki Kaisha. She is believed to be the world's second catamaran fireboat, the first being the smaller BP Firemaster in the UK. She is 90·2ft long and 34·1ft broad over the twin hulls, giving a stable platform for her 49·2ft fire fighting tower, at the same time having very shallow draught, namely 6·9ft. With engines and screws in each of the twin hulls, she is very manoeuvrable, capable of making a complete circle in one spot, with one engine going ahead and the other astern. She is equipped with 7 firefighting nozzles, 2 for water, 2 for foam, 2 for either water or chemical foam, and 1 that can be used for either, alternatively. Each hull has a 1,100bhp Mercedes Benz MB820Db diesel engine, driving a controllable pitch propeller.*

HIROSHIMA MARU. *Japanese*. Tanker. Built by Taihei Kogyo, Hiroshima, for Okada Kaiun KK, Osaka. 3,531 tons gross, 5,900 tons dw, 333ft loa × 49·33ft breadth × 22·75ft draught, 6-cyl Hanshin diesel, 3,000bhp, knots na.

HOEGH MINERVA. *Norwegian*. Bulk carrier/cars. Built by Kaldnes M/V A/S, Tonsberg, for Lief Hoegh & Co A/S, Oslo. 15,743 tons gross, 24,215 tons dw, 591·09ft loa × 75·18ft breadth × 33·33ft draught, 6-cyl Sulzer diesel, cpp, 10,500bhp, 15·5 knots.

HOEGH MIRANDA. *Norwegian*. Bulk carrier. Built by Kaldnes M/V A/S, Tonsberg, for Leif Hoegh & Co A/S, Oslo. 15,744 tons gross, 25,250 tons dw, 591·5ft loa × 75·18ft breadth × 33·5ft draught, 6-cyl Sulzer diesel, 10,599bhp, knots na.

Hohkokusan Maru. *Japan's largest grain carrier at 55,000 tons deadweight is jointly owned by the Mitsui-OSK Kisen Kaisha and the Matsuoka Steamship Co. She has been designed for the N America-Japan grain trade, with the maximum capacity permitted by the Panama Canal. There are 3 motor driven 5-ton jib cranes for cargo handling, and as well as the usual ballast tanks, each cargo hold is provided with hopper tanks exclusively for ballast to maintain 50% of full load conditions when in ballast. The main engine is a Mitsui-B & W 7K74EF developing 13,100bhp at 124rpm, giving a maximum trial speed of 16·75 knots.*

HOEGH SHIELD. *Norwegian.* LPG carrier. Built by Moss Vaerft & Dokk A/S, Moss, for Leif Hoegh & Co A/S, Oslo. 6,817 tons gross, 8,645 tons dw, 403·18ft loa × 60·84ft breadth × 28·81ft draught, 6-cyl Horten-Sulzer diesel, 8,000bhp, 17·5 knots.

HOEI MARU. *Japanese.* Cargo. Built by Hashihama Zosen, Imabari, for Bibo KKK, Namikata. 2,999 tons gross, 5,200 tons dw, 295·25ft lbp × 51·25ft breadth × 21·33ft draught, 6-cyl Kobe Hatsudoki diesel, 2,700bhp, 12·75 knots.

Hornmeer. *The Horn Linie's latest ship is here shown on charter to Pioneer Shipping (a Reed Paper Group subsidiary) discharging reels of liner boards at Samuel Williams' terminal at Dagenham, before, the last stage of her maiden homeward journey from Central America, the West Indies and the USA to Europe. She is specially designed to take general cargo from Europe to the West Indies, and the carriage of paper products homeward from the Gulf of Mexico.*

HOHKOKUSAN MARU. *Japanese.* Bulk carrier. Built by Mitsui Zosen, Tamano, for Mitsui OSK Lines KK & Matsuoka KKK, Kobe. 34,064 tons gross, 54,400 tons dw, 731·58ft loa (incl bb) × 105·75ft breadth × 38·84ft draught, 7-cyl Mitsui-B & W diesel, 13,100bhp, knots na.

HOJO MARU. *Japanese.* Cement carrier. Built by Setoda Zosen, Setoda, for Kinkai Yusen KK, Tokyo. 3,938 tons gross, 6,897 tons dw, 351·18ft loa × 53·92ft breadth × 22·33ft draught, 6-cyl Hitachi-B & W diesel, 3,300bhp, 12·5 knots.

HONG KONG MAIL. *USA.* Cargo, ref (part container ship). Built by Newport News SB & DD Co, Newport News, for American Mail Line Ltd, Portland Ore. 15,949 tons gross, 22,208 tons dw, 605ft loa × 82·18ft breadth × 35·05ft draught, GEC turbs, 21,600shp, 20·75 knots.

H

Honmoku Maru. *A sister ship of the* Bluebird (*Showa SS Co*), Oppama Maru (*Mitsui-OSK*) *and* Zama Maru (*Showa*), *all 4 vessels are engaged in carrying Datsun Bluebird and other export cars to the USA from Japan, bringing back mainly grain. 1,200 Datsun cars can be accommodated in the hold of each. The cars are driven on board under their own power, by means of a special ramp, and drive off in a similar manner. As these vehicles are filled one-quarter full in their petrol tanks, very complete fire detection and fighting equipment is provided as well as a mechanized exhaust ventilation system and vent pipes to disperse the cars' exhaust fumes. The ships have both removable decks, hinged decks and fixed grating decks for the cars, in order not to interfere with their bulk loading capacity. The Hitachi diesel engine is a B & W 662-VT2BF-140 type, developing 7,200bhp and giving a maximum trial speed of 16·919 knots. Dimensions, etc, are in Volume XVII.*

HOPE ISLE. *German.* Cargo OSD. Built by Van der Giessen-De Noord, Alblasserdam, for H. Wurthmann, Elsfleth. 999 tons gross, 2,400 tons dw. 313·66ft loa × 52·84ft breadth × 13·78ft draught, 8-cyl Atlas-MaK diesel, 3,500bhp, knots na.

HORNMEER. *German.* Cargo, ref. Built by Howaldtswerke-Deutsche Werft, Hamburg, for Horn Linie, Hamburg. 4,522 tons gross, 7,200 tons dw, 434·5ft loa (incl bb) × 65·25ft breadth × 24·84ft draught, 6-cyl MAN diesel, 7,200bhp, 17·5 knots.

HORNWIND. *German.* Cargo, ref. Built by Howaldtswerke-Deutsche Werft, Hamburg, for Horn Linie, Hamburg. 4,525 tons gross, 7,500 tons dw, 437·58ft loa × 65·09ft breadth × 24·33ft draught, 6-cyl MAN diesel, 7,200bhp, knots na.

HORTA BARBOSA. *Brazilian.* Tanker. Built by Odense Staalskibs A/S, Lindo, for Petrobras Frotas Nacional de Petroleos, Rio de Janeiro. 60,900 tons gross, 114,800 tons dw, 891·25ft loa × 138ft breadth × 49·23ft draught, 9-cyl B & W diesel, 25,200bhp, knots na.

HOVERINGHAM V. *British.* Sand suction dredger. Built by Appledore SB Ltd, Appledore, for Hoveringham Gravels Ltd, Hull. 879 tons gross, 1,359 tons dw, 208·25ft loa × 59·58ft breadth × 12·58ft draught, 8-cyl Ruston Hornsby diesel, cpp, 1,050bhp, 11 knots.

HRVATSKA (ex CASSOPEIA). *Yugoslavian.* Cargo, ref. Built by Brodogradiliste 3rd Maj, Rijeka, for Jugoslavenska Linijska Plovidba, Rijeka. 6,952 tons gross, 10,845 tons dw, 508·58ft loa × 67·41ft breadth × 26·77ft draught, 6-cyl Stork diesel, 10,500bhp, 18 knots.

HUGO OLDENDORFF. *German.* Cargo. Built by AG 'WESER' Werk Seebeck, Bremerhaven, for Egon Oldendorff, Lubeck. 9,786 tons gross, 16,260 tons dw, 489ft loa × 69·5ft breadth × 30·33ft draught, 8-cyl MAN diesel, 8,690bhp, knots na.

HWASONG. *S. Korean.* Bulk carrier. Built by Italcantieri SpA, Spezia, for Korea United Lines Inc, Inchon. 9,235 tons gross, 15,156 tons dw, 481ft loa × 70ft breadth × 29·66ft draught, 6-cyl Ansaldo-B & W diesel, 7,200bhp, 15 knots.

HYPOLITE WORMS. *French.* LPG carrier. Built by Cons Nav & Ind del La Mediteranee, (CNIM), La Seyne, for Cie Havraise & Nantaise Peninsulaire (CHNP), Dunkirk. 18,667 tons gross, 22,291 tons dw, 583·66ft loa × 80·5ft breadth × 34·18ft draught, 6-cyl CCM-Sulzer diesel, 13,800bhp, 17 knots.

ICHIZAN ISE. *Japanese.* Cargo. Built by Kurushima Dk Co Ltd, Imabari, for Ichizan Kinkai KKK, Kikuma. 2,996 tons gross, 5,450 tons dw, 326·41ft loa (incl bb) × 52·5ft breadth × 21·55ft draught, 6-cyl Akasaka Tekkosho diesel, 3,000bhp, 12 knots.

IDA ISLE (ex IDA BLUNMENTHAL). *German.* Cargo. Built by Schiffs Unterweser, Bremerhaven, for Johann K Blumenthal Reederei, Kiel. 2,228 tons gross, 3,530 tons dw, 311·58ft loa × 45·92ft m breadth × 18·75ft draught, 8-cyl Deutz diesel, 3,000bhp, knots na.

IKTINOS

The Iktinos built by the Doxford & Sunderland Shipbuilding & Engineering Co Ltd for a partnership of Messrs Lyras and Fafalios Lineas Interoceanicos SA) is fitted with Macgregor single-pull hatch covers.

IDAHO. *USA.* Cargo, ref (general plus 216 × 20ft containers). Built by Avondale Shipyards Inc, Avondale La, for States Steamship Co, San Francisco. 9,493/13,053 tons gross, 12,500/14,077 tons dw, 579ft loa (incl bb) × 82·18ft breadth × 32·07ft draught, cyl na, GEC turbs, 24,000shp, 23 knots.

IGINIA. *Italian.* Ferry. Built by Cantieri Nav Del Tirrenio e Riuniti, Ancona, for Italian State Railways, Messina. 4,900 tons gross, 2,120 tons dw, 464·25ft loa × 61·66ft breadth × 17ft draught, four 6-cyl tw sc Fiat diesel, 10,800bhp, 20 knots.

IGUAPE. *Liberian.* Cargo (1st Mitsui MM 14 Lib rep). Built by Mitsui HI Ltd, Shimonoseki, for Maranave SA, Monrovia. 10,430 tons gross, 15,850 tons dw, 495·92ft loa × 69·75ft breadth × 31·09ft draught, 6-cyl Mitsubishi-Sulzer diesel, 7,200bhp, 14·5 knots.

IKTINOS. *Greek.* Cargo (35-ton derrick). Built by Doxford & Sunderland SB & E Co Ltd, Pallion, for Lineas Interoceanicos SA, Piraeus Lyras/ Fafalios). 11,489 tons gross, 16·350 tons dw, 539·5ft loa × 70·18ft breadth × 31·64ft draught, 7-cyl Clark-Sulzer diesel, 11,200bhp, 16·5 knots.

ILICHEVSK. *Russian.* Stern trawler, fish factory, ref (ATLANTIK class). Built by Volkswerft Stralsund, Stralsund, 1968, for USSR. 2,657 tons gross, 1,152 tons dw, 269·58ft loa × 44·75ft breadth × 16·41ft draught, two 8-cyl s sc Liebknecht diesel, cpp, 2,320bhp, 13·25 knots.

ILMEN. *Russian.* Stern trawler, fish factory (ATLANTIK class) ref. Built by Volkswerft Stralsund, Stralsund, for USSR. 2,657 tons gross, 1,152 tons dw, 269·58ft loa × 44·75ft breadth × 16·41ft draught, two 8-cyl s sc Liebknecht diesel, 2,320 bhp, 13·25 knots.

ILOVAJSK. *Russian.* Cargo. Built by Warnowwerft, Warnemunde, 1968, for USSR, Odessa. 9,748 tons gross, 12,882 tons dw. 496·92ft loa × 66·66ft breadth × 28·88ft draught, 8-cyl DMR-MAN diesel, 9,600bhp, 16·5 knots.

ILYA KULIN. *Russian.* Cargo. Built by Kherson Shipyard, Kherson, for USSR. 9,547 tons gross, tons dw na, 501·33ft loa × 67·58ft breadth × 29·59ft draught, 6-cyl Bryansk B & W diesel, 9,000bhp, 17 knots.

IMA. *Liberian.* Bulk carrier. Built by Nippon Kokan, Tsurumi, 1968, for Alcyonia Corpn, Monrovia. 27,989 tons gross, 57,650 tons dw, 742·84ft loa × 102·25ft breadth × 39·05ft draught, 8-cyl Uraga-Sulzer diesel, 17,600bhp, knots na.

IMANT SUDMALIS. *Russian.* Stern trawler, fish factory, ref. Builder na, Russia, for USSR, Riga. 3,162 tons gross, 1,428 tons dw, 277·92ft loa × 46ft breadth × 18·73ft draught, 8-cyl Skoda diesel, bhp na, 12·25 knots.

IMENI 61 KOMMUNARA. *Russian.* Fish carrier, ref. Built by '61 Kommunar' Shipyard, Nikolayev, 1968, for USSR. 5,942 tons gross, tons dw na, 426·5ft loa × 55·25ft breadth × 23·66ft draught, four 10-cyl tw sc diesel electric (Russian), bhp na, 16·5 knots.

IMPERIAL BEDFORD. *Canadian.* Tanker, ice strengthened. Built by Davie SB Ltd, Lauzon, for Imperial Oil Co Ltd, Halifax. 9,500 tons gross, 14,000 tons dw, 485·41ft loa × 70·18ft breadth × 26ft draught, 5-cyl MAN diesel, 6,500bhp, 14 knots.

INCA. CAPAC YUPANQUI. *Peruvian.* Cargo CSD. Built by Soc Espanola de Const Navales, Bilbao, for Cia Peruana de Vapores Callao. 9,624 tons gross, 13,250 tons dw, 514·5ft loa × 64·66ft breadth × 29·7ft draught, 6-cyl SECN-Sulzer diesel, 9,600bhp, 18 knots.

INCA HUAYNA CAPAC. *Peruvian.* Cargo CSD. Built by Soc Espanola de Cons Nav, Bilbao, for Corporacion Peruana de Vapores, Callao. 9,624 tons gross, 12,971 tons dw, 514·5ft loa × 64·66ft breadth × 29·77ft draught, 6-cyl SECN-Sulzer diesel, 9,600bhp, 16·5 knots.

INCA YAHUAR HUACA. *Peruvian.* Cargo. Built by Soc Espanola de Cons Nav, Bilbao, for Corporacion Peruana de Vapores, Callao. 9,624 tons gross, 12,971 tons dw, 514·5ft loa × 64·66ft breadth × 29·7ft draught, 6-cyl SECN-Sulzer diesel, 9,600bhp, 16 knots.

Innisfallen. *Costing £2,500,000, the* Innisfallen *is the third ship of British and Irish revised drive on and off fleet, the other 2 being the* Leinster *and* Munster *(together with the 2 container ships* Tipperary *and* Kildare*). Opening the new service in May, 1968 the* Munster, *in 7 months carried 175,000 passengers and 37,500 cars between Liverpool-Dublin, as well as a considerable amount of drive on and off freight. This intensive service necessitated a 1 hour turn round at each end ferry port, and the ship operated 10 trips per week, her capacity being 220 cars and 1,000 passengers, with a 22 knot speed.* Leinster, *with her, will provide 16 round trips per week, offering accommodation for 17,600 persons and 3,600 cars. The* Innisfallen *inaugurated the new Cork-Swansea service, giving a daily sailing in each direction during the summer. The total investment in this 'B & I Motorway' is £10,000,000. As to the ship herself. She can accommodate 1,200 passengers and 232 cars, with 6 trucks, and operates at a speed of 24 knots. She is of Swedish design, but has detailed improvements on the* Munster *from experience with that ship. All internal bulkheads are of non-combustible material, all air conditioning*

Innisfallen—cont.
is automatically controlled, and all spaces fitted with new rule fire detecting apparatus. Steel doors and stair cases are fitted throughout, and all large windows near lifeboats and rafts have steel shutters. Denny Brown AEG-stabilizers of the fore and aft folding type are fitted. The wheelhouse contains the main control console, into which are set the main items of bridge equipment. There are 2 KaMeWa controllable pitch propellers, and a KaMeWa bow thrust. The 4 main engines are MAN type R7V 40/54 diesels. Navigational equipment consists of an Arma-Brown compass with Arkas automatic steering, Mark 12 Decca Navigator, Marconi-Argus 12 True Motion Radar and Raytheon 12 High-definition Radar, with Lodestar Direction Finding and Sal Log.

The first ship of the B72 series from Gdynia, the International *has been delivered to her Soviet owners. She has 19 cargo tanks arranged to carry either crude oil or products, with three automatically controlled cargo pumps, together with ancilliary remote control tank gauges. This automation is the principal difference to the B70 class. The engine is a Cegielski-Sulzer type 6RD76.*

INDUS. *Swedish.* Cargo, ref. Built by Eriksbergs M/V A/S, Gothenburg, for A/B Svenska Ostasiatiske Kompaniet, Gothenburg. 6,150/9,640 tons gross, 9,025/12,800 tons dw, 458ft loa × 70·66ft breadth × —/31ft draught, two 10-cyl s sc Eriksbergs-Pielstick diesel, bhp na, knots na.

INDUS MARU. *Japanese.* Cargo. Built by Kanazashi Zosensho, Shimizu, for Takuyo KKK, Osaka. 9,935 tons gross, 16,000 tons dw, 488·5ft loa × 72·25ft breadth × 29·18ft draught, 6-cyl Mitsui-B & W diesel, 7,200bhp, 14 knots.

INDUSTRIAL TRANSPORT. *Canadian.* Tanker (chemicals). Built by Davie SB Ltd, Lauzon, for Hall Corporation of Canada, Toronto. 4,980 tons gross, 8,000 tons dw, 391ft loa × 55·33ft breadth × 21·73ft draught, two 10-cyl tw sc Fairbanks-Morse diesel, 3,332bhp, 12·5 knots.

INITIATOR. *Russian.* Stern trawler, fish factory, ref (ATLANTIK class). Built by Volkswerft Stralsund, Stralsund, 1968, for USSR. 2,657 tons gross, 1,152 tons dw, 269·58ft loa × 44·75ft breadth × 16·41ft draught, two 8-cyl s sc Liebknecht diesel, cpp, 2,594bhp, 13·5 knots.

INNISFALLEN. *Eire.* Pass/car ferry. Built by Werft Nobiskrug, Rendsburg, for British & Irish SP Co Ltd, Cork. 4,849 tons gross, 936 tons dw, 387·75ft loa (incl bb) × 58·5ft breadth × 14·5ft draught, four 7-cyl tw sc MAN diesel, cpps, btp, 16,000bhp, 23 knots.

IRIS. *German.* Cargo CSD. Built by Scheeps 'De Biesbosch' Dordrecht, for Gerhard Schepers, Aschendorf. 1,000 tons gross, 2,475 tons dw, 276·41ft loa × 47·18ft breadth × 16·75ft draught, 8-cyl MWM diesel, bhp na, knots na.

IRIS. *German.* Cargo OSD. Built by Husumer Schiffsw, Husum, for Johannes Thode, Hamburg. 500 tons gross, tons dw na, 250·33ft loa × 39·18ft breadth × 12·92ft draught, 8-cyl Deutz diesel, bhp na, knots na.

IRMA DELMAS. *French.* Cargo, ref, CSD. Built by Ch Nav de La Ciotat, La Ciotat, for Soc Navale Delmas Vieljeux, Dunkerque. 10,171 tons gross, 13,281 tons dw, 528·41ft loa × 69·33ft breadth × 29·75ft draught, 6-cyl CCM-Sulzer diesel, 15,180bhp, 17·5 knots.

IRON ENDEAVOUR. *British.* Bulk carrier. Built by Doxford & Sunderland SB & E Co Ltd (J. L. Thompson), Sunderland, for Nile SS Co Ltd (J. & J. Denholm Mgrs), Newcastle. 40,316 tons gross, 69,115 tons dw, 798·41ft loa (incl bb) × 120·25ft breadth × 39·3ft draught, 8-cyl Doxford diesel, 20,000bhp, 15 knots.

ISABELLA. *German.* Cargo (part container ship). Built by J. J. Sietas, Hamburg, for Peter Dohle, Hamburg. 3,251 tons gross, 4,100 tons dw, 329·75ft loa × 50·09ft breadth × 22·2ft draught, 8-cyl Atlas-MaK diesel, 3,500bhp, knots na.

ISAKOGORKA. *Russian.* Cargo. Built by A. Zhdanov, Leningrad, 1968, for USSR, Archangel. 4,896 tons gross, tons dw na, 400·09ft loa × 54·92ft breadth × 22·2ft draught, 9-cyl Bryansk-B & W diesel, bhp na, knots na.

ISAR. *German.* Cargo 63 × 20ft containers (chartered for UK-Spain container trade). Built by J. J. Sietas Schiffsw, Hamburg, for Schepers Rhein-See Linie, Hamburg. 499 tons gross, 1,271 tons dw, 242·33ft loa × 35·41ft m breadth × 12·64ft draught, 8-cyl Deutz diesel, 1,320bhp, 13 knots.

ISFAHAN. *Swedish.* Cargo, ref. Built by Eriksbergs M/V A/S, Gothenburg, for A/B Svenska Ostasiatiske Kompaniet, Gothenburg. 6,149/9,640 tons gross, 9,025/12,800 tons dw, 459·41ft loa × 70·66ft breadth × 25·89/31·23ft draught, two 10-cyl s sc Eriksbergs-Pielstick diesel, cpp, 8,800bhp, 16·5 knots.

ISKRA. *Russian.* Tanker. Built by Stocznia im Komuny Paryskiej, Gdynia, for USSR. 14,164 tons gross, 20,000 tons dw, 581·58ft loa × 73·5ft breadth × 30·75ft draught, 6-cyl Cegielski-Sulzer diesel, 9,600bhp, 16 knots.

IVAN CHERNYKH. *Russian.* Cargo. Built by A. Zhdanov, Leningrad, 1968, for USSR, Leningrad. 4,896 tons gross, tons dw na, 400·09ft loa × 54·92ft breadth × 22·2ft draught, 9-cyl Bryansk-B & W diesel, bhp na, knots na.

IVONDRO. *French.* Cargo, ref. Built by At & Ch de Dunkerque-Bordeaux (France-Gironde), Dunkerque, 1968, for Cie Havraise & Nantaise Peninsulaire (CHNP), Dunkerque. 8,581 tons gross, tons dw, 472·41ft loa (incl bb) × 65·84ft breadth × 24·58ft draught, 6-cyl Creusot-B & W diesel, 12,600bhp, 20·5 knots.

Isfahan. *This latest class of ships of the Swedish East Asiatic Company, with names beginning with 'I' are composed of four 4 hold ships, the foremost 1 of which is arranged for carrying refrigerated cargo and vegetable oils. Out of a total of 570,000cu ft (bale), the refrigerated capacity is 37,100cu ft. Vegetable oil tanks hold 17,800cu ft. In the upper tween deck in holds 2-4 are wing tanks designed for use as ballast tanks. The ship is an 'open ship' with 4 pairs of hatches on the main and tween decks. The main deck hatches are hydraulically operated, with the tween deck ones being mechanically operated. There are three 12-ton and one 5-ton deck cranes, the main mast carrying one 100-ton and two 22-ton swinging derricks. Three 3-ton derricks are also provided, 2 of which are for handling provisions. The two 4 stroke Pielstick engines built by Eriskberg drive a stainless steel KaMeWa controllable pitch propeller, giving the ship a speed of 16¾ knots at 24ft draught. The sister ship is the* Indus*, the other 2 are to operate for the Svenska Orient Line, the first being named* Birkaland.

I

Italian Reefer. *Lead ship of a new large series of 4 refrigerated ships for Messrs Lauritzen, she has a capacity of 420,000cu ft. She has the now usual bulbous forefoot and transom stern, and there are 4 holds divided into 15 insulated compartments. The forward 3 holds have 4 decks and the after hold 3; and she can carry all refrigerated food products, meat or fruit, cooled or frozen. Of her 3 independent electric thermometer units, 2 can be read on the bridge, and 1 in the engine room. Each hatch is served by a Velle crane, 1 man control of all operations for each being fitted. There are 2 fibreglass lifeboats, and 2 'Floating Igloo' plastic rafts, together with an ordinary inflatable raft. Complete modern electronic navigational aids are fitted in the combined chart and wheelhouse, with a small room adjacent housing the fire control equipment. A swimming pool is fitted. All the accommodation is fitted and decorated in the latest Scandinavian style, 1 bulkhead of the crew smoking room, being entirely covered with a typical Jutland landscape, photographed into a plastic laminate. The ship is highly automated, with bridge control of the main engines, which are B & W type 8K74EF, 2 stroke single acting crosshead direct reversible with turbocharge. Maximum continuous rating is 16,300ihp equal to 15,000ehp at 124rpm, whilst service power is 13,700 effective horse power at 120rpm, giving a service speed of 22¾ knots. The engine room may be unmanned. The sister ship* Nippon Reefer *has also been completed. She has her name in Japanese characters also on the side of the bridge.*

IZHORA. *Russian.* Cargo. Built by Warnowwerft, Warnemunde, 1968, for USSR, Odessa. 9,455 tons gross, 12,882 tons dw, 496·92ft loa × 66·66ft breadth × 28·88ft draught, 8-cyl DMR-MAN diesel, 9,600bhp, 16·5 knots.

IZMAIL. *Russian.* Cargo. Built by Warnowwerft, Warnemunde, 1968, for USSR, Odessa. 9,727 tons gross, 12,882 tons dw, 496·92ft loa × 66·66ft breadth × 28·88ft draught, 8-cyl DMR-MAN diesel, 9,600bhp, knots na.

IZMAIL. *Russian.* Stern trawler, fish factory, ref (ATLANTIK class). Built by Volkswerft Stralsund, Stralsund, 1968, for USSR. 2,657 tons gross, 1,152 tons dw, 269·58ft loa × 44·75ft breadth × 16·41ft draught, two 8-cyl s sc Liebknecht diesel, cpp, 2,320bhp, 13·5 knots.

J

JAG DARSHAN. *Indian.* Bulk carrier (B1V Pioneer class, Sis JAG DEV). Built by Blohm & Voss AG, Hamburg, for Great Eastern Shipping Co Ltd, Bombay. 13,341 tons gross, 21,550 tons dw, 531·58ft loa (incl bb) × 74·92ft breadth × 34·08ft draught, 18-cyl B & V-Pielstick diesel, 9,000bhp, 16·5 knots.

JAMAICA MARU. *Japanese.* Cargo, ref. Built by Hitachi Zosen, Mukaishima, for Kawasaki KKK, Kobe. 8,816 tons gross, 12,000 tons dw, 462·66ft loa × 68·33ft breadth × 30·09ft draught, 6-cyl Hitachi-B & W diesel, 7,200bhp, 15·5 knots.

JANEY. *Liberian.* Cargo. Built by Austin & Pickersgill Ltd, Sunderland, for Mavroleon Bros (Ship Management) Ltd, Monrovia. 9,072 tons gross, 15,000 tons dw, 462·57ft loa × 67·11ft breadth × 29·05ft draught, 5-cyl Hawthorn-Sulzer diesel, 5,500bhp, knots na.

JAPAN AMBASSADOR. *Japanese.* Cargo. Built by Mitsubishi HI Ltd, Kobe, for Japan Lines Ltd, Tokyo. 9,957 tons gross, 11,800 tons dw, 503·5ft loa × 72·25ft breadth × 30·5ft draught, 7-cyl Mitsubishi-Sulzer diesel, 11,200bhp, 19 knots.

JAPAN CANNA. *Japanese.* Tanker. Built by Mitsubishi HI Ltd, Nagasaki, for Japan Lines Ltd, Tokyo. 116,457 tons gross, 209,800 tons dw, 1,036ft loa × 164·18ft breadth × 62·33ft draught, Mitsubishi turbs, 36,000shp, 16·25 knots.

JAPAN CEDAR. *Japanese.* Bulk carrier. Built by Mitsubishi HI Ltd, Kobe, for Japan Line Ltd, Tokyo. 33,264 tons gross, 57,700 tons dw, 734·92ft loa (incl bb) × 104·41ft breadth × 40ft draught, 6-cyl Mitsubishi-Sulzer diesel, 15,000bhp, 15·5 knots.

JAPAN MAGNOLIA. *Japanese.* Bulk/oil carrier. Built by Mitsubishi HI Ltd, Hiroshima, for Japan Line Ltd, Tokyo. 54,857 tons gross, 94,000 tons dw, 820·25ft loa (incl bb) × 126·5ft breadth × 47·38ft draught, 9-cyl Mitsubishi diesel, 21,600bhp, knots na.

JAPAN MARGUERITE. *Japanese.* Tanker. Built by Ishikawajima-Harima HI, Yokohama, for Japan Line Ltd, Tokyo. 117,404 tons gross, 208,500 tons dw, 1,036·41ft loa × 164·25ft breadth × 62·33ft draught, Ishikawajima turbs, 36,000shp, knots na.

JARAMA. *Norwegian.* Ore/oil carrier. Built by Nippon Kokan, Tsurumi, for Anders Jahre, Sandefjord. 57,850 tons gross, 95,700 tons dw, 867·25ft loa (incl bb) × 124·66ft breadth × 47·96ft draught, 9-cyl Mitsui-B & W diesel, 23,200bhp, knots na.

JASMINE. *Dutch* (*Antilles*). Cargo OSD. Built by Schps & Mach Welgelegen, Haarlem, for NV Stoomvaart Maats. 'Oostzee' Curacao, Willemstad (Vinke & Co). 499 tons gross, 1,260 tons dw, 257·5ft loa × 43·33ft breadth × draught na, 8-cyl MAN diesel, 2,260bhp, knots na.

JAWAHARLAL NEHRU. *Indian.* Tanker. Built by Brodogradiliste 'Split', Split, for The Shipping Corporation of India Ltd, Bombay. 47,343 tons gross, 88,000 tons dw, 843·25ft loa (incl bb) × 113·41ft breadth × 46ft draught, 9-cyl MAN diesel, 20,700bhp, knots na.

JEANNE LABOURBE. *Russian.* Cargo CSD. Built by Stocznia Gdanska, Gdansk for USSR. 10,380 tons gross, 12,725 tons dw, 507·41ft loa × 67·66ft breadth × 29·5ft draught, 6-cyl Cegielski-Sulzer diesel, 9,600bhp, 18·25 knots.

JEANNIE. *Chinese* (*Taiwan*). Bulk carrier. Built by Taiwan Shipbuilding Corpn, Keelung, for Eddie Steamship Co Ltd, Kaohsiung. 17,300 tons gross, 28,100 tons dw, 594·84ft loa × 82ft m breadth × 33·6ft draught, 7-cyl IHI-Sulzer diesel, 11,200bhp, knots na.

J

JELCZ II. *Polish.* Cargo. Built by G. Dimitrov Shipyard, Varna, 1968, for Polish SS Co, Szczecin. 2,468 tons gross, 3,428 tons dw, 314·58ft loa × 45·09ft breadth × 18·5ft draught, 6-cyl Zgoda-Sulzer diesel, 2,250bhp, 13 knots.

JENKA. *Norwegian.* Cargo (part container ship). Built by Schiffswerft Neptun, Rostock, for J. Brunvall, Bergen. 3,044 tons gross, 4,340 tons dw, 337·75ft loa × 47·92ft m breadth × 19ft draught, 8-cyl Atlas-MaK diesel, 3,000bhp, 13·5 knots.

JO-RIVKA. *Norwegian.* Cargo, ref. Built by At & Ch du Havre, Havre, for Lars Rej Johansen, Oslo. 499/1,191 tons gross, 950/1,700 tons dw 247·92ft loa × 42·84ft breadth × 13·11/16·77ft draught, 8-cyl Atlas-MaK diesel, 3,000bhp, knots na.

JOANA. *Liberian.* Bulk carrier. Built by Mitsui Zosen, Fujinagata, for Regina Sea Transport Corp SA, Monrovia (J. Livanos). 15,869 tons gross, 26,560 tons dw, 551·25ft lbp × 75·18ft breadth × 32·92ft draught, 6-cyl IHI-Sulzer diesel, 9,600bhp, 14·5 knots.

JOHN A. McCONE. *Liberian.* Tanker. Built by Kockums M/V A/B, Malmo, for Equitable Life Assurance Soc of the USA, Monrovia. 96,997 tons gross, 212,018 tons dw, 1,037ft loa × 160·18ft breadth × 62·38ft draught, Koskums-Stal Laval turbs, 30,000shp, 15·5 knots.

JOHN WULFF. *German.* Cargo OSD/CSD 63 × 20ft containers. Built by J. J. Sietas Schiffsw, Hamburg, for Hermann Wulff, Hamburg. 499/999 tons gross, 1,270/2,000 tons dw, 242·33ft loa × 35·41ft m breadth × 13/—ft draught, 8-cyl Deutz diesel, 1,400bhp, 13 knots.

JOINVILLE. *French.* Cargo, ref. Built by Ch Nav de La Ciotat, La Ciotat, for Cie Maritime des Chargeurs Reunis, Dunkerque. 10,618 tons gross, 13,750 tons dw, 515·09ft loa × 71·58ft breadth × 31·88ft draught, 6-cyl CCM-Sulzer diesel, 13,800bhp, 19 knots.

JOQUITA. *Norwegian.* Cargo, ref OSD/CSD. Built by At & Ch du Havre, Havre, for Lars Rej Johansen, Oslo. 499/1,200 tons gross, 950/1,700 tons dw, 278·84ft loa × 42·58ft breadth × 13·09/16·72ft draught, 8-cyl Atlas-MaK diesel, 3,000bhp, 15 knots.

JORG KRUGER. *German.* Cargo OSD/CSD (part container ship, 202 × 20ft containers, chartered to DART Line for Europe-Canada service). Built by Elsflether Werft AG, Elsfleth, for Hans Kruger GmbH, Hamburg. 5,383 tons gross, 7,150 tons dw, 385·84ft loa × 59·5ft breadth × 25·97ft draught, 12-cyl Blohm & Voss-Pielstick diesel, 6,950bhp, 17·25 knots.

JOSELIN. *German.* Cargo (typ 451). Built by Schiffsw Neptun, Rostock, for H. F. Cordes & Co, Bremen. 4,202 tons gross, 6,043 tons dw, 376·25ft loa × 53·84ft m breadth × 21·14ft draught, 6-cyl Halberstadt-MAN diesel, 4,000bhp, 14·75 knots.

JOTINA (launched as SIGYN). *Norwegian.* Cargo. Built by Schiffsw Neptun, Rostock, for Lars Rej Johansen, Oslo. 4,192 tons gross, 6,043 tons dw, 376·41ft loa × 53·84ft m breadth × 21·13ft draught, 6-cyl Halberstadt-MAN diesel, 4,000bhp, 14·5 knots.

JOULLA. *Norwegian.* Cargo. Built by Schiffsw Neptun, Rostock, for Lars Rej Johansen, Oslo. 4,068 tons gross, 6,043 tons dw, 376·41ft loa × 53·84ft breadth × 21·09ft draught, 6-cyl Halberstadt-MAN diesel, 4,000bhp, knots na.

JOWOOD. *Norwegian.* Cargo. Built by Schiffsw Neptun Rostock, for J. Brunvall, Bergen. 2,916 tons gross, 4,165 tons dw, 334·58ft loa × 47·92ft m breadth × 19·22ft draught, 8-cyl Atlas-MaK diesel, 3,000bhp, knots na.

JULIAN MARCHLEVSKI. *Russian.* Fish factory, ref, OSD (B69-1 class). Built by Stocznia Gdanska, Gdansk, 1968, for USSR. 13,600 tons gross, 10,000 tons dw, 537·33ft loa × 69·75ft breadth × 26·5ft draught, 6-cyl Cegielski-B & W diesel, 7,200bhp, 15·25 knots.

JULIUS FOCK. (Sis JULIUS PICKENPACK). *German.* Stern trawler CSD. Built by Rickmers Werft Bremerhaven, for Reederei Hans Pickenpack KG, Hamburg. 1,568 tons gross, tons dw, na 266ft loa × 44·75ft breadth × 19ft draught, 8-cyl MAN diesel, 2,260bhp, 15 knots.

JUNEAU MARU. *Japanese.* Cargo (timber). Built by Setoda Zosen, Setoda, for Yamashita-Shinnihon KKK & Futaba KKK, Tokyo. 10,598 tons gross, 15,800 tons dw, 469·25ft lbp × 71·58ft breadth × 28·5ft draught, 6-cyl Hitachi-B & W diesel, 7,200bhp, 14·25 knots.

JUNO. *German.* Cargo OSD/CSD. Built by Werft Nobiskrug, Rendsburg, for Flensburger Schiffssp: Vereing AG, Flensburg. 5,035 tons gross, 5,520/7,320 tons dw, 410ft loa × 56·58ft breadth × 21·38/25ft draught, 8-cyl Atlas-MaK diesel, 4,000bhp, knots na.

John A. McCone. *The first of a new series of 212,000 ton tankers for the Standard Oil Co of California's subsidiary Chevron Transport Corpn, and at the time the largest ship built by the builders. She was instrumented by the University of Arizona and the American Bureau of Shipping for a major strength analysis covering the hull structure, known as the Displacement Automated Integral System, during her trials and for her first ballast trip to the Middle East. Propulsion is by remotely-operated Kockum-Stal Laval advanced-propulsion type turbines rated at 30,000shp at 83rpm giving a contract sea speed of 15·8 knots, 16·09 being obtained on trials. She is the first mammoth tanker constructed by Kockum's computerized production in their new building dock. Mainly constructed of strong simplified hull sections of up to 800 tons each, the after superstructure for instance, is composed of a small number of entirely square assemblies. She is made of 100 block sections ranging up to 475 tons in steel and 175 tons in equipment.*

J

JUPITER. *German.* Cargo OSD/CSD. Built by Werft Nobiskrug, Rendsburg, for Flensburger Schiffsparten Vereinigung AG, Flensburg. 5,025 tons gross, 7,500 tons dw, 410ft loa × 56·58ft breadth × 21·41/25·18ft draught, 8-cyl Atlas-MaK diesel, 4,000bhp, knots na.

JUYO MARU. *Japanese.* Cargo ref. Built by Hayashikane Zosen, Shimonoseki, 1968, for Taiyo Shosen KK, Tokyo. 3,411 tons gross, 4,513 tons dw, 364·5 ft loa × 53·25ft breadth × 22·5ft draught, 7-cyl Hatsudoki diesel, 6,000bhp, 16 knots.

K

KAIOZAN MARU. *Japanese.* Cargo. Built by Kusushima Dock Co Ltd, Imabari, for Tamao KKK, Namikata. 10,033 tons gross, 15,800 tons dw, 446·18ft lbp × 71·58ft breadth × 28ft draught, 6-cyl Kawasaki-MAN diesel, 7,500bhp, knots na.

KAISEI MARU. *Japanese.* Tanker. Built by Imabari Zosen, Imabari, for Fuso KKK, Kobe. 1,500 tons gross, 3,100 tons dw, 246ft lbp × 41·09ft breadth × 18·75ft draught, two 8-cyl s sc Daihatsu diesel, 2,000bhp, 13 knots.

KAKUYU MARU. *Japanese.* Tanker. Built by Geibi Yosen Kogyo, Kure, for Tsurumi Yuso KK, Tokyo. 1,497 tons gross, 2,451 tons dw, 249·33ft loa × 38·84ft breadth × 17·58ft draught, 6-cyl Daihatsu diesel, 2,400bhp, knots na.

KALININGRAD. *Russian.* Cargo. Built by Valmet O/Y Pansion Telakka, Abo, for USSR. 2,920 tons gross, 3,500 tons dw 335·66ft loa × 46·09ft breadth × 19·66ft draught, 5-cyl Valmet-B & W diesel, 2,900bhp, knots na.

KAMCHADAL. *Russian.* Cargo (timber). Built by Nystads Varv A/B, Nystad, 1968, for USSR. 2,920 tons gross, 3,400 tons dw, 335ft loa × 46·09ft breadth × 18·75ft draught, 5-cyl Valmet-B & W diesel, 2,900bhp, 13·75 knots.

KAMOGANA MARU No 18. *Japanese.* Cargo. Built by Shin Yamamoto Zosen, Kochi, 1968, for Shimozaki KKK, Kobe. 2,956 tons gross, 5,100 tons dw, 308·41ft lbp × 49·33ft breadth × 21·18ft draught, 6-cyl Ito Tekkosho diesel, 3,200bhp, 14·5 knots.

KANEYOSHI MARU. *Japanese.* Cargo/cars. Built by Kanazashi Zosensho, Shimizu, for Kinsei KKK, Tokyo. 9,853 tons gross, 15,705 tons dw, 488·58ft loa × 72·25ft breadth × 29·18ft draught, 6-cyl Mitsui-B & W diesel, 7,200bhp, 14 knots.

KAPITAN KUSHNARENKO. *Russian.* Cargo. Built by Nosenko Shipyard, Nikolayev, 1967, for USSR. 11,670 tons gross, 16,584 tons dw, 556·5ft loa × 71·58ft breadth × 32·81ft draught, 6-cyl Bryansk-B & W diesel, 12,000bhp, knots na.

KAPITAN VISLOBOKOV. *Russian.* Cargo, ref. Built by Nosenko Shipyard, Niolayev, 1967, for USSR. 11,801 tons gross, tons dw na, 510·75ft loa × 67·92ft breadth × 29·75ft draught, 7-cyl Bryansk-B & W diesel, bhp na, knots na.

KARA. *Russian.* Cargo (timber). Built by Valmet O/Y Helsingin Telakka, Helsingfors, for USSR, Archangel. 2,914 tons gross, 3,541 tons dw, 335ft loa × 46ft breadth × 19·33ft draught, 5-cyl Valmet-B & W diesel, 3,250bhp, 13·75 knots.

KARAGANDA. *Russian.* Cargo. Built by Warnowwerft, Warnemunde, for USSR, Leningrad. 9,748 tons gross, 12,882 tons dw, 496·92ft loa × 66·66ft breadth × 28·89ft draught, 8-cyl DMR-MAN diesel, 9,600bhp, 16·5 knots.

KARL KRUSHTEYN. *Russian.* Cargo. Built by Angyalfold Shipyard, Budapest, for USSR. 1,248 tons gross, 1,299 tons dw, 244·33ft loa × 37·18ft breadth × 13·13ft draught, 8-cyl Lang diesel, 1,000bhp, 11·5 knots.

KASTAV. *Yugoslavian.* Cargo, ref. Built by Italcantieri SpA, Monfalcone, for Jugoslavenska Linijska Plovidba, Rijeka. 8,555 tons gross, 8,575 tons dw, 499·41ft loa (incl bb) × 65·75ft breadth × 25·43ft draught, 7-cyl CRDA-Fiat diesel, 10,500bhp, 18·75 knots.

KATHE WIARDS. *German.* Cargo. Built by P. Lindenau, Kiel for Kauffahrtei Seereederei Adolf Wiards & Co, Lubeck. 5,079 tons gross, tons dw na, 410·18ft loa × 56·84ft breadth × 25ft draught, 8-cyl MAN diesel, 4,450bhp, knots na.

KATRINA. *Liberian*. Bulk carrier. Built by Sanoyasu Dockyard Ltd, Osaka, for East Coast Maritime Corpn, Monrovia (Oak SS Co, Hong Kong). 9,385 tons gross, 16,769 tons dw, 471·5ft loa × 71·66ft breadth × 28·92ft draught, 6-cyl Uraga-Sulzer diesel, 7,200bhp, 14·5 knots.

KAZATIN. *Russian*. Cargo. Builder na, Russia, for USSR. 3,172 tons gross, tons dw na, measurements na, cyl na, diesel, bhp na, knots na.

KEIGO MARU. *Japanese*. Bulk carrier. Built by Mitsubishi HI Ltd, Hiroshima, for Yamashita-Shinnihon KK, Tokyo. 34,084 tons gross, 57,900 tons dw, 734·92ft loa × 104·5ft breadth × 40·09ft draught, 6-cyl Mitsubishi diesel, 15,000bhp, knots na.

KEIYO MARU. *Japanese*. Tanker. Built by Mitsubishi HI Ltd, Nagasaki, for Taiyo Shosen KK, Tokyo. 116,457 tons gross, 206,500 tons dw, 1,036ft loa (incl bb) × 164·18ft breadth × 62·33ft draught, Mitsubishi turbs, 36,000shp, knots na.

KHERSONES. *Russian*. Tanker. Built by Rauma-Repola O/Y Rauma, 1968, for USSR. 3,674 tons gross, 4,600 tons dw, 348·25ft loa × 63·09ft breadth × 21·33ft draught, 5-cyl Bryansk-B & W diesel, 2,900bhp, 14 knots.

KHIAN HILL. *Greek*. Cargo (IHI Freedom type). Built by Ishikawajima-Harima HI, Tokyo, for Freedom Sea Transport SA, Piraeus (J. Carras). 10,016 tons gross, 15,178 tons dw, 466·75ft loa (incl bb) × 65·09ft breadth × 28·8ft draught, 12-cyl IHI-Pielstick diesel, 5,130bhp, 14·25 knots.

KHIAN ISLAND. *Greek*. Cargo. Built by Ishikawajima-Harima HI, Tokyo, for Tramp Tankers Enterprises SA, Piraeus (J. C. Carras). 10,016 tons gross, 14,939 tons dw, 465·75ft loa (incl bb) × 65·09ft breadth × 29·7ft draught, 12-cyl IHI-Pielstick diesel, 5,130bhp, 14 knots.

KHIAN SEA. *Greek*. Cargo. Built by Ishikawajima-Harima HI, Tokyo, for Islander Shipping Enterprises SA, Piraeus (J. C. Carras). 10,015 tons gross, 14,939 tons dw, 466·75ft loa (incl bb) × 65·09ft breadth × 29·7ft draught, 12-cyl IHI-Pielstick diesel, 5,130bhp, 14 knots.

KHIAN STAR. *Greek*. Cargo. Built by Ishikawajima-Harima HI, Tokyo, for Associated Bulk Carriers SA, Piraeus (J. C. Carras). 10,016 tons gross, 15,178 tons dw, 465·92ft loa (incl bb) × 65·09ft breadth × 29·63ft draught, 12-cyl IHI-Pielstick diesel, 5,130bhp, 14 knots.

KHIAN SUN. *Greek*. Cargo. Built by Ishikawajima-Harima HI, Tokyo, for Freedom Pacific Tramping SA, Piraeus (J. C. Carras). 10,016 tons gross, 15·163 tons dw, 465·92ft loa (incl bb) × 65ft breadth × 29·66ft draught, 12-cyl IHI-Pielstick diesel, 5,130bhp, 14 knots.

KHIAN ZEPHYR. *Greek*. Cargo. Built by Ishikawajima-Harima HI, Tokyo, for Freedom General Shipping SA, Piraeus (J. C. Carras). 10,015 tons gross, 15,163 tons dw, 466·84ft loa (incl bb) × 65·09ft breadth × 29·62ft draught, 12-cyl IHI-Pielstick diesel, 5,130bhp, 14 knots.

KHRUSTALNYY. *Russian*. Tanker. Builder na, for USSR. 1,722 tons gross, tons dw na, measurements na, cyl na, diesel, bhp na, knots na.

KICCHO MARU. *Japanese*. Cargo (timber). Built by Onomichi Zosen, Onomichi, 1968, for Satokuni KKK, Kobe. 3,990 tons gross, 6,073 tons dw, 329·5ft lbp × 53·92ft breadth × 22·18ft draught, 6-cyl Hatsudoki diesel, 3,800bhp, 12·75 knots.

KIMI MARU. (Sis JAPAN CEDAR). *Japanese*. Bulk carrier. Built by Mitsubishi HI, Kobe, for Mitsui-OSK Lines KK, Osaka. 37,179 tons gross, 61,400 tons dw, 780·84ft loa (incl bb) × 105·84ft breadth × 40ft draught, 8-cyl Mitsubishi-Sulzer diesel, 18,400bhp, 15·25 knots.

KIMITSUSAN MARU *Japanese*. Ore/oil carrier. Built by Mitsui Zosen, Chiba, 1968, for Mitsui-OSK Lines KK, Osaka. 56,702 tons gross, 99,605 tons dw, 831·41ft loa (incl bb) × 127·75ft breadth × 48·25ft draught, 9-cyl Mitsui-B & W diesel, 20,700bhp, 16 knots.

KIMRY. *Russian*. Cargo (timber). Built by F. W. Hollming O/Y, Rauma, for USSR, Archangel. 2,920 tons gross, 3,400 tons dw, 335 ft loa × 46·09ft breadth × 19·66ft draught, 5-cyl Bryansk-B & W diesel, 2,900bhp, 13·75 knots.

KINTAI MARU. *Japanese*. Cargo. Built by Hashihama Zosen, Imabari, for Sanoyasu Shoji KK, Osaka. 6,038 tons gross, 9,500 tons dw, 390·41ft lbp × 60·09ft breadth × 24·58ft draught, 6-cyl Hatsudoki diesel, 5,400bhp, knots na.

KIS SKOU (Sis TEGELHOLMEN). *Danish*. Tanker. Built by Aarhus Flydk & Msk, Aarhus, for Ove Skou, Copenhagen. 499 tons gross, 1,050 tons dw, 196·5ft loa × 33·75ft breadth × 12·79ft draught, 6-cyl Atlas-MaK diesel, 1,100bhp, 11 knots.

Kanimbla. *Associated Steamships Pty of Melbourne operate through their subsidiary Bulkships Ltd, the coastal feeder container services connecting with the overseas container ships. They have 2 new ships, Kanimbia and her sister Manoora, both famous names on the Australian coast. They have a predecessor in the fleet, the 6,500 ton dw Kooringa, claimed the world's first cellular container ship, designed as such from the keel upwards. Her success has prompted the building of the 2 larger vessels. Together the two maintain a door to door container service between Brisbane, Sydney, Melbourne and Fremantle, whilst the Kooringa maintains a weekly Seatainer service between Melbourne, Sydney and Brisbane. They are designed to carry below deck 172 × 20ft ISO containers, 40 open type half height, 20ft ones, and 20 full height open type 20ft ones, together with 1,340 Australian standard type 'D' fully enclosed containers. Above decks 140 × 20ft ISO containers are carried in 2 tiers, 8 athwartships on Nos 3, 4, 5 and 6 hatches plus 14 in a single tier 7 wide on No 2. Normally 79 are refrigerated. The only non cellular hold is No 1, which, with 3 decks is designed to carry 74 motor vehicles. Fully loaded they carry dw of 13,000 tons on a 27ft 9in draught. As soon as 1 cell has been discharged, loading and discharge can be carried out simultaneously, maintaining twin lifts of 20ft containers, 600 tons per hour can be handled on a 4 minute cycle. Except No 1, all cargo is handled by shore Portainer type cranes. No 1 is worked by the ship's electric 5-ton crane. Main engines are Sulzer 7RD76 type, partly constructed at the Commonwealth Government Engineering Works at Port Melbourne. The engine in each ship is rated at 11,200bhp (metric) at 123rpm, on a consumption of 35 tons fuel per day and 17½ knots service speed. Bridge control is employed, with additional alternative controls in the engine room. The anchor windlass is remotely controlled from the wheelhouse by Clarke Chapman gear. They each have bow thrust propellers. Of the complement of 29, there are 12 'general purpose' seamen.*

KISOGAWA MARU. *Japanese*. Tanker. Built by Hitachi Zosen, Sakai, for Kawasaki KKK & Ilno Kaiun KK, Kobe. 104,008 tons gross, 187,500 tons dw, 1,026ft loa (incl bb) × 166·75ft breadth × 57·09ft draught, Kawasaki turbs, 34,000shp, 17 knots.

KIYO MARU. *Japanese*. Cargo (timber). Built by Namura Zosensho, Osaka, 1968, for Taiheyo Kaiun KK, Tokyo. 11,315 tons gross, 18,700 tons dw, 491·75ft loa × 74·58ft breadth × 30ft draught, 16-cyl Mitsubishi-MAN diesel, 8,690bhp, 14·75 knots.

KLAUS BLOCK. *German*. Cargo OSD (71 × 20ft containers). Built by J. J. Sietas Schiffsw, Hamburg, for Heinrich Block, Hamburg. 499 tons gross, 1,460 tons dw, 252·66ft loa × 36·75ft m breadth × 13·27ft draught, 6-cyl Deutz diesel, 1,700bhp, 13 knots.

KLONDIKE. *Canadian*. Container ship (shipboard gantry crane, 200 × 20ft containers). Built by Canadian Vickers Shipyards Ltd, Montreal, for British Yukon Navigation Co Ltd, Vancouver. 8,040 tons gross, 6,900 tons dw, 394·09ft loa × 71·75ft breadth × 20ft draught, two 7-cyl tw sc Nydqvist & Holm diesel, 5,700bhp, 13·5 knots.

KLORTE LAGOON (Sis SUBIN RIVER). *Ghanaian*. Cargo. Built by Soc Espanola de Cons Nav, Cadiz, for Black Star Line, Takoradi. 7,155 tons gross, 9,600 tons dw, 455ft loa × 62·59ft breadth × 27·92ft draught, 6-cyl SECN-Sulzer diesel, 7,200bhp, 16 knots.

KOA MARU. *Japanese*. Tanker. Built by Tokushima Zosen, Tokushima, for Mitsubishi Shoji Kaisha, Tokyo. 2,153 tons gross, 3,550 tons dw, 269ft lbp × 44·84ft breadth × 18·33ft draught, 6-cyl Hatsudoki diesel, 3,500bhp, knots na.

KOAN MARU NO 7. *Japanese*. Tanker. Built by Hayashikane Zosen Nagasaki, 1968, for Idemitsu Kosan KK, Tokyo. 2,189 tons gross, 3,500 tons dw, 293·75ft loa × 42ft breadth × 19·66ft draught, two 6-cyl s sc Fuji diesel, 1,500bhp, 13 knots.

KOBE MARU. *Japanese*. Cargo. Built by Hashihama Zosen, Imabari, for Kobe Sempaku KK, Kobe. 2,991 tons gross, 5,200 tons dw, 295·25ft lbp × 51·25ft breadth × 21·33ft draught, 6-cyl Hatsudoki diesel, 3,200bhp, knots na.

KOHO MARU. *Japanese*. Tanker. Built by Ishikawajima-Harima HI, Kure, for Kawasaki KKK & Iino KKK. 89,367 tons gross, 155,000 tons dw, 998·33ft loa (incl bb) × 142·18ft breadth × 58·41ft draught, 12-cyl IHI-Sulzer diesel, 28,800bhp, 15 knots.

King Alfred. *See Volume XVII for particulars. This 53,250 ton deadweight ship was launched as the* Angelus of Oslo *by Eriksbergs of Gothenburg, and renamed* Hemsefjell. *On changing hands for the third time, being bought for the King Line section of the British and Commonwealth company, she received her present name.*

KOHO MARU. *Japanese.* Cargo. Built by Hayashikane Zosen, Nagasaki, 1968, for Fukuho Kaiun Sangyo KK, Nagasaki. 2,997 tons gross, 5,200 tons dw, 333·92ft loa × 51·25ft breadth × 20·92ft draught, 6-cyl Akasaka Tekkosho diesel, 3,200bhp, 12·25 knots.

KOJO MARU. *Japanese.* Cargo. Built by Hayashikane Zosen, Nagasaki, for Ueno Shokai KK, Kitakyushu. 3,901 tons gross, 6,048 tons dw, 356·84ft loa × 53·92ft breadth × 21·66ft draught, 6-cyl Mitsui-B & W diesel, 3,300bhp, 12·5 knots.

KOLYA MYAGOTIM. *Russian.* Cargo. Built by Schiffsw Neptun, Rostock, for USSR, Vladivostok. 3,684 tons gross, 4,638 tons dw, 346·75ft loa × 51·33ft breadth × 22·18ft draught, 6-cyl Halberstadt-MAN diesel, 3,250bhp, knots na.

KOMAHIME MARU. *Japanese.* Molasses tanker. Built by Hayashikane Zosen, Shimonoseki, 1968, for Manno KKK, Osaka. 2,376 tons gross, 4,400cu metres, 308ft loa × 45·33ft breadth × 18·84ft draught, 6-cyl Akasaka Tekkosho diesel, 3,200bhp, 13·5 knots.

KOMET. *German.* Survey ship. Built by Jadewerft GmbH, Wilhelmshaven, for Deutsches Hydrographisches Institut, Hamburg. 1,200 tons gross, tons dw na, 221·84ft loa × 38·09ft breadth × 13·11ft draught, two 16-cyl tw sc Maybach diesel, cpp, 1,800bhp, 15 knots.

KOMPAS. *Russian.* Fish factory, ref (training: 121 apprentices). Built by Burmeister & Wain, Copenhagen, 1968, for USSR, Murmansk. 4,734 tons gross, 2,480 tons dw, 337ft loa × 52·66ft breadth × 18·25ft draught, 6-cyl B & W diesel, cpp, 3,100bhp, 14 knots.

KOMSOMOLETS LENINGRADA. *Russian.* Tanker. Builder na, Leningrad, 1968, for USSR. 32,334 tons gross, 50,000 tons dw, 756·33ft loa × 101·75ft breadth × draught na, turbs, 19,000shp, knots na.

KOMSOMOLSKAYA SLAVA. *Russian.* Cargo. Built by Kherson Shipyard, Kherson, 1968, for USSR. 9,547 tons gross, tons dw na, 501·33ft loa × 67·58ft breadth × 29·62ft draught, 6-cyl Bryansk-B & W diesel, 9,000bhp, 17 knots.

KONDRATIY BULAVIN. *Russian.* Cargo. Built by Angyalfold Shipyard, Budapest, for USSR. 1,505 tons gross, 1,923 tons dw na, 255·25ft loa × 37·75ft breadth × 16·27ft draught, 6-cyl Jugoturbina-Sulzer diesel, 1,500bhp, 12·5 knots.

KONG HAAKON VII. *Norwegian.* Tanker. Built by A/S Akers M/V, Stord, for Hilmar Reksten, Bergen. 109,423 tons gross, 219,000 tons dw, 1,068·66ft loa × 152·41ft breadth × 67ft draught, GEC turbs, shp na, knots na. NB. Severely damaged by explosion 31.12.69 whilst tank cleaning off West African coast.

KONIN. *Polish* Cargo, ref, OSD/CSD. Built by Stocznia Gdanska, Gdansk, 1968, for Polish Ocean Lines, Gdansk 6,382/10,063 tons gross, 9,596/12,056 tons dw, 504·92ft loa × 67·58ft breadth × —/29·42ft draught, 6-cyl Cegielski-Sulzer diesel, 9,600bhp, knots na.

KONPIRA MARU. *Japanese.* Ferry (Catamaran hull) Built by Nippon Kokan, Shimizu, for Udaka Kokudo Ferry KK, Takamatsu. 2,700 tons gross, tons dw na, 272·33ft loa × 82·09ft breadth × 15·33ft draught, four 8-cyl tw sc Daihatsu diesel, bhp na, knots na.

KONSTANTIN SAVELYEV. *Russian.* Cargo. Builder na, Vyborg, for USSR. 1,813 tons gross, 2,260 tons dw, 269ft loa × 41ft breadth × draught na, cyl na, diesel, bhp na, knots na.

KOPALNIA KLEOFAS. *Polish.* Cargo. Built by A/S Nakskov Skibsv, Nakskov, for Polish SS Co, Szczecin. 8,405 tons gross, 11,500 tons dw 465·09ft loa × 63ft breadth × 26·9ft draught, 6-cyl Cegielski-B & W diesel, 7,200bhp, knots na.

Korea Rainbow. *This ship is equipped with the latest type of Vac-U-Vator pneumatic conveying machine. Previously it had been found that whilst grain could be handled successfully in bulk, rice was susceptible of kernel breakage when moved pneumatically. Otherwise gearless, the ship, with 7 holds and hatches unloaded on her main voyage at Inchon, by this means, successfully, 4 holds of Californian 'Calrose' rice, and 3 holds of pearl rice without undue damage to the rice kernels.*

KOPALNIA MARCEL. *Polish.* Cargo. Built by A/S Nakskov Skibsv, Nakskov, for Polish SS Co, Szczecin. 8,400 tons gross, 12,480 tons dw, 465·09ft loa × 63·09ft breadth × 28·08ft draught, 6-cyl Cegielski-B & W diesel, 7,200bhp, knots na.

KOPALNIA SOSNICA. *Polish.* Cargo. Built by A/S Nakskov Skibsv, Nakskov, for Polish SS Co, Szczecin. 8,383 tons gross, 11,594 tons dw, 465·09ft loa × 63ft breadth × 26·9ft draught, 6-cyl Cegielski-B & W diesel, 7,200bhp, knots na.

KOPALNIA SZCZYGLOWICE. *Polish.* Cargo. Built by A/S Nakskov Skibsv, Nakskov, for Polish SS Co, Szczecin. 8,407 tons gross, 11,500 tons dw, 465·09ft loa × 63·18ft breadth × 26·9ft draught, 6-cyl Cegielski-B & W diesel, 6,550bhp, knots na.

KOPALNIA WIREK. *Polish.* Cargo. Built by A/S Nakskov Skibsv, Nakskov, for Polish SS Co, Szczecin. 8,404 tons gross, 11,500 tons dw, 465·09ft loa × 63ft breadth × 26·9ft draught, 6-cyl Cegielski-B & W diesel, 7,200bhp, 15·25 knots.

KORABLESTROITYEL KLOPOTOV. *Russian.* Fish factory, ref Built by Admiralteiski Shipyard, Leningrad, 1967, for USSR, Vladivostok· 13,528 tons gross, 7,316 tons. dw, 531·5ft loa × 65·58ft breadth × 22·96ft draught, two 8-cyl tw sc Russki diesel, 4,000bhp, 12 knots.

KOREA PACIFIC. *South Korean* Bulk carrier. Built by Ishikawajima-Harima HI, Aioi, for Far Eastern Marine Transport Co Ltd, Inchon. 28,199 tons gross, 40,900 tons dw, 692·25ft loa (incl bb) × 98·5ft breadth × 33·92ft draught, 8-cyl IHI-Sulzer diesel, 12,800bhp, knots na.

KOREA RAINBOW. *South Korean.* Bulk carrier. Built by Ishikawajima-Harima HI, Aioi, 1968, for Far Eastern Marine Transport Co Ltd, Inchon. 28,493 tons gross, 40,900 tons dw, 692·25ft loa (incl bb) × 98·58ft breadth × 33·9ft draught, 8-cyl IHI-Sulzer diesel, 12,800bhp, 15·5 knots.

KOREAN FRONTIER. *South Korean.* Cargo, ref. Built by Kasado Dock Co Ltd, Kudamatsu, 1968, for Korea Shipping Corpn, Pusan 9,745 tons gross, 12,280 tons dw, 518·33ft loa × 71·66ft breadth × 31·09ft draught, 8-cyl Kawasaki-MAN diesel, 10,000bhp, 21·5 knots.

KOREAN MAIL. *USA.* Cargo, ref, part containership. Built by Newport News SB & DD Co, Newport News, 1968, for American Mail Line, Portland, Ore.; 11,559/15,949 tons gross, 18,000/22,273 tons dw, 605ft loa×82·18ft breadth×3[illegible]·18/35·05ft draught, GEC turbs, 21,600shp, 21 knots.

KOREAN TRADER. *South Korean.* Cargo, ref. Built by Kasado Dock Co Ltd, Kudamatsu, 1968, for Korea Shipping Corpn, Pusan 9,760 tons gross, 12,280 tons dw, 518·33ft loa×71·66ft breadth×31·09ft draught, 8-cyl Kawasaki-MAN diesel, 10,000bhp, 21 knots.

KORMORAN ISLE. *German.* Cargo OSD. Built by Gebr Schurenstedt, Bardenfleth, for Partenreederei 'Kormoran Isle', Bremen. 700 tons gross, 1,523 tons dw, 269·33ft loa×42ft m breadth×12·5ft draught, 6-cyl Atlas MaK diesel, 2,400bhp, knots na.

KORRIZ. *Russian.* Cargo. Builder na, Russia, 1968, for USSR. 3,172 tons gross, tons dw na, measurements na, cyl na, diesel, bhp na, knots na.

KORYU MARU. *Japanese.* Bulk nickel carrier. Built by Ishikawajima-Harima HI, Aioi, 1968, for Taiheiyo KKK, Tokyo. 9,618 tons gross, 15,300 tons dw, 482·33ft loa (incl bb)×67·33ft breadth×26·92ft draught, 6-cyl IHI-Sulzer diesel, 7,200bhp, 14 knots.

KORYU MARU. *Japanese.* Cargo. Built by Imabari Zosen, Imabari, for Kinriki KKK, Hakata. 2,629 tons gross, 4,600 tons dw, 282·18ft lbp×36·18ft breadth×draught na, two 6-cyl s sc Daihatsu diesel, 1,500bhp, knots na.

KOSHO MARU. *Japanese.* Cargo. Built by Onomichi Zosen, Onomichi, for Kenko KKK, Kobe. 10,800 tons gross, 17,100 tons dw, 505·5ft loa×72·92ft breadth×29·5ft draught, 6-cyl Hitachi-B & W diesel, 7,200bhp, knots na.

KOSHO MARU. *Japanese.* Cargo. Built by Hashihama Zosen, Imabari, 1968, for Eguchi KK, Kobe. 2,982 tons gross, 5,100 tons dw, 308·33ft lbp×49·33ft breadth×20·92ft draught, 6-cyl Ito Tekkosho diesel, 3,000bhp, knots na.

KOSHO MARU. *Japanese.* Cargo. Built by Kurushima Dockyard, Imabari, 1968, for Toda KKK, Iyomishima. 2,502 tons gross, 4,192 tons dw, 272·33ft lbp×47·33ft breadth×draught na, 6-cyl Akasaka Tekkosho diesel, 2,200bhp, 12 knots.

KOSMONAUT KOMAROV. *Russian.* Fish carrier, ref. Builder na, Russia, 1968, for USSR. 6,455 tons gross, 4,270 tons dw, 429·18ft loa×55·33ft breadth×25·29ft draught, four 10-cyl tw sc Russian made diesel electric, bhp na, knots na.

KOTEL. *Bulgarian.* Cargo. Built by I. Dimitrov Shipyard, Rousse, for Navigation Maritime Bulgare, Varna. 1,833 tons gross, tons dw na, 264·18ft loa×39·09ft breadth×14·27ft draught, 6-cyl Zgoda-Sulzer diesel, 1,320bhp, knots na.

KOTOKU MARU. *Japanese.* Cargo. Built by Shin Yamamoto Zosen, Kochi, for Maeda Unyu KK, Yawatahama. 3,910 tons gross, 6,300 tons dw, 333·09ft lbp×53·25ft breadth×21·92ft draught, 6-cyl Hatsudoki-diesel, 3,800bhp, 12·5 knots.

KOYO MARU. *Japanese.* Cargo. Built by Imabari Zosen, Imabari, for Hashimoto KKK, Shimokamagari. 2,994 tons gross, 5,500 tons dw, 308·41ft lbp×51·58ft breadth×21·66ft draught, 6-cyl Hatsudoki diesel, 3,800 bhp,14·5 knots.

KOYO MARU. *Japanese.* Salvage tug. Built by Mitsubishi HI Ltd, Shimonoseki, 1967, for Nippon Koyo Eisen KK, Tokyo 2,062 tons gross, 1,880 tons dw, 280·5ft loa×46ft breadth×19·66ft draught, two 9-cyl s sc Mitsubishi-MAN diesel, cpp, btp, bhp na, 19·6 knots.

KOYO MARU. *Japanese.* LPG carrier. Built by Taiheiyo Kogyo, Hiroshima, 1968, for Abo Shoten KK, Onomichi. 1,270 tons gross, 1,200 tons dw, 220·84ft loa×35·5ft breadth×14·8ft draught, two 12-cyl tw sc Daihatsu diesel, 1,400bhp, knots na.

KRASNAYA GORKA. *Russian.* Cargo. Built by A. Zhdanov, Leningrad, 1968, for USSR, Leningrad. 4,676 tons gross, tons dw na, 400·09ft loa×54·92ft breadth×22·2ft draught, 9-cyl Bryansk-B & W diesel, bhp na, knots na.

KRASNOARMEYSK. *Russian.* Cargo. Builder na, Russia, 1968, for USSR. 3,172 tons gross, tons dw na, measurements na, cyl na, diesel, bhp na, knots na.

Koyo Maru. *To meet the demand for prompt assistance to distressed mammoth bulk carriers and tankers in remote areas, the Japan Ocean Tug Co has been formed by leading Japanese shipowners and insurance companies. The* Koyo Maru *is claimed to be the largest ocean-going salvage tug of her kind in the world, and has been bareboat chartered to the* Nippon Salvage Co. *She has 2 sets of Yokohama-MAN diesel engines of type R9V 40/54, with reduction gearing to a single screw shaft, giving a maximum free running speed of 19·6 knots. The ship has a range of 18,000 miles, or when towing at 5 knots, 5,000 miles. She is capable of towing a 300,000 tonner. She has a KaMeWa controllable pitch propeller and a 350hp bow thrust unit. She has equipment to cope with any type of salvage operation, an electric towing winch capable of withstanding a strain of 150 tons and accommodation for a crew of 31 plus 43 salvage hands. She is based at Moji and now has a plain funnel (no black top) with a device of 2 vertical entwined cable links.*

KRASNOPOLIE. *Russian.* Cargo. Builder na, Russia, for USSR. tonnage na, measurements na, cyl na, diesel, bhp na, knots na.

KRASNOTURINSK. *Russian.* Cargo. Builder na, Russia, for USSR. 3,172 tons gross, tons dw na, measurements na, cyl na, diesel, bhp na, knots na.

K

Kuwait Horizon. *One of the Freedom class of Ishikawajima Liberty Replacements and an early member of the expanding fleet of Kuwait ships.*

KULOY. *Russian.* Cargo. Builder na, Vyborg, 1967, for USSR, Archangel. 4,896 tons gross, 6,357 tons dw. 400·09ft loa × 54·92ft breadth × 22·2ft draught, 9-cyl Bryansk-B & W diesel, bhp na, knots na.

KUMSONG. *South Korean.* Bulk carrier. Built by Italcantieri SpA, Monfalcone, 1968, for Korean United Lines, Inchon. 9,164 tons gross, 15,400 tons dw, 459·33ft loa × 69ft breadth × 30·41ft draught, 6-cyl Ansaldo-B & W diesel, 7,200bhp, 15 knots.

KURS. *Russian.* Fish carrier, ref. Built by Burmeister & Wain, Copenhagen, for USSR. 4,700 tons gross, 2,500 tons dw, 356ft loa × 52·58ft breadth × 18ft draught, 6-cyl B & W diesel, 3,100bhp, 14 knots.

KUSUNOKI MARU. *Japanese.* Bulk carrier (5 Mitsubishi 20-ton derricks). Built by Mitsubishi HI Ltd, Kobe, for Mitsubishi Shoji KK, Tokyo. 10,084 tons gross, 16,860 tons dw, 479ft loa × 71ft breadth × 30·66ft draught, 6-cyl Mitsubishi-Sulzer diesel, 8,000bhp, 17 knots.

KUWAIT HORIZON. *Kuwait.* Cargo (Freedom). Built by Ishikawajima-Harima HI, Tokyo, for National Maritime & Agencies Co WLL, Kuwait. 9,650 tons gross, 14,099 tons dw, 465ft loa (incl bb) × 65·18ft breadth × 28·66ft draught, 12-cyl IHI-Pielstick diesel, 5,130bhp, 14·25 knots.

K

KYOGO MARU. *Japanese.* Cargo. Built by Imai Zosen, Kochi, 1968, for Kamishio KKK, Kasaoka. 2,950 tons gross, 5,000 tons dw, 285·5ft lbp × 49·33ft breadth × 20·84ft draught, 6-cyl Hatsudoki diesel, 2,700bhp, 11·5 knots.

KYORYU MARU. *Japanese.* Cargo. Built by Ujina Zosensho, Hiroshima, 1968, for Kotaka KKK, Osaka. 1,967 tons gross, 3,407 tons dw, 294·33ft loa × 42·09ft breadth × 18·84ft draught, 6-cyl Ito Tekkosho diesel, 2,200bhp, 12·25 knots.

KYOWA MARU. *Japanese.* Cargo. Built by Ujino Zosensho, Hiroshima, 1968, for Sankyo KKK, Tokyo. 2,999 tons gross, 5,100 tons dw, 326·18ft loa × 49·92ft breadth × 20·84ft draught, 6-cyl Hatsudoki diesel, 3,500bhp, 12·75 knots.

L

LA GAVOTTE. *French.* Cargo OSD. Built by At & Ch du Havre, Havre, for Finnfran Line, Caen. 499 tons gross, 1,525 tons dw, 296ft loa × 46ft m breadth × draught na, 6-cyl Werkspoor diesel, 3,000bhp, 15 knots.

LA HACIENDA. *British.* Oil/chemical tanker. Built by N. V. Wilton-Fijenoord, Schiedam, for Buries Markes Ltd, London. 1,452 tons gross, 2,328 tons dw, 264·18ft loa × 41·58ft breadth × 17·18ft draught, two 6-cyl s sc Ruston-Hornsby diesel, 2,000bhp, 13 knots.

LA QUINTA. *British.* Oil/chemical tanker. Built by N. V. Wilton-Fijenoord, Schiedam, for Buries Markes Ltd, London. 1,452 tons gross, 2,300 tons dw, 264·09ft loa × 41·58ft breadth × 17ft draught, two 6-cyl s sc Ruston-Hornsby diesel, cpp, 2,000bhp, 13 knots.

LADY CATHERINE. *Liberian.* Oil rig supply ship. Built by Verolme United Shipyards, Heusden, for International Offshore Services (UK) Ltd, Monrovia. 479 tons gross, 750 tons dw, 159·09ft loa × 33ft breadth × 11ft draught, two 10-cyl tw sc Werkspoor diesel, 2,600bhp, knots na.

LADY SOPHIE. *Dutch (Antilles).* Cargo CSD. Built by Schps & Masch 'Holland', Hardinxveld, for van der Laan's Scheepv & Handel Mij, Willemstad. 752 tons gross, tons dw na, 283·66ft loa × 45·41ft breadth × 11·35ft draught, two 12-cyl tw sc Caterpillar diesel, 850bhp, knots na.

LADY VALERIE (Sis LADY MARGARET). *Liberian.* Oil rig supply ship (35-ton gantry; stern ramp). Built by Verolme United Shipyards, Heusden, for International Offshore Services (UK) Ltd, Monrovia. 479 tons gross, 750 tons dw, 159·09ft loa × 33ft breadth × 11ft draught, two 10-cyl tw sc Werkspoor diesel, 2,600bhp, 12·5 knots.

LAKESHELL. *Canadian.* Tanker. Built by Marine Industries Ltd, Sorel, for Shell Canada Ltd, Toronto. 5,900 tons gross, 8,120 tons dw, 399·75ft loa × 60·75ft breadth × 23·31ft draught, 8-cyl Ruston Hornsby diesel, btp, 4,000bhp, 13 knots.

LARA MIKHEENKO. *Russian.* Cargo. Built by Schiffswerft Neptun Rostock, 1968, for USSR Vladivostok. 3,685 tons gross, 4,638 tons dw, 346·75ft loa × 51·33ft breadth × 22·18ft draught, 6-cyl Halberstadt-MAN diesel, 3,250bhp, 13·75 knots.

LAROUCO. *Portuguese.* Tanker. Built by A. G. 'Weser', Bremerhaven, for Lisnave Estaleiros Navais de Lisboa, S.a.r.l, Lisbon. 46,690 tons gross, 80,000 tons dw, 822ft loa (incl bb) × 123·84ft breadth × 42·07ft draught, 9-cyl B & W diesel, 20,700bhp, 16 knots.

LASKARA. *Polish.* Stern trawler, ref. Built by Stocznia im Komuny Paryskiej, Gdynia, 1968, for PPDiUR 'Gryf', Szczecin. 1,479 tons gross, 915 tons dw, 247·75ft loa × 41·66ft breadth × 16·39ft draught, 12-cyl Cegielski-Fiat diesel, cpp, 2,500bhp, 14·5 knots.

LAURELWOOD. *British.* Tanker. Built by Doxford & Sunderland SB & E Co, Deptford, Sunderland, for John I. Jacobs & Co Ltd, London. 15,100 tons gross, 24,800 tons dw, 557ft loa × 81·33ft breadth × 32ft draught, 6-cyl Doxford diesel, 12,000bhp, knots na.

LAURITA. *Norwegian.* Cargo (cars roll on and off). Built by Blohm & Voss AG, Hamburg, for J. M. Ugland, Grimstad. 7,220 tons gross, tons dw na, 521·5ft loa × 84·58ft breadth × 22·33ft draught, two 16-cyl s sc Pielstick diesel, 7,440bhp, 21 knots.

LAWRENTIAN. *British.* Bulk carrier. Built by Austin & Pickersgill Ltd, Sunderland, for Oregon SS Co Ltd, London. 14,807 tons gross, 22,800 tons dw, 575·75ft loa × 75·18ft breadth × 32ft draught, 7-cyl Clark-Sulzer diesel, 11,200bhp, knots na.

The Lakeshell *is designed to carry mainly petrol, jet fuels and heating oils on the Canadian lakes and Eastern Seabord. She is fitted with an 8-cyl Ruston 8A 0M diesel engine developing 4,000bhp at 450rpm reduced to driving a controllable pitch propeller at 150rpm, through an MWD type R10 gearbox. She replaces a tanker of the same name which has given 30 years service, and was built by the same builders at Sorel.*

LEINSTER. *Eire*. Pass/car ferry. Built by Verolme Cork Dockyard Ltd, Cork, for British & Irish SP Co Ltd, Dublin. 4,849 tons gross, 1,034 tons dw, 388·18ft loa × 58·5ft breadth × 14·59ft draught, four 18-cyl tw sc MAN diesel, cpps, btp, 11,400bhp, 21·75 knots.

LENINOGORSK. *Russian*. Stern trawler, fish factory, ref (ATLANTIK class). Built by Volkswerft Stralsund, Stralsund, 1967, for USSR. 2,657 tons gross, 1,152 tons dw, 269·58ft loa × 63·75ft breadth × 16·41ft draught, two 8-cyl s sc Liebknecht diesel, cpp, 2,320bhp, 13·5 knots.

LIMAN. *Russian*. Stern trawler, fish factory, ref (ATLANTIK class). Built by Volkswerft Stralsund, Stralsund, 1968, for USSR. 2,657 tons gross, 1,152 tons dw, 269·58ft loa × 44·75ft breadth × 16·41ft draught, two 8-cyl s sc Liebknecht diesel, cpp, 2,320bhp, 13·5 knots.

LINDBLAD EXPLORER. *Norwegian*. Passenger. Built by Nystads Varv A/B, Nystad, for L. Usterud-Svenson & Co, Oslo. 2,484 tons gross, 550 tons dw, 249·33ft loa × 46·92ft breadth × 13·77ft draught, two 8-cyl s sc Atlas-MaK diesel, cpp, btp, 3,600bhp, 15 knots.

LINDINGER PEARL. *Danish*. Cargo OSD (one 15-ton derrick). Built by Husumer Schiffsw, Husum, for Rederiet Lindinger A/S, Copenhagen 499 tons gross, 1,305 tons dw, 228·18ft loa × 36·75ft breadth × 13·05ft draught, 8-cyl Deutz diesel, 1,500bhp, 13 knots.

Lans. *A modern Belgian built and owned stern trawler of 418 tons gross. She is owned by Redery Lans of Ostende. On a length of 140·1ft overall and a 975bhp Deutz engine, her speed is 13 knots.*

LISE NIELSON. *Danish.* Cargo. Built by Schps Gebr van Diepen, Waterhuizen, for O. Amsinck, Copenhagen. 1,400 tons gross, 2,500 tons dw, 262·84ft loa × 41ft breadth × 17·77ft draught, 6-cyl Atlas-MaK diesel, 2,000bhp, knots na.

LITIJA. *Yugoslavian.* Cargo. Built by Empresa Nacional 'Bazan' Ferrol, for Splosna Plovba, Koper. 8,502 tons gross, tons dw, na, 448·41ft lbp × 65·58ft m breadth × draught, na, 6-cyl Ast de Cadiz-Sulzer diesel, 9,900bhp, knots na.

LOKATOR. *Russian.* Fish carrier, ref. Built by Burmeister & Wain, Copenhagen, 1968, for USSR. 4,700 tons gross, 2,500 tons dw, 356ft loa × 52·58ft breadth × draught na, 6-cyl B & W diesel, 100bhp, 14 knots.

LONG CHARITY. *Norwegian.* Bulk carrier. Built by Rheinstal Nordsee Werke, Emden, for Einar Lange, Oslo. 14,095 tons gross, tons dw na, 554·5ft loa × 71ft breadth × 33·2ft draught, 7-cyl Borsig-Fiat diesel, bhp na, knots na.

LORINA. *Liberian.* Bulk carrier. Built by Mitsui Zosen, Osaka, for Lorina Shipping Inc, Monrovia (Ednasa Co, Hong Kong). 15,919 tons gross, 27,041 tons dw, 585·66ft loa (incl bb) × 75·09ft breadth × 34·68ft draught, 6-cyl Mitsui-B & W diesel, 11,600bhp, knots na.

LOTTE NIELSEN. *Danish.* Cargo OSD. Built by Aarhus Flydk & Mak, Aarhus, for O. Amsinck, Copenhagen. 1,181 tons gross, tons dw na, 231·09ft loa × 37·92ft breadth × 12·25ft draught, 8-cyl Atlas-MaK diesel, 1,400bhp, knots na.

Laskara. *The prototype B29 type trawler from Gdynia looks at first glance almost a passenger ship. She is designed for operation on the North Sea and Central Atlantic fishing grounds, and is reinforced for navigation in ice. Her main machinery is controlled either from the control room or from the bridge console, the engine being a Cegielski-Fiat B 3012 SS 4-stroke diesel driving through a gearbox the controllable pitch propeller and 2 generators, 1 for the trawl winch, and 1 for the ship's mains.*

LOYOLA. *Spanish.* Tanker. Built by Soc Espanola de Constr Nav, Sestao, for Naviera Artola SA, Bilbao. 51,388 tons gross, 97,350 tons dw, 871·66ft loa (incl bb) × 128·18ft breadth × 45·67ft draught, 9-cyl SECN-Sulzer diesel, 20,700bhp, 16·5 knots.

LUBECK. *German.* Cargo, ref, CSD. Built by Lubecker Flender-Werke AG, Lubeck, for Lubeck Linie AG, Lubeck. 8,999 tons gross, tons dw na, 485·58ft loa × 69·25ft breadth × 30·9ft draught, 8-cyl MAN diesel, 11,200bhp, knots na.

Leinster. *The third of the new British & Irish Steam Packet Co's reorganized service ships, and the first to be built in the Republic of Ireland, is a development of both the* Munster *and* Innisfallen. *The former, bought on the stocks whilst building for a Scandinavian firm had an ice strengthened bow, (retained in the* Leinster) *is of the same breadth, but this ship is 26ft longer, with a very slightly deeper (2in) draught. The* Leinster *is more generally similar to the German built* Innisfallen, *the machinery excepted. Car capacity is about 240 units, with 1,200 passengers (252 in 2 and 4 berth cabins, 252 in reclining seats) and a crew of 84. She is a drive through ship, ie with bow and stern doors. 2 decks are utilized for passenger cabins, with the main public rooms on the promenade deck, above the garage space. On this deck are a full width cafeteria seating 300 (forward), amidships the main hall, aft a lounge with 180 reclining seats. Also on this deck are a bar, nursery, pursers' office and shop. On the boat deck above are (forward) the Shamrock restaurant, seating 63, with adjacent cocktail bar separated from it by decorative screens, amidships a lounge with seats for 150. Aft of this are 14 double and 2 de luxe cabins. 2 decks up, and above the officers' cabins is the oval Skybar with 72 seats arranged around a central bar, giving wide panoramic views. There are 8 fibreglass lifeboats, 4 of which are motor driven, and 2 tiers of self inflating liferafts. An AEG-Denny Brown folding fin stabilizer is fitted. The main machinery consists of 4 MAN V9V30/45 diesel engines running at 430rpm, which can be used flexibly 2, 3 or 4 at a time. These drive twin KaMeWa controllable pitch propellers through 2 Renk gearboxes, bridge controlled, giving a maximum speed of 24 knots. The exterior colour scheme now adopted by the B & I line is white funnel with a black top and a red device, white superstructure, topsides and name bright blue with green boot topping.*

L

LUDOGORETZ. *Bulgarian.* Bulk carrier. Built by Setoda Zosen, Setoda, for Navigation Maritime Bulgare, Varna. 9,145 tons gross, 13,611 tons dw, 458·75ft loa × 63·84ft breadth × 29·5ft draught, 6-cyl Maizuru-B & W diesel, 7,200bhp, 15 knots.

LUDWIG. *German.* Tanker. Built by Krogerwerft GmbH, Rendsburg, for Leth & Co, Hamburg. 999 tons gross, 2,608 tons dw, 266·09ft loa × 42·66ft breadth × 16·31ft draught, 6-cyl MWM diesel, 1,650bhp, knots na.

LYRA. *Polish.* Stern trawler, fish factory, ref. Built by Stocznia Gdanska, Gdansk, for PPDiUR 'DALMOR', Gdynia. 2,687 tons gross, 1,977 tons dw, 288·58ft loa × 47·66ft breadth × 18·37ft draught, 12-cyl Cegielski-Fiat diesel, cpp, 2,500bhp, 13·75 knots.

M

M. G. TSANGARIS. *Greek.* Bulk carrier. Built by Ishikawajima-Harima HI, Aioi, 1968, for Actis Co Ltd, Piraeus (J. C. Carras). 25,168 tons gross, 46,628 tons dw, 665ft loa (incl bb) × 95·18ft m breadth × 40·26ft draught, 9-cyl IHI-Sulzer diesel, 14,400bhp, 15·5 knots.

MACTRA. (N.B. badly damaged by explosion in tanks on 30 12 69 off E. African coast.) *British.* Tanker. Built by Howaldtswerke-Deutsche Werft, Kiel, for Shell Tankers (UK) Ltd, London. 104,723 tons gross, 208,560 tons dw, 1,067·33ft loa (incl bb) × 154·92ft breadth × 62·39ft draught, AEG turbs, 28,000shp, 15·5 knots.

MADELEINE. *German.* Cargo, ref. Built by Jos L. Meyer, Papenburg, for Transmarin Hamburg GmbH, Hamburg. 3,070 tons gross, tons dw na, 393·66ft loa × 56·75ft breadth × 24·92ft draught, two 8-cyl s sc Deutz diesel, 7,000bhp, knots na.

MAHENO. *New Zealand.* Cargo (stern door loading plus three 30-ton cranes). Built by Robb Caledon SB Ltd, Dundee, for Union SS Co of New Zealand, Wellington. 4,510 tons gross, 6,053 tons dw, 429·75ft loa × 63·09ft breadth × 22ft draught, two 14-cyl tw sc Crossley Pielstick diesel, btp, 13,020bhp, 18 knots.

MAISTROS. *Liberian.* Bulk carrier. Built by Mitsui Zosen, Tamano, for Aurura Borealis Armadora Cia SA, Monrovia. 18,923 tons gross, 32,900 tons dw, 599ft loa (incl bb) × 84·18ft breadth × 35·9ft draught, 7-cyl Mitsui-B & W diesel, 11,500bhp, knots na.

Maheno (see next page)

MAKHTUM KULI. *Russian*. Cargo. Built by Brodogradiliste 3rd Maj, Rijeka, for USSR, Vladivostok. 11,290 tons gross, 13,780 tons dw, 522·92ft loa × 69·84ft breadth × 31·56ft draught, 8-cyl 3rd Maj-Sulzer diesel, 12,000bhp, knots na.

MALAGA. *Spanish*. Tanker. Built by Ast de Cadiz SA, Cadiz, for Emp Nac 'ELCANO' de la Marina Mercante, Cadiz. 80,000 tons gross, 146,360 tons dw, 944·84ft loa × 149·5ft breadth × 56·41ft draught, 12-cyl Cadiz (Manises)-Sulzer diesel, 27,600bhp, 16·5 knots.

MALMO. *Swedish*. Ferry (Copenhagen-Malmo service 700 pass). Built by Husumer Schiffsw, Husum, for Rederi A/B Centrumlinjen, Malmo. 1,172 tons gross, 143 tons dw, 187ft loa × 40·33ft breadth × 9·5ft draught, two 6-cyl tw sc Atlas-MaK diesel, cpps, 1,800bhp, 15 knots.

Maheno. *This ship, with her sister,* Marama, *are of advanced design for the trans-Tasman service of the owners, 1 operating from Sydney to New Zealand ports, and the other a similar service from Melbourne. She is the first ship to be completed by the merged Robb-Caledon company. A roll on and off vessel, she is driven by 2 Crossley-Pielstick 14 PC2V diesels, each developing 6,510bhp at 465rpm, reduced by a Hindmarch gearbox to 215rpm, and giving just under 20 knots on trials. A conventional stern-loader, she has been specially designed to transport palletized cargoes of the USNZ Co's Seafreighter units, which are handled by heavy shore based forklift trucks. Cargo is transferred from the main deck to the lower hold by 2 hydraulically operated scissors type lifts, capable of coping with 30 tons weight. Fork lift trucks finally do the stowing in the lower hold. There is a similar lift for transferring cargo to the upper deck, where there is a large well ventilated deck house (enclosed) for cargo. Unaccompanied motor vehicles can also be carried, and in another deck house aft, horses in stalls. A crew of 36 hands is carried. There is a comprehensive system of supply and exhaust ventilation, mechanically operated, with considerable fire precautions of* CO_2 *and drencher types. Trimming and heeling tanks are incorporated in the hull, with wing ballast and fresh water tanks, and a bow thruster unit. Between the engine room and the cargo hold passive roll damping flume tanks are positioned.*

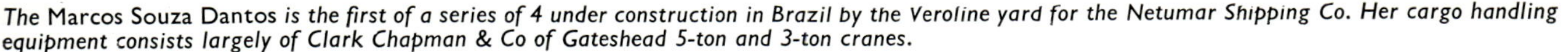
The Marcos Souza Dantos *is the first of a series of 4 under construction in Brazil by the Veroline yard for the Netumar Shipping Co. Her cargo handling equipment consists largely of Clark Chapman & Co of Gateshead 5-ton and 3-ton cranes.*

Frontispiece
Possibly the most significant maritime event of the year—even, perhaps, more so than the advent of the LASH ship, is the voyage of the ice-breaking tanker Manhattan *through the NW passage to Prudhoe Bay in Alaska. Converted into the world's largest ice-breaker with a weight of 150,000 tons and with a new type bow at an 18° angle to the water surface, she was rammed into the ice until the sheer weight forced her through. The experiment conducted by the Humble Oil Co, BP and Atlantic Richfuel is still under evaluation as to its utility as a trade route, it cost £12,000,000. She was assisted by a Canadian ice-breaker. She was originally a 65,740 gross ton conventional tanker of 108,588 tons deadweight owned by a Niarchos subsidiary (but lately by the Hudson Waterways Corpn of New York) and built in 1962 at Quincy, Mass by the Bethlehem Steel Co with dimensions of 940·4ft × 132·5ft × 50ft (draught) she has a speed of 17½ knots with 43,000shp turbines driving twin screws. Conversion added 65ft to her length, the ice-breaking bow making her 1,005ft long, whilst her breadth has been increased by 16ft to 148ft. Her weight has been increased by 9,000 tons of steelwork (extra bulkheads, helicopter platform, underwater guards for her twin rudders, etc). Her new draught is 52·8ft. She has many new advanced navigational aids, including a digital computer for utilising positional data from satellites. Several shipyards were occupied in working on her various parts when she was cut into three sections for conversion, and the adding of a 9ft wide steel belt around the hull in way of her tanks.*

MANCHESTER CONCORDE. *British*. Container ship (Ice class 1). Built by Smith's Dock Co Ltd, Middlesborough, for Nile SS Co Ltd (for long term charter to Manchester Liners, Manchester). 11,899 tons gross, 12,124 tons dw, 529·75ft loa × 63·75ft breadth × 27·11ft draught, two 18-cyl s sc Crossley Pielstick, cpp, 16,380bhp, 19·5 knots.

MANCHESTER COURAGE. *British*. Container ship (500 × 210ft containers). Built by Smiths Dock Co Ltd, Middlesborough, for Manchester Liners Ltd, Manchester. 11,899 tons gross, tons dw na, 529·75ft loa × 63·75ft breadth × 27·1ft draught, two 18-cyl s sc Crossley-Pielstick diesel, 16,380bhp, 19·5 knots.

MANGAN (Sis MERIAN). *German*. Cargo, ref, OSC/CSD (two 30-ton; one 50-ton derricks). Built by Lubecker Flenderwerke AG, Lubeck, for Komrowski Befrachtung-kontor KG, Hamburg. 7,817/11,383 tons gross, 12,386/15,283 tons dw, 551·25ft loa × 75·33ft breadth × 26·22/29·75ft draught, 6-cyl MAN diesel, 16,500bhp, 19 knots.

MANGEN. *Dutch*. Cargo (packaged timber). Built by Schpsw 'Friesland' NV, Lemmer, for Vereenigd Cargasdoorkantoor, Amsterdam. 575 tons gross, 1,577 tons dw, 254·75ft loa × 39·18ft breadth × 13·58/19·14ft draught, 8-cyl Atlas-MaK diesel, 1,500bhp, 12·5 knots.

MANOORA. *Australian*. Container ship. Built by Whyalla SB & E Works, Whyalla, for Bulkships Ltd (Associated Steamships Pty Ltd), Sydney 13,300 tons gross, 14,900 tons dw, 514ft loa × 72·18ft breadth × 30ft draught, 7-cyl Commonwealth Govt E Wks-Sulzer diesel, 11,200bhp, knots na.

MARAMA (Sis MAHENO). *New Zealand*. Cargo (stern door loading by fork lift truck plus three 30-ton cranes). Built by Robb-Caledon SBS Ltd, Dundee, for Union SS Co of New Zealand, Ltd Auckland. 4,500 tons gross, 6,350 tons dw, 429·75ft loa × 63·09ft breadth × 21·41ft draught, two 14-cyl tw sc Crossley-Pielstick diesel, 13,020bhp, 18 knots.

MARCOS SOUZA DANTAS. *Brazilian*. Cargo. Built by Verolme Est Reunidos do Brazil, Jacuacanga, for Cia de Navegacao Maritima Netumar, Rio de Janeiro. 4,500 tons gross, 6,850 tons dw, 390·58ft loa × 55·66ft breadth × 25·29ft draught, 6-cyl Pesada-MAN diesel, 5,400bhp, 15·75 knots.

MARCOSA 1. *Spanish*. Cargo (timber; one 40-ton, one 20-ton, ten 10-ton derricks). Built by Union Navale de Levante, Valencia, for Cia Mar. Continental y Comercio SA (MARCOSA), Valencia. 5,729 tons gross, 8,640 tons dw, 431ft loa (incl bb) × 57·33ft breadth × 24·6ft draught, 8-cyl Cadiz-B & W diesel, 6,150bhp, 17·5 knots.

MARIA OLDENDORFF. *German*. Cargo OSD/CSD. Built by Bremer Vulkan, Vegesack, for E. L. Oldendorff & Co GmbH, Lubeck. 6,550/9,400 tons gross, —/15,300 tons dw, 459·18ft loa × 68·92ft m breadth × 26·96/30·12ft draught, 6-cyl Br Vulkan diesel, 8,400bhp, knots na.

MARIAECK. *German*. Cargo (Basle via Rhine. Ro-Ro, 100-ton derrick). Built by T. van Duivendijks Schps, Lekkerkerk, for DDG 'Hansa', Bremen. 499 tons gross, 1,083 tons dw, 252·58ft loa × 42·92ft breadth × 9·35ft draught, two 16-cyl tw sc Caterpillar diesel, btp, 2,360bhp, 13 knots

MARIANNE. *Swedish*. Cargo, ref. Built by Jos L. Meyer, Papenburg, for A/B Transmarin, Helsingborg. 3,068/5,069 tons gross, —/6,715 tons dw, 393·66ft loa × 56·92ft breadth × —/24·92ft draught, two 8-cyl s sc Deutz diesel, 7,500bhp, 16·5 knots.

MARIGO R. *Greek*. Cargo (one 60-ton derrick). Built by Doxford & Sunderland SB & E Co Ltd, Sunderland, for Cia de Nav Golfo Azul SA, Syros (Rethymnis & Kulukundis). 10,816 tons gross, 16,480 tons dw, 522·92ft loa × 70·33ft breadth × 31·61ft draught, 6-cyl B & W diesel, 11,600bhp, 17·5 knots.

MARKO ORESKOVIC. *Yugoslavian*. Cargo. Built by Cockerill Yards Hoboken, Hoboken, for Jadranska Slobodna Plovidba, Split. 9,333 tons gross, tons dw na, 461ft loa × 67·33ft breadth × 30·37ft draught, 5-cyl Stork diesel, 5,500bhp, knots na.

MARPESSA. *Dutch*. Tanker. (Sank following explosion in tank on 15-12-69 in 16 30N 17.45W whilst tank cleaning) Built by Ishikawajima-Harima HI, Yokohama, for N. V. Curacaosche Sv (Shell Tankers NV). 104,373 tons gross, 206,600 tons dw, 1,067·41ft loa (incl bb) × 154·92ft breadth × 62·22ft draught, cyl na, IHI turbs, 28,000shp, knots na.

MARSOUIN. *French*. Cargo, ref. Built by At & Ch de Dunkerque & Bordeaux France-Gironde, Dunkerque, for Societe Courtage & Transport, Dunkerque 8,570 tons gross, tons dw na, 436·41ft loa (incl bb) × 65·84ft breadth × 24·62ft draught, 6-cyl Creusot-B & W diesel, 12,600bhp, knots na.

MARY ANN. *Liberian*. Ore/oil carrier. Built by Hitachi Zosen, Innoshima, for Global Bulk Carriers, Inc, Monrovia. 35,684 tons gross, 69,900 tons dw, 792·58ft loa (incl bb) × 106·09ft breadth × 45·75ft draught, 8-cyl Hitachi-B & W diesel, 18,400 bhp,knots na.

MASTER PETROS. *Greek*. Bulk carrier. Built by Rheinstal Nordseewerke GmbH, Emden, for Maistros Corpn Piraeus (Phocean Agency, London). 22,391 tons gross, 40,501 tons dw, 672·41ft loa × 89·5ft breadth × 37·31ft draught, 6-cyl Sulzer diesel, 13,800bhp, 15·75 knots.

MATINA (Sis MORANT and MOTAGUA). *British*. Cargo, ref. Built by Kawasaki Dkyd Co Ltd, Kobe, for Fyffes Group Ltd (Elders & Fyffes), London. 8,400 tons gross, 5,860 tons dw, 474ft loa (incl bb) × 67·09ft breadth × 24·33ft draught, 10-cyl Kawasaki-MAN diesel, 12,600bhp, knots na.

MATSU MARU No. 5. *Japanese*. Tanker. Built by Imabari Zosen, Imabari, 1968, for Matsufuji Shoji GK, Nagasaki. 990 tons gross, 2,150 tons dw, 213·18ft lbp × 36·18ft breadth × 17·09ft draught, two 6-cyl s sc Daihatsu diesel, 1,500bhp, 12 knots.

MATSUBARA MARU. *Japanese*. Cargo. Built by Usuki Tekkosho, Saiki, for NYK & Tanda Sangyo KK, Tokyo. 9,719 tons gross, 15,000 tons dw, 482·33ft loa × 69·58ft breadth × 28·5ft draught, 16-cyl IHI-Pielstick diesel, 7,440bhp, 14·25 knots.

MAYA. *Mexican*. Bulk carrier. Built by Stocznia Szczecinska, Szczecin, for Transportacion Maritime Mexicana SA, Veracruz. 16,066 tons gross, 25,800 tons dw, 610·25ft loa (incl bb) × 75ft breadth × 34·66ft draught, 6-cyl Cegielski-Sulzer diesel, 9,600bhp, 15·5 knots.

In this photograph of the Marsouin *of the Societe Courtage et transports, of Dunkirk is seen the* Atlantic Crown *lying astern. The* Marsouin *is 1 of a class of 8 delivered to various French owners.*

MAYMAKSA. *Russian*. Cargo. Builder na, Vyborg, 1968, for USSR. 4,896 tons gross, tons dw na, 400·09ft loa × 54·92ft breadth × 22·22ft draught, 9-cyl Bryansk-B & W diesel, bhp na, knots na.

MEIJUN MARU. *Japanese*. Cargo. Built by Nipponkai Heavy Industries Co Ltd, Toyama, for Japan Line & Meiji Tochi Tatemono KK, Kobe. 10,318 tons gross, 16,245 tons dw, 491ft loa × 74·25ft breadth × 29·75ft draught, 16-cyl IHI-Pielstick diesel, 7,440bhp, knots na.

MEISHUN MARU. *Japanese*. Cargo, ref. Built by Nipponkai HI Co Ltd, Toyama, for Yasuda Shintaku Ginko KK, Tokyo. 10,321 tons gross, 16,332 tons dw, 488·84ft loa × 74·25ft breadth × 29·84ft draught, 16-cyl Nippon Kokan diesel (Pielstick?), 7,440bhp, knots na.

The Matina *is the lead ship of a class of 3, the first Elders & Fyffes ships to be built in Japan. Lacking the graceful lines of the traditional Fyffes ships, who have abandoned their former pleasant livery for that of the parent company, the American owned United Fruit Co of Boston, she is nevertheless a fine fast banana carrier of 354,500cu ft refrigerated capacity. Her Kawasaki-MAN K10Z70/120E diesel engine develops 12,600bhp at 140rpm, giving her a 20·5 knots service speed.*

Melania. *The first 'mammoth' of over 200,000 tons completed in Holland, this ship, the 209,400dwt Shell tanker* Melania *(vide* Vol XVII*), one of the 22 of the class ordered by Shell, was built in two halves and joined up afloat.*

M

MEITEN MARU. *Japanese*. Cargo. Built by Ishikawajima Harima HI, Aioi, for Meiji Tochi Tatamono KK, Kobe. 11,912 tons gross, 17,450 tons dw, 487·25ft loa × 76·5ft breadth × 28·75ft draught, 5-cyl IHI-Sulzer diesel, 7,200bhp, knots na.

MEKHANIK AFANASYEV. *Russian*. Tanker. Built by Admiralteiski Shipyard, Leningrad, 1968, for USSR. 32,483 tons gross, 60,000 tons dw, 772·5ft loa × 101·75ft breadth × 38·05ft draught, turbs, 19,000shp, 17 knots.

MEKHANIK RYBACHUK. *Russian*. Cargo (Timber: 64th in B45 series, one 50-ton derrick). Built by Stocznia Gdanska, Gdansk, 1968 for USSR. 4,689 tons gross, 6,000 tons dw, 382·09ft lr × 54·92ft breadth × 23·05ft draught, 5-cyl Gdansk-B & W diesel, 5,450bhp, 13 knots.

MELCHOR OCAMPO. *Mexican*. Tanker. Built by Ishikawajima-Harima HI, Nagoya, 1968, for Petroleos Mexicanos, Salina Cruz. 12,753 tons gross, 20,402 tons dw, 560·18ft loa × 72·41ft breadth × 30ft draught, 7-cyl IHI-Sulzer diesel, 8,000bhp, 15·5 knots.

MELO. *British*. Tanker. Built by Kawasaki HI Ltd, Sakkaide, for Shell Tankers (UK) Ltd, London. 105,138 tons gross, 207,000 tons dw, 1,067·25ft loa (incl bb) × 154·92ft breadth × 62ft draught, Kawasaki turbs, 28,000shp, knots na.

MESANA. *Spanish*. Cargo. Built by Ast Celaya, Bilbao, for Extramar SA, Bilbao. 610 tons gross, 1,038 tons dw, 196ft loa × 33·5ft m breadth × 12·58ft draught, 8-cyl Naval-Stork-Werkspoor diesel, 1,100bhp, knots na.

MESSIDOR. *French*. Tanker. Built by Ch Naval de La Ciotat, La Ciotat, for Soc des Transports Maritimes Petroliers, Dunkerque 48,054 tons gross, 80,000 tons dw, 832·84ft loa × 116·58ft breadth × 44ft draught, 9-cyl Atlantique diesel, 20,790bhp, knots na.

MESSINAIKI AIGLI. *Greek*. Tanker. Built by Ishikawajima-Harima HI, Aioi, for Amigos Cia Nav SA, Pireaus. 18,263 tons gross, tons dw na, 561ft loa (incl bb) × 85·33ft m breadth × 36·11ft draught, 7-cyl IHI-Sulzer diesel, 11,200bhp, knots na.

METEORIT. *Russian*. Stern trawler, fish factory, ref (ATLANTIK class). Built by Volkswerft Stralsund, Stralsund, 1968, for USSR. 2,657 tons gross, 1,152 tons dw, 269·58ft loa × 44·66ft breadth × 16·41ft draught, two 8-cyl s sc Leibknecht diesel, cpp, 2,320bhp, 13·5 knots.

MICHIGAN. *USA*. Cargo (incl 216 × 20ft containers). Built by Avondale Shipyards Inc, Avondale, La, for States SS Co, San Francisco. 9,493/13,053 tons gross, —/14,149 tons dw, 579ft loa (incl bb) × 82·18ft breadth × 32·07ft draught, GEC turbs, 24,000shp, 23 knots.

MIIKE MARU. *Japanese*. Cargo. Built by Kurushima Dock Co Ltd, Imabari, for Tanda Sangyo KK, Tokyo. 5,087 tons gross, 7,750 tons dw, 377·3ft lbp × 55·84ft breadth × 23·66ft draught, 6-cyl Mitsubishi-Sulzer diesel, 4,600bhp, knots na.

MINA L CAMBANIS (ex EAST BREEZE) (Sis FRUMENTON). *Greek*. Bulk carrier. Built by Hakodate Dock Co Ltd, Hakodate, for Mareblama Nav SA (S G Embiricos, London) (originally for J Manners, Hong Kong). 16,413 tons gross, 28,131 tons dw, 591·58ft loa × 75·18ft breadth × 31·97ft draught, 6-cyl IHI-Sulzer diesel, 9,600bhp, 14 knots.

MINI LACE. *Liberian*. Cargo (44 × 20ft containers). Built by Hakodate Dock Co Ltd, Hakodate, for Elmini Lace Inc, Monrovia (Livanos). 1,572 tons gross, 3,150 tons dw, 214·84ft loa × 50·25ft breadth × 16·22ft draught, two 6-cyl tw sc Daihatsu diesel, 1,000bhp, 10·25 knots.

MINI LADY. *Liberian*. Cargo. Built by Hakodate Dock Co Ltd, Hakodate, for Elmini Lady Inc, Monrovia. 1,569 tons gross, 3,150 tons dw, 214·84ft loa × 50·25ft breadth × 16·22ft draught, two 6-cyl tw sc Daihatsu diesel, 1,000bhp, 10·5 knots.

MINI LANCE. *Liberian*. Cargo. Built by Hakodate Dock Co Ltd, Hakodate, for Elmini Lance Inc, Monrovia. 1,572 tons gross, 3,150 tons dw, 214·84ft loa × 50·25ft breadth × 16·22ft draught, two 6-cyl tw sc Daithatsu diesel, 1,000bhp, 10·25 knots.

MINI LORD. *Liberian*. Cargo. Built by Hakodate Dock Co Ltd, Hakodate, for Elmini Lord Inc, Monrovia. 1,565 tons gross, 3,150 tons dw, 214·84ft loa × 50·25ft breadth × 16·22ft draught, two 6-cyl tw sc Daihatsu diesel, 1,000bhp, 10·5 knots.

M

MINI LUCK. *Liberian*. Cargo. Built by Hakodate Dock Co Ltd, Hakodate, for Elmini Luck Inc, Monrovia. 1,560 tons gross, 3,150 tons dw, 214·84ft loa × 50·25ft breadth × 16·22ft draught, two 6-cyl tw sc Daihatsu diesel, 1,000bhp, 10·5 knots.

MIRALDA. *French*. Tanker. Built by Ch de l'Atlantique, St Nazaire, for Soc Maritime Shell, Havre. 105,317 tons gross, 212,000 tons dw, 1,065·33ft loa × 154·92ft breadth × 62·29ft draught, Atlantique-Stal Laval turbs, 28,000shp, knots na.

MISHIMA MARU. *Japanese*. Cargo. Built by Shikoku Dock Co, Takamatsu, for Yashima KKK, Tokyo. 2,684 tons gross, 3,456 tons dw, 306·75ft lbp × 47·58ft breadth × 21·5ft draught, 7-cyl Akasaka Tekkosho diesel, 4,400bhp, 15·5 knots.

MISS PAPALIOS. *Cypriot*. Cargo (SD 14). Built by Hellenic Shipyards, Skaramanga, for Aktor Shipping Co, Famagusta. 9,241 tons gross, 14,200 tons dw, 440ft loa × 67ft breadth × 28·5ft draught, 5-cyl Sulzer diesel, 5,500bhp, knots na.

MITRA. *British*. Tanker. Built by Odense Staalskibs, Lindo, for Shell Tankers (UK) Ltd, London. 98,876 tons gross, 195,500 tons dw, 1,077·09ft loa (incl bb) × 143·75ft breadth × 62·3ft draught, Kockum-Stal Laval turbs, 28,000shp, 15·75 knots.

MOBIL PEGASUS. *British*. Tanker. Built by Sasebo HI, Sasebo, for Mobil Shipping Co Ltd, London. 112,657 tons gross, 211,000 tons dw, 1,069ft loa (incl bb) × 158·25ft breadth × 54·18ft draught IHI-GEC turbs, 30,000shp, 16·75 knots.

MOBILITA. *Greek*. Tanker. Built by Ishikawajima-Harima HI, Aioi, for PanOceanic Navigation Corpn, Piraeus. 47,958 tons gross, 79,820 tons dw, 872·75ft loa (incl bb) × 127·58ft m breadth × 39ft draught, IHI turbs, 21,000shp, knots na.

MOKSONG. *South Korean*. Bulk carrier. Built by Ansaldo SpA, Spezia, for Korea United Lines, Inchon. 9,235 tons gross, 16,060 tons dw, 481·18ft loa × 69ft m breadth × 29·66ft draught, 6-cyl Ansaldo-B & W diesel, 7,200bhp, 15 knots.

MOKUSEI MARU. *Japanese*. Cargo. Built by Tohoku Zosen, Shiogama, for Sanko KKK, Amagaski. 6,359 tons gross, 10,125 tons dw, 418·6ft loa × 62·41ft breadth × 24·66ft draught, 8-cyl Hitachi diesel, 5,000bhp, knots na.

MOLODAYA GVARDIYA. *Russian*. Fish carrier. Built by '61 Kommun' Shipyard, Nikolayev, 1967, for USSR, Sevastopol. 5,942 tons gross, 5,170 tons dw, 426·5ft loa × 55·25ft breadth × 25·92ft draught, two 10-cyl tw sc diesel-electric, bhp na, 16·5 knots.

MOLODOGVARDEYSK. *Russian*. Cargo. Built by Stocznia Gdanska, Gdansk, 1967, for USSR, Odessa. 9,904 tons gross, 12,388 tons dw, 508·66ft loa × 66·41ft breadth × 29·6ft draught, 6-cyl Cegielski-Sulzer diesel, 9,600bhp, 17·5 knots.

MOMMARK. *Danish*. Ferry, 550 passengers. Built by Husumer Shiffsw, Husum, 1968, for Rederiet Union I/S, Sonderborg. 493 tons gross, 140 tons dw, 177·09ft loa × 33·84ft breadth × 8·23ft draught, two 12-cyl tw sc MWM diesel, 1,960bhp, 16 knots.

MONICA. *British*. Cargo. Built by E. J. Smit & Zns' Scheeps, Westerbroek, for Turnbull Scott (Management) Ltd, London. 1,598 tons gross, 2,700 tons dw, 275·58ft loa × 39·09ft breadth × 18·5ft draught, 9-cyl Atlas-MaK diesel, 2,450bhp, knots na.

MONIKA WIARDS. *German*. Cargo (container facilities: 1st Weser type 36). Built by A. G. 'Weser' Werk Seebeck, Bremerhaven, for Kauff Seereederei Adolf Wiards & Co, Bremen. 6,515/9,312 tons gross, —/15,433 tons dw, 463·25ft loa × 69ft breadth × 30·25ft draught, cyl na, MAN diesel, 6,250bhp, 15·25 knots.

MONTE CINTO. *French*. Vehicle carrier, part wine tanker, stern doors 170 cars plus 18 × 36-ton trailers. Built by At & Ch du Havre, Havre, for Cie Generale Transatlantique. 2,080 tons gross, 3,248 tons dw, 327ft loa × 48·75ft m breadth × 19·75ft draught, two 8-cyl tw sc Ruston-Hornsby diesel, btp, 4,260bhp, 15·5 knots.

MONTE ZAMBURO. *Spanish*. Bulk carrier. Built by Cia Euskalduna, Bilbao, for Naviera Aznar Soc Anom, Bilbao. 15,650 tons gross, 27,000 tons dw, 599ft loa × 73·66ft breadth × 34·48ft draught, 7-cyl Euskalduna-MAN diesel, 9,800bhp, knots na.

The 211,666 ton dw tanker Mobil Pegasus *is the first of a class of 4. Though her service speed is 15·8 knots, she obtained 16·9 on trials. She is distinguished from all other large tankers by having a double bottom for the whole length of the cargo space. Cargo lines and remote control equipment are located in the duct keel, whilst the double bottom will be used for ballast. It is hoped to reduce port time considerably by ballasting the double bottom tanks whilst unloading.*

MONTELEON. *Spanish.* Tanker (asphalt). Built by Union Navale de Levante, Valencia, for Compania Espanola de Petroles SA, Valencia. 5,780 tons gross, 8,220 tons dw, 404·75ft loa (incl bb) × 55·25ft breadth × 23·95ft draught, 6-cyl Maq Terre y Mar-B & W diesel, 3,300bhp, 13 knots.

MONTENAKEN. *Belgian.* Cargo (4 pass). Built by Cockerill Yards Hoboken, Hoboken, for Cie Maritime Belge (Lloyd Royale) SA, Antwerp. 7,081/11,519 tons gross, 11,174/16,304 tons dw, 527·58ft loa × 76·25ft breadth × 26·02/32·47ft draught, 6-cyl Cockerill-B & W diesel, 13,800bhp, 20 knots.

MONTESA (Sis LA RABIDA). *Spanish.* Tanker. Built by Ast de Cadiz, Cadiz, for Refineria de Petroles de Escombreras SA, Cadiz 55,000 tons gross, 98,000 tons dw, 883·66ft loa (incl bb) × 128·18ft breadth × 46·18ft draught, 9-cyl Ast de Cadiz-Sulzer diesel, 20,700bhp, 16 knots.

MONTFORT. *Belgian.* Cargo (4 pass). Built by Cockerill Yards Hoboken, Hoboken, for Cia Mar Belge (Lloyd Royale) SA, Antwerp 7,081/11,519 tons gross, 11,143/16,300 tons dw, 527·58ft loa × 76·25ft breadth × 26/32·48ft draught, 6-cyl Cockerill-B & W diesel, 13,800bhp, 20 knots.

MONTIGNY. *Liberian.* Bulk carrier. Built by Sanoyasu Dkyd Co Ltd, Osaka, for San Antonio Inc, Monrovia. 10,397 tons gross, 18,000 tons dw, 508·58ft loa (incl bb) × 75ft breadth × 29·18ft draught, 7-cyl IHI-Sulzer diesel, 8,400bhp, 14·75 knots.

MONTSOREAU. *French.* Tanker. Built by At & Ch de Dunkerque & Bordeaux (France-Gironde), Dunkerque, for Soc Maritime des Petroles BP, Dunkerque. 67,280 tons gross, 124,082 tons dw, 900ft loa (incl bb) × 137·84ft m breadth × 50·84ft draught, Atlantique-Stal Laval turbs, 24,000shp, 16 knots.

MORETON BAY. *British.* Container ship, ref (1,300 × 20ft containers incl 300 ref). Built by Blohm & Voss AG, Hamburg, for P & O SN Co Ltd, London (Mgrs Oversea Containers Ltd). 26,876 tons gross, 29,100 tons dw, 752·41ft loa (incl bb) × 100·25ft breadth × 35·09ft draught, Stal-Laval turbs, 32,450shp, 22 knots.

MORMACSEA. *USA.* Container ship RoRo (824 × 20ft containers) CSD. Built by Ingalls SB Corpn, Pascagoula, for Moore-McCormack Lines Inc. New York. 11,757 tons gross, 15,694 tons dw, 601·58ft loa (incl bb) × 90·18ft breadth × 34·1ft draught, GEC turbs, 30,000shp, 25 knots.

MORMACSKY. *USA.* Container ship. Built by Ingalls SB Corpn, Pascagoula, for Moore-McCormack Lines Inc, New York. 11,757 tons gross, 15,694 tons dw, 601·5ft loa (incl bb) × 90·18ft breadth × 34·1ft draught, GEC turbs, 30,000shp, 25 knots.

MORMACSTAR. *USA.* Container ship. Built by Ingalls SB Corpn, Pascagoula, for Moore-McCormack Lines Inc, New York 11,757 tons gross, 15,694 tons dw, 602ft loa × 90·18ft breadth × 34ft draught, GEC turbs, 30,000shp, 25 knots.

MORSKOI 16. *Russian.* Cargo. Built by Reposaaren Konepaja O/Y, Bjorenborg, 1968, for USSR. 1,700 tons gross, 1,800 tons dw, 296·25ft loa × 40·66ft breadth × 10·84ft draught, two 8-cyl tw sc Russki diesel, 1,400bhp, 11 knots.

MORSKOI 17. *Russian.* Cargo. Built by O/Y Laivateollisuus A/B, Abo, 1968, for USSR. 1,500 tons gross, 1,810 tons dw, 288·75ft loa × 40·66ft breadth × 10·84ft draught, two 6-cyl Russki diesel, 1,400bhp, 11 knots.

Montaigle. *With her sisters* Montfort *and* Montenaken, *this ship completes the series of 10 cargo liners, whose names begin with* Mo, *for the African & Persian Gulf Trades.They have gained a very high reputation for reliability and efficiency. On her trials in October, 1968, the* Montaigle *attained a speed of 20 knots. The holds are so designed as to be easily convertible for container carrying, while the hatches are strengthened for carrying containers on deck. She is of the 'Open Ship' type at Nos 3 and 4 hatches, with 3 openings abreast. These holds are divided athwartships into three compartments, with a view to solving technical problems regarding stowage, loading and discharging in numerous ports. The loading gear consists of Velle derricks with a lifting capacity of 30-tons at holds 2, 3 and 4, and of 10-tons at 5. By working 2 derricks together at No 3, 60 tons can be lifted. The other derricks are 10-ton capacity. The 33 man crew are accommodated in single air conditioned cabins. She is an intensively automated ship, and manoeuvring of the engines and casting anchor can all be carried out from the bridge. She is intended to run eventually with an unmanned engine room, and is equipped with an alarm system covering 192 different conditions.* Montaigle *herself is in the register in Vol XVII.*

Montesa. *This 98,000 tonner built at Cadiz is powered by a Manises-Sulzer type 9RD90 diesel giving a service speed of 16½ knots at 20,700bhp. She is a sister to* La Rabida (vide *Vol XVII*).

MORTEN MOLS (Sis MIKKEL MOLS). *Danish*. Pass/car ferry (800 pass, 110 cars). Built by Aalborg Vaerft A/S, Allborg, for Mols Linien A/S, Copenhagen (DFDS) 2,430 tons gross, 790 tons dw, 304ft loa × 54·84ft breadth × 13·66ft draught, four 14-cyl tw sc B & W diesels, cpp, btp, 11,200bhp, 19·5 knots.

MOSA PIJADE. *Yugoslavian*. Cargo Built. by Cockerill Yards (Hoboken), Hoboken, for Jadranska Slobodna Plovidba, Split. 6,132/9,333 tons gross, —/15,370 tons dw, 461ft loa × 67·33ft breadth × 30·41ft draught, 5-cyl Stork diesel, 5,500bhp, knots na.

MOSEL EXPRESS. *German*. Container ship (728 × 20ft containers). Built by Bremer Vulkan, Vegesack, for Norddeutscher Lloyd, Bremen 13,396 tons gross, 11,050 tons dw, 560·41ft loa (incl bb) × 81·18ft breadth × 25·92ft draught, 9-cyl BV-MAN diesel, 15,750bhp, 20·5 knots

MOUNT EDEN (Sis MOUNT KATHARINA). *Liberian*. Bulk carrier. Built by Furness SB Co Ltd, Haverton Hill on Tees, for Transatlantic Tramp Ships Inc, Monrovia (Maritime Overseas Corpn, NY). 35,843 tons gross, 77,250 tons dw, 809ft loa (incl bb) × 104·25ft breadth × 47·45ft draught, 8-cyl H & W-B & W diesel, 18,400bhp, 15·5 knots.

Mormacsea. *Claimed to be America's first roll on and off container ship, she left New York on her maiden voyage on 5th May. She, with her sisters, the* Mormacsky, Star and Sun *have been found deficient in stability, and it has been necessary to add 1,400 tons of fixed mud ballast to all of them, at a cost of £66,000 per ship, as a compromise solution. They are fast ships of 25 knot service speed, and are vehicle carriers, as well as container ships, of which they can carry 800 × 20ft units.*

MOZART. *Liberian.* Ore/oil carrier. Built by Ishikawajima-Harima HI, Kure, for General Overseas Financing Inc, Monrovia. 43,456 tons gross, 84,631 tons dw, 835ft loa (incl bb) × 120·18ft breadth × 45·97ft draught, 8-cyl IHI-Sulzer diesel, 18,400bhp, 15·25 knots.

MUI KIM. *British.* Cargo, ref. Built by Hayashikane Zosen, Nagasaki, for Hong Kong-Borneo Shipping Co Ltd, Hong Kong 4,952 tons gross, 7,292 tons dw, 383·84ft loa × 56·58ft breadth × 23·13ft draught, 7-cyl Mitsui-B & W diesel, 3,850bhp, 12·5 knots.

MUMBLES. *British.* Tug. Built by Richard Dunston (Hessle) Ltd, Hessle, for Alexandra Towing Co Ltd, Swansea. 291 tons gross, 187 tons dw, 112·5ft loa × 31ft breadth × 12·75ft draught, 9-cyl Ruston & Hornsby diesel, 2,190bhp, 13·25 knots.

Morten Mols. *Last of a class of 4 (Maren and Mette Mols 1966, and Mikkel Mols, late 1968) for the Ebeltoft-Odden ferry service. The first 2 ships opened this service, which became so successful that 2 more ships became necessary. The Mols line is a subsidiary of DFDS of Copenhagen. Ice strengthened ships, they carry 1,200 passengers as well as cars and lorries on the short crossing, at a speed of 19·5 knots. Of conventional Scandinavian ferry silhouette, they can be navigated either from the bridge in the normal way, as well as from a wheel house aft, being comprehensively equipped with electronic navigational aids, including 3 radar sets. On the after tween deck is the crew accommodation, as well as that for lorry drivers, who have a small saloon to themselves. On the tween deck forward are passenger cabins and those of the catering staff, together with a special room for mothers and children. From the car deck are stairs and lifts to the saloon deck, where amidships is the entrance hall, with a childrens' play room centrally placed, with a kiosk and telephone room adjacent. The hall is comfortably furnished with chairs. From the hall, large glass doors lead to the cafeteria saloons, placed forward and aft, with panoramic views through large windows.*
Manoeuvring is helped by twin spade rudders aft, a bow rudder and KaMeWa bow thrust propeller, and 2 main twin KaMeWa controllable pitch propellers. The 4 main engines are 14-cyl B & W type 26 MTBF-40V, 4-stroke single acting, non reversible with exhaust turbo charging. They are controlled from either the fore or aft wheelhouse, or the engine rooms. Service revolutions are 271rpm at 2,520ehp for each engine. Bow and stern doors are fitted for embarking and disembarking vehicles.

MUNDOGAS ATLANTIC. *Norwegian.* LPG carrier. Built by A/S Framnaes M/V, Sandefhord, for Oivind Lorentzen, Oslo 6,804 tons gross, 8,645 tons dw, 402·58ft loa × 60·66ft m breadth × 28·88ft draught, 6-cyl Akers-B & W diesel, 7,200bhp, 16 knots.

MUROMSK. *Russian.* Stern trawler, fish factory, ref. Built by Stocznia im Komuny Pariskiej, Gydnia, 1967, for USSR. 2,976 tons gross, 1,321 tons dw, 256ft lr × 45·41ft breadth × 18·09ft draught, 8-cyl Zgoda-Sulzer diesel, 2,400bhp, 13 knots.

MUTSU MARU. *Japanese.* Bulk carrier. Built by Ishikawajima-Harima HI, Nagasaki, for Nippon Yusen Kaisha, Tokyo. 25,168 tons gross. 41,300 tons dw, 634·84ft loa (incl bb) × 96·66ft breadth × 37·25ft draught, 7-cyl IHI-Sulzer diesel, 11,200bhp, knots na.

Mumbles. *This ship, the largest tug yet built for the Alexandra Towing Co, has been specially designed to handle the large ore carriers in the new Port Talbot tidal harbour, which are expected to have a draught of 47 feet initially. She has a 4 bladed propeller in a Kort nozzle, driven by a Ruston & Hornsby type 9 ACTM diesel engine. With a bollard pull of 33¾ tons, her free running speed is 13·25 knots. She was delivered 6 weeks before her contract date, and is to have a sister ship.*

MUTSO MARU No. 1. *Japanese.* Ferry. Built by Taguma Zosen, Innoshima, for Higashi Nippon Ferry KK, Hakodate 1,250 tons gross, 420 tons dw, 245ft loa × 46·58ft breadth × 10·41ft draught, two 8-cyl tw sc Daihatsu diesel, 6,400bhp, knots na.

MYOKO MARU. *Japanese.* Cargo. Built by Imabari Zosen, Imabari, for Niigata Rinko Kairiku Unso KK, Niigata. 2,990 tons gross, 5,500 tons dw, 308·41ft lbp × 51·58ft breadth × 21·66ft draught, 6-cyl Mitsubishi-Sulzer diesel, 3,300bhp, 12·25 knots.

MYSIA. *British.* Tanker. Built by Mitsubishi HI, Nagasaki, for Shell Tankers (UK) Ltd, London. 105,248 tons gross, 207,000 tons dw, 1,067·25ft loa (incl bb) × 154·92ft breadth × 62·2ft draught, Mitsubishi turbs, 28,000bhp, knots na.

MYTILUS. *British.* Tanker. Built by Hitachi Zosen, Sakai, for Shell Tankers (UK) Ltd, London. 105,521 tons gross, 207,000 tons dw, 1,066ft loa (incl bb) × 154·92ft breadth × 62·25ft draught, Mitsubishi turbs, 28,000bhp, knots na.

N

N. R. CRUMP. *British*. Bulk carrier (three 18-ton travelling gantry cranes). Built by Mitsubishi HI, Hiroshima, for Canadian Pacific Steamships Ltd, Hamilton, Bermuda. 21,445 tons gross, 28,947 tons dw, 593·84ft loa × 95·92ft breadth × 34·25ft draught, 7-cyl Mitsubishi-Sulzer diesel, 10,500bhp, 14·75 knots.

NAGATO MARU. *Japanese*. Bulk carrier. Built by Mitsui Zosen, Tamano, for Sanko KKK, Amagasaki. 11,682 tons gross, 18,970 tons dw, 508·66ft loa × 74·92ft breadth × 30ft draught, 7-cyl Mitsui-B & W diesel, 9,400bhp, 15 knots.

NAKAOKI MARU. *Japanese*. Cement carrier. Built by Kasado Dock Co Ltd, Kudamatsu, for Ube Kosan KK, Ube. 13,952 tons gross, 21,932 tons dw, 528·25ft loa × 80·09ft breadth × 30·75ft draught, 9-cyl Ube Tekkosho diesel, 12,150bhp, 16 knots.

NANIWA MARU No 68. *Japanese*. Tanker. Built by Hashihama Zosen, Imabari, for Naniea Tanker KK, Osaka. 2,861 tons gross, 4,000 tons dw, 288·75ft lbp × 46ft breadth × draught na, 6-cyl Hanshin diesel, 2,400bhp, 12 knots.

NARVA. *Russian*. Tanker. Builder na, Kerch, 1967, for USSR, Klaipeda. 1,772 tons gross, 1,634 tons dw, 274·18ft loa × 39·5ft breadth × 15·25ft draught, 8-cyl Skoda diesel, bhp na, 13·25 knots.

NARVSKAYA ZASTAVA. *Russian*. Stern trawler, fish factory, ref. Built by Stocznia im Komuny Pariskiej, Gydnia, 1968, for USSR 2,944 tons gross, 1,321 tons dw, 272·66ft loa × 45·41ft breadth × draught na, 8-cyl Zgoda Sulzer diesel, 2,400bhp, knots na.

NARWAL. *Polish*. Stern trawler, fish factory (B 18-1 series). Built by Stocznia im Komuny Pariskiej, Gdynia, 1968, for PPDIUR 'Odra', Swinoujscie. 2,480 tons gross, 1,300 tons dw, 285·66ft loa × 46·5ft breadth × 17·58ft draught, 6-cyl Zgoda-Sulzer diesel, cpp, 2,250bhp, 14 knots.

NAVIPESA UNO (Sis NAVIPESA OOS, building). *Spanish*. RoRo heavy cargo ship, OSD, hydraulic ramps (extending over side) for lifts up to 600 tons. Built by Ast de T. Ruiz de Velasco SA, Bilbao, for Naviera Quimica SA, Bilbao. 499 tons gross, 1,100 tons dw, 252·5ft loa × 42·75ft breadth × 9·33ft draught, cyl na, tw sc Caterpillar diesel, btp, 2,250bhp, 13 knots.

NAZAR GUBIN. *Russian*. Cargo. Built by A. Zdhanov, Leningrad, 1968, for USSR. 4,996 tons gross, tons dw na, 400·09ft loa × 54·92ft breadth × 22·22ft draught, 9-cyl Bryansk-B & W diesel, bhp na, knots na.

NEA HELLAS. *Cypriot*. Cargo (SD 14). Built by Hellenic Shipyards Co, Skaramanga, for Nea Hellas Shipping Co, Famagusta. 9,241 tons gross, 15,136 tons dw, 462·58ft loa × 67·5ft breadth × 29ft draught, 5-cyl Sulzer diesel, 5,500bhp, 14 knots.

NEPTUNE AMETHYST. *Singapore*. Cargo OSD/CSD. Built by Warnowwerft, Warnemunde, for Neptune Orient Lines Ltd, Singapore. 5,350/8,715 tons gross, 10,800/12,725 tons dw, 494·41ft loa × 65·92ft breadth × na/29·58ft draught, 8-cyl MAN diesel, 11,200bhp, 20 knots,

NEPTUNE AQUAMARINE. *Singapore*. Cargo OSD/CSD. Built by Warnowwerft, Warnemunde, for Neptune Orient Lines, Singapore. 5,630/8,715 tons gross, 10,800/12,725 tons dw, 494·41ft loa × 65·75ft breadth × 29·58ft draught, 8-cyl DMR-MAN diesel, 11,200bhp, 20 knots.

NEW CALEDONIA MARU. *Japanese*. Ore carrier (nickel). Built by Sanoyasu Dkyd Ltd, Osaka, for Osaka Sempaku KK & Mitsui-OSK Lines KK, Osaka. 12,251 tons gross, 20,800 tons dw, 509·66ft loa × 74·92ft breadth × 30·09ft draught, 7-cyl Uraga-Sulzer diesel, 8,400bhp, 13·75 knots.

N

N

New Bahama Star. *Not a new ship, and not in the register of this volume, but an interesting conversion. Originally the ZIM liner Jerusalem, then chartered as the Miami, she was ultimately purchased by the Miami Steamship Co, a Liberian registered company, for Caribbean cruising out of Miami. The conversion was planned by Technical Marine Planning Ltd, of London, and carried out by the Jacksonville Shipyards South Side Division, Jacksonville, Florida, under the planners' supervision. The ship was built in 1957, at Hamburg, and after conversion complies with the latest SOLAS regulations with 1966 IMCO amendments, and with the requirements of the US Coastguard for fire precautions, for foreign flag vessels operating from US ports. The conversion entailed the removal of the swimming pool, all derrick posts and cargo gear, enlarging some public rooms, creation of new stairways and extension of some deck areas, new cabins and modernization and refurnishing of other passenger accommodation, the creation of a lido and gallery deck around a new swimming pool aft. Crew accommodation was modified to meet the needs of an increased complement of about 250. The main public room on the lounge deck is the Star lounge, with changes in ceiling height to create a visual effect of a night club, bar, dance floor and lounge area. There is luxury seating for 280 passengers, increasing to 360 on gala occasions. All main rooms have been modernized and re-decorated. The forward Bahama lounge features a bar draped in chain mail, the former gallery is now a games room; the reading and writing rooms have been redecorated. The new lido area and swimming pool have a tiled beach effect surround with underwater lighting and access from the Star lounge by large glass doors. There are new de luxe cabins on the navigation deck and on either side of the swimming pool area. Siting the deck house further aft with the new cabins provided an 80ft extension of the sun and sports deck. All cabins have been modernized, and 79 new ones added. The 100 seat cinema on the Caribbean deck has been refurnished, and the dining-room modernized to take 300 passengers at 1 sitting, as well as 2 private dining-rooms for parties of 30 and 16 respectively. The galley area has been entirely redesigned and re-equipped with the latest American stainless steel equipment. The air conditioning machinery, adequate for the North Atlantic run has been replaced by a more elaborate system. The life saving equipment is sufficient for 830 persons. The entire hull was shotblasted and epoxy coated whilst in the dock company's hands. I have written fairly extensively on this ship to indicate how a ship can be modernized and given a useful life in a new sphere, and also because otherwise this book is liable to become a tedious catalogue of bulk carriers and mammoth tankers. She now has a gross tonnage of 8,312 tons and is operated by the Bahamas Shipping Corporation.*

NEW MUI KIM. *Liberian*. Bulk carrier. Built by Osaka Zosensho, Osaka, for Pacific Shipping Co Ltd, Monrovia 9,776 tons gross, 16,950 tons dw, 475·84ft loa × 73·41ft breadth × 28·66ft draught, 6-cyl IHI-Sulzer diesel, 7,200bhp, 17 knots.

NEW STAR (Sis SEA STAR). *South Korean* Tanker. Built by A/B Gotaverken, Gothenburg, for Samyang Navigation Co Ltd, Inchon. 63,989 tons gross, 120,250 tons dw, 893·18ft loa (incl bb) × 127·92ft breadth × 53·25ft draught, 11-cyl Gotaverken diesel, 26,400bhp, 16knots.

NICOLA SPECCHIO. *Italian*. Stern trawler, ref. Built by Soc Esercizio Cant, Viareggio, for Soc Atlas Pesca Molfetta, Bari. 850 tons gross, 620 tons dw, 208·75ft loa × 34·18ft breadth × 14·18ft draught, 8-cyl Deutz diesel, 2,350bhp, knots na.

NIENBURG. *East German*. Cargo (XD series) ref, OSD/CSD. Built by Warnowwerft Warnemunde, for Deutsche Seereederie, Rostock. 5,578/8,812 tons gross, 8,210/10,080 tons dw, 492·58ft loa × 66·41ft breadth × 23·88/26·96ft draught, 8-cyl DMR-MAN diesel, 11,200bhp, 19·25 knots.

NIKIEL. *Russian*. Stern trawler, fish factory, ref. Built by Stocznia Gdanska, Gdansk, for USSR. 2,944 tons gross, 1,366 tons dw, 272·66ft loa × 45·41ft breadth × 18·04ft draught, 8-cyl Sulzer diesel, 2,400bhp, knots na.

NIKOLAI BAUMAN. *Russian*. Cargo. Built by Angyalfold Shipyard, Budapest, for USSR. 1,501 tons gross, 1,923 tons dw, 255·25ft loa × 37·75ft breadth × 16·27ft draught, 6-cyl Jugoturbina-Sulzer diesel, 1,500bhp, 12·5 knots.

N

New Star. *The South Korean merchant fleet has taken delivery of a number of modern ships, with more building.* New Star *of the Samyang Navigation Co, a sister of the* Sea Star, *is with her, 1 of the 2 largest to fly the South Korean ensign; as well as having one of the highest powered European built marine diesel engines.*

N

NIKOLAI BROVTSEV. *Russian.* Stern trawler, fish factory, ref (ATLANTIK class). Built by Volkswerft Stralsund, Stralsund, 1967, for USSR. 2,657 tons gross, 1,152 tons dw, 269·58ft loa × 44·75ft breadth × 16·41ft draught, two 8-cyl s sc Liebknecht diesel, cpp, 2,320 bhp, 13·5 knots.

NIKOLAI KARAMZIN. *Russian.* Cargo. Built by Brodogradiliste 3rd Maj, Rijeka, for USSR, Vladivostok. 10,401 tons gross, 14,000 tons dw, 522·92ft loa × 69·84ft breadth × 31·56ft draught, 8-cyl 3rd Maj-Sulzer diesel, 12,000bhp, 18·5 knots.

NIKOLAI KREMIANSKY. *Russian.* Cargo CSD (B40-1 series) one 60-ton derrick (plus others). Built by Stocznia Gdanska, Gdansk, 1968, for USSR. 10,183 tons gross, 12,725 tons dw, 507·41ft loa × 67·66ft breadth × 29·5ft draught, 6-cyl Cegielski-Sulzer diesel, 9,600bhp, 18·25 knots.

NIKOLAI SHCHORS. *Russian.* Cargo, ref. Built by Cantieri Naval Breda, Venice, 1968, for USSR, Odessa. 4,970 tons gross, 4,400 tons dw, 400ft loa × 55·92ft breadth × 24·6ft draught, 7-cyl Fiat diesel, 8,400bhp, 19 knots.

NIKOLOZ BARATASHVILI. *Russian.* Tanker. Built by Brodogradiliste 'Split', Split, for USSR, Batumi. 15,250 tons gross, 22,144 tons dw, 610·25ft loa × 77ft breadth × 31·84ft draught, 7-cyl Uljanik-B & W diesel, 10,500bhp, knots na.

NIMOS (ex BERKEL) *British.* Cargo (containers) RoRo. Built by J. J. Sietas Schiffsw, Hamburg, for Common Bros (Management) Ltd, Newcastle. 2,634/4,974 tons gross, 4,232/6,112 tons dw, 372·41ft loa × 56·33ft breadth × 20·55/24·62ft draught, 10-cyl MAN diesel, cpp, btp, 5,430 bhp, 15·75 knots.

NIPPON REEFER. *Danish.* Cargo, ref, OSD. Built by Aalborg Vaerft A/S, Aalborg, for J. Lauritzen, Copenhagen. 6,010 tons gross, 8,500 tons dw, 477·66ft loa × 69ft breadth × 28·33ft draught, 8-cyl B & W diesel, 15,000bhp, knots na.

NIPPONHAM MARU No 2. *Japanese.* Cargo, ref. Built by Shikoku Dock Co, Takamatsu, 1968, for Shikoku Dock KK, Takamatsu. 2,661 tons gross, 3,476 tons dw, 342·84ft loa × 47·58ft breadth × 19·07ft draught, 8-cyl IHI diesel, 3,500bhp, 15 knots.

NJORD. *Swedish.* Icebreaker. Built by O/Y Wartsila A/B, Helsingfors, 1968, for Swedish Government. 3,970 tons gross, 865 tons dw, 283·85ft loa × 69·58ft breadth × draught na, four 9-cyl tw sc Wartsila-Sulzer diesel-electric (2 screws fwd, 2 aft), 9,000bhp, 18 knots.

NORDWELLE. *German.* Cargo. Built by Schlichting Werke, Travemunde, for Reederei 'NORD' Klaus E. Oldendorff, Hamburg. 4,800 tons gross, 7,350 tons dw, 382·58ft loa × 56·41ft m breadth × 24·7ft draught, 8-cyl Atlas-MaK diesel, 4,000bhp, knots na.

NORMANNIA. *German.* Cargo (bulk/cars i.e. 1,563 Volkswagen) (PIONEER 11/111 series). Built by Blohm & Voss AG, Hamburg, 1968, for Christian F. Ahrenkiel, Hamburg. 12,348 tons gross, 20,418 tons dw, 532·09ft loa (incl bb) × 74·92ft breadth × 33·99ft draught, 18-cyl Ottensener-Pielstick diesel, 9,000bhp, 16·5 knots.

NOSHIRO MARU. *Japanese.* Cargo. Built by Hitachi Zosen, Mukaishima, for Nippon Yusen Kaisha, Tokyo. 9,465 tons gross, 11,150 tons dw, 493·5ftl oa × 78·33ft breadth × 27·5ft draught, 6-cyl Hitachi-B & W diesel, 8,300bhp, 17 knots.

NOTO MARU. *Japanese.* Cargo. Built by Hitachi Zosen, Mukaishima, 1968, for Nippon Yusen Kaisha, Tokyo. 9,463 tons gross, 11,500 tons dw, 493·5ft loa × 68·33ft breadth × 27·5ft draught, 6-cyl Hitachi-B & W diesel, 8,300bhp, 17 knots.

NJORD

Njord. *Of conventional north European ice breaker appearance, this view gives an excellent idea of an ice breaker's bow propeller shafting, etc. Similar basically to the Finnish* Varma *(1968) and Swedish* Tor, *she is fitted with remote controlled highly automated diesel electric engines. There are 4 main Wartsila-Sulzer 9MH51 diesels providing a total output of 13,820bhp at 330rpm. 4 propellers (2 forward, 2 aft) are driven by electric propulsion motors, the latter developing 3,400kw each, and the former 2,200kw. Direct control is exercised either from the wheelhouse, the bridge wings, or the after control station when towing. She also has an automatic heeling system for working through pack ice.*

Normannia. *The second Blohm & Voss* Pioneer *multi class ship fitted with their hoistable car deck system. She can by these removable temporary decks carry over 1,000 Volkswagen and 500 transporters. This photograph shows very clearly the enormous bow bulb and unorthodox angular hull construction.*

N

For particulars of the Norris Castle *see Vol XVII. The latest ship on the Southampton-Cowes route, now being served experimentally with hydrofoils and hovercraft, she can carry either 500 passengers, or 300 passengers and 45 cars, or a total weight of 150 tons at 14 knots.*

Novomirgorod. *First of a series of 7 ships from the Wartsila yard, she is driven by a Wartsila-Sulzer 6RD76 diesel of 9,600bhp driving a KaMeWa controllable pitch propeller to give a loaded speed of 18 knots. Cargo handling gear includes five 5-ton Wartsila-Kampnagel electric cranes, with fittings in 2 places for the installation of 80-ton booms. A bow thruster is fitted, and the vessel can be operated with an unmanned engine room.*

NOVAYA LADOGA. *Russian.* Cargo. Built by A Zdhanov, Leningrad, 1967, for USSR, Leningrad. 4,676 tons gross, tons dw na, 400·09ft loa × 54·92ft breadth × 22·22ft draught, 9-cyl Bryansk-B & W diesel, bhp na, knots na.

NOVOMIRGOROD. *Russian.* Cargo CSD. Built by O/Y Wartsila A/B, Abo, for USSR. 9,150 tons gross, 12,500 tons dw, 495ft loa × 67·66ft breadth × 29·5ft draught, 6-cyl Wartsila-Sulzer diesel, 9,600bhp, knots na.

NOVOPOLOTSK. *Russian.* Cargo CSD. Built by O/Y Wartsila A/B, Abo, for USSR. 9,150 tons gross, 12,500 tons dw, 495ft loa × 67·75ft breadth × 29·53ft draught, 6-cyl Wartsila-Sulzer diesel, 9,600bhp, knots na.

O

OB. *Russian*. Fishing, ref. Built by Mathias Thesen Werft, Wismar, 1968, for USSR. 1,110 tons gross, tons dw na, 214·92ft loa × 37·41ft m breadth × 11·84ft draught, 8-cyl Liebknecht diesel, 825bhp, knots na.

OCEANIC. *German*. Salvage tug. Built by F. Schichau GmbH, Bremerhaven, for Bugsier Reederei & Bergungs AG, Hamburg. 2,047 tons gross, 1,550 tons dw, 286·18ft loa × 48·5ft breadth × 21ft draught, two 16-cyl tw sc Deutz diesel, btp, 14,400bhp, 19·5/22 knots.

OCEANO INDICO (ex ATLANTIC REEFER). *Cuban*. Cargo, ref. Built by Cant Nav Apuania, Marina di Carrara , for Flota Bananera Ecuatoriana Israeli, Haifa (Transferred to Emp Nav Mambisa, Havana). 6,632 tons gross, 5,600 tons dw, 456ft loa × 58·5ft breadth × 24·92ft draught, 7-cyl Fiat diesel, 10,500bhp, 20 knots.

OCEANO PACIFICO (ex PACIFIC REEFER). *Cuban*. Cargo, ref. Built by Cant Nav Apuania, Marina di Carrara, for Flota Bananera Ecuatoriana, Israeli (transferred to Empresa Nav Mambisa, Havana). 6,652 tons gross, 5,600 tons dw, 456ft loa × 58·5ft breadth × 24·92ft draught, 7-cyl Fiat diesel, 10,500bhp, 20 knots.

OCEANUS. *Swedish*. Tanker. Built by Eriksbergs M/V A/B, Gothenburg, for A/B Nynas Petroleum, Stockholm. 67,535 tons gross, 132,900 tons dw, 923·18ft loa × 135·18ft breadth × 54·88ft draught, three 18-cyl s sc Eriksbergs-Pielstick diesel, 22,380bhp, 16 knots.

ODA MARU. *Japanese*. Cargo. Built by Kurushima Dock Co, Imabari, for Oda KKK, Iyo. 2,500 tons gross, 4,100 tons dw, 272·33ft lbp × 47·33ft breadth × 19·33ft draught, 6-cyl Akasaka Tekkosho diesel, 4,100bhp, 11·75 knots.

ODER. *German*. Cargo, ref. Built by Lubecker Flender Werke AG, Lubeck for Friedrich A. Detjen, Hamburg. 8,999 tons gross, 15,300 tons dw, 487·58ft loa (incl bb) × 69·25ft breadth × 30·94ft draught, 8-cyl MAN diesel, 11,200bhp, knots na.

ODESSA MARU. *Japanese*. Ore/oil carrier. Built by Mitsubishi HI, Ltd Yokohama, for Sanko KKK. 45,236 tons gross, tons dw na, measurements na, cyl na, bhp na, knots na.

ODIN. *British*. Barge (for UK-east coast Eire service). Built by Akers Nylands Verksted, Oslo, for Anchorage Ferrying Services Ltd (J. Fisher & Sons, Barrow Mgrs), Barrow. 1,844 tons gross, 3,380 tons dw, 242ft loa × 41·09ft breadth × 18·81ft draught, two 8-cyl tw sc Rolls Royce diesel, directional props, 1,000bhp, 9 knots.

OGDEN WABASH. *USA*. Tanker. Built by Bethlehem Steel Corpn, Sparrow's Point, for Wabash Transport Inc, New York. 20,884 tons gross, 37,853 tons dw, 660·18ft loa × 90·18ft breadth × 36·73ft draught, GEC turbs, 15,000shp, 16·25 knots.

OGDEN WILLAMETTE. *USA*. Tanker. Built by Bethlehem Steel Corpn, Sparrow's Point, for Willamette Transport Inc, New York. 20,884 tons gross, 37,853 tons dw, 660·18ft loa × 90·18ft breadth × 36·63ft draught, GEC turbs, 15,000shp, 16·25 knots.

OHTSU MARU. *Japanese*. Ore carrier. Built by Nippon Kokan, Tsurumi, for Nippon Yusen Kaisha, Tokyo. 58,262 tons gross, 107,020 tons dw, 852·09ft loa (incl bb) × 124·84ft breadth × 51ft draught, 8-cyl Mitsui-B & W diesel, 20,000bhp, knots na.

OKA. *Russian*. Fishing, ref. Built by Mathias Thesen Werft, 1968, for USSR. 1,110 tons gross, tons dw na, 214·92ft loa × 36·41ft m breadth × 11·84ft draught, 8-cyl Liebknecht diesel, 825bhp, knots na.

OKITAMA MARU. *Japanese*. Tanker. Built by Imabari Zosen, Imabari, 1968, for Tamai Shosen KK, Kobe. 999 tons gross, 2,150 tons dw, 213·18ft lbp × 36·18ft breadth × 17·09ft draught, two 6-cyl s sc Daihatsu diesel, 1,500bhp, 12 knots.

OKTYABSKOYE. *Russian*. Stern trawler, fish factory, ref (ATLANTIK class). Built by Volkswerft Stralsund, Stralsund, 1968, for USSR. 2,657 tons gross, 1,152 tons dw, 269·58ft loa × 44·66ft breadth × 16·41ft draught, two 8-cyl s sc Liebknecht diesel, cpp, 2,320bhp, 13·5 knots.

OKUTOMI MARU No 28. *Japanese*. Tanker. Built by Imamura Zosen, Kure, for Kido KKK, Shimonoseki. 994 tons gross, 2,000 tons dw, 226·41ft loa × 36·18ft breadth × 17·08ft draught, 6-cyl, Hanshin diesel, 1,800bhp, knots na.

Oceanic. This ship can only be described as a 'Supertug' and salvage ship. Built to be capable of handling ships up to 500,000 tons deadweight, she is of 17,500hp, derived from 2 supercharged 16-cyl Deutz RBV 16 M 540 type, each geared to a single shaft. Each engine indicates 8,750hp at 600rpm, geared down to 148rpm shaft speed. The twin shafts are each connected to variable pitch propellers, controlled from the bridge. She is also provided with a bow thrust unit. Her free running speed is 22 knots, and her bollard pull 150 tons. She has a range of 20,000 nautical miles, with bunker capacity of 1,250 tons. Her crew consists of 26, including 2 divers. Her 2 electric-hydraulic towing winches are furnished with 2,000 metres of $7\frac{1}{2}$in special towing wire, with a third drum in reserve. Her salvage hold is served by a 15-ton derrick, of 20 metres length, which can also deposit salvage equipment such as pumps and compressors on board a casualty. She is equipped with a spacious and comprehensive workshop, including a cement mixer and underwater welding apparatus. There is a second control position abaft the funnel, with duplicated bridge controls. Navigation and communication instruments are extremely comprehensive, and a continuous radio watch is kept. There are 2 motor driven lifeboats, each holding 35 persons, 4 life rafts, and an air conditioned hospital in the shipwreck survivors' section of the accommodation. She can operate under any conditions from polar to tropical. When her sister ship Arctic is completed, the Bugsier tug fleet will total some 50 units.

O

OLAU NORD. *Danish*. Tanker. Built by Helsingor Skibs & Msk, Helsingor, for Ole Lauritzen, Ribe. 5,650 tons gross, 8,000 tons dw, 462·92ft loa × 59·25ft breadth × 24·66ft draught, 7-cyl B & W diesel, 9,400bhp, knots na.

OLENEOGORSK. *Russian*. Stern trawler, fish factory, ref. Built by Stocznia im Komuny Pariskiej, 1968, for USSR. 2,934 tons gross, 1,321 tons dw, 272·75ft loa × 45·41ft breadth × 18·09ft draught, 8-cyl Jugoturbina-Sulzer diesel, 2,400bhp, 12·5 knots.

OLIVIA MAERSK. *Danish*. Bulk carrier. Built by Burmeister & Wain, Copenhagen, for A. P. Moller, Copenhagen. 30,039 tons gross, 50,850 tons dw, 718ft loa × 100·25ft breadth × 39·66ft draught, 8-cyl B & W diesel, 15,000bhp, knots na,

OLYMPIC ARMOUR. *Greek*. Tanker. Built by Hitachi Zosen, Sakai, for A. Onassis, Piraeus. 109,579 tons gross, 216,508 tons dw, 1,057·41ft loa (incl bb) × 158·25ft breadth × 63·62ft draught, Mitsubishi turbs, 30,000shp, 15·75 knots.

OLYMPIC ATHLETE. *Liberian*. Tanker. Built by Hitachi Zosen, Sakai, for Durango Marine Panama SA, Monrovia (A. Onassis). 97,468 ton gross, 213,000 tons dw, 1,057ft loa (incl bb) × 158·33ft breadth × 53·84ft draught, Mistbishhi turbs, 30,000shp, knots na.

OLYMPIC PEACE. *Liberian*. Bulk carrier. Built by Nippon Kokan, Shimizu, for Kinsdale Panama SA, Monrovia (A. Onassis). 15,688 tons gross, 27,023 tons dw, 576·09ft loa × 75·18ft breadth × 35·98ft draught, 8-cyl IHI-Sulzer diesel, 12,000bhp, knots na.

OLYMPIC PRESTIGE. *Liberian*. Bulk carrier. Built by Nippon Kokan, Shimizu, for Olinda Panama SA, Monrovia (A. Onassis). 15,808 tons gross, 26,998 tons dw, 576·09ft loa × 75·18ft breadth × 35·98ft draught, 8-cyl IHI-Sulzer diesel, 12,000bhp, 16·25 knots.

OLYMPIC PROGRESS. *Liberian*. Bulk carrier. Built by Nippon Kokan, Shimizu, for Howland Panama SA, Monrovia (A. Onassis). 15,668 tons gross, 26,000 tons dw, 576·09ft loa × 75·18ft breadth × 35·98ft draught, 8-cyl IHI-Sulzer diesel, 12,000bhp, knots na.

OMSK. *Russian*. Tanker. Built by Rauma-Repola O/Y, Rauma, for USSR. 3,500 tons gross, 5,000 tons dw, 348·25ft loa × 50·66ft breadth × 21·33ft draught, 5-cyl Bryansk-B & W diesel, 2,900bhp, 12·75 knots.

OOSADO MARU (particulars courtesy of *Fairplay*). *Japanese*. Passenger/car ferry. Built by Ishikawajima-Harima HI, Ltd, for Sado Kisen Kaisha. 1,864 tons gross, 402 tons dw, 269ft loa × 51·8ft breadth × 11·3ft draught, cyl na, make and type na, 2,000bhp, 16·5 knots.

ORANJELAND. *German*. Cargo, ref (180-ton Stulcken derrick). Built by Blohm & Voss AG, Hamburg, for Globus Reederei GmbH, Hamburg. 8,260/11,372 tons gross, 11,690/15,590 tons dw, 536·09ft loa (incl bb) × 78·75ft m breadth × 26·75/31·18ft draught, 7-cyl MAN diesel, 2,250bhp, 19 knots.

OSHIMA MARU. *Japanese*. Train ferry. Built by Hakodate Dock Co Ltd, Hakodate, for Department of Railways, Tokyo. 7,400 tons gross, 2,380 tons dw, 474·41ft loa × 60·5ft breadth × draught na, two 16-cyl tw sc Kawasaki-MAN diesel, bhp na, knots na.

OSHIMA MARU. *Japanese*. Cargo. Built by Kurushima Dkyd Co Ltd, Imabari, for Ebisu KKK, Nagahama. 2,999 tons gross, 5,800 tons dw, 308·41ft lbp × 52·5ft breadth × 22·18ft draught, 6-cyl Hatsudoki diesel, 3,800bhp, knots na.

OSMUSSAAR. *Russian*. Cargo. Built by Angyalfold Shipyard, Budapest, 1968, for USSR, Tallinn. 1,248 tons gross, 1,299 tons dw, 244·41ft loa × 37·18ft breadth × 13·13ft draught, 8-cyl Lang diesel, 1,000bhp, 11·5 knots.

OSTERBEK (Sis ISEBEK). *German*. Tanker. Built by J. G. Hitzler, Lauenberg, 1968, for Knohr & Burchard, Hamburg. 999 tons gross, 1,658 tons dw, 221·5ft loa × 35·09ft breadth × 15·18ft draught, 8-cyl MWM diesel, 1,150bhp, 11·5 knots.

OSTROV LISYANSKOGO. *Russian*. Fish carrier, ref. Built by A/B Lindhomens Varv, Gothenburg, for USSR, Vladivostok. 9,790 tons gross, 10,200 tons dw, 497·5ft loa × 67·33ft breadth × 24·5ft draught, two 12-cyl Lindholmens-Pielstick diesel, 6,000bhp, knots na.

OSTROV OSHAKOVA. *Russian*. Fish carrier, ref, CSD. Built by A/B Lindholmens Varv, Gothenburg, for USSR, Kaliningrad. 9,660 tons gross, 9,600 tons dw, 497ft loa × 67·41ft breadth × 24·41ft draught, two 12-cyl s sc Lindholmens-Pielstick diesel, 6,000bhp, knots na.

O

Olympic Armour. *The first of 5 sister 200,000 tonners from Sakai for Mr A. Onassis, she is the largest size capable of transiting the Suez Canal in ballast. Her Mitsubishi steam turbine develops 30,000shp at 87rpm of the propeller, giving a trial speed of 16·55 knots. She can take 2 different types of cargo in the ratio 50:50 or 25:75. A helicopter landing platform is fitted aft. The ships are designed for the Persian Gulf-European route, and remote control of the machinery is from the engine room control station.*

OSTROV RUSSKITY. *Russian.* Fish carrier, ref, CSD. Built by A/B Lindholmens Varv, Gothenburg, 1968, for USSR, Kaliningrad. 9,660 tons gross, 9,600 tons dw, 497ft loa × 67·41ft breadth × 24·41ft draught, two 12-cyl s sc Lindholmens-Pielstick diesel, cpp, 6,000bhp, 18 knots.

OSTROV SHOKALSKOGO. *Russian.* Fish carrier, ref, CSD. Built by A/B Lindholmens Varv, Gothenburg, for USSR, Kaliningrad 9,660 tons gross, 9,600 tons dw, 497ft loa × 67·41ft breadth × 24·41ft draught, two 12-cyl s sc Lindholmens-Pielstick diesel, 6,000bhp, 18 knots.

Oosado Maru. *This ship, owned by the Sado Kisen Kaisha is designed for operation between Niigata Port, on the west coast of Honshu, and Sado Island, 34 miles west of Honshu (the main island of Japan). She can carry 1,791 passengers, 55 of their cars (or 12 large buses) and 48 containers, at a service speed of 16·5 knots. She has a crew of 33. Sado Island has an annually increasing tourist industry, which will be facilitated by the thrice daily voyages she will make. Cars can be loaded and discharged from either end of the ship, she has twin screws and a bow thrust propeller, whilst the stern has a hinge-up bow door, giving a rapid turn round.*

OSTROV SIBIRYAKOVA. *Russian.* Fish carrier, ref, CSD. Built by A/B Lindholmens Varv, Gothenburg, for USSR, Kaliningrad. 9,660 tons gross, 9,600 tons dw, 497ft loa × 67·41ft breadth × 24·41ft draught, two 12-cyl s sc Lindholmens-Pielstick diesel, 6,000bhp, 18 knots.

OSTSEE. *German.* Passenger ferry (416 pass). Built by Husumer Werft, Husum, for Forde-Reederei GmbH, Flensburg. 375 tons gross, tons dw na, 128·09ft loa × 29·58ft breadth × 6·92ft draught, two 8-cyl s sc MAN diesel, 1,020bhp, 14 knots.

Otto Hahn. *Europe's first nuclear powered cargo ship is operated experimentally by the* Gesellschaft fur Kernenergieverwertung in Schiffbau und Schiffahrt, *that is the Society for the Evaluation of Nuclear Energy in Shipbuilding and Navigation. She is claimed to have a more compact reactor plant than either the* Savannah *or* Lenin, *which reduces the danger in collision. Costing £5·5 million, she was launched in 1964 and completed in 1968. Her particulars are in the register of Vol XVII. She originally made a trial run in the Baltic before her reactor was fitted, using conventional auxiliary engines.*

OTARU. *Swedish*. Chemical tanker. Built by A/B Lodose Varf, Lodose, for Lars Johansson, Skarhamn. 2,678 tons gross, 4,130 tons dw, 324·84ft loa × 41·33ft breadth × 20ft draught, 8-cyl MWM diesel, 2,200bhp, 12 knots.

OTELIA. *Swedish*. Asphalt. tanker Built by Lodose Varf Lodose, for Lars Johansson, Skarhamn. 2,671 tons gross, 4,235 tons dw, 324·84ft loa × 41·09ft breadth × 21·09ft draught, 8-cyl MWM diesel, 2,200bhp, knots na.

OTELLO. *Swedish*. Oil/asphalt tanker. Built by A/B Lodose Varf, Lodose, for Lars Johansson, Skarhamn. 2,671 tons gross, 4,376 tons dw, 324·84ft loa × 41·18ft breadth × 20·09ft draught, 9-cyl Ruston-Hornsby diesel, cpp, 2,460bhp, 12 knots.

OTTERCLIFFE HALL. *Canadian*. Bulk carrier. Built by Davie SB Ltd, Lauzon, for Hall Corpn of Canada, Toronto 17,800 tons gross, 26,850 tons dw, 729·75ft loa × 75·25ft breadth × 26·48ft draught, three 6-cyl s sc Mirrlees National diesel, 8,310bhp, 14·75 knots.

OVERBECK. *German*. Car carrier (480 Volkswagen). Built by Orenstein Koppel & Lbcr Masch, Lubeck, for Lubeck Linie AG, Lubeck. 999/1,599 tons gross, 1,772/3,306 tons dw, 253ft loa × 46·18ft m breadth × 16·62/22·46ft draught, 9-cyl Atlas-MaK diesel, btp, 2,000bhp, 13·5 knots.

OVERSEAS VIVIAN. *USA*. tanker. Built by Bethlehem Steel Corpn Inc, Sparrow's Point, for Ocean Tankships Corpn, Wilmington Del. 20,879 tons gross, 37,250 tons dw, 660·18ft loa × 90·09ft breadth × 36·41ft draught, GEC turbs, 15,000 shp 16·5 knots.

OWARI MARU (Sis FURYU MARU). *Japanese*. Ore Carrier Built by Mitsui Zosen, Chiba for Nippon Yusen Kaisha, Tokyo 58,800 ton gross 10,6495 tons dw, 849·75ft loa × 137·66ft breadth 46·5ft draught, 9-cyl Mitsui-B & W diesel 23,200 bhp 15·25 knots.

P

PABLO GARNICA. *Spanish*. Tanker. Built by Astano del Noreste, Ferrol, for Naviera de Castilla SA, Santander. 51,819 tons gross, 97,735 tons dw, 878ft loa (incl bb) × 128·18ft breadth × draught na, GEC turbs, 22,000shp, 16·5 knots.

PACIFIC LOGGER. *British*. Cargo. Built by Sanoyasu Dkyd Ltd, Osaka, for Canadian Pacific (Bermuda) Ltd, Hong Kong. 10,324 tons gross, 15,900 tons dw, 459·33ft lbp × 69·5ft m breadth × 28·41ft draught, 7-cyl Sumitomo -Sulzer diesel, 8,000bhp, 15 knots.

PACIFIC VOYAGER. *British*. Tanker. Built by Schps 'De Waal', Zaltbommel, for Dilmun Nav Co Ltd, London. 675 tons gross, 1,060 tons dw, 210ft loa × 35·41ft breadth × 11ft draught, 8-cyl Deutz diesel, 1,060bhp, knots na.

PAG (ex LOGATEC). *Yugoslavian* Cargo, ref. Built by Empresa Nacional 'Bazan', Ferrol, for Splosna Plovba, Koper. 7,800 tons gross, tons dw na, 448·41ft lbp × 65·6ft m breadth × draught na, 6-cyl Ast de Cadiz-Sulzer diesel, 9,600bhp, 18 knots

PAJALA (Sis FLOWERGATE). *Swedish*. Ore/oil carrier. Built by A/B Gotaverken, Gothenburg, for Trafik A/B Grangesberg-Oxelsound, Stockholm. 58,808 tons gross, 106,700 tons dw, 830·09ft loa × 131·41ft breadth × 47·5ft draught, 8-cyl Gotaverken diesel, 19,200bhp, 15·25 knots.

PANAMERICA. *Norwegian*. Ferry (see PANATLANTIC). Built by A/S Ankerlkken Verft, Glommen A/S, Frederiksstad, for Odd Berg, Oslo. 499 tons gross, 975 tons dw, 258·58ft loa × 44·66ft breadth × 10·25ft draught, two 16-cyl tw sc Caterpillar diesels, cpp, 2,000bhp, 13.5 knots.

PANATLANTIC. *Norwegian*. Ferry (RoRo bow, bow door and port side door, capable of beaching. 28 × 40ft trailers, strengthened bottom for Miami-Virgin Island run). Built by Ankerlokken Verft Glommen A/S, Frederiksstad, for Odd Berg & Co, Oslo 499 tons gross, 975 tons dw, 258·58ft loa × 44·66ft breadth × 10·25ft draught, two 16-cyl tw sc Caterpillar diesel, cpp, 2,000bhp, 13·5 knots.

PANGANI (ex BRUNSHAGEN). *German*. Cargo. Built by Kherson Shipyard, Kherson, 1968, for DAL Deutsche-Afrika Linien GmbH & Co, Hamburg. 6,486/9,890 tons gross, na/12,740 tons dw, 484·41ft lr × breadth na × draught na, 6-cyl Bryansk-B & W diesel, 9,000bhp, knots na.

PARALLAKS. *Russian* Stern trawler, fish factory, ref. Built by Stocznia Gdanska, Gdansk, 1967, for USSR, Murmansk. 2,994 tons gross, 1,239 tons dw, 272·33ft loa × 45·41ft breadth × 18·04ft draught, 8-cyl Jugoturbina-Sulzer diesel, 2,400bhp, 12·5 knots.

PARINAS (Sis PIMENTEL). *Peruvian*. Tanker. Built by Servicio Ind de la Armada Peruana, Callao, 1968, for Ministry of Marine, Callao. 6,926 tons gross, 10,000 tons dw, 440·58ft loa × 62·18ft breadth × 23·88ft draught, 7-cyl Helsingor-B & W diesel, 5,400bhp, 14 knots.

PARKHOMENKO. *Russian*. Cargo, ref. Built by Cantieri Naval Breda, Venice, 1968, for USSR, Odessa. 4,059 tons gross, 4,400 tons dw, 400ft loa × 55·92ft breadth × 24·62ft draught, 7-cyl Fiat diesel, 8,400bhp, 19 knots.

PASSAT. *German* Cargo OSD/CSD (Liberty replacement type). Built by Flensburger Schiffs Ges, 1968, Flensburg, for Hugo Stinnes Transozean Schiffahrt GmbH, Hamburg. 6,542/9,296 tons gross, na/15,000 tons dw, 458·41ft loa × 69·09ft breadth × na/29·58ft draught, 6-cyl Bremer-Vulkan-MAN diesel, 7,200 bhp,15·5 knots.

PASSAT. *Russian*. Hydrographic survey ship. Built by Stocznia Szczecinska, Szczecin, 1967, for USSR. 3,214 tons gross, 928 tons dw, 318·58ft loa × 45·41ft breadth × 17·09ft draught, two 8-cyl tw sc Zgoda-Sulzer diesel, 4,800bhp, 14 knots.

PATUDA. *Ghanaan*. Stern trawler, ref. Built by Newport SB & E Co Ltd, Newport, for Ghana Government, Takoradi. 1,083 tons gross, 884 tons dw, 239·18ft loa × 38·09ft breadth × 15·5ft draught, 6-cyl Mirrlees National diesel, 2,308bhp, 15 knots.

PAULA HOWALDT. *German*. Cargo OSD/CSD. Built by Bremer Vulkan, Vegesack, for Bernhard Howaldt Reederei, Hamburg. 9,416 tons gross, 15,200 tons dw, 457·66ft loa × 68·92ft m breadth × 30·09ft draught, 6-cyl Bremer-Vulkan diesel, 8,400bhp, knots na.

PAZIN. *Yugoslavian* Cargo, ref. Built by Italcantieri SpA, Monfalcone, for Jugoslavenska Linijska Plovidba, Rijeka. 6,275 tons gross, 8,439 tons dw, 497·41ft loa (incl bb) × 65·75ft breadth × 25·42ft draught, 7-cyl CRDA-Fiat diesel, 10,500bhp, knots na.

Pacific Shore. *This supply ship has a tank capacity of 248 tons of fuel cargo, 136 tons of fresh water, and 236 tons of ballast or drill water, in addition to three 1,230cu ft pressure tanks which are designed for dry material such as cement. 2 further tanks can be accommodated on deck, which is strengthened for loads up to 347 tons. Refrigerated storage capacity comprises a 270cu ft deep freeze, and a 300cu ft cool store. A high degree of manoeuvrability is provided by a Dorman 264bhp water cooled diesel bow thrust unit running at 1,290rpm and driving a Series 1 White Gill bow thruster manufactured at Cowes. This unit can in addition supplement the main propulsion system.*

PELENGATOR. *Russian.* Fish factory, ref, training ship for 110 cadets. Built by Burmeister & Wain, Copenhagen, 1968, for USSR, Murmansk. 4,734 tons gross, 2,500 tons dw, 339ft loa × 52·66ft breadth × draught na, 6-cyl B & W diesel, cpp, 3,100bhp, 14 knots.

PELLEAS. *Greek* Bulk carrier. Built by Ishikawajima-Harima HI, Nagoya, for Pelleas Shipping Co SA, Piraeus (Faros). 10,010 tons gross, 14,930 tons dw, 466·75ft loa (incl bb) × 65·09ft breadth × 29·66ft draught, 12-cyl IHI-Pielstick diesel, 5,180bhp, 14·25 knots.

P

Pajala. *This 106,400 ton ship is the largest in the Grangesberg-Oxelosund firm's fleet. She is an ore/oil carrier, with 585,000cu ft of clean water ballast capacity. She is extensively automated, and it is planned to run her with an unmanned engine room for 16 hours out of 24. Her KaMeWa controllable pitch propeller is bridge controlled, with very extensive monitoring and automation arrangements in the engine room control room, which includes a data logger. There are 4 centre line ore/oil compartments, flanked on each side by 5 oil cargo only. Fore and afterpeak tanks, together with a pair of midship wing tanks are arranged for water ballast. The pump room contains 3 vertical steam turbine centrifugal pumps, rated at 2,500 tons per hour each, and is situated between Nos 2 and 3 centre holds. Steam for the cargo pumps and other services is supplied by two Gotaverken-Babcock & Wilcox water tube boilers of type M11, in port, whilst steam requirements at sea are met by a Gotaverken exhaust boiler. She is the third ship of her name in the owner's fleet, and the 59th built for them by Gotaverken.*

P

PELLWORM. *German.* Asphalt tanker. Built by Werft Nobiskrug, Rendsburg, for Carl W. Hanssen Tankschiffahrt, Hamburg. 1,692 tons gross, 2,805 tons dw, 283·18ft loa × 41ft breadth × 16·5ft draught, 6-cyl Atlas-MaK diesel, 1,550bhp, 11·75 knots.

PENN CHAMPION. *USA.* Tanker. Built by Bethlehem Steel Corpn, Sparrow's Point, for Penn Shipping Co Inc, Wilmington, Del. 21,000 tons gross, tons dw na, 660·18ft loa × 90·18ft breadth × 36·41ft draught, GEC turbs, bhp na, knots na.

PEREDOVIK. *Russian.* Stern trawler, fish factory, ref (ATLANTIK class). Built by Volkswerft Stralsund, Stralsund, 1967, for USSR, Sevastopol. 2,657 tons gross, 1,152 tons dw, 269·58ft loa × 44·75ft breadth × 16·41ft draught, two 8-cyl s sc Liebknecht diesel, 2,320bhp, 13·5 knots.

PERUSTICA. *Bulgarian.* Cargo. Builder na, Bulgaria, for Navigation Maritime Bulgare, 1,812 tons gross, tons dw na, measurements na, cyl na, diesel, bhp na, knots na.

PETR KAHOVSKY. *Russian.* Cargo. Built by Angyalfold Shipyard, Budapest, for USSR. 1,440 tons gross, 1,923 tons dw, 255·25ft loa × 37·75ft breadth × 16·3ft draught, 6-cyl Jugoturbina-Sulzer diesel, 1,500bhp, 12·5 knots.

PETROSANI. *Roumanian.* Bulk carrier. Built by Santierual Naval, Galatz, 1968, for NAVROM Roumanian Maritime & Fluvial Navigation, Constantza. 9,557 tons gross, 12,680 tons dw, 487·75ft lr × 64·84ft breadth × 25·97ft draught, 6-cyl Cegielski-Sulzer diesel, 7,200bhp, 15 knots.

PETROZAVODSK. *Russian.* Cargo. Builder na, Vyborg, 1968, for USSR. 4,796 tons gross, tons dw na, 400·09ft loa × 54·92ft breadth × draught na, cyl na, diesel, bhp na, knots na.

PHILIPPINE LEADER. *Philippine.* Tanker. Built by Mitsubishi HI Ltd, Hiroshima, for United Philippine Carriers Inc, Manila. 47,485 tons gross, 93,900 tons dw, 841·5ft loa (incl bb) × 128ft breadth × 46·35ft draught, 9-cyl Mitsubishi-Sulzer diesel, 20,700bhp, 15·5 knots.

PHILLIPS ARKANSAS. *Liberian.* LPG carrier, ref. Built by Kockums M/V A/B, Malmo, for Philtankers Inc, Monrovia. 18,013 tons gross, 20,000 tons dw, 606·09ft loa (incl bb) × 83·84ft breadth × 30·84ft draught, 9-cyl Kockums-MAN diesel, 15,750bhp, 17 knots.

PHOSPHORE CONVEYOR. *Liberian.* Bulk carrier. Built by Mitsubishi HI Ltd, Hiroshima, for Naviteck Co, Monrovia. 36,500 tons gross, 72,060 tons dw, 851·41ft loa (incl bb) × 105·84ft breadth × 42·97ft draught, two 18-cyl s sc Mitsubishi-MAN diesel, 19,560bhp, knots na.

PIMENTAL. *Peruvian.* Tanker. Built by Servicio Ind de La Armada Peruana, Callao, for Ministry of Marine. 7,000 tons gross, tons dw na, 440·58ft loa × 62·18ft breadth × 23·84ft draught, 7-cyl Helsingor-B & W diesel, 5,390bhp, 14 knots.

PINGVIN. *Bulgarian.* Stern trawler, fish factory, ref (ATLANTIK class). Built by Volkswerft Stralsund, Stralsund, 1968, for Okeansky Ribolov, Bourgas. 2,657 tons gross, 1,152 tons dw, 269·58ft loa × 44·75ft breadth × 16·41ft draught, two 8-cyl s sc Liebknecht diesel, cpp, 2,594bhp, 13·5 knots.

PIONER. *Russian.* Cargo. Built by Shiffsw Neptun, Rostock, 1967, for USSR, Vladivostok. 3,685 tons gross, 4,638 tons dw, 346·75ft loa × 51·33ft breadth × 22·2ft draught, 6-cyl DMR-MAN diesel, 3,250bhp, 13·75 knots.

PIONERSKAYA PRAVDA. *Russian.* Cargo. Built by Schiffsw Neptun, Rostock, for USSR, Vladivostok. 3,684 tons gross, 4,638 tons dw, 346·75ft loa × 51·33ft breadth × 22·2ft draught, 8-cyl Halberstadt-MAN diesel, 3,250bhp, knots na.

PIOTRKOW TRYBUNALSKI. *Polish.* Cargo. Built by G. Dimitrov Shipyard, Varna, for Polish SS Co, Szcecin. 2,423 tons gross, 3,615 tons dw, 314·75ft loa × 45·09ft breadth × 18·56ft draught, 6-cyl Zgoda-Sulzer diesel, 2,250bhp, knots na.

PITZUNDA. *Russian.* Stern trawler, fish factory, ref (ATLANTIK class). Built by Volkswerft Stralsund, Stralsund, 1967, for USSR, Kertch. 2,650 tons gross, 1,152 tons dw, 269·58ft loa × 44·75ft breadth × 16·92ft draught, two 8-cyl s sc Liebknecht diesel, 2,320bhp, 13·5 knots.

Phillips Arkansas. *This liquid petroleum gas tanker is of the atmospheric pressure and refrigerated type, and is ice strengthened. The hull is divided into 3 cargo compartments, with small apertures for the tank domes and access. Only 2 grades of gas can be carried at 1 time. She has a double bottom and sloping wing ballast tanks. In her bulbous bow is a KaMeWa bow thrust unit. The main propulsion is by means of a Kockums-MAN diesel of type K9Z 78/155E. The contract service speed at 27ft draught is 18·4 knots, with 13,375bhp and 116rpm, but 19 knots can be achieved with 15,750bhp at 122rpm. Electronic bridge control is fitted. She is designed to carry gases with a boiling temperature of 46·45°C or above with a max specific gravity of 0·72. Cargo gas is discharged by six 300 cu m p.h. electrically driven submerged centrifugal deep well pumps, 2 located in each tank. All the cargo can be discharged in 16 hours.*

PLAYA BIANCA (Sis PLAYA DE NAOS). *Spanish*. Cargo, ref. Built by Astano SA, Ferrol, for Naviera de Canarias SA, Las Palmas. 2,622 tons gross, 3,500 tons dw, 360·84ft loa (incl bb) × 50·18ft breadth × 21·2ft draught, 7-cyl SECN-B & W diesel, 5,400bhp, 16·25 knots.

PLAYA DE GURES. *Spanish*. Cargo OSD. Built by Ast Sicar, Corcubion, for Perfecto y Marcelo Castro Rial, Corcubion, 558 tons gross, 1,053 tons dw, 181·92ft loa × 27·92ft m breadth × draught na, 6-cyl Atlas-MaK diesel, 850bhp, 12·25 knots.

P

Polar Alaska. (*Not illustrated.*) *Of conventional liquid gas carrier appearance, this ship (as with her sister* Arctic Tokyo*), will carry each trip 450,000 barrels of liquid natural gas between Cook Inlet in SW Alaska and Negishi on the Bay of Tokyo, and they are scheduled to do this for 15 years. During this period they will supply the equivalent of 50 billion cubic feet of methane gas per year to the Tokyo Electric Power Co and Tokyo Gas Co. They are owned by separate companies, but the Marathon Oil Co will operate them. Moored stem to stern at Kockums, they were jointly christened from platforms decorated with American, Japanese, Liberian and Swedish flags by the wives of the Chairmen of Marathon Oil Co, Findlay, Ohio and Phillips Petroleum Co, Bartlesville, Oklahoma. They are designed externally for Arctic conditions, and for internal cryogenic conditions. The cargo is carried at atmospheric temperature and boiling temperature (—260°F). There are 6 heavily insulated cargo tanks, and the boil off of the gas is used as fuel in the dual fired ship's boilers, amounting to 0·3% of a full cargo per day. In dimensions, they are equivalent to a 70,000 ton dw tanker. The main turbines develop 20,000 metric shp at 106rpm, and service speed is 18·25 knots at 18,000shp and 103rpm. The hull is double skinned and provided with Class 3 ice strengthening. Ballast capacity is sufficient to maintain the same draught empty as when loaded. The cargo tanks, of the membrane type, were manufactured by the Gaz Transport Co, of Paris. Each cargo tank has 2 main pumps, and a full cargo can be unloaded by 6 pumps in 15 hours. Cargo piping is of stainless steel, and a remote control inert gas generator is fitted to control the prevention of fire and explosion. A 1,000hp bow thrust propeller is fitted.*

PLAYA DE NAOS (launched as PLAYA NAOS). *Spanish.* Cargo, ref. Built by Astano SA, Ferrol, for Naviera de Canarias SA, Las Palmas. 2,622 tons gross, 3,250 tons dw, 360·84ft loa (incl bb) × 50·18ft breadth × 21·2ft draught, 7-cyl SECN-B & W diesel, 5,400bhp, 16·25 knots.

PLAYA LARGA. *Cuban.* Cargo, ref. Built by Uddevallavarvet, A/B, Uddevalla, for Empresa Navigacion Mambisa, Havana. 10,972 tons gross, 15,550 tons dw, 531·09ft loa × 67·41ft breadth × 32ft draught, 7-cyl Uddevalla-B & W diesel, 11,900bhp, knots na.

PLEIADES. *Italian.* Ore carrier. Built by Italcantieri SpA, Genoa, for 'SIDERMAR' SpA, Genoa. 45,000 tons gross, 79,200 tons dw, 820·58ft loa (incl bb) × 125·5ft breadth × 41·73ft draught, 8-cyl CRDA-Sulzer diesel, 18,400bhp, 16·5 knots.

PLESETSK. *Russian.* Cargo. Builder na, Vyborg, for USSR, Archangel. 4,796 tons gross, tons dw na, 400·09ft loa × 54·92ft breadth × draught na, cyl na, Bryansk diesel, bhp na, knots na.

PLUTON. *Russian.* Stern trawler, fish factory, ref (ATLANTIK class). Built by Volkswerft Stralsund, Stralsund, 1967, for USSR, Kertch. 2,657 tons gross, 1,152 tons dw, 269·58ft loa × 44·75ft breadth × 16·92ft draught, two 8-cyl s sc Liebknecht diesel, 2,320bhp, 13·5 knots.

POBEDA OKTYABRYA. *Russian.* Tanker. Built by Baltic SB & E Works, Leningrad, 1968, for USSR. 12,000 tons gross, 15,200 tons dw, 532·5ft loa (incl bb) × 70·25ft breadth × 27·92ft draught, 6-cyl Bryansk- B & W diesel, 9,900bhp, 16·5 knots.

POINTE ALLEGRE. *French.* Cargo, ref. Built by Cons Nav & Ind de La Mediterranee (CNIM) la Seyne, for Cie Generale Transatlantique, Dunkerque. 6,800 tons gross, 8,620 tons dw, 448·58ft loa × 69ft breadth × 26·25ft draught, two 18-cyl s sc Atlantique-Pielstick diesel, 16,740bhp, knots na.

POINTE DES COLIBRIS (Sis POINTE MARIN). *French.* Cargo, ref. Built by Cons Nav & Ind de La Mediteranee (CNIM) La Seyne, for Cie Generale Transatlantique, Dunkerque. 9,700 tons gross, 8,620 tons dw, 448·58ft loa × 69ft breadth × 26·25ft draught, two 18-cyl s sc Atlantique diesel, 16,740bhp, knots na.

POLAR ALASKA. *Liberian.* LNG carrier, ref. Built by Kockums M/V A/B, Malmo, 1968 for Polar LNG Shipping Corpn, Monrovia (Phillips & Marathon Oil Cos USA). 44,089 tons gross, 32,359 tons dw, 799ft loa × 111·66ft breadth × 32·75ft draught, Kockums turbs, 20,000bhp, 18·25 knots.

POMONA (Sis PONTOS). *Belgian.* Cargo, ref. Built by N. V. Boelwerf SA, Tamise, for Bureau Maritime HG Ahlers, SA. 5,853 tons gross, 7,340 tons dw, 489·5ft loa (incl bb) × 63·84ft breadth × 30·64ft draught, 9-cyl ACEC-MAN diesel, 12,600bhp, 22 knots.

Princess Astrid. *This is the latest of the Belgian Dover-Ostend car ferries, which can accept lorries up to 59ft long, 8·2ft wide and 13ft high, weighing up to 36 tons. She can accommodate 172 vehicles. The Belgian Government now operate 6 passenger ships, each carrying 1,700 passengers, and 5 car ferries, 1 of which carries 100 vehicles, and the others about 160, between Ostend and Harwich-Ostend and Dover. This ship is described in the register of Vol XVII, as she came into service in 1968, but no illustration was available at the time that volume went to press. To recapitulate her dimensions, they are 387ft × 52·5ft × 12·5ft overall, twin 12-cyl Sulzer engines of total 9,600bhp, speed 22 knots, gross tonnage 3,148. A bow thrust propeller is fitted.*

Prinsessan Christina. *Owned by the Gothenburg-Frederikshaven Company of Gothenburg, this ship was named by HRH Princess Christina of Sweden. Capable of carrying 1,400 passengers and 300 cars, she has a more attractive profile than the recent Baltic ferries. She has an active tank stabilizer system for preventing excessive rolling, and a KaMeWa bow thrust propeller to aid in manoeuvring. In light colour Scandinavian style, there are 30 cabins, each 2 berth, for passengers, below the car deck. In the forepart of the saloon deck is a small intimate bar with seating for 50 passengers, and connected with this, on the starboard side are 2 conference rooms, accommodating 12 and 16 persons, and on the port side, a card room with 4 bridge tables. Coffee, tea and sandwiches may be bought at the bar. Aft of this, abaft the entrance hall with kiosks, is a cafeteria, on the starboard side of which is a lorry drivers' saloon. Aft of these again is the main dining saloon, seating 146 persons, decorated in modern Scandinavian style, with a dance floor in the centre, covered with brass. On the boat deck is a small hall with first class cabins, with toilets and bathrooms. The propelling machinery consists of 8 Nohab Polar 12-cyl 4-stroke turbo charged type SF 112 V-SE engines with a total maximum output of 15,600bhp at 750rpm; through gearboxes and couplings, these revolutions are reduced to 280 for the twin KaMeWa controllable pitch propellers.*

POMORZE. *Polish.* Fish factory, ref. Built by Stocznia Gdanska, Gdansk, 1968, for Dalekomorskie Bazy Rybackie, Szczecin. 13,875 tons gross, 9,600 tons dw, 538ft loa × 69·92ft breadth × 25·58ft draught, 6-cyl Cegielski-B & W diesel, 7,200bhp, 15·25 knots.

PONGOLA (Sis TUGELA and another). *South African.* Cargo. Built by Barens SB & E Corpn Ltd, Durban, for Grindrod Gersigny & Co Ltd, Durban (African Coasters Pty Ltd). 2,900 tons gross, 3,500 tons dw, 314ft loa × 47·58ft breadth × 21·52ft draught, 6-cyl Sulzer diesel, 3,000bhp, 13 knots.

PONOY. *Russian.* Cargo. Builder na, Vyborg, for USSR. 4,796 tons gross, tons dw na, 400·09ft loa × 54·92ft breadth × draught na, cyl na, Bryansk diesel, bhp na, knots na.

P

PONTOS. *Belgian*. Cargo, ref. Built by N. V. Boelwerf SA, Tamise, for Bureau Maritime HG Ahlers SA, Antwerp (Mgrs F. Laeisz). 5,824 tons gross, 7,340 tons dw, 489·5ft loa (incl bb) × 63·84ft breadth × 25·66ft draught, 9-cyl ACEC-MAN diesel, 12,800bhp, 22 knots.

PRAG. *German*. Bulk carrier. Built by Bremer Vulkan, Vegesack, for Alfred C. Toepfer Schiffahrtsges mbH, Hamburg. 24,400 tons gross, 43,000 tons dw, 666·09ft loa × 93·5ft m breadth × 37·75ft draught, 9-cyl Bremer Vulkan diesel, 12,600bhp, knots na.

PRINCE MARU No 5. *Japanese*. Vehicle carrier. Built by Kanazashi Zosensho, Shimizu, for Mitsui Muromachi KK, Tokyo. 2,114 tons gross, 3,198 tons dw, 300·92ft loa × 46ft breadth × 19·41ft draught, 6-cyl Hitachi-B & W diesel, 2,950bhp, 13·25 knots.

PRINSESSAN CHRISTINA. *Swedish*. Passenger and car ferry. Built by Aalborg Vaerft A/S, Aalborg, for Rederi A/B Gothenburg-Frederikshavn Linjen, Gothenburg. 6,000 tons gross, tons dw na, 404·33ft loa × 69·09ft breadth × 17ft draught, eight 12-cyl tw sc Nydqvist & Holm Polar diesels, cpp, bow thrust cpp, 15,600bhp, knots na.

PRODROMOS. *Greek*. Cargo. Built by Bartram & Sons Ltd, Sunderland, for Sampsa Cia Nav SA, Piraeus. 9,023 tons gross, 15,000 tons dw, 462·58ft loa × 67·09ft breadth × 29·05ft draught. 5-cyl Clark-Sulzer diesel, 5,500bhp, knots na.

PROLETARSKAYA POBEIDA. *Russian*. Tanker. Built by Stocznia im Komuny Pariskiej, Gdynia, for USSR. 14,203 tons gross, 20,000 tons dw, 581·58ft loa × 73·5ft breadth × 30·75ft draught, 6-cyl Cegielski-Sulzer diesel, 9,600bhp, 16 knots.

PULKOVO. *Russian*. Cargo. Builder na, Vyborg, for USSR. 4,796 tons gross, tons dw na, 400·09ft loa × 54·92ft breadth × draught na, cyl na. Bryansk diesel, bhp na, knots na.

PUMARIN. *Spanish*. Cargo. Built by Corbasa, Santander, for Andres Ruiz de Velasco, Santander. 1,138 tons gross, 1,900 tons dw, 240·5ft loa × 38·09ft breadth × 15·09ft draught, 6-cyl Barreras-Deutz diesel, bhp na, knots na.

PURPLE DOLPHIN. *British*. Cargo. Built by Mitsubishi HI Ltd, Shimonoseki, for Chung Shek Enterprises Co Ltd, Hong Kong (Jebmel S, Mangrs). 9,420 tons gross, 13,450 tons dw, 452ft loa (incl bb) × 65·66ft breadth × 30·5ft draught, 6-cyl Mitsubishi-MAN diesel, 5,600bhp, knots na.

PUSTOZERSK. *Russian*. Cargo. Builder na, Vyborg, for USSR. 4,796 tons gross, tons dw na, 400·09ft loa × 54·92ft breadth × draught na, cyl na, Bryansk diesel, bhp na, knots na.

PYATIDYESYATILYETIYE KOMSOMOLA. *Russian*. Cargo. Built by A. Zdhanov, Leningrad, 1968, for USSR, Zhdanov. 6,630 tons gross, tons dw na, 426·5ft loa × 58·5ft breadth × draught na, 7-cyl Bryansk-B & W diesel, 5,400bhp, knots na.

PYATIDYESYATILYETIYE KOMSOMOLA. *Russian*. Cargo. Built by Volodarsky Shipyard, Rybinsk, 1968, for USSR. 3,500 tons gross, tons dw na, 394ft loa × breadth na × draught na, cyl na, diesel, bhp na, knots na.

PYATIGORSK. *Russian*. Stern trawler, fish factory, ref (ATLANTIK class). Built by Volkswerft Stralsund, Stralsund, 1968, for USSR. 2,567 tons gross, 1,152 tons dw, 269·58ft loa × 44·75ft breadth × 16·41ft draught, two 8-cyl s sc Liebknecht diesel, 2,594bhp, 13·5 knots.

Q

QUEEN ELIZABETH 2. *British*. Passenger (2,025 pass). Built by Upper Clyde Shipbuilders, Clydebank division, Clydebank, for Cunard Line Ltd, Southampton. 65,863 tons gross, 15,724 tons dw, 963ft loa (incl bb) × 105·25ft breadth × 32·64ft draught, tw sc Brown turbs (Pametrada) 2 btp, 110,000shp, 28·5 knots.

Queen Elizabeth 2. *So much has appeared in the press concerning the QE2, that it seems anti-climax to write about her. However, the Cunard Line state that she is operating very satisfactorily, though her first season's cruising from New York to the West Indies has pointed to the need for some minor modifications in decor, with still a little vibration in some cabins. It is hoped to cure these items during her next refit. To describe the accommodation first. The numerous rooms were designed by many internationally known artists and designers, the whole being co-ordinated by Dennis Lennon & Partners in addition to their design of the restaurants. The 4 main staircases are identical in design, with blue, white red and yellow colours extending beyond the staircases to the lift doors, and with matching carpets, in order to assist passenger orientation. Door furniture is common throughout the ship, with the aluminium sections being anodised a soft gold. Of the 13 decks, the top 5 are given over to public rooms, in addition to the bridge and officers' cabins with those below being mainly accommodation. Passengers usually board through the midships lobby, circular in form, with a sunken central seating area. Hide, navy and green are the predominating colours here, with cedar veneered passageways leading away. On the next door down is the sports deck.*

(1) 

(2) 

(1) Theatre Bar. (2) The look out.

Q

with a large area devoted to the needs of children (creche, cinema, and childrens' room), the latter designed by two students of the Royal College of Arts, and which has a shallow pool, cupboards with blackboard doors, chequerboard plastic top tables, and stools which double as large building bricks. The same 2 designed the coffee shop on the boat deck (also for use as a discotheque) the floor is white with a large brown and black bullseye marking the dancing area. Red, black and white with stainless steel are the colours here. On one side and leading aft is a raised gallery with booths and tables and windows on to the promenade deck, with views seaward and at one end a juke box, pin tables, etc. Forward of this is the 763 Club (after the shipyard number of the ship). Designed by Stefan Buzas and Alan Irvine, this aims at a shiplike, warm intimate interior. Tan coloured upholstery with wood veneers and a rich blue/green carpet, with seating in 2 banks around a lowered dance floor is the scheme for this room. These 2 designers designed the London Gallery, designed for picture exhibitions, which runs down the opposite side of the ship to the 'teenagers' arcade. Between this and the arcade is the balcony of the theatre, with arcades and shops by the same designers.

Queen Elizabeth 2. *The Queens' Room.*

Beyond all these is the Double Room (top level), designed by Jon Bannenberg, one of the largest and most dramatic rooms on the ship, seating 800 and covering 20,000sq ft. Used for every activity from morning coffee, drinks, dancing, cabaret, etc., it is the central pivot of the accommodation. Furnished in various shades of red, with flexible lighting and with a great stainless steel curved staircase sweeping down to the lower level, the room has two bars, 1 at each level, the lower one also serving the deck space adjacent above the open air swimming pool. On the opposite side to the Upper Deck Library, the Theatre Bar contrasts with bright red glassfibre. The Theatre was designed by Gaby Schreiber and seats over 500. It has 4 principal functions, namely those of a theatre, a cinema, a conference room, and on Sundays, a church. The type of atmosphere required is obtained by various forms of lighting.

Glassfibre predominates in this room, with the seats being provided with removable flap down trays for conference use, and pockets for short wave receivers for simultaneous interpretation. Seating 815, the Britannia Restaurant with a red, white and blue colour scheme occupies the full width of the ship, with white glassfibre bulkheads, and panoramic views. The ceiling is in cedar veneer. Beyond its double glass doors in the main entrance, is the Look Out, a 2 level room where passengers are able to look forward out to sea and simulate the Bridge. Light movable chairs in glassfibre, bulkheads faced with cedar of Lebanon and an olive green carpet are the features here. On the Quarter Deck below, the fore end of the ship is occupied by the Columbia Restaurant and the main kitchen. Designed by Dennis Lennon & Partners, it seats 500, and is divided into smaller areas. It also extends the full width of the ship. Just forward, and discreetly inaccesible (as it can only be reached from its own bar by a circular staircase from the deck below), is the 100 seat Grill Room. Aft of the Columbia Bar is the Midships Bar, which acts as ante room to the restaurant, and is luxuriously furnished with sofas in sumptuous rice green leather and mohair velvet, with walls lined with the same material. The promenade area outside has white rubber floors, magnolia Formica facings, and brilliant open weave green curtains with dark green

Queen Elizabeth 2. *Main engine control room.*

upholstery. On the port side are the Card Room and the Quarter Deck Library. The latter room, designed by Michael Inchbald, has a peaceful, masculine atmosphere with wood and brass fittings, with wood roller shutters hiding the books when not in use. Bannenberg's Card Room is in shades of green. Further aft is the Queens' Room (designed by Inchbald), which spans the ship, and has a sunny garden like atmosphere. Open screen walls, rather than solid ones are suggested fore and aft in this almost square room by walnut veneer in 3 planes inset with mirrors, flanked by vertical mirrors. A slotted silver plastic ceiling, with lighting behind, gives an airy trellised effect, and the structural columns are encased in great inverted trumpets of white glass-fibre. Abaft this is the Q4 Room, designed by David Hicks. This is a night club opening on to the swimming pool. It has walls panelled in grey flannel in polished aluminium frames, separated by strips of gold leaf. The quarter deck pool is in 5 shades of blue, with a canopy formed by the deck above. The accommodation cabins are of every variety ranging from 1, 2 and 3 main room suites through family cabins to small single berth rooms. Cunard Naval Architects designed the cabins, each with its own lavatory and bath or shower, and all corridors and rooms have fitted carpets. The more expensive suites have been designed by the designers of the Public Rooms. All are air conditioned and fitted with a 6 channel radio console for shipboard and shore programmes and have individual telephones. Officers have been given 5 different colour schemes, and crew cabins are gay, tough and most comfortable. 1,200 tons of fresh water per day can be distilled, there are drive on/off facilities with 2 car lifts for 80 cars belonging to passengers, of whom the ship can accommodate 2,025, with 906 crew. Deck areas comprise 6,000 square yards, there are 2 outdoor and 2 indoor swimming pools and 22 lifts. She is the first ship to have an all purpose computer system, based on the Ferranti Argus 400, which though mainly for data logging and alarm scanning and continuous control of some machinery, also deals with weather routing, hotel stock control and fresh water requirement predictions, and can accept special programmes.

There are 3 Foster Wheeler ESD boilers providing steam for the 2 sets of John Brown-Pametrada turbines, designed to operate at a maximum efficiency at 94,000shp for $28\frac{1}{2}$ knots. The maximum propulsive power is 110,000shp. Design work overall for a replacement Queen Elizabeth started in 1955, and a weight saving exercise was carried out in the Sylvania, building at that time many new ideas being tried, such as lightweight furniture, plastic piping, new deck coverings, etc, were experimented with, so that a decade of service was utilized before being placed into this ship. Two 31·6-ton propellers, 6 bladed, of a special high duty propeller alloy were provided by the Stone Manganese firm, each one having to absorb 55,000shp at 174rpm. The various automatic controls of the engines are carried out by AEI Marecon pneumatic equipment from the turbine control room, the damage control room and the main control room. Entire control of the propulsion machinery is carried out from a turbine control console by the engineers.

On the Bridge are 3 control panels in the Wheelhouse. The pilotage console takes charge of the 2 Stone Manganese bow thrust controls, whistle (Tyfon) controls, Kwant engine room telegraphs, IMR VHF radio telephone system, secondary steering controls and the gyro repeater, loud speaking intercom systems to the fore and aft docking positions, and a GEC-AEL Escort radar. There are 2 auxiliary control panels in the wings. The radar control contains a new type GEC-AEI Compact track computing radar with a range of 48 miles. This set has a computer giving predicted tracks of a given number of targets. Also fitted is a Decca Navigator Mark 12 and a system for using the existing Polar orbiting satellites of the USN System, giving accurate fixes to within 0·1 nautical miles.

The third console has the loud speaker telephones in various parts of the ship, bridge lighting, navigation lights indicator, watertight door controls and indicators, stopping of ventilation fans, stabilizer controls and general alarms.

The ship is also fitted with the new Omega 1 relative navigation receiver of the Northrop Corporation system produced for the USN (mercantile type). There are 4 shore based transmitters operating at present, giving a position fixing of about 2 miles accuracy with full coverage of the North Atlantic; when the remaining 4 stations are completed, global coverage will be achieved.

There are over 3,000 items of fire prevention and protection equipment used throughout the ship, with 34,000ft of the latest fire fighting hose. In her navigation and communication systems, the ship incorporates a number of 'firsts'. The safety control room is manned by a trained operator at all times, and the fire fighting water supply is entirely independent of all other water circuits. A wide variety of detection devices, alarms and extinguishers are controlled from this 24 hour a day manned centre with a complex system of instruments and an illuminated master plan of the ship. The ship has her *own fire brigade. Each cabin is surrounded by incombustible bulkheads, and the structure is entirely incombustible. All furnishing materials conform to low flame spread specifications and all stairways are surrounded by incombustible bulkheads, with remotely controlled doors. She is divided into 15 watertight compartments with electro-hydraulic doors, either closing by the men on the spot, or remotely from the Bridge. The hotel services, galleys, etc, hospital and laundry have every possible facility and modern equipment, 16 kennels for dogs are situated near the funnel, with an airing and exercise space under cover, and there are a number of printing machines for printing the QE2 edition of the Daily Telegraph. It is quite impossible within the limited compass of this book to describe all the details of the radio and hotel and other components, which are all of specially designed and advanced practice, much being of special design for the ship. One might call the whole ship a vast test bed, but for the fact that the equipment has been thoroughly tested in advance, but she has no relation in design to previous ships, being a major floating hotel designed to follow the sun. With a hull somewhat smaller than the earlier Queens, she can do far more and with a superior standard of amenities and accommodation, and with her lighter draught enter many more ports than they. With the experiments successfully carried out in the Carmania and Franconia, the pursers' department as such is phased out. He is replaced by the Hotel Manager who has the combined pursers, stewards and entertainment services under his organization, he being responsible to the Captain.*

RAGNA. *German*. Cargo-container feeder ship (64×35ft containers. 5 years sea-land charter). Built by J. J. Sietas, Hamburg, 1968, for Freidrich Osterwisch, Hamburg. 499 tons gross, 1,160 tons dw, 244·58ft loa×42·09ft m breadth×12·18ft draught, 8-cyl Deutz diesel, 1,500bhp, 13 knots.

RAUMA. *Russian*. Tanker. Built by Rauma-Repola O/Y, Rauma, 1967, for USSR. 3,359 tons gross, 4,600 tons dw, 348·25ft loa×50·66ft breadth× 21·33ft draught, 5-cyl Bryansk-B & W diesel, 2,900bhp, 14 knots.

RAZLOG. *Bulgarian*. Cargo. Builder na, Bulgaria, for Navigation Maritime, Bulgare. 1,346 tons gross, tons dw na, measurements na, cyl na, diesel, bhp na, knots na.

REINHART LORENZ RUSS. *German*. Bulk carrier. Built by Lubecker Flender Werke AG, Lubeck, for Ernst Russ, Hamburg. 26,500 tons gross, tons dw na, 709·09ft loa (incl bb)×92·25ft breadth×38·94ft draught, 6-cyl MAN diesel, 13,800bhp, knots na.

RESEARCHER. *USA*. Oceanographic ship. Built by American SB Co, Lorain, for Dept of Commerce. 2,750 tons gross, tons dw na, 278·25ft loa×51ft breadth×16ft draught, 2-cyl tw sc American Locomotive Co diesels, cpp, 3,200bhp, 15 knots.

RHEIN MARU. *Japanese*. Bulk carrier. Built by Sanoyasu Dockyard Co Ltd, Osaka, for Sanko KKK, Amagasaki. 11,654 tons gross, 18,900 tons dw, 508·5ft loa (incl bb)×74·92ft breadth×29·92ft draught, 7-cyl IHI-Sulzer diesel, 8,400bhp, 14·75 knots.

RIGHTEOUS. *Liberian*. Bulk carrier. Built by Taiwan Shipbuilding Corpn, Keelung, for Righteous Navigation Inc, Monrovia (Taiwan). 17,941 tons gross, 28,158 tons dw, 594·84ft loa×82·18ft breadth×33·66ft draught, 7-cyl Uraga-Sulzer diesel, 11,200bhp, 15·25 knots.

RIGOLETTO. *Swedish*. Bulk carrier. Built by Baltic SB & E Works, Leningrad, for Rederi AB Soya, Stockholm (O. Wallenius). 23,361 tons gross, 35,000 tons dw, 660·5ft loa×91·41ft breadth×35ft draught, 8-cyl Bryansk-B & W diesel, 13,200bhp, 16 knots.

RINGSTAD. *Norwegian*. Bulk carrier. Built by A/S Frederiksstad M/V, Frederiksstad, for Olav Ringdal. 21,820 tons gross, 36,700 tons dw, 635·09ft loa×86·18ft breadth×33·66ft draught, 8-cyl Frederiksstad-Gotaverken diesel, 10,700bhp, knots na.

RINSEI MARU. *Japanese*. Cargo. Built by Tohoku Zosen, Shiogama, for Sanko KKK, Amagasaki. 6,362 tons gross, 10,157 tons dw, 418·58ft loa×62·66ft breadth×24·5ft draught, 8-cyl Hitachi-B & W diesel, 5,000bhp, knots na.

R

RITSA. *Russian*. Fish factory, ref. Built by NV Kon Maats 'De Schelde', Flushing, for USSR, Kertch. 4,199 tons gross, 2,600 tons dw, 340·09ft loa × 54·58ft breadth × 18·11ft draught, 8-cyl De Schelde-Sulzer diesel, cpp, 3,000bhp, 14 knots.

RIVADEMAR. *Spanish*. Cargo. Built by Ast del Cantabrico & Riera, Gijon, for Vapores Suardiaz SA, Gijon. 4,700 tons gross, tons dw na, 429·75ft loa × 57·5ft breadth × draught na, 6-cyl Terrestre y Mar-B & W diesel, 4,600bhp, knots na.

RIVER ETHIOPE. *Nigerian*. Cargo. Built by Rheinstahl Nordseewerke, Emden, for Nigerian National Shipping Line Ltd, Lagos. 5,373/7,827 tons gross, 8,130/10,360 tons dw, 447·92ft loa × 62·5ft breadth × na/31·33ft draught, 6-cyl Cockerill-B & W diesel, 7,200bhp, 16·5 knots.

RIZHSKIY ZALIV. *Russian*. Fish carrier, ref. Built by Dubigeon-Normandie, Nantes, for USSR. 13,000 tons gross, tons dw na, 540ft loa × 72·33ft breadth × 26·25ft draught, two 12-cyl s sc Bretagne-Pielstick diesel, 11,160bhp, 17·5 knots.

ROBERT L. D. *French*. Ore carrier. Built by Ch de l'Atlantique, St Nazaire, for SA Louis Dreyfus & Cie, Dunkerque. 12,705 tons gross, 19,081 tons dw, 498·58ft loa × 74·25ft breadth × 31·46ft draught, two 12-cyl s sc Atlantique Pielstick diesel, 11,160bhp, 16 knots.

ROKKO MARU. *Japanese*. Vehicle carrier (Catamaran hull). Built by Nippon Kokan, Shimizu, for Kansai KKK, Osaka. 2,700 tons gross, tons dw na, 272·33ft loa × 82·09ft breadth × 15·33ft draught, four 8-cyl tw sc Daihatsu diesel, 6,400bhp, knots na.

ROKKO MARU. *Japanese*. Cargo. Built by Hashihama Zosen, Imabari, 1968, for Daiichi Sempaku KK, Kobe. 2,951 tons gross, 5,014 tons dw, 308·41ft lbp × 49·33ft breadth × 20·92ft draught, 7-cyl Hatsudoki diesel, 3,000bhp, 12 knots.

ROSA LUXEMBURG. *Russian*. Cargo CSD. Built by Stocznia Gdanska, Gdansk, for USSR. 10,183 tons gross, 12,725 tons dw, 507·41ft loa × 67·66ft breadth × 29·5ft draught, 6-cyl Cegielski-Sulzer diesel, 9,600bhp, 18·25 knots.

RUGWARDERSAND. *German*. Cargo, part containers (two 20-ton derricks). Built by Elsflether Werft A/G, Elsfleth, for Helmut Meyer, Brake. 814/1,596 tons gross, na/2,900 tons dw, 259·84ft loa × 42·33ft breadth × 14·97/19·82ft draught, 8-cyl Atlas-MaK diesel, 3,000bhp, 14 knots.

RUPERT DE LARRINAGA. *British*. Cargo. Built by Austin & Pickersgill Ltd, Sunderland, for Larrinaga SS Co Ltd, Liverpool. 9,268 tons gross, 15,000 tons dw, 462·58ft loa × 67·09ft breadth × 29·05ft draught, 5-cyl Hawthorn-Sulzer diesel, 6,100bhp, knots na.

RYUHAKU MARU. *Japanese*. Cargo. Built by Onomichi Zosen, Onomichi, 1968, for Maruni Shokai KK, Fukuoka. 3,980 tons gross, 5,900 tons dw, 329·41ft lbp × 53·92ft breadth × 22·18ft draught, 6-cyl Mitsubishi-Sulzer diesel, 3,500bhp, 12·75 knots.

RYUKO MARU. *Japanese*. Cargo. Built by Osaka Zosensho, Osaka, for Sanko KKK, Amagasaki. 11,631 tons gross, 18,000 tons dw, 506·33ft loa (incl bb) × 74·84ft breadth × 29·92ft draught, 7-cyl IHI-Sulzer diesel, 8,700bhp, knots na.

RYUSHO MARU. *Japanese*. Cargo. Built by Kanazashi Zosen, Shimizu, for Ryuku KKK, Naha. 3,842 tons gross, 6,206 tons dw, 361·25ft loa × 53·25ft breadth × 21·66ft draught, 6-cyl Ito Tekkosho diesel, 3,400bhp, knots na.

S

S. A. MORGENSTAR. *South African*. Cargo, ref. Built by Mitsui Zosen, Fujinagata, for South African Marine Corpn, Cape Town. 7,343/10,596 tons gross, na/13,225 tons dw, 551·18ft loa × 75ft breadth × 30/31·72ft draught, 6-cyl Uraga-Sulzer diesel, 15,000bhp, 20 knots.

S. A. VERGELEGEN. *South African*. Cargo, ref. Built by Mitsui Zosen, Fujinagata, for South African Marine Corpn, Cape Town. 10,600 tons gross, 11,470 tons dw, 551·84ft loa (incl bb) × 75ft breadth × 30ft draught, 6-cyl Uraga-Sulzer diesel, 15,000bhp, 20 knots.

SAAR. *German*. Cargo. Built by Lubecker Flender Werke AG, Lubeck, for Friedrich A. Detjen, Hamburg. 9,000 tons gross, 15,300 tons dw, 487·58ft loa × 69·25ft breadth × 30·94ft draught, 8-cyl MAN diesel, 11,200bhp, knots na.

Last of 3 sister ships from Mitsui, the S. A. Vergelegen can carry in addition to general and refrigerated cargoes 209 ISO 20ft containers. The other 2 ships are the S. A. Constantia and S. A. Morgenstea. Designed for the Cape-New York route they are powered by Uraga-Sulzer 6RD90 diesels, giving a trial speed of 23 knots at 122rpm (15,000bhp) (service speed 21½ knots at 116rpm, 12,750bhp). Remote control of the main machinery and cargo temperature recording system is fitted. Eighteen 5-ton derricks and two 30-ton derricks are fitted, and temperatures from 12°C to —30°C can be maintained in the refrigerated holds (4 holds out of 6).

S

SABOGAL. *Peruvian.* Cargo. Built by OY Wartsila A/B, Abo, for Corporacion Peruana de Vapores, Callao. 7,000/9,464 tons gross, 10,000/13,700 tons dw, 492·18ft loa × 64·75ft breadth × draught na, 6-cyl Wartsila-Sulzer diesel, 9,600bhp, 17 knots.

SACHIKAZE MARU. *Japanese.* Fish meal carrier. Built by Setoda Zosen, Setoda, for Nippon Suisan KK, Tokyo. 2,860 tons gross, 4,300 tons dw, 295·35ft lbp × 48·58ft breadth × 20·33ft draught, 8-cyl IHI-Sulzer diesel, 3,360bhp, knots na.

SAGANOSEKI MARU. *Japanese.* Ore carrier (nickel). Built by Maizuru Jugkogyo Ltd, Maizuru, for Nissho KK, Tokyo. 12,093 tons gross, 19,304 tons dw, 492·18ft lbp × 74·25ft breadth × 29·5ft draught, 6-cyl Maizuru-Sulzer diesel, 7,200bhp, 14 knots.

ST LAWRENCE MARU. *Japanese.* Bulk carrier. Built by Sanoyasu Dkyd Ltd, Osaka, for Sanko KKK, Amagasaki. 12,700 tons gross, 19,800 tons dw, 514·66ft loa × 74·92ft breadth × 32·41ft draught, 8-cyl Hitachi-B & W diesel, 10,700bhp, knots na.

ST MARTIN. *Philippine.* Cargo. Built by Tohoku Zosen, Shiogama, for Oceanic Shipping Corpn, Manila. 3,880 tons gross, 5,977 tons dw, 358·92ft loa × 52·84ft breadth × 21·66ft draught, 6-cyl Hatsudoki diesel, 3,800bhp, 15 knots.

SAINT MICHEL. *French.* Cargo, ref. Built by Warnowwerft, Warnemunde, for Soc Navale de l'Ouest, Dunkerque. 8,718 tons gross, 12,710 tons dw, 494·41ft loa × 65·84ft breadth × 29·05ft draught, 8-cyl DMR-MAN diesel, 9,600bhp, knots na.

SAINTONGE (Sis DAUPHINE). *French.* Tanker. Built by Ch de l'Atlantique (Penhoet-Loire), St Nazaire, for Soc Francaise de Transports Petroliers, Dunkerque. 60,104 tons gross, 115,418 tons dw, 902ft loa × 135·5ft breadth × 49·41ft draught, 10-cyl Atlantique-B & W diesel, 23,100bhp, 16·75 knots.

SAIPEM LINCE (Sis SAIPEM ORSA). *Italian.* Oil rig supply vessel. Built by Cant Nav M & B Benetti, Viareggio, for Societa Azione Italiana Perforazione e Montaggi (Mgrs 'SNAM' Soc Nazionale Metanoditti SpA, Genoa). 758 tons gross, 994 tons dw, 184ft loa × 37·5ft breadth × 13·5ft draught, two 8-cyl tw sc Fiat diesel, 2,700bhp, 14 knots.

SAN JUAN VANGUARD. *Liberian.* Ore/oil carrier. Built by Kawasaki HI Ltd, Kobe, for San Juan Vanguard Corpn, Monrovia (San Juan Carriers, San Francisco). 75,048 tons gross, 130,668 tons dw, 948·18ft loa (incl bb) × 138ft breadth × 52·33ft draught, Kawasaki turbs, 23,500shp, 16 knots.

SAN JUAN VENTURER. *Liberian.* Ore/oil carrier. Built by Mitsubishi HI Ltd, Yokohama, for San Juan Venturer Corpn, Monrovia. 75,269 tons gross, 131,322 tons dw, 957·33ft loa (incl bb) × 138ft breadth × 52·33ft draught, Mitsubishi turbs, 23,500bhp, 16 knots.

SANDAR. *Norwegian.* Bulk carrier. Built by A/S Frederiksstad M/V, Frederiksstad, for Harald Virik, Sandefjord. 21,836 tons gross, 36,650 tons dw, 635ft loa × 86·18ft breadth × 37·64ft draught, 8-cyl Frederiksstad-Gotaverken diesel, 10,700bhp, 14·75 knots.

SANTAGATA. *Italian.* Bulk carrier. Built by Italcantieri SpA, Genoa, 1967, for 'NEREIDE' Soc per Azione di Navigazione, Palermo. 39,665 tons gross, 66,841 tons dw, 800ft loa (incl bb) × 106·09ft breadth × 42·63ft draught, 8-cyl Ansaldo-Fiat diesel, 18,400bhp, 16 knots.

SANTANDER. *Spanish.* Tanker. Built by Astano SA, Ferrol, for Naviera Castilla SA, Santander. 53,000 tons gross, tons dw na, 871·5ft loa × 127·92ft breadth × draught na, 9-cyl SECN diesel, bhp na, knots na.

SAO MARCOS (launched as DENIB). *Brazilian.* OSD/CSD. Built by Estaleiro So, Porto Alegre, 1968, for L. Figueirido Navegacao SA, Santos 1,308/1,996 tons gross, 2,165/2,992 tons dw, 259·58ft loa × 41·09ft breadth × 16·64/20·37ft draught, 7-cyl Ishibras-Sulzer diesel, 1,680bhp, 12 knots.

SASHA KONDRATYEV. *Russian.* Cargo. Built by Schiffsw Neptun, Rostock, 1968, for USSR, Vladivostok. 3,684 tons gross, 4,638 tons dw, 346·75ft loa × 51·33ft breadth × 22·18ft draught, 6-cyl Halberstadt-MAN diesel, 3,250bhp, knots na.

S

SASHA KOVALYOV. *Russian*. Cargo. Built by Schiffsw Neptun, Rostok, 1968, for USSR, Murmansk. 3,685 tons gross, 4,638 tons dw, 347·75ft loa × 51·33ft breadth × 22·18ft draught, 6-cyl Halberstadt-MAN diesel, 3,250bhp, 13·75 knots.

SCHLESWIG-HOLSTEIN. *German*. Ferry. Built by D. W. Krehmer Sohn, Elmshorn, for Grune Kustenstrasse GmbH & Co KG, Brunsbuttel. 700 tons gross, tons dw na, 199·18ft loa × 39·75ft breadth × 13·2ft draught, two 8-cyl s sc Atlas-MaK diesel, 2,500bhp, 15 knots.

SCILLA. *German*. Cargo. Built by Schps 'De Hoop', Lobith, for Partenreederei Hamburg, Elsfleth. 999 tons gross, 2,400 tons dw, 266·41ft loa × 48·84ft breadth × 22·66ft draught, 8-cyl Atlas-MaK diesel, 3,000bhp, knots na.

SCOTSPARK. *British*. Bulk carrier. Built by Upper Clyde Shipbuilders (Scotstoun Div), Scotstoun, for J. & J. Denholm (Management) Ltd Glasgow. 16,743 tons gross, 26,000 tons dw, 580ft loa × 75·18ft breadth × draught na, 6-cyl Kincaid-B & W diesel, 11,600bhp, knots na.

SEA HORSE. *Belgian*. Tug. Built by N. V. Boelwerf SA, Tamise, for Union de Remorquage & Sauvetage SA, Antwerp. 200 tons gross, tons dw na, 116·84ft loa × 32·75ft breadth × 12·8ft draught, two 8-cyl Anglo-Belgian Co SA, directional propeller, bhp na, knots na.

SEA SOVEREIGN. *Swedish*. Tanker. Built by Kockums M/V A/B, Malmo, for Salenrederiana A/B, Stockholm. 107,286 tons gross, 210,000 tons dw, 1,037ft loa × 160ft m breadth × 62·37ft draught, Kockums-Stal Laval turbs, 32,000shp, knots na.

SEAFALCON. *Norwegian*. Tanker. Built by Smith's Dock Co Ltd, Middlesborough, for Graff-Wang & Evjen, Oslo. 1,999 tons gross, 5,200 tons dw, 354ft loa × 50·92ft breadth × 21·33ft draught, 16-cyl Smit & Bolnes diesel, cpp, 3,200bhp, knots na.

SEA FREEZE ATLANTIC. (Sis SEA FREEZE PACIFIC). *USA*. Stern trawler, ref (processes 124tp day fish fillets plus 5tpd fishmeal). Built by Maryland SB & DD Co, Baltimore, for American Stern Trawlers Inc, Wilmington, Del. 1,593 tons gross, 1,692 tons dw, 295ft loa × 44·33ft breadth × 18·66ft draught, two 12-cyl; one 8-cyl, tw sc General Motors diesel-electric, 3,975bhp, 14·5 knots.

SEA FREEZE PACIFIC. *USA*. Stern trawler, ref. Built by Maryland SB & DD Co, Baltimore, for American Stern Trawlers Inc, Wilmington, Del. 1,593 tons gross, 1,692 tons dw, 295ft loa × 44·33ft breadth × 18·66ft draught, two 12-cyl; one 8-cyl, tw sc General Motors diesel-electric, 3,975bhp, 14·5 knots.

SEATERN. *Norwegian*. Tanker. Built by Smith's Dock Co Ltd, Middlesborough, for Graff-Wang & Evjen, Oslo. 1,999 tons gross, 5,200 tons dw 354ft loa × 50·92ft breadth × 21·33ft draught, 16-cyl Smit & Bolnes diesel, cpp, 3,200bhp, knots na.

SEEFELDERSAND. *German*. Cargo, part container ship OSD/CSD. Built by C. Luhring, Brake, for Helmut Meyer, Brake. 999/1,999 tons gross, 2,200/3,400 tons dw, 304·75ft loa × 44·25ft m breadth × 15·25/20ft draught, 12-cyl Deutz diesel, 3,000bhp, 15 knots.

SEIHA MARU. *Japanese*. Salvage tug, Built by Hashihama Zosen, Imabari, for Nippon Salvage KK, Tokyo. 1,000 tons gross, tons dw na, 187ft lbp × 34·75ft m breadth × draught na, 6-cyl Aksasaka Tekkosho diesel, bhp na, knots na.

SEIKAN MARU. *Japanese*. Ferry. Built by Taguma Zosen, Hiroshima, 1967, for Donan KKK, Hakodate. 850 tons gross, 340 tons dw, 206·75ft lbp × 39·41ft breadth × 9·66ft draught, two 6-cyl tw sc Daihatsu diesel, 2,600bhp, knots na.

SEIKAN MARU No 2. *Japanese*. Ferry. Built by Taguma Zosen, Innoshima, 1968, for Donan KKK, Hakodate. 990 tons gross, 353 tons dw, 206·75ft lbp × 39·41ft breadth × 10ft draught, two 8-cyl Daihatsu diesel, 2,660bhp, knots na.

SEIKAN MARU No 5. *Japanese*. Ferry. Built by Taguma Zosen Innoshima, 1968, for Higashi Nippon Ferry KK, Hakodate. 999 tons gross, 407 tons dw, 206·75ft lbp × 46·58ft breadth × 10ft draught, two 8-cyl tw sc Daihatsu diesel, 2,600bhp, 16 knots.

SEIKO MARU. *Japanese*. Tanker. Built by Imabari Zosen, Imabari, for Shoei KKK, Imabari. 999 tons gross, 2,486 tons dw, 234·75ft loa × 37·5ft breadth × 17·96ft draught, 6-cyl Daihatsu diesel, 1,500bhp, knots na.

Scotspark. *Built for the Scotspark Shipping Co under the management of Messrs J. & J. Denholm (Management) Ltd of Glasgow. This firm manages a large number of ships of sizes from small and moderate to mammoth, for various owners, including Wm Brandts (Leasing) of London, Advanport Ltd, London, British Steam Shipping Co Ltd of Cardiff, The Denholm Line Steamers, Hopepark Shipping Co Ltd, St Andrew Shipping Co Ltd, H. Clarkson & Co Ltd, London, Falkland Shipowners Ltd, Light Shipping Co Ltd, Glasgow, Scottish Ore Carriers Ltd, Naess Denholm Ltd (with various other Naess companies), Buckingham Tanker Co Ltd, Anglo-Norness Shipping Co, being the main ones, with recently, the packaged lumber carriers of the British section of the SCANSCOT pool. Due to a large amount of equipment being installed before launching, this ship was completed in 10 weeks after launch. She is a self trimmer, designed for loading ore in alternate holds. Cargo is carried in 7 holds (one of which is a short deep tank/hold), with topsides arranged for carrying water ballast or grain. The double bottom forms hoppered sides for water ballast. In addition to the 7 large hatches, there are 40 small grain loading hatches fitted to the topside tanks. The main hatch covers are of the Macgregor electrically operated chain drive type. There are 5 electro-hydraulic deck cranes of 8 tons capacity, with two 3-ton store derricks aft. There is an engine room control room, air conditioned, and the main and auxiliary machinery is arranged for automatic control to unmanned engine room standard. The complement of 36 have extensive accommodation, ratings having a smoke room, bar and dining room, officers a lounge, lounge-bar and dining room, with a laundry, hospital and owners' suite.*

Sea Horse. *The Towage & Salvage Union of Antwerp, normally engaged in towage in that port area, has taken delivery of the first of 2 tugs for sea towage. The* Sea Horse *is driven by 2 diesel engines powering 1 controllable pitch propeller in a Kort nozzle, with a total of 3,000bhp. She is fully automated, and her engines can run for 24 hours without any attendance, the master having full bridge control at hand. She is equipped with most extensive communication and navigation equipment, with a hydraulic towing winch capable of a static pull of 120 tons, and she can tow 3 objects at once or each individually. 2 fire extinguishing monitors are carried, capable of foam or water ejection. The towing hook is provided with a hydraulic quick release arrangement. With the new tugs, the Company, besides covering most Belgian ports, will now be able to undertake open sea work in European waters.*

SEIKO MARU No 8. *Japanese*. Tanker. Built by Kishimoto Zosen, Kinoe, for Konan Shoji YK, Shimizu. 999 tons gross, 2,000 tons dw 233·92ft loa × 36·18ft breadth × 16·41ft draught, 8-cyl Daihatsu diesel, 2,000bhp, knots na.

SEINE MARU. *Japanese*. Cargo. Built by Onomichi Zosen, Onomichi, 1968, for Shinko KK, Himeji. 10,878 tons gross, 16,300 tons dw, 504·84ft loa (incl bb) × 73ft breadth × 28·75ft draught, 7-cyl Hitachi-B & W diesel, 8,400bhp, 14·75 knots.

SEISHO MARU. *Japanese*. Cargo. Built by Imabari Zosen, Imabari, for Shoei KKK, Imabari. 2,998 tons gross, 5,800 tons dw, 314·92ft lbp × 53·5ft breadth × 22ft draught, 6-cyl Hatsudoki diesel, 3,800bhp, knots na.

S

SEMARANG MARU. *Japanese*. Cargo. Built by Mitsubishi HI, Shimonoseki, for Tokyo Sempaku KK, Tokyo. 6,750 tons gross, 9,700 tons dw, 433·92ft loa × 60·5ft breadth × 27·25ft draught, two 6-cyl s sc Mitsubishi-MAN diesel, 6,720bhp, knots na.

SEMYON KOSINOV. *Russian*. Cargo. Built by A. Zhdanov, Leningrad, 1968, for USSR, Leningrad. 4,896 tons gross, tons dw na, 400·09ft loa × 54·92ft breadth × 22·22ft draught, 9-cyl Bryansk-B & W diesel, bhp na, knots na.

SERANTES. *Spanish*. Bulk carrier. Built by Cia Euskalduna, Bilbao, for Nav Vascongada SA & Nav Bilbaina SA, Bilbao. 15,494 tons gross, 26,700 tons dw, 599ft loa × 73·58ft breadth × 32ft draught, 7-cyl Euskalduna-MAN diesel, 9,800bhp, 15·5 knots.

SEREBRYANSK. *Russian*. Cargo. Builder na, owner na. 9,547 tons gross, tons dw na, measurements na, cyl na, make na, bhp na, knots na.

SEROV. *Russian*. Cargo. Built by Kherson Shipyard, Kherson, for USSR. 9,547 tons gross, tons dw na, 501·33ft loa × 67·58ft breadth × 29·59ft draught, 6-cyl Bryansk-B & W diesel, 9,000bhp, 17 knots.

SERVUS. *Swedish*. Container feeder ship (12 pass), stern door. Built by Jos L. Meyer, Papenburg, for Stockholms Rederi A/B Svea, Stockholm. 2,232 tons gross, 2,775 tons dw, 358·41ft loa (incl bb) × 54·92ft breadth × 16·29ft draught, two 8-cyl tw sc Deutz diesel, cpp, btp, 5,000bhp, 17 knots.

SEVAN. *Russian*. Cargo. Built by Kherson Shipyard, Kherson, for USSR. 9,547 tons gross, tons dw na, 501·33ft loa × 67·58ft breadth × 29·59ft draught, 6-cyl Bryansk-B & W diesel, 9,000bhp, 17 knots.

SEVEN SEAS. *Dutch*. Cargo OSD/CSD. Built by Schps 'Harlingen', Harlingen, 1968, for Rederij 'Bothnia', Harlingen. 499/1,259 tons gross, 1,200/2,184 tons dw, 239·58ft loa × 37·41ft breadth × 11·2/17·2ft draught, 6-cyl Industrie diesel, 1,500bhp, 13 knots.

SEVER. *Russian*. Stern trawler, fish factory, ref. Builder na, Russia, 1967, for USSR, Murmansk. 1,941 tons gross, 695 tons dw, 233ft loa × 43ft breadth × 16·44ft draught, three 6-cyl s sc Russian diesel-electric, bhp na, 13·25 knots.

SEVERNAJA PALMIRA. *Russian*. Stern trawler, fish factory, ref. Builder na, Russia, 1967, for USSR, Leningrad. 3,162 tons gross, 1,428 tons dw, 277·92ft loa × 46ft breadth × 18·69ft draught, 8-cyl Skoda diesel, bhp na, 12·5 knots.

SEVERODONETSK. *Russian*. Cargo. Built by Kherson Shipyard, Kherson, 1968, for USSR. 9,457 tons gross, tons dw na, 501·33ft loa × 67·58ft breadth × 29·59ft draught, 6-cyl Bryansk-B & W diesel, 9,000bhp, 17 knots.

SEZELA. *South African*. Cargo. Built by Barens SB & E Co Ltd, Durban, for African Coasters Pty (Grindrod, Gersigny & Co Pty Ltd), Durban. 3,100 tons gross, 4,500 tons dw, 314ft loa × 47·58ft breadth × 22ft draught, 6-cyl Sulzer diesel, 3,000bhp, knots na.

SHIMA MARU. *Japanese*. Wood chip carrier (2 travelling cranes). Built by Uraga HI Ltd, Yokosuka, for Nippon Yusen Kaisha & Chiyoda KKK, Tokyo. 31,899 tons gross, 39,300 tons dw, measurements na, cyl na, make na, bhp na, knots na.

SHIMA MARU. *Japanese*. Cargo. Built by Shin-Yamamoto Zosen, Kochi, for Shimaya KKK, Tokushima. 3,999 tons gross, tons dw na, 333·09ft lbp × 53·92ft breadth × draught na, 6-cyl Mitsubishi-Sulzer diesel, 4,600bhp, knots na.

SHINEI MARU No 1. *Japanese*. Cargo. Built by Imabari Zosen, Imabari, for Imabari Sempaku KK, Miyakubo. 2,996 tons gross, 5,800 tons dw, 314·92ft lbp × 53·5ft breadth × 22ft draught, 6-cyl Hanshin diesel, 3,500bhp, knots na.

SHINFUKUSHO MARU. *Japanese*. Cargo. Built by Ujina Zosensho, Hiroshima, 1968, for Fukusho KK, Ube. 2,691 tons gross, 4,576 tons dw, 311ft loa × 47·58ft breadth × 20·18ft draught, 6-cyl Akasaka-Tekkosho diesel, 3,000bhp, 14 knots.

SHINJU MARU. *Japanese*. Cargo. Built by Miho Zosen, Shimizu, for Kuribayashi Shosen KK, Tokyo. 2,176 tons gross, 3,084 tons dw, 313ft loa × 48ft breadth × 19·66ft draught, 9-cyl Nippon-Kokan diesel, 4,185bhp, knots na.

Servus. The Svea Line's new ship Servus is employed on the joint Svea-Ellerman Wilson between Hull and Gothenburg supplementing the latters' passenger carrying Spero. Though she can carry 12 passengers she will be employed solely in her role of a roll on-roll off cargo container ship, loading through her stern doors 124 ISO 20ft containers, or an equivalent number of flats, packaged timber trailers or other wheeled cargo. She carries a 25-ton fork lift truck for stowing these containers 2 high. Her crew consists of 17 men, and her twin KaMeWa propellers are bridge controlled, and driven by two 8-cyl Deutz diesels SBV8M358 each developing 2,500bhp at 284rpm.

SHINKO MARU. *Japanese.* Cargo (timber). Built by Hayashikane Zosen, Shimonoseki, for Horie Sempaku KK, Kitakuyushu. 10,479 tons gross, 16,500 tons dw, 486·92ft loa × 73·92ft breadth × 29·25ft draught, 6-cyl Mitsubishi-Sulzer diesel, 8,000bhp, 15·5 knots.

SHINNAN MARU. *Japanese.* Cargo. Built by Kurushima Dock Co Ltd, Imabari, 1968, for Kitanihon KKK, Tokyo. 2,960 tons gross, 5,000 tons dw, 295·25ft lbp × 51·25ft breadth × 20·92ft draught, 6-cyl Mitsubishi-Sulzer diesel, 3,500bhp, 12·5 knots.

SHINSUI MARU No 1. *Japanese.* Tanker. Built by Taihei Kogyo, Hiroshima, for Toshin Yusosen KK, Tokyo. 1,501 tons gross, 3,041 tons dw, 264·25ft loa × 40·41ft breadth × 18·7ft draught, 6-cyl Hanshin diesel, 2,400bhp, knots na.

SHINTAI MARU. *Japanese.* Cargo. Built by Hashihama Zosen, Imabari, for Shinko KKK, Osaka. 6,082 tons gross, 9,500 tons dw, 390·41ft lbp × 60·09ft breadth × 24·58ft draught, 6-cyl Hatsudoki diesel, 5,400bhp, knots na.

SHINYO MARU. *Japanese.* Cargo (timber). Built by Onomichi Zosen, Onomichi, 1968, for Kokyuo KKK, Kobe. 4,598 tons gross, 7,150 tons dw, 373·66ft loa × 57·18ft breadth × 22·66ft draught, 6-cyl Mitsubishi-Sulzer diesel, 4,600bhp, 13·5 knots.

SHOAN MARU. *Japanese.* Cargo. Built by Koyo Dock, Mihara, 1968, for Kihara Shoji KK, Tokyo. 1,998 tons gross, 3,547 tons dw, 286·33ft loa × 44·33ft breadth × 18·75ft draught, 6-cyl Hatsudoki diesel, 2,200bhp, 14·5 knots.

SHOEI MARU No 1. *Japanese.* Cement carrier. Built by Kanmon Zosen, Shimonoseki for Kitakyushu Unyu KK, Kitakyushu. 903 tons gross, 1,350 tons dw, 199·41ft loa × 33·84ft breadth × 15·09ft draught, 6-cyl Daihatsu diesel, 1,200bhp, knots na.

SHOEN MARU. *Japanese.* Tanker. Built by Kawasaki HI Ltd, Sakkaide, for Showa KKK, Tokyo. 102,598 tons gross, 198,940 tons dw, 990·84ft lbp × 165·5ft breadth × 59·75ft draught, Kawasaki turbs, 34,000shp, knots na.

S

SHOJU MARU. *Japanese*. Tanker. Built by Ishikawajima-Harima HI, Yokohama, for Idemitsu Tanker KK, Tokyo. 109,080 tons gross, 202,400 tons dw, 1,034·66ft loa (incl bb) × 164·18ft breadth × 61·84ft draught, IHI turbs, 33,000shp, 15·75 knots.

SHOKYO MARU. *Japanese*. Ore carrier. Built by Nippon Kokan, Tsurumi, for Showa KKK, Tokyo. 44,876 tons gross, 78,571 tons dw, 813·75ft loa (incl bb) × 120·18ft breadth × 41·41ft draught, 6-cyl Uraga-Sulzer diesel, 15,000bhp, 14 knots.

SHOYO MARU. *Japanese*. Cargo. Built by Kurushima Dock Co Ltd, Imabari, for Yamato KKK, Mikame. 2,999 tons gross, 5,450 tons dw, 301·84ft lbp × 52·5ft breadth × 18·25ft draught, 6-cyl Akasaka-Tekkosho diesel, 3,000bhp, knots na.

SHOZUI MARU. *Japanese*. Bulk carrier. Built by Nippon Kokan, Tsurumi, for Showa KKK, Tokyo. 32,940 tons gross, 58,026 tons dw, 746·92ft loa (incl bb) × 104·18ft breadth × 38·92ft draught, 6-cyl Uraga-Sulzer diesel, 15,000bhp, 15 knots.

SHUN HING. *Liberian*. Cargo. Built by Ujina Zosensho, Hiroshima, for Mutual SN (Liberia) Corpn, Monrovia. 3,046 tons gross, 5,009 tons dw, 326·09ft loa × 50ft breadth × 20·86ft draught, 6-cyl Hatsudoki diesel, 3,500bhp, 13·5 knots.

SHUNYO MARU. *Japanese*. Bulk carrier. Built by Namura Zosensho, Osaka, for Taiheiyo Kinkai Sempaku KK & Dainikko Sempaku KK, Tokyo. 9,463 tons gross, 15,480 tons dw, 474·84ft loa × 71·25ft breadth × 28·18ft draught, 14-cyl Mitsubishi-MAN diesel, 7,600bhp, knots na.

SHUSEI MARU. *Japanese*. Cargo. Built by Kanazashi Zosensho, Shimizu, for Itochu Shoji KK, Tokyo. 4,020 tons gross, 6,100 tons dw, 361·25ft loa × 53·25ft breadth × 21·33ft draught, 8-cyl IHI-Pielstick diesel ,3,200bhp, 12·5 knots.

SIBENIK. *Yugoslavian*. Cargo. Built by Cockerill Yards (Hoboken), Hoboken, for Splobodna Plovidba, Sibenik. 9,333 tons gross, tons dw na, 461ft loa × 67·33ft breadth × 30·37ft draught, 5-cyl Stork diesel, 5,500bhp, knots na.

SIBOTO. *Norwegian*. Ore/bulk/oil carrier. Built by A/B Gotaverken, Gothenburg, 1968, for Tschudi & Eitzen, Oslo. 44,326 tons gross, 76,500 tons dw, 848·58ft loa × 105·92ft breadth × 45·07ft draught, 8-cyl Gotaverken diesel, 17,600bhp, 16 knots.

SIBOTRE. *Norwegian*. Ore/bulk/oil carrier. Built by A/B Gotaverken, Gothenburg, for Tschudi & Eitzen, Oslo. 44,327 tons gross, 76,500 tons dw, 848·58ft loa × 105·84ft breadth × 47·04ft draught, 8-cyl Gotaverken diesel, 17,600bhp, 16 knots.

SILVEREID. *British*. Chemical tanker. Built by Hall, Russell & Co Ltd, Aberdeen, for Silver Chemical Tankers Ltd, London. 1,596 tons gross, 2,470 tons dw, 300ft loa × 40·09ft breadth × 16ft draught, 6-cyl Mirrlees National diesel, cpp, 2,520bhp, 13 knots.

SILVERHAWK. *British*. Tanker. Built by Cammell Laird & Co (SB & E) Ltd, Birkenhead, for Nile SS Co Ltd (Silver Line Ltd Managers), London. 6,771 tons gross, 9,760 tons dw, 427·18ft loa × 66ft breadth × 24·25ft draught, 14-cyl Crossley-Pielstick diesel, 6,510bhp, knots na.

SIMSMETAL. *Greek*. Bulk carrier (strengthened for ore). Built by Doxford & Sunderland SB & E Co Ltd, Deptford yard, Sunderland, for Zante Navegacion SA, Piraeus. 12,748 tons gross, 20,410 tons dw, 525ft loa (incl bb) × 75ft breadth × 30ft draught, 6-cyl Hawthorn-Sulzer diesel, 10,200bhp, 15·5 knots.

SINGAPORE PRIDE. *Singapore*. Cargo, ref. Built by Uraga HI Ltd, Yokosuka, for Malaysia Marine Corpn, Singapore (C. Y. Tung). 11,208 tons gross, 13,599 tons dw, 529·84ft loa (incl bb) × 76·92ft breadth × 32·46ft draught, 9-cyl Uraga-Sulzer diesel, 14,400bhp, 21 knots.

SINGAPORE TRIUMPH. *Singapore*. Cargo, ref. Built by Uraga HI, Ltd, Yokosuka, for Malaysia Marine Corpn, Singapore (C. Y. Tung) 11,208 tons gross, 13,593 tons dw, 529·84ft loa (incl bb) × 76·92ft breadth × 32·5ft draught, 9-cyl Uraga-Sulzer diesel, 14,400bhp, 21 knots.

SIVASH. *Russian*. Stern trawler, fish factory, ref (ATLANTIK class). Built by Volkswerft Stralsund, Stralsund, for USSR, Kerch. 2,657 tons gross, 1,152 tons dw, 269·58ft loa × 44·75ft breadth × 16·41ft draught, two 8-cyl s sc Liebknecht diesel, cpp, 2,320bhp, 13·5 knots.

SKLERION. *Greek*. Cargo (SD 14), CSD. Built by Bartram & Sons, Ltd Sunderland, for N. & J. Vlassopoulos, Chios. 9,057 tons gross, 15,005 tons dw, 462·75ft loa × 67·18ft breadth × 29·04ft draught, 5-cyl Clark-Sulzer diesel, 5,500bhp, 15 knots.

Shinju Maru. (*Not illustrated.*) *One of the most versatile cargo ships afloat, this roll on/off lift on/off ship is especially designed for a short turn round. She is designed for a crew of 15 for the 600 mile run between Tomakai (Hokkaido) and Tokyo, carrying newsprint rolls whilst southbound, and cars containers and pallets northbound. She carries over 3,000 rolls of newsprint and more than 100 medium size passenger cars. The design also calls for loading and unloading to be completed within 10 hours, cargo handling to be unaffected by rain, and a one-third reduction in shore labour normally employed. Similar in appearance to the high box like car carriers employed elsewhere in the world with accommodation and 2 funnels abreast right aft, and a very low poop, she has 2 masts with a single large hatchway from forward to amidships. The masts carry one 5-ton (forward), one 9-ton and one 10-ton derrick (aft mast). Overhead cranes are placed in the tween deck, especially designed for the ship with the power plant in a separate compartment. This is considered more economical than fork lift trucks by the owners. The 10-ton derrick can be reversed to place containers abaft the hatchway. The roll on/off ramps are an integral part of the ship, folding jack knife fashion for stowing, in which position they form watertight doors to the stern entrance. They lower at an angle to the fore and aft line of the ship on each quarter. Newsprint rolls coming on board via trailers are lifted off and stowed by the tween deck cranes. The main engine is an NKK-Pielstick 9PC2L type developing 4,185bhp at 500rpm, and is arranged for bridge control. Trial speed was 15·8 knots, giving a service speed of 14·5 knots at 15 tons fuel consumption per day, and a maximum range of 4,500 miles.*

Silvereid. *The first chemical tanker to be built by Messrs Hall, Russell at Aberdeen, and owned by William Brandts (Leasing) Ltd, is leased to Silver Chemical Tankers Ltd. They in turn have chartered her to Ethyl International of the Ethyl Corporation. She is designed for the carriage of anti-knock compounds and ethyl dibromide. Her main engine is a Mirrlees K major, coupled to a Stone-KaMeWa controllable pitch propeller. She will load mainly at the charterer's plant at Houston, Texas, for their European terminal, but with occasional voyages to South America and the Caribbean.*

SOKOL. *Russian.* Cargo. Built by Kherson Shipyard, Kherson, for USSR. 9,547 tons gross, tons dw na, 501·33ft loa × 67·58ft breadth × 29·58ft draught, 6-cyl Bryansk-B & W diesel, 9,000bhp, knots na.

SOKOLINOYE. *Russian.* Stern Trawler, fish factory, ref (ATLANTIK class). Built by Volkswerft Stralsund, Stralsund, for USSR, Sevastopol. 2,657 tons gross, 1,152 tons dw, 269·58ft loa × 44·75ft breadth × 16·41ft draught, two 8-cyl s sc Liebknecht diesel, 2,320bhp, 13·5 knots.

SOLHEIM. *Norwegian.* Tanker. Built by P. Lindenau, Kiel, for Helm & Co, Larvik. 1,985 tons gross, 3,445 tons dw, 308·09ft loa × 44·18ft breadth × 18·55ft draught, 8-cyl MAN diesel, cpp, 2,050bhp, 12·5 knots.

Singapore Triumph. *The fifth ship in the series of semi-submerged ship theory design of the builders, which is claimed to produce less wave making resistance. First was the* Oriental Queen *(1966), followed by the* Ling Yung *and* Yeh Yung *in 1968 and the* Singapore Pride *in 1969, all for members of the C. Y. Tung Group. She is propelled by a 9RD76 Uraga-Sulzer diesel, developing 14,400bhp at 119rpm giving a service speed of 21·17 knots, and a trials speed of 22·86. Her cargo gear consists of Ebel system* $22\frac{1}{2}$ *ton derricks, remote control of the hydraulically operated hatch covers, extensive automation and remote control of the main machinery, including the refrigeration units. She has the ability to carry ordinary and refrigerated containers and general cargo.*

SOLNOEDER. *Russian*. Stern trawler, fish factory, ref (ATLANTIK class). Built by Volkswerft Stralsund, Stralsund, for USSR. 2,657 tons gross, 1,152 tons dw, 269·58ft loa × 44·75ft breadth × 16·41ft draught, two 8-cyl s sc Liebknecht diesel, cpp, 2,320bhp, 13·5 knots.

SOLSTREIF. *Norwegian*. Tanker (solvents). Built by P. Lindenau, Kiel, for Helm & Co, Larvik. 1,985 tons gross, 3,445 tons dw, 308·09ft loa × 44·18ft breadth × 18·45ft draught, 8-cyl MAN diesel, cpp, 2,050bhp, 12·5 knots.

SONNE. *German*. Stern trawler, ref, CSD. Built by Rickmers Werft, Bremerhaven, 1968, for Hochseefischerei Nordstern AG, Bremerhaven. 2,678 tons gross, tons dw na, 283·84ft loa × 46·66ft breadth × 19ft draught, four 8-cyl s sc Atlas-MaK diesel-electric, 4,000bhp, 15·5 knots.

SONNEBERG. *East German*. Cargo OSD/CSD. Built by Mathias Thesen Werft Wismar, 1968, for Deutsche Seereederei, Rostock, 2,918/5,969 tons gross, 5,428/6,840 tons dw, 424·41ft loa × 56·84ft breadth × 22·1/24·94ft draught, 7-cyl Halberstadt-MAN diesel, 7,000bhp, 16 knots.

SORMOVSKY 2, 4, 5, 6, 7, 11, 12, 13. *Russian*. Cargo. Builder na, Russia, 1968-69, for USSR. 2,292 tons gross, tons dw na, measurements na, cyl na, diesel ('Dvigatel Revolyutsli' works, Gorky), bhp na, knots na.

SOTETSU MARU No 1. *Japanese*. Cargo. Built by Wakamatsu Zosen KK, Wakamatsu, 1968, for Sagami Tetsudo KK, Yokohama. 997 tons gross, 2,000 tons dw, 232·75ft loa × 37·09ft breadth × draught na, 6-cyl Hanshin diesel, 2,000bhp, 12 knots.

SOUND OF JURA. *British*. Ferry (cars and 202 passengers). Built by Hatlo Verksted A/S, Ulsteinvik, for Western Ferries (Harrisons, Clyde, Managers), Campbeltown. 558 tons gross, 155 tons dw, 161·84ft loa × 36·25ft breadth × draught na. two 8-cyl tw sc Lister-Blackstone diesels, cpp, btp, 2,000bhp, 14 knots.

SOUTHELLA. *British*. Stern trawler. Built by Hall, Russell & Co Ltd, Aberdeen, for J. Marr & Son Ltd, Hull. 1,144 tons gross, 830 tons dw, 246ft loa × 41·58ft breadth × 15ft draught, 8-cyl Mirrlees National diesel, cpp, 2,880 bhp, knots na.

SOUTHERN CROSS. *Kenya*. Tanker. Built by Krogerwerft GmbH, Rensburg, for Southern Line Ltd, Mombasa. 758 tons gross, 1,588 tons dw, 228ft loa × 36·09ft breadth × 14·19ft draught, 8-cyl MWM diesel, 1,400bhp, 12·5 knots.

SPARTA. *Liberian*. Cargo. Built by Ishikawajima-Harima HI, Tokyo, for Sparta Shpg Co Ltd, Monrovia (c/o Crystal Maritime Agency, New York). 8,825 tons gross, 14,937 tons dw, 466·66ft loa (incl bb) × 65·18ft breadth × 29·62ft draught, 12-cyl IHI-Pielstick diesel, 5,130bhp, knots na.

SPARTAK. *Russian*. Cargo. Built by Angyalfold Shipyard, Budapest, for USSR. 1,505 tons gross, 1,923 tons dw, 255·25ft loa × 37·75ft breadth × 16·27ft draught, 6-cyl Jugoturbina-Sulzer diesel, 1,500bhp, 12·75 knots.

SPERO. *Norwegian*. Bulk carrier. Built by Rheinstahl Nordsee Werke, Emden, for E. B. Aaby's Rederi AS, Oslo. 14,318 tons gross, 21,640 tons dw, 536·58ft loa × 75ft breadth × 32·2ft draught, 7-cyl Borsig-Fiat diesel, 10,500bhp, 16 knots.

SPEY BRIDGE. *British*. Bulk carrier. Built by Sumitomo SB & Machy Co Ltd, Yokosuka, for H. Clarkson & Co Ltd, London (J. & J. Denholm Mgrs). 66,126 tons gross, tons dw na, 849·75ft loa (incl bb) × 134ft breadth × 52·09ft draught, 10-cyl Sumitomo-Sulzer diesel, bhp na, knots na.

STAINLESS TRANSPORTER. *Danish*. Chemical Tanker. Built by E. Menzer Schiffsw, Geesthacht, for A. H. Basse Rederi A/S, Copenhagen. 1,399 tons gross, 2,800 tons dw, 284·5ft loa (incl bb) × 40·18ft breadth × 18·43ft draught, 6-cyl Atlas-MaK diesel, cpp, 1,995bhp, 13·5 knots.

STAR ATLANTIC. *Norwegian*. Bulk carrier (lumber). Built by Akers A/S Bergens M/V, Bergen, for Kom Star Shipping Group (B. Ostervold & Per Waaler), Bergen. 19,166 tons gross, 29,240 tons dw, 564ft loa × 85·18ft breadth × 35·31ft draught, two 12-cyl s sc Kockums-MAN diesel, cpp, 13,040bhp, 15·75 knots.

S

Sound of Jura. *(Not illustrated.) Western Ferries of Glasgow having achieved success with the* Sound of Islay *(Vol XVII) have now placed this ship in service between West Loch Tarbert and Port Askaig on Islay. They also employ the small* Sound of Gigha *between Islay and Gigha. The* Sound of Islay *which opened up the service to Port Askaig was intended for mainly goods and agricultural traffic, and though she has achieved success on this route, she proved neither large nor fast enough to meet the growing potential. The new ship has been designed to cope with the service. She can accommodate 200 passengers in 1 class and 2 spacious lounges. On the boat deck is a spacious and comfortable observation lounge, with seating for 50, whilst below the vehicle deck (accommodating 35-40 vehicles) is a saloon divided into smoking and non smoking sections, with seating for 68 and 72 passengers respectively. Here there is a refreshment section, with facilities for mothers with children and the usual amenities. Vehicles board through a visor type bow ramp, and leave over a stern ramp. It is intended to operate the ship on a year round basis. Due to her deck covering being a special 'Intergrip', cattle can be safely transported in normal conditions, and the headroom in the garage space is adequate for the commercial vehicles in use in the islands. At 14 knots she makes the crossing in less than 2 hours, propelled by 2 Lister-Blackstone 4-stroke unidirectional EWSL8M engines rated each at 1,000bhp at 900rpm, and each coupled to a Liaaen controllable pitch propeller through a reduction gearbox giving 300rpm. A hydraulic Brunvoll bow thrust is fitted. She makes 4 round trips per day when required.*

Spey Bridge. *This very large OBO Carrier of 113,460 tons dw is owned by the H. Clarkson section of Seabridge Carriers, who are amassing a large fleet of mammoth bulk carrying ships through their various members. The main propulsion is an Uraga-Sulzer diesel engine of 10RND90 type, giving an output of 25,000bhp at 119rpm. Service speed is 15¾ knots, though 17 was achieved on trials.*

STAR PINEWOOD. *British*. Bulk carrier (lumber) (for charter to Star Shipping Group). Built by Cammell Laird & Co (SB & E Ltd), Birkenhead for Wm France, Fenwick & Co Ltd, London. 19,577 tons gross, 29,200 tons dw, 564ft loa × 85·5ft breadth × 35·37ft draught, two 12-cyl s sc MAN diesel, 12,010bhp, 15·75 knots.

STELLA KARINA. *Faroese*. Stern trawler, ref. Built by Soviknes Verft A/S, Syvikgrend, for P/f Stells Shipping & Commercial Co Ltd, Klakksvik 834 tons gross, 701 tons dw, 201·25ft loa × 33·58ft breadth × 16·3ft draught, 8-cyl MWM diesel, cpp, 2,200bhp, knots na.

STELLA KRISTINA. *Faroese*. Stern trawler, ref. Built by Soviknes Verft A/S, Syvikgrend, for P/f Stella Shipping & Commercial Co Ltd. Klakksvik. 834 tons gross, 701 tons dw, 202·58ft loa × 33·58ft breadth × 16·31ft draught, 8-cyl MWM diesel, cpp, 2,200bhp, knots na.

STENA DANICA. *Swedish*. Passenger/car ferry. Built by A. G. 'Weser' Werke Seebeck, Bremerhaven, for Stena A/B, Gothenburg. 5,537 tons gross, 870 tons dw, 410·09ft loa × 67·58ft breadth × 15·92ft draught, two 16-cyl tw sc MAN diesel, 15,600bhp, knots na.

STEPANKERT. *Russian*. Tanker. Builder na, for USSR. 1,723 tons gross, tons dw na, measurements na, cyl na, diesel, bhp na, knots na.

STOLLHAMMERSAND. *German*. Cargo OSD/CSD. Built by C. Luhring, Brake, for Helmut Meyer, Brake. 999/1,999 tons gross, 2,200/3,400 tons dw, 302·5ft loa (incl bb) × 45·18ft breadth × 15·25/20·04ft draught, 12-cyl Deutz diesel, 3,000bhp, 15·5 knots.

STOVE TRADITION. *Norwegian*. Bulk carrier. Built by A/S Frederiksstad M/V, Frederiksstad, for Stove Shipping, Oslo. 11,294 tons gross, 17,900 tons dw, 543·41ft loa × 67·58ft breadth × 30·55ft draught, 6-cyl Frederiksstad-Gotaverken diesel, 7,500bhp, 15·5 knots.

STRAAT AGULHAS. *Dutch*. Cargo, ref. Built by van der Giessen-De Noord NV, Krimpen, for Kon Java-China Paketvaart Lijnen NV, Amsterdam. 7,282/10,484 tons gross, 10,119/13,719 tons dw, 527·58ft loa × 75·66ft breadth × 28·92/33·5ft draught, 6-cyl Stork diesel, 13,500bhp, 20 knots.

STRAAT ALGOA. *Dutch*. Cargo, ref. Built by Verolme United Shipyards, Rozenburg, for Kon Java-China Paketvaart Lijnen N/V, Amsterdam. 7,282/10,485 tons gross, 10,281/13,824 tons dw, 527·66ft loa × 75·66ft breadth × 28·92/33·5ft draught, 6-cyl Stork diesel, 13,500bhp, 20 knots.

STRYMON. *Liberian*. Bulk carrier. Built by Hakodate Dock Co Ltd, Hakodate, for Strymon Shpg Co Ltd, Monrovia (S. Livanos). 16,475 tons gross, 28,699 tons dw, 593·18ft loa (incl bb) × 76ft breadth × 34·7ft draught, 7-cyl IHI-Sulzer diesel, 11,200bhp, 18 knots.

SUBIN RIVER. *Ghanaian*. Cargo. Built by Soc Espanola de Constr Nav, Cadiz, for Black Star Line Ltd, Takoradi. 7,155 tons gross, 9,600 tons dw, 455ft loa × 62·58ft breadth × 27·92ft draught, 6-cyl SECN-Sulzer diesel, 8,000bhp, 17 knots.

SUKHINICHI. *Russian*. Fish carrier, ref. Builder na, Russia, 1965, for USSR, Vladivostok. 3,556 tons gross, 2,485 tons dw, 326ft loa × 46·09ft breadth × 18·44ft draught, four 6-cyl s sc diesel-electric, bhp na, 14·5 knots.

SULFURICO. *Spanish*. Tanker (LPG). Built by Ast T. Ruiz de Velasco, Bilbao, for Naviera Quimico SA, Bilbao. 1,215 tons gross, tons dw na, 253·66ft loa × 40ft m breadth × 15·75ft draught, 6-cyl Naval-Stork Werkspoor diesel, 1,550bhp, 12 knots.

SUMAURA MARU. *Japanese*. Bulk carrier (ore). Built by Ishikawajima-Harima HI, Kure, for Shinwa KKK, Tokyo. 38,985 tons gross, 64,400 tons dw, 754·66ft loa (incl bb) × 119·5ft breadth × 38·18ft draught, 6-cyl IHI-Sulzer diesel, 15,000bhp, knots na.

SUN YANG. *South Korean*. Cement carrier. Built by Tohoku Zosen, Shiogama, 1968, for Keumsung Shipping Co Ltd, Pusan. 3,328 tons gross, 5,045 tons dw, 343ft loa × 49·33ft breadth × 20·41ft draught, 6-cyl Hanshin diesel, 2,500bhp, 12·5 knots.

SUNCAPRI (launched as BERTHA FISSER). *German*. Cargo OSD/CSD. Built by Flensburger Schiffs Ges, Flensburg, for Fisser & Van Dornum, Hamburg. 6,635/9,402 tons gross, 12,817/15,138 tons dw, 458·18ft loa × 68·92ft m breadth × 30·23ft draught, 6-cyl Br Vulkan-MAN diesel, 7,800bhp, 16 knots.

STAR PINEWOOD
LONDON
CAMMELL LAIRD
& Co (S&E) LTD

S

Star Pinewood. *The largest ship yet built for Messrs Wm France, Fenwick & Co, has been fixed on long term charter to the Star Bulk Group, she is the first of a new series being constructed by Bergens Mek. Verksted, Verolme Cork & Cammell Laird for operation by Star Bulk. A development of the Malmanger series (vide Vol XVII) she was on completion considered the largest fully 'open' ship to be yet built, designed for operation as contract carriers of forestry products (pulp, paper, lumber, plywood), unitized steel, containers, unitized semi-bulk (metals, etc),and bulk cargoes. Of her 5 cargo holds, all except No 1, are covered by 69ft 7in wide Kvaerner 'piggy-back' covers, the largest yet made, and straddled by 2 Munck travelling gantry cranes, also the largest yet shipboard cranes so far installed in a ship. Wing ballast tanks are formed by the downward extensions of the hatch coamings, providing first an entirely open hold, a working alleyway immediately below the main deck, and with ballast compartments under. Holds 1, 3 and 5 are suitable for the carriage of ore at about 24cu ft to the ton, whilst 2 and 4 are arranged for a partial load of water ballast. Hatches 2-5 measure 80ft× 69·6ft, making the ship really 'open'. The Munck loaders have a safe working load of 25 tons, and can travel the length of the hatches. The lower lifting yoke is designed for a variety of fittings, including magnets for handling scrap, electro-hydraulic grabs for bulk cargo, and pulp bale clamps for timber products. Propulsion is by 2 MAN 12-cyl V6V 40/54 type diesels, each developing 6,520bhp at 400rpm, reduced through clutches and gearbox to a Stone-KaMeWa stainless steel controllable pitch propeller.*

SUNDBUS BARONEN. *Danish*. Ferry (275 pass). Built by Schiffb Unterweser, Bremerhaven, for Moltzau Tanksibsrederi Dansk-Norsk A/S, Helsingor. 213 tons gross, 40 tons dw, 119·09ft loa×25·58ft breadth×7·55ft draught, two 6-cyl tw sc Daimler-Benz diesel, 500bhp, 13 knots.

SURREY. *Danish*. Cargo OSD. Built by Helsingor Skibs & Masch, Helsingor, for Det forenede Dampskibsselskab A/S, Esbjerg. 3,000 tons gross, 3,220 tons dw, 375·5ft loa×63·33ft breadth×18·92ft draught, two 8-cyl tw sc Helsingor diesel, 8,800bhp, knots na.

SUSONG. *South Korean*. Bulk carrier. Built by Italcantieri SpA, Monfalcone, 1968, for Korea United Lines Inc, Inchon. 9,164 tons gross, 15,400 tons dw, 457·66ft loa×70ft breadth×30·41ft draught, 6-cyl Ansaldo-B & W diesel, 7,200bhp, 15 knots.

SUSSEXBROOK. *British*. Cargo. Built by Cochrane & Sons Ltd, Selby, for Comben Longstaff & Co. Ltd, London. 1,599 tons gross, 1,800 tons dw, 283ft loa×42·41ft breadth×16·5ft draught, 8-cyl Ruston diesel, 2,100bhp, 12·5 knots.

SUVARNABHUMI. *Thai*. Tanker. Built by Robb Caledon SB Co Ltd, Dundee, for Thai Petroleum Transport Co Ltd, Bangkok. 3,300 tons gross, 3,800 tons dw, 348·09ft loa×49·75ft breadth×15·25ft draught, two 8-cyl tw sc English Electric (Kelvin) diesel, 2,400bhp, knots na.

SUZUKA MARU. *Japanese*. Tanker. Built by Ishikawajima-Harima HI, Aioi, for Daikyo Seikyu KK, Tokyo. 86,200 tons gross, 155,100 tons dw, 931·84ft loa (incl bb)×144·5ft breadth×58·41ft draught, 12-cyl IHI-Sulzer diesel, 27,600bhp, knots na.

SYDNEY TRADER. *Australian*. Ferry, stern door, side ports, vehicles and containers. Built by Evans Deakin & Co Pty Ltd, for Australian Coastal Shipping Commission, Melbourne. 9,000 tons gross, 4,000 tons dw, 448ft loa×70·58ft breadth×20·25ft draught, two 8-cyl tw sc MAN diesel, 10,650bhp, 17·5 knots.

SYLVANIA. *Norwegian*. Tanker. Built by Akers A/S Stord Verft, Lervik, 1968, for Onstad Shipping Co, Oslo. 46,417 tons gross, 84,385 tons dw, 820·84ft loa (incl bb)×127·92ft breadth×43·92ft draught, 10-cyl Akers-Nylands-B & W diesel, 23,000bhp, 16·25 knots.

Straat Accra. *1 of a class of 6, of which she and* Straat Adelaide, Straat Amsterdam *and* Straat Auckland *are in the register of Vol XVII, but which are illustrated and described in this volume with* Straat Agulhas *and* Straat Algoa. *The ships have a bale capacity of 698,222cu ft, with a refrigerated space of 49,201cu ft, together with tanks for edible oil and latex. A bulb has not been fitted to the bow, and a transom stern has been built. The ships have a very full midships section, with fine bow and stern lines, giving a block coefficient of 0·577 at 95% draught. Hatches No 3 and 4 are of the 'open' type, each having 3 hatches abreast. These holds are so designed that 65 containers can be carried in each hold with tween deck hatches open. Hatches 2, 3 and 4 can take another 36 on deck, with 8 on deck adjoining No 2, and 16 in No 2 lower hold and tween deck. In order to facilitate the loading of insulated cargo, separate insulated hatches are provided at No 4 hold and in No 5 bridge space for independent loading. Nos 2, 3 and 4 lower holds and No 4 tween deck wings are specially strengthened for heavy cargoes, such as ore, with No 2 lower hold specially arranged for ferro-silicon ore. A duct keel between the engine room and the palm oil pump room forward carries the bilge, ballast, oil fuel, steam and fresh water lines. Cargo handling is mainly by a Hensen 21·5-ton twin crane at Nos 3 and 4 hatches, with the remaining deck cranes being 3-8 ton low pressure hydraulik/Braatvag units. There is also one set of 10-ton and one of 15-ton derricks. The shell plating is protected by Hughes-Guardian Cematic cathodic equipment. 2 fibreglass boats are carried, 1 with an engine, 1 with hand propelling gear. The engine control room is fitted with Sperry/TKS monitoring and recording gear covering 186 points, with alarm coverage to 87. The main engine is a Stork type SW6 80/160 diesel giving a service speed of 20 knots with the Lips propeller turning at 117 rpm.*

Surrey. (Not illustrated.) A development of her near sister ships Somerset *and* Stratford, *she is* $6\frac{1}{2}$*ft beamier and slightly longer, being the broadest ship capable of entering the lock at Grimsby. She is designed mainly for the Danish bacon and butter trade which is handled at that port from Esbjerg. Her return cargoes consist of normal UK manufactures, with cars and foodstuffs such as chocolate predominating. She can carry 215 containers or 196 bacon trailers and 42 containers. She accommodates on her container deck 42 containers, on her upper trailer deck either 73 containers or 83 trailers, on her lower trailer deck either 72 containers or 85 trailers, and in the trailer hold, 28 trailers or 28 containers. This is considerably more than the other 2 ships* (vide *Vol XVI*)*, because her engines have been moved aft from amidships. She has twin funnels abreast instead on 1 centrally placed, and her crew quarters have been moved to the upper container deck. An additional space saver is a 39-ton hydraulic lift 39×10ft, which loads the trailer hold. There are no ramps within the ship, loading being direct by outside ramps or by crane. Loading is through a stern door. The ship carries a container crane designed in Norway and made in Denmark. Sperry Gyrofin stabilizers are fitted, which are intended to reduce rolling by 75%. The Bridge or engine room controlled machinery is a twin screw B & W DM8S45HU set of diesels, giving an 18 knot service speed. A KaMeWa bow thrust is also fitted. Crew consists of 27 hands.*

S

T

T. AKASAKA. *British*. Bulk carrier. Built by Nippon Kokan, Yokohama, for Canadian Pacific (Bermuda) Ltd, Hong Kong. 33,328 tons gross, 57,188 tons dw, 744·33ft loa (incl bb)×102·18ft breadth×40·35ft draught, 7-cyl Mitsui-B & W diesel, 17,500bhp, knots na.

TABARISTAN. *British*. Cargo, ref (150-ton Stulcken derrick). Built by Swan Hunter Sbldrs (Readhead yard), S. Shields, for F. C. Strick & Co Ltd, London. 6,416/9,627 tons gross, —/14,158 tons dw, 510·84ft loa (incl bb)×69·84ft breadth×30·20ft draught, 6-cyl Doxford diesel, 12,000bhp, 17·5 knots.

TAI FONG No 2. *Chinese* (*Taiwan*). Cargo. Built by Kurushima Dock Co Ltd, Imabari, 1967, for Taiwan Maritime Transportation Co Ltd, Keelung. 4,026 tons gross, 6,354 tons dw, 363·84ft loa×53·92ft breadth×21·97ft draught, 6-cyl Mitsubishi-Sulzer diesel, 3,500bhp, 13 knots.

TAI SUN. (Sis TAI NING). *Chinese* (*Taiwan*). Cargo, ref. Built by Mitsubishi HI Ltd, Kobe, for Taiwan Navigation Co Ltd, Keelung. 10,016 tons gross, 12,300 tons dw, 508·5ft loa (incl bb)×71·58ft breadth×31ft draught, 6-cyl Mitsubishi-MAN diesel, 10,000bhp, 19 knots.

TAISEI MARU No 31. *Japanese*. Tanker. Built by Tokushima Zosen, Tokushima, for Kyowa Sangyo KK, Osaka. 1,000 tons gross, 2,032 tons dw, 230·41ft loa×34·5ft breadth×17·09ft draught, 6-cyl Niigata diesel, 1,500bhp, 11 knots.

TAKAMINE MARU. *Japanese*. Tanker. Built by Mitsubishi HI Ltd, Nagasaki, for Nippon Yusen Kaisha, Tokyo. 99,376 tons gross, 179,800 tons dw, 987·66ft loa (incl bb)×158·33ft breadth×59·09ft draught, Mitsubishi turbs, bhp na, 16 knots.

TAKASAGO MARU No 8. *Japanese*. Cargo. Built by Kurushima Dkyd Co Ltd, Imabari, 1968, for Horiuchi KKK, Hojyo. 999 tons gross, 2,000 tons dw, 213·25ft lbp×36·09ft breadth×16·41ft draught, 6-cyl Akasaka Tekkosho diesel, 1,500bhp, 11·5 knots.

TAKASAGO MARU No 11. *Japanese*. Cargo. Built by Kurushima Dock Co Ltd, Imabari, 1968, for Horiuchi KKK, Hojyo. 2,959 tons gross, 5,000 tons dw, 295·25ft lbp×51·18ft m breadth×20·92ft draught, 6-cyl Akasaka Tekkosho diesel, 3,000bhp, 12 knots.

TAKHUNA. *Russian*. Cargo. Built by Angyalfold Shipyard, Budapest, 1968, for USSR. 1,248 tons gross, 1,299 tons dw, 244·41ft loa×37·18ft breadth×13·13ft draught, 8-cyl Lang diesel, 1,000bhp, 11·5 knots.

TANBA MARU. *Japanese*. Cargo (timber). Built by Onomichi Zosen, Onomichi, for Sanko KKK, Osaka. 10,894 tons gross, 16,300 tons dw, 504·84ft loa (incl bb)×73ft breadth×28·75ft draught, 7-cyl Hitachi-B & W diesel, 8,400bhp, 14·5 knots.

TABARISTAN

Tabaristan is the latest of the series built by Readheads of South Shields for the Strick Line (member of the P & O group) and also the 45th ship they have built for Messrs Strick. She was delivered 7 weeks ahead of schedule. Her Doxford 67J6 diesel engine develops 12,000bhp at 124rpm, and she achieved a speed of 21 knots on trials. Her Stulcker derrick can lift 150 tons. There are 5 holds. No 2 lower hold also acts as a deep tank. There are 5 insulated compartments. There are 5 cranes of 10-20 ton capacity and 6 derricks of 5-tons. Main engines are bridge controlled. On her maiden voyage she carried one 110-ton barge, one 110-ton tug and one 53-ton light float all on the fore deck and lifted on board by her own equipment. She is the first in the P & O group to have her draught in metric figures as well as in feet. Her voyage to Persia via the Cape takes about 30 days instead of 19 via Suez and adds 4,750 miles to the distance steamed. Her sister Nigaristan *is building at the same yard.*

TARANGER. *Norwegian.* Bulk carrier. Built by A/S Bergens M/V, Bergen, for Westfal-Larsen & Co AS, Bergen. 19,024 tons gross, 29,200 tons dw, 563·58ft loa × 85·09ft breadth × 35·3ft draught, two 12-cyl s sc Kockums-MAN diesel, cpp, 13,040bhp, knots na.

TARNTANK. *Swedish.* Tanker (chemical). Built by C. Luhring, Brake, for Sven Olof Kristensson, Donso. 1,599 tons gross, 2,805 tons dw, 282·09ft loa × 41·66ft breadth × 16·9ft draught, 8-cyl Atlas-MaK diesel, cpp, 1,500bhp, 12·5 knots.

TATSUMI MARU No 28. *Japanese.* Caustic soda carrier (chemical tanker). Built by Taihei Kogyo, Hiroshima, for Tatsumi Shokai KK, Osaka, 2,990 tons gross, 5 080 tons dw, 320ft loa × 49·33ft breadth × 21·41ft draught. 6-cyl Hanshin diesel, 2,800bhp, knots na.

TAVRIDA. *Russian.* Stern trawler, fish factory, ref (ATLANTIK class). Built by Volkswerft Stralsund, Stralsund, for USSR. 2 657 tons gross. 1,152 tons dw, 269·58ft loa × 44·75ft breadth × 16·5ft draught, two 8-cyl s sc Liebknecht diesel, 2,594 bhp,13·5 knots.

TEGELERSAND. *German.* Cargo OSD/CSD part container ship (two 20-ton derricks). Built by Schiffsw Heinrich Brand KG, Oldenburg, for Helmut Meyer, Brake. 999/1,999 tons gross, 2,200/3,400 tons dw, 302·92ft loa × 45·09ft breadth × 15·25/20ft draught, 12-cyl Deutz diesel, 3,000bhp, 15 knots.

TEGURASAN MARU. *Japanese.* Tanker. Built by Mitsui Zosen, Chiba, for Mitsui-OSK Lines KK, Osaka. 99,137 tons gross, 181,881 tons dw, 984·33ft loa (incl bb) × 162·58ft breadth × 58·5ft draught, 12-cyl Mitsui-B & W diesel, 30,900bhp, 15·75 knots.

TEMPLE ARCH. *British.* Bulk carrier. Built by A/S Horten Verft, Horten, for Euxine S Co (Lambert Bros [Shipping] Ltd, London) (Mgrs Scottish Ship Management Ltd). 13,543 tons gross, 21,350 tons dw, 527·66ft loa × 75·18ft breadth × 32ft draught, two 9-cyl s sc English Electric (Ruston) diesel, 10,000bhp, knots na.

TETIN. *Greek.* Cargo (Freedom type). Built by Ishikawajima-Harima HI, Tokyo, for Seabird Shipping Co SA, Piraeus. 10,008 tons gross, 15,175. tons dw, 466·7ft loa × 65·09ft breadth × 29·7ft draught, 12-cyl IHI-Pielstick diesel, 5,130bhp, 14·25 knots.

TEXACO CHIEF. *Canadian.* Tanker. Built by Collingwood Shipyards, Collingwood, for Texaco (Canada) Ltd, Toronto. 4,700 tons gross, 6,500 tons dw, 400·5ft loa × 54·18ft breadth × 21·5ft draught, two 12-cyl s sc Fairbanks Morse (Canada) diesel, 4,000bhp, 13·75 knots.

TEXACO FRANKFURT. *British.* Tanker. Built by Howaldtswerke-Deutschewerft, Kiel, for Regent Petroleum Tankship Co Ltd, London. 104,616 tons gross, 205,800 tons dw, 1,067·33ft loa (incl bb) × 154·92ft breadth × 62·3ft draught, AEG turbs, 28,000shp, knots na.

TEXACO HAMBURG. *British.* Tanker. Built by Howaldtswerke-Deutschewerft, Kiel, for Texaco Overseas Tankship Co Ltd, London. 104,616 tons gross, 206,000 tons dw, 1,067·33ft loa (incl bb) × 154·92ft breadth × 62·29ft draught, AEG turbs, 28,000shp, knots na.

TEXACO NORTH AMERICA. *British.* Tanker. Built by Howaldtswerke-Deutschewerft, Kiel, for Texaco Overseas Tankship Ltd, London. 104,616 tons gross, 205,800 tons dw, 1,067·33ft loa (incl bb) × 154·92ft breadth × 62·3ft draught, AEG turbs, 28,000shp, knots na.

The Texaco Bogota, *built in 1960 by Eriksberg at Gothenburg as a 19,800 ton tanker, suffered a major explosion in the Baltic in 1968, causing major damage amidships, with total destruction of the deckhouse. She was temporarily repaired and towed to Gothenburg where she was not only reconstructed but enlarged by 1 tank section 11 metres long, raising her cargo capacity to 22,100 tons, and giving her an entirely different silhouette by removing the bridge house aft. She left the shipyard for the second time on 14th December, 1968 for trials. (Not included in the register of this Volume.)*

T

TEXADA QUEEN. *Canadian*. Ferry. Built by Allied Shipbuilders Ltd, Vancouver, for British Columbia Dept of Highways, Victoria. 800 tons gross, tons dw na, 159·5ft loa × 48·18ft breadth × 7·92ft draught, two 6-cyl tw sc Ruston Hornsby diesel, 1,200bhp, knots na.

THORHAGEN. *German*. Oil/chemical tanker. Built by Werft Nobiskrug, Rendsburg, for Tankreederei De Vries & Co KG, Hamburg. 1,591 tons gross, 3,200 tons dw, 309·41ft loa × 44·41ft breadth × 17·38ft draught, 6-cyl MAN diesel, 3,350bhp, 15 knots.

THORSHAMMER. *Norwegian*. Tanker. Built by Uddevallavarfet A/B, Uddevalla, for A/S Thor Dahl, Sandefjord. 120,000 tons gross, 230,000 tons dw, 1,066·18ft loa × 158·09ft breadth × 67ft draught, GEC turbs, 32,400shp, 15·75 knots.

THUNTANK 6. *British*. Tanker. Built by Clelands SB Co Ltd, Wallsend, for Thun Tankers Ltd, Newcastle. 3,000 tons gross, tons dw na, 322·5ft loa × 47ft breadth × 21·33ft draught, 12-cyl Ruston diesel, 2,900bhp, knots na.

TIDE CROWN (launched as BUTANGA). *Liberian*. Tanker. Built by Oresundsvarvet A/B, Landskrona, for Tide Marine Corpn, Monrovia. 43,981 tons gross, 90,800 tons dw, 845·33ft loa (incl bb) × 127·92ft breadth × 44·29ft draught, 8-cyl Gotaverken diesel, 19,200bhp, 16·25 knots.

TIDE HAL I, II, III, IV. *Dutch*. Oil rig supply vessels. Built by Verolme Schpsw Alblasserdam, 1968, for Tidewater-Halcyon Marine Service NV, Rotterdam. 713 tons gross, 990 tons dw, 165ft loa × 38·92ft breadth × 12·46ft draught, two 12-cyl tw sc Caterpillar diesel, btp, 1,700bhp, 11 knots.

TIISKERI. *Finnish*. Tanker. Built by Rheinstal Nordseewerke, Emden, for Neste O/Y, Naantali/Nadendal. 62,357 tons gross, 110,000 tons dw, 853ft lbp × 127·92ft breadth × 50·22ft draught, 10-cyl Wartsila-Sulzer diesel, cpp, 26,000bhp, 17 knots.

TINA. *German*. Container ship (63 × 20ft containers). Built by J. J. Sietas Schiffsw, Hamburg, for Peter Dohle & Co, Hamburg. 499 tons gross, tons dw na, 242·33ft loa × 35·41ft m breadth × 13ft draught, 8-cyl Atlas-MaK diesel, 1,400bhp, 12·5 knots.

TINNES. *Norwegian*. Cargo. Built by Fr Lurssen, Vegesack, for A/S Kristian Jebsen's Rederi, 2,806 tons gross, 4,416 tons dw, 314·33ft loa × 45·66ft breadth × 20·92ft draught, two 8-cyl s sc Normo diesel, cpp, 2 080bhp, knots na.

TIPPERARY (Sis KILDARE). *Eire*. Cargo (containers, 74 × 20ft). Built by Schlichting Werft, Travemunde, for Shelbourne Shipping Co, Dublin 622 tons gross, 1,331 tons dw, 256·09ft loa × 43·84ft breadth × 11·88ft draught, 6-cyl Atlas-MaK diesel, 1 550bhp, 13 knots.

TKVARCHELI. *Russian*. Fish factory, ref. Built by N. V. Kon Maats 'De Schelde', Flushing, 1968, for USSR, Kertch. 4,234 tons gross, 2,600 tons dw, 339·92ft loa × 54·58ft breadth × 18·04ft draught, 8-cyl Schelde-Sulzer diesel, cpp, 3,000bhp, 14·5 knots.

TOBOL. *Russian*. Cargo. Built by Nystads Varv A/B, Nystad, for USSR, Kholmsk. 2,873 tons gross, 3,400 tons dw, 335ft loa × 46·09ft breadth × 18·75ft draught, 5-cyl Valmet-B & W diesel, 2,900bhp, knots na.

TOHKOHSAN MARU. *Japanese*. Tanker (chartered to Idemitsu Tanker Co). Built by Mitsui Zosen, Chiba, for Mitsui-OSK Lines KK, Osaka. 81,744 tons gross, 137,325 tons dw, 961·33ft loa × 144·41ft breadth × 52·84ft draught, 12-cyl Mitsui-B & W diesel, 27,600bhp, 16 knots.

TOKAI MARU. *Japanese*. Cargo. Built by Kurushima Dock Co Ltd, Imabari, for Toko KKK, Kobe. 10,028 tons gross, 15,800 tons dw, 446·18ft lbp × 71·58ft breadth × 28ft draught, 6-cyl Kawasaki-MAN diesel, 7,500bhp, knots na.

TOKEI MARU. *Japanese*. Cargo. Built by Kurushima Dock Co Ltd, Imabari, for Tokei KKK, Namikata. 4,267 tons gross, 6,700 tons dw, 339·5ft lbp × 55·25ft breadth × 22·18ft draught, 6-cyl Hatsudoki diesel, 3,800bhp, knots na.

TOKYO MARU. *Japanese*. Cargo, ref, pass. Built by Onomichi Zosen, Onomichi, for Ryuku Kaiun KK, Naha. 3,510 tons gross, 1,700 tons dw, 333·09ft lbp × 49·92ft breadth × 18ft draught, 8-cyl Maizuru-Sulzer diesel, 6,150bhp, knots na.

T

Texaco Hamburg. *This 200,000 tonner was at the time of delivery, the largest in the cargo fleet, with 3 sister ships being constructed at Kiel, of which 2 have been handed over, the* Texaco Frankfurt *and* North America. *Also for operation under the British flag for Texaco Overseas Tankship Co Ltd under construction are 4 additional 255,000 ton deadweight ships, 1 at Swan Hunters and 3 at Odense. The AEG turbines develop 28,000shp at 85rpm, with centralized machinery control from the bridge, with a lift from the lower engine room to the upper Bridge deck. There are 13 tanks holding about 1,500,000 barrels of liquid cargo, of which 2 grades can be carried. The ship is fitted with permanent ballast tanks, as well as 2 tanks for the residue from tank cleaning for subsequent pumping ashore. The engine room has separator tanks for oily bilge water. The main cargo pumps and tank valves, with tank gauges, are controlled from a centralized cargo control room and the cargo pump room is provided with a lift. A flume stabilizing system is installed, the lifeboats are fully enclosed, and a most complete electronic navigation system fitted, including a sonar/doppler docking system.*

Tiiskeri. *The largest vessel yet from the builders, and the first of 2 sisters building at Emden. She has an inert gas system for safety for the cargo tanks. The Bridge has a 360° vision from the wheelhouse, and several television cameras for monitoring from the Bridge. Amongst the navigation equipment are a weather chart printer and doppler sonar, whilst she is also fitted with a bow thrust propeller and a water jet system aft for manoeuvring. The Wartsila-Sulzer 10RND90 main engine develops 26,000 metric bhp at 122rpm, giving a trial speed of 17 knots, with a variable pitch propeller.*

The Tipperary is the second of 2 ships — Kildare is her sister ship — built at Travemunde for the Shelbourne Shipping Co of Dublin for long term bareboat charter to the British & Irish Steam Packet Co, for service between Eire and England (Dublin and Liverpool), carrying 74×20ft standard ISO containers.

TOKYO VENTURE. *Liberian.* Bulk carrier. Built by Hitachi Zosen, Mukaishima, for Cosmopolitan Carriers, Monrovia. 11,186 tons gross, 19,088 tons dw, 512·33ft loa×74·33ft breadth×31·29ft draught, 7-cyl Hitachi-B & W diesel, 8,400bhp, 15·25 knots.

TONAMI MARU. *Japanese.* Bulk carrier (wood chips). Built by Maizuru Jugogyo Ltd, Maizuru, for Yamashita-Shinnihon & Tamai Zosen KK. 34,944 tons gross, 42,000 tons dw, 646·33ft loa (incl bb)×99ft breadth×36·09ft draught, 7-cyl Hitachi-B & W diesel, 11,500bhp, 14·5 knots.

TONICHI MARU. *Japanese.* Cargo, ref. Built by Shikoku Dock Co, Takamatsu, for Towa KKK. 2,659 tons gross, 3,463 tons dw, 306·75ft lbp×47·58ft breadth×19·18ft draught, 8-cyl IHI-Pielstick diesel, 3,520bhp, 17·5 knots.

TORNADO. *Greek.* Ore/oil carrier. Built by Ishikawajima-Harima HI, Aioi, for Western Navigation Corpn, Piraeus. 41,000 tons gross, 73,300 tons dw, 794ft loa (incl bb)×105·58ft m breadth×47·18ft draught, 8-cyl IHI-Sulzer diesel, 17,600bhp, knots na.

T

TORO. *Norwegian*. Cargo, ref. Built by Sasebo HI, Sasebo, for Wilh Wilhelmsen, Tonsberg. 5,490/8,256 tons gross, 9,145/10,445 tons dw, 452·84ft loa × 65·66ft breadth × 25·31/27·55ft draught, two 10-cyl s sc Nippon Kokan-Pielstick diesel, 8,000bhp, knots na.

TOROS. *Russian*. Stern trawler, fish factory (B26 class). Built by Stocznia in Komuny Pariskiej, Gydnia, 1968, for USSR. 2,979 tons gross, 1,321 tons dw, 256ft lr × 45·41ft breadth × draught na, 8-cyl Zgoda-Sulzer diesel, 2,400bhp, 12·75 knots.

TOSONG. *South Korean*. Bulk carrier. Built by Ansaldo SpA Spezia, for Korea United Lines, Inchon. 9,235 tons gross, 16,770 tons dw, 481·09ft loa × 69ft breadth × 29·58ft draught, 6-cyl Ansaldo-B & W diesel, 7,200bhp, knots na.

TOYO MARU No 12. *Japanese*. Cargo (14 pass). Built by Shin Yamamoto Zosen, Kochi, 1968, for Mazda Unyu KK, Hiroshima. 688 tons gross, 658 tons dw, 219ft lbp × 34·18ft breadth × 10·84ft draught, 6-cyl Hanshin diesel, 1,250bhp, knots na.

TOYO MARU No 18. *Japanese*. Vehicle carrier. Built by Shin Yamamoto Zosen, Kochi, for Nisihara KKK, Matsuyama. 699 tons gross, tons dw na, 214·92ft lbp × 34·25ft breadth × 10·84ft draught, 6-cyl Hanshin diesel, 1,500bhp, knots na.

TOYO MARU No 30. *Japanese*. Vehicle carrier. Built by Ujino Zosensho, Hiroshima, 1968, for Shinwa KKK, Tokyo. 1,148 tons gross, 1,437 tons dw, 283·84ft loa × 40·09ft breadth × 14·66ft draught, 6-cyl Hanshin diesel, 2,500bhp, knots na.

TOYOTA MARU No 2 (Sis TOYOTA MARU No 1). *Japanese*. Bulk carrier (vehicles). Built by Kawasaki Dockyard Co Ltd, Kobe, for Kawasaki KKK, Kobe. 12,411 tons gross, 18,257 tons dw, 521·75ft loa (incl bb) × 72·41ft breadth × 31·33ft draught, 7-cyl Kawasaki-MAN diesel, 8,750bhp, 14·5 knots.

TOYOTA MARU No 3. *Japanese*. Bulk carrier (vehicles). Built by Kawasaki Dockyard Co Ltd, Kobe, for Nippon Kisen KK, Kobe. 12,409 tons gross, 18,320 tons dw, 521·75ft loa (incl bb) × 72·92ft breadth × 31·33ft draught, 7-cyl Kawasaki-MAN diesel, 8,750bhp, 14·5 knots.

TOYOTA MARU No 5. *Japanese*. Bulk carrier (vehicles). Built by Namura Zosensho, Osaka, for Nippon Yusen Kaisha, Tokyo. 12,087 tons gross, 18,300 tons dw, 492·18ft loa × 74·5ft breadth × 31·84ft draught, 6-cyl Mitsubishi-Sulzer diesel, 8,200bhp, 14·5 knots.

TOYOTA MARU No 6. *Japanese*. Bulk carrier (vehicles). Built by Namura Zosensho, Osaka, for Nippon Yusen Kaisha, Tokyo. 12,102 tons gross, 18,300 tons dw, 492·09ft loa × 74·5ft breadth × 31·75ft draught, 6-cyl Mitsubishi-Sulzer diesel, 8,200bhp, knots na.

TRANSCONTAINER 1. *French*. 36 pass./vehicles/containers. Built by Const Nav & Ind de la Mediteranee (CNIM), La Seyne, 1968, for Soc Nationale des Chemins de Fer Francais, Dunkerque. 2,692 tons gross, 1,800 tons dw, 341·25ft loa × 61·33ft breadth × 15·41ft draught, two 8-cyl tw sc MWM diesel, btp, 4,400bhp, 16 knots.

TRANSMUNDUM 1. *German*. Trailing suction hopper dredger. Built by Cammell Laird & Co (SB & E) Ltd, Birkenhead, for R. Boltje & Zonen GmbH, Bremen. 2,400 tons gross, 5,000 tons dw, 311·66ft loa × 52·5ft m breadth × 16·39ft draught, three 12-cyl tr sc English Electric diesel, 2,481bhp, knots na.

TRANSMUNDUM II. *British*. Trailing suction Hopper dredger. Built by Cammell Laird & Co (SB & E) Ltd, Birkenhead, for Taylor Woodrow (International) Ltd, London. 2,400 tons gross, 5,000 tons dw, 311·66ft loa × 52·66ft breadth × 16·39ft draught, three 12-cyl tr sc English Electric diesel, 2,481bhp, knots na.

TRANSMUNDUM III. *German*. Suction dredger. Built by Norderwerft J. R. Koser, Hamburg, for R. Boltje & Zonen GmbH, Hamburg. 2,600 tons gross, tons dw na, 311·66ft loa × 52·5ft m breadth × 17·23ft draught, three 12-cyl tr sc Dorman diesel, 2,481bhp, knots na.

TRANSMUNDUM IV. *German*. Trailing suction hopper dredger. Built by Nordewerft J. R. Koser, Hamburg, for R. Boltje & Zonen GmbH, Hamburg. 2,690 tons gross, tons dw na, 311·66ft loa × 52·56ft m breadth × 17·23ft draught, three 12-cyl tr sc English Electric Dorman Div) diesel, 2,481bhp, knots na.

Transcontainer I. *First of 2 sister ships, this ship is used on the Harwich-Dunkerque route of the Societe Nationale des Chemins de Fer Francais, connecting the freightliner service at the French end. The ship has bridge controlled engines. Cargo capacity is 192 trans-containers of 20ft length, or 125 of 30ft, or any combination of 20ft, 30ft and 40ft units. The containers are handled by slave trailers, which are loaded by 2 gantry cranes in the garage deck, thus achieving a similar load to a cellular ship. Containers on the upper deck remain on their trailers for the crossing. Although she will operate from a roll on and off link span, she is also suitable for operations with a dockside container crane, as openings have been made in the upper deck. She can thus be used for all types of cargo, road vehicles, freight on wheels, and flats and unit loads. She can accommodate 36 passengers, but as this route is exclusively for freight, these will be mainly lorry drivers.*

TRAVIATA. *Swedish.* Bulk carrier. Built by Baltic SB & E Works, Leningrad, for Olof Wallenius, Stockholm. 23,360 tons gross, 35,000 tons dw, 660·41ft loa × 91·41ft breadth × 34·97ft draught, 8-cyl Bryansk-B & W diesel, 12,000bhp, knots na.

TROPIC SHORE (Sis ATLANTIC SHORE). *British.* Oil rig supply ship, ref. Built by N. V. Isselwerf, Rotterdam, for Offshore Marine Ltd, London (Cunard Group). 500 tons gross, 762 tons dw, 166·66ft loa × 36·92ft breadth × 12·41ft draught, two 12-cyl tw sc Lister Blackstone diesel, twin rudders, bow jet pump, 2,400bhp, 12 knots.

TRURO (launched as BELE). *German.* Container ship (for long term charter to Ellerman-Wilson Line). Built by Martin Jansen, Leer, for Johannes Bos, Leer. 680/1,490 tons gross, 1,510/2,780 tons dw, 247·66ft loa × 38·66ft m breadth × 13·84/19·68ft draught, 6-cyl Deutz diesel, 2,200bhp, 14 knots.

TSCHIL BO SAN. *North Korean.* Fish factory, ref. Built by Verolme Scheepsw Heusden, for Korean Fishing Owners' Industry. 10,236 tons gross, 7,050 tons dw, 453ft loa × 65·75ft breadth × 22·33ft draught, 6-cyl Verolme-MAN diesel, 5,500bhp, knots na.

T

TSUGARU MARU. *Japanese*. Cable Ship. Built by Mitsubishi HI Ltd, Shimonoseki, for Nippon Denshin Denwa Kosha, Tokyo. 1,660 tons gross, 1,090 tons dw, 277·41ft loa × 41·41ft breadth × 15·09ft draught, 7-cyl Hatsudoki diesel, 3,000bhp, knots na.

TSUKIKAWA MARU. *Japanese*. Cargo. Built by Kurushima Dock Co Ltd, Imabari, for Kawasaki KKK, Kobe. 3,982 tons gross, 5,450 tons dw, 331·41ft lbp × 53·25ft breadth × draught na, 6-cyl Hatsudoki diesel, 3,800bhp, knots na.

TULA. *Russian*. Cargo. Built by Warnowwerft, Warnemunde, for USSR, Leningrad. 9,748 tons gross, 12,882 tons dw, 496·92ft loa × 66·66ft breadth × 28·86ft draught, 8-cyl DMR-MAN diesel, 9,600bhp, 16·5 knots.

TULEN KABILOV. *Russian*. Stern trawler, fish factory, ref (ATLANTIK class). Built by Volkswerft Stralsund, Stralsund, 1968, for USSR, Kaliningrad. 2,657 tons gross, 1,152 tons dw, 269·58ft loa × 44·75ft breadth × 16·41ft draught, two 8-cyl s sc Liebknecht diesel, 2,320bhp, 13·5 knots.

TWEED (launched as HINRICH BEHRMANN). *German*. Cargo OSD (part containers, 21 × 20ft). Built by J. J. Sietas Schiffsw, Hamburg, for Albert Behrmann, Hamburg. 499 tons gross, 1,460 tons dw, 252·66ft loa × 36·75ft breadth × 13·27ft draught, 8-cyl Atlas-MaK diesel, 1,500bhp, 12·5 knots.

U

UNDEN. *Dutch*. Cargo (baled paper and packaged lumber). Built by Fa. C. Amels & Zn Schpsw & Mchfbk 'Wegelegen', Makkun, 1968, for Vereenigd Cargadoorskantoor, Amsterdam. 575/1,534 tons gross, 1,577/2,809 tons dw, 254·75ft loa × 39·09ft breadth × 13·58/19·13ft draught, 8-cyl Atlas-MaK diesel, 1,500bhp, 12 knots.

UNION EAST. *Chinese* (*Taiwan*). Cargo, ref. Built by Ishikawajima-Harima HI Aioi, 1968, for China Union Lines, Keelung. 10,481 tons gross, 12,700 tons dw, 523·33ft loa (incl bb) × 73·5ft breadth × 32·18ft draught, 8-cyl IHI-Pielstick diesel, 12,800bhp, 19 knots.

UNION EVERGREEN. *Chinese* (*Taiwan*). Cargo, ref, OSD/CSD. Built by Taiwan SB Corpn, Keelung, 1968, for China Union Lines, Keelung, 3,629/5,000 tons gross, 5,669/— tons dw, 351·09ft loa × 54·18ft breadth × 23·25/—ft draught, 6-cyl Kawasaki-MAN diesel, 4,200bhp, 14·5 knots.

UNION FRIENDSHIP. *Liberian*. Bulk carrier. Built by Namura Zosensho, Osaka, for International Union Lines Ltd, Monrovia. 9,759 tons gross, 16,941 tons dw, 477·33ft loa × 71ft breadth × 30·48ft draught, 6-cyl Mitsubishi-Sulzer diesel, 8,000bhp, 14·75 knots.

UNION WISDOM. *Liberian*. Bulk carrier. Built by Sanoyasu Dkyd Co Ltd, Osaka, for International Union Lines, Monrovia. 9,968 tons gross, 16,644 tons dw, 470·92ft loa × 71·66ft breadth × 30·09ft draught, 7-cyl IHI-Sulzer diesel, 8,000bhp, 14·75 knots.

UNIVERSE IRAN. *Liberian*. Tanker. Built by Mitsubishi HI Ltd, Nagasaki, for Bantry Transportation Co, Monrovia (National Bulk Carriers, NY, for charter to Gulf Oil Co). 149,623 tons gross, 326,933 tons dw, 1,132·84ft loa (incl bb) × 175·18ft breadth × 81·41ft draught, tw sc IHI turbs, 37,400shp, 15 knots.

UNIVERSE JAPAN. *Liberian*. Tanker. Built by Ishikawajima-Harima HI, Yokohama, for Bantry Transportation Co, Monrovia. 149,623 tons gross, 326,562 tons dw, 1,132·92ft loa (incl bb) × 175·18ft breadth × 81·41ft draught, tw sc IHI turbs, 37,400shp, 15 knots.

UNIVERSE KOREA. *Liberian*. Tanker. Built by Ishikawajima-Harima HI, Yokohama, for Bantry Transportation Co, Monrovia. 149,623 tons gross, 326,676 tons dw, 1,132·84ft loa (incl bb) × 175·09ft breadth × 81·41ft draught, tw sc IHI turbs, 37,400shp, 15 knots.

Universe Aztec. *Believed to be the world's largest bulk carrier at 160,242 tons deadweight, the vessel will be employed in the carriage of industrial salt from Mexico to Japan. She is fitted with side rolling hatch covers with quick acting cleats, developed at the Kure yard. The machinery consists of a main GEC steam turbine developing 27,500shp at 98rpm, the normal output being 25,000shp at 95rpm giving a service speed of 15½ knots, though on trials, she reached a maximum of 18·3 knots.*

UNIVERSE PORTUGAL. *Liberian*. Tanker. Built by Mitsubishi HI Ltd, Nagasaki, for Bantry Transportation Co, Monrovia. 149,623 tons gross, 326,676 tons dw, 1,132·84ft loa (incl bb) × 175·18ft breadth × 81·41ft draught, tw sc IHI turbs, 37,400shp, 15 knots.

UREA MARU. *Japanese*. Bulk carrier (internal conveyor; for urea carrying). Built by Nippon Kokan Shimizu, 1968, for Showa KKK, Tokyo. 11,220 tons gross, 14,200 tons dw, 459·33ft loa × 72·33ft breadth × 28·25ft draught, 12-cyl NK-Pielstick diesel, 5,580bhp, 13·5 knots.

Universe Kuwait (*Vol XVII*) *second of the class of six 326,000 tonners now in commission shown loading at the new man-made Sea Island loading terminal 10 miles off the Kuwait coast and especially built to accommodate these huge ships. It is the only berth in the world where they can load a complete cargo.*

V

VALDES (launched as GEERTIEN BOS). *German*. Cargo OSD (71 × 20ft containers) (for charter to MacAndrews Liverpool-Bilbao service). Built by Schps 'Hoogezand' J. Bodewes, Bergum, for Johannes Bos, Hamburg. 500 tons gross, 1,350 tons dw, 248·33ft loa × 36·09ft breadth × 11·62ft draught, 8-cyl MWM diesel, 1,400bhp, 13·75 knots.

VALLE DE NERVION. *Spanish*. LPG carrier, ref. Built by As de T. Ruiz de Velasco, SA, Bilbao, for Vasco Madrilena de Navegacion SA, Bilbao. 1,760 tons gross, 2,226 tons dw, 248·18ft loa × 39·5ft breadth × 18·05ft draught, 8-cyl Naval-Stork-Werkspoor diesel, 2,000bhp, 15 knots.

VALLEJO. *Peruvian*. Cargo. Built by O/Y Wartsila A/B, Abo, for Cia Peruana de Vapores, Callao. 5,792/9,464 tons gross, —/13,700 tons dw, 493·84ft loa × 64·75ft breadth × 30·33ft draught, 6-cyl Wartsila-Sulzer diesel, 9,600bhp, 17 knots.

VAN ENTERPRISE. *Liberian*. Bulk carrier. Built by Osaka Zosensho, Osaka, for Alberti Navigation Co, Monrovia (Vanshipping Co, Hong Kong). 10,192 tons gross, 16,780 tons dw, 454·41ft lbp × 73·92ft breadth × 29·09ft draught, 7-cyl Mitsubishi-Sulzer diesel, 8,700bhp, knots na.

VAN FORT. *Liberian*. Bulk carrier. Built by Osaka Zosensho, Osaka, for Victoria Shipping Co Inc, Monrovia. 10,524 tons gross, 17,080 tons wd, 484·25ft loa × 73·33ft breadth × 29·12ft draught, 7-cyl Mitsubishi-Sulzer diesel, 8,700bhp, 15 knots.

VAN HATTUM EN BLANKEVOORT 20. *British*. Trailing suction dredger. Built by Schps & Mach De Merwede, Hardinxveld, for Nash Dredging & Reclamation Co Ltd, London. 4,821 tons gross, 6,065 tons dw, 343·33ft loa × 59ft m breadth × 24·09ft draught, two 12-cyl tw sc Smit-Bolnes diesel, btp, 4,400bhp, 12·5 knots.

VAN UNION. *Liberian*. Cargo. Built by Onomichi Zosen, Onomichi, for Kalgrad Navigation Co, Monrovia (Vanshipping Co, Hong Kong). 10,207 tons gross, 16,700 tons dw, 490ft loa × 73ft breadth × 29·5ft draught, 7-cyl Hitachi-B & W diesel, 8,400bhp, knots na.

VANCOUVER FOREST. *British*. Bulk carrier/timber (ore strengthened). Built by Upper Clyde Shipbuilders, Clydebank Div, Clydebank, for J. & J. Denholm (Management) Ltd, Glasgow. 17,659 tons gross, 26,700 tons dw, 575ft loa × 87·41ft breadth × 31·84ft draught, cyl na, Barclay-Curle-Sulzer diesel, cpp, 10,500bhp, 15·5 knots.

VANGUARD. *Liberian*. Bulk carrier. Built by Osaka Zosensho, Osaka, for Montreal Shipping Co Inc, Monrovia (Vanshipping Co, Hong Kong). 10,524 tons gross, 17,089 tons dw, 484·25ft loa × 73·33ft breadth × 29·38ft draught, 7-cyl IHI-Sulzer diesel, 8,700bhp, 15 knots.

VASILY GOLOVKIN. *Russian*. Stern trawler, fish factory, ref (ATLANTIK class). Built by Volkswerft Stralsund, Stralsund, 1968, for USSR. 2,657 tons gross, 1,152 tons dw, 269·58ft loa × 44·75ft breadth × 16·41ft draught, two 8-cyl s sc Liebknecht diesel, cpp, 2,320bhp, 13·5 knots.

VASILY KOZENKOV. *Russian*. Stern trawler, fish factory, ref. Built by Stocznia Gdanska, Gdansk, for USSR. 2,944 tons gross, 1,366 tons dw, 272·66ft loa × 45·41ft breadth × 18·05ft draught, 8-cyl Sulzer diesel, 2,400bhp, 11·75 knots.

VASYA SHISHKOVSKY. *Russian*. Cargo. Built by Schiffsw Neptun, Rostock, for USSR, Murmansk. 3,684 tons gross, 4,638 tons dw, 346·75ft loa × 51·33ft breadth × 22·18ft draught, 6-cyl Halberstadt-MAN diesel, 3,250bhp, knots na.

VEGA. *South Korean*. Cargo (8 pass). Built by Hayashikane Zosen, Nagasaki, 1968, for Korea Shipping Corpn, Pusan. 5,992 tons gross, 8,234 tons dw, 422·58ft loa × 59·18ft breadth × 24·84ft draught, 7-cyl Kawasaki-MAN diesel, 6,440bhp, 14·75 knots.

VELIKYE POCHIN. *Russian*. Cargo. Builder na, Roumania, for USSR. 2,292 tons gross, tons dw na, measurements na, tw sc diesel, cyl na, bhp na, knots na.

Valdes. *Messrs Macandrews have started a new weekly container service between Liverpool and Bilbao with the chartered German ship renamed as above. A somewhat similar ship, renamed* Velazquez *is employed on a similar service from Liverpool every 16 days to Barcelona and Valencia direct carrying 102×20ft containers at 12½ knots. The names perpetuate the famous white hulled liners which formerly served the London-Gibraltar-Barcelona run which they performed for so many years, with passengers and cargo. The new services are part of the 'Macpak' service, the third leg of which is the passenger/car service run from Southampton in conjunction with the Swedish Lloyd ships. The ship recently made a record turn round in less than 12 hours, discharging 35 containers and loading 53. She holds 71 containers. These services replace a 200 year old conventional service operated by these owners.*

VELIKYE USTJUG. *Russian.* Cargo. Built by F. W. Hollming O/Y, Rauma, for USSR. 2,920 tons gross, 3,400 tons dw, 335ft loa×46·09ft breadth×19·66ft draught, 5-cyl Valmet-B & W diesel, 2,900bhp, knots na.

VENERA I. V. *Russian.* Stern trawler, fish factory, ref (ATLANTIK class). Built by Volkswerft Stralsund, Stralsund, 1967, for USSR, Odessa. 2,657 tons gross, 1,152 tons dw, 269·58ft loa×44·75ft breadth×16·41ft draught, two 8-cyl s sc Liebknecht diesel, 2,320bhp, 13·5 knots.

Valle de Ibaizabal. *Typical of the small liquid natural gas carriers being built in Spain, this ship was sold to Italian owners on completion and renamed* Andalusia.

VENEZUELA MARU. *Japanese*. Cargo, ref. Built by Hitachi Zosen, Mukaishima, for Kawasaki KKK, Kobe. 8,816 tons gross, 12,000 tons dw, 462·58ft loa × 68·33ft breadth × 30ft draught, 6-cyl Hitachi-B & W diesel, 7,200bhp, knots na.

VENUSTIANO CARRANZA. *Mexican*. Tanker (5 pass). Built by Ishikawajima Harima HI, Tokyo, for Petroleos Mexicanos, Tampico. 10,086 tons gross, 15,577 tons dw, 475ft loa (incl bb) × 70ft breadth × 28·45ft draught, 6-cyl IHI-Sulzer diesel, 7,200bhp, 14 knots.

VERONA. *Norwegian*. Bulk carrier. Built by Oresundsvarvet A/B, Landskrona, for Sverre Ditlev-Simonsen & Co, Oslo. 22,600 tons gross, 38,000 tons dw, 656ft loa × 885ft m breadth × 36·66ft draught, 7-cyl Gotaverken diesel, 13,700bhp, knots na.

VICTORIA DE GIRON. *Cuban*. Cargo, ref. Built by Uddevallavarvet A/B, Uddevalla, for Emp. Nacional Mambisa, Havana. 10,972 tons gross, 15,120 tons dw, 531·09ft loa × 67·25ft breadth × 32ft draught, 7-cyl Uddevalla-B & W diesel, 11,900bhp, 18 knots.

Varma. For particulars see Vol XVII. Similar to the 1963 built Tarmo, but 2 metres longer, and built by Oy Wartsila A/B for the Finnish Board of Navigation. She is fitted with quadruple screws, 2 forward for ice breaking and 2 aft. Her Wartsila-Sulzer 8M451 diesels give her an open water speed of 18 knots, each of the 4 main engines having an output of 3,440bhp, her total shp is 12,000. This Helsinki yard is well known as the world's major ice breaker constructor and designer.

V

Vassijaure. *An unusual step for these owners is entering the acid carrying trade. Formerly a large ore/oil carrier, constructed in 1954, she is the first of 3 similar Grangesberg-Oxelosund ships to be converted for carrying commercial phosphoric acid in bulk, and on her first trip delivered the largest shipment of the acid yet sent by sea, at Rotterdam, produced at the Fertilizer complex at Coatzacoalcos, Mexico. The ship is now a chemical and oil carrier capable of carrying 23,500 tons of cargo. She has been chartered to the producing firm, Fertilizantes Fosfatados Mexicanos SA for 10 years, and will deliver acid to Brazil, India, Europe and Australia. The other ships are the Viris and Virihaure, also chartered for 10 years, which will come into service in 1970. (Not in register.) The converted ships carry the letters FFM in front of their names.*

VICTORIASAND. *German*. Tanker. Built by Busumer Werft GmbH, Busum, for A. F. Harmstorf & Co, Hamburg. 499 tons gross, 1,330 tons dw, 241·09ft loa × 39·33ft m breadth × 12ft draught, 4-cyl Atlas-MaK diesel, 1,000bhp, 12 knots.

VIGSNES. *Norwegian*. Cargo. Built by Fr Lurssen, Vegesack, for A/S Kristian Jebsen's Rederi, Bergen. 2,866 tons gross, 4,405 tons dw, 314·33ft loa × 45·75ft breadth × 21·7ft draught, two 8-cyl s sc Akers diesel, cpp, 2,080bhp, 12·5 knots.

VIKINGFJORD. *German*. Ferry OSD. Built by Jos L. Meyer, Papenburg, for Nordland Reederei Heinz Schmidt-Wiking, Cuxhaven. 4,300 tons gross, tons dw na, 354·66ft loa × 57·09ft breadth × 14·96ft draught, two 6-cyl tw sc MAN diesel, 13,400bhp, knots na.

VILLE DE REIMS. *French*. Cargo, ref. Built by Warnowwerft, Warnemunde, for Cie Havraise & Nantaise Peninsulaire (CHNP), Dunkerque. 9,435 tons gross, 12,520 tons dw, 494·41ft loa × 65·58ft m breadth × 29·66ft draught, 8-cyl DMR-MAN diesel, 11,200bhp, 15 knots.

VINDEMIA. *Swedish*. Wine tanker. Built by Vaagen Verft, Kryksaeterora, for Rederi A/B Svenska Lloyd, Gothenburg. 700 tons gross, tons dw na, 239·33ft loa × 34·84ft breadth × draught na, 6-cyl Deutz diesel, 1,600bhp, knots na.

VIRTSU. *Russian*. Cargo. Built by Angyalfold Shipyard, Budapest, 1967, for USSR, Tallinn. 1,248 tons gross, 1,285 tons dw, 244·41ft loa × 37·18ft breadth × 13·12ft draught, 8-cyl Lang diesel, 1,000bhp, 11·5 knots.

VIRTUS. *Liberian*. Cargo. Built by Bartram & Sons Ltd, Sunderland, for International Navigation Corpn, Monrovia. 8,938 tons gross, 15,000 tons dw, 462·58ft loa × 67·09ft breadth × 29·05ft draught, 5-cyl Hawthorn-Sulzer diesel, 5,500bhp, knots na.

VISAYAN. *Japanese*. Chemical tanker (molasses). Built by Hayashikane Zosen, Nagasaki, for Nagai KKK, Tokyo. 1,800 tons gross, 2,900 tons dw, 272·25ft loa × 41·41ft breadth × 18·09ft draught, 6-cyl Akasaka-Tekkosho diesel, 2,200bhp, 12·5 knots.

VISHVA BINDU. *Indian*. Cargo, ref. Built by Stocznia Szczecinska, Szczecin, for The Shipping Corpn of India Ltd, Bombay. 5,350/8,120 tons gross, 8,210/11,560 tons dw, 476·92ft loa × 61·84ft breadth × 24·64/28·8ft draught 7-cyl Cegileski-Sulzer diesel, 8,000bhp, knots na.

VISHVA CHETANA (ex VISHVA CHETNA, launched as ZYGMUNT AUGUST). *Indian*. Cargo, ref. Built by Stocznia Szczecinska, Szczecin, for The Shipping Corpn of India, Bombay. 5,353/8,119 tons gross, 8,222/11,572 tons dw, 476·92ft loa × 61·92ft breadth × 24·16/29·84ft draught, 7-cyl Cegielski-Sulzer diesel, 8,000bhp, 17·5 knots.

VISHVA SANDESH. *Indian*. Cargo, ref. Built by Stocznia Szczecinska, Szczecin, for The Shipping Corpn of India Ltd, Bombay. 5,391/8,119 tons gross, —/11,565 tons dw, 476·92ft loa × 61·92ft breadth × 24·16/29·86ft draught, 7-cyl Cegielski-Sulzer diesel, 8,000bhp, 17·5 knots.

VISHVA SHAKTI. *Indian*. Cargo, ref. Built by Hindustan Shipyard, Visakhapatnam, for The Shipping Corpn of India Ltd, Bombay. 9,320 tons gross, 12,970 tons dw, 505·09ft loa × 64ft breadth × 30·3ft draught, 6-cyl Cegielski-Sulzer diesel, 8,000bhp, knots na.

VISHVA SHOBHA. *Indian*. Cargo, ref. Built by Hindustan Shipyard, Visakhapatnam, for The Shipping Corpn of India, Bombay. 9,200 tons gross, 12,970 tons dw, 505·09ft loa × 64ft breadth × 30·3ft draught, 6-cyl Cegielski-Sulzer deisel, 9,600bhp, 16·75 knots.

VISHVA VIKAS (launched as WLADYSLAW JAGIELIO). *Indian*. Cargo, ref. Built by Stocznia Szczecinska Szczecin, 1968, for The Shipping Corpn of India, Bombay. 5,528/8,422 tons gross, —/11,378 tons dw, 476·92ft loa × 61·84ft breadth × 24·16/29·75ft draught, 7-cyl Cegielski-Sulzer diesel, 8000,bhp, 17·5 knots.

VLADIMIR KOROLENKO. *Russian*. Cargo. Built by Brodogradiliste 'Uljanik', Pula, 1968, for USSR, Vladivostok. 10,457 tons gross, 14,200 tons dw, 524·58ft loa × 69·33ft breadth × 31·75ft draught, 8-cyl Uljanik-B & W diesel, 12,000bhp, 18·5 knots.

Victoria de Giron *is the first of 3 ships being built in Sweden for the European Navigacion Mambisa of Havana, and is fitted with a 7K74EF type of Uddevallavarvet-B & W engine developing 11,900bhp at 120rpm giving a speed of 18 knots. She has eighteen 10-ton derricks, with 2 heavy lift derricks of 30 and 60-tons respectively. The second ship is the somewhat inelegantly named* Bahia de Cochinos *(but probably a notable name in recent Cuban history).*

Vladivostok. *Last of 5 ships of the* Moskva *class built by Wartsila O/Y for the USSR, and amongst the world's most powerful ice breakers with conventional machinery, with their 22,000shp diesel-electric engines being the most powerful yet installed. She has accommodation for 122 persons; an automatic electric towing winch with a pull of 60 tons and a heeling tank set which can pump 180 tons of water from 1 side to the other in 2 minutes, to lessen the risk of the ship being caught in the ice. The main propelling plant consists of 8 Wartsila-Sulzer 9MH51 units, each developing 3,250bhp. There are 3 electric propulsion motors, each driving its own propeller. The centre motor develops 8,400kw, whilst the 2 wing ones each develop 4,050. These motors exert high torque at low revolutions to prevent the propellers being stuck in the ice. In open water 18 knots can be maintained.*

Volnay. Carrying on the 'V' nomenclature of the now defunct firm, well known in pre-war days, of Gow, Harrison & Co Ltd of Glasgow, this ship was in April 1969, the largest British car/bulk carrier. Delivered by Upper Clyde Shipbuilders 2 weeks ahead of schedule, she has been fitted at a cost of about £500,000 with Blohm & Voss portable car decks at Hamburg. In each of Nos 1-3 and 5-7 holds are fitted 2 steel platform decks and 5 hanging or hoistable steel decks. In No 4 hold, also a ballast compartment, are fitted 6 platform decks. She has been chartered to the Star Shipping Group for service between Japan and the USA. On her first voyage from Tilbury to the West Coast of the USA she loaded 2,540 vehicles in 4 days. When not used for cars, the pontoon car decks are taken out of the cargo holds and stowed in stowage racks on deck. She is a versatile ship, being designed for the carriage of all kinds of grain without shifting boards, cement, iron ore, coke, etc. She is also designed to carry packaged lumber in the holds, and on deck up to a height of 22ft 6in. She has seven 10-ton ASEA design electric cranes, mounted on pillars, to be well clear of packaged lumber on deck. She has a ram bow and transom stern, the double bottom tanks are extended up the ship's sides to form hoppers in order to make her self-trimming. The hatch covers are hydraulically operated, a duct keel carries piping through the holds, and the holds, originally naturally ventilated are to be fitted with mechanical ventilation. The main engine is a Sulzer large bore RD 90 built by the builder of the ship (John Brown & Co, Clydebank). She cost (without the car decks), £2,250,000 approximately. En route Hamburg to be fitted with the decks, she took a coke cargo from Baltimore to Ijmuiden, before commencing her 6 year charter, carrying Toyota cars from Japan to the USA.

VLAS CHUBAR. *Russian*. Cargo. Builder na, Giurgiu, 1968, for USSR. 1,865 tons gross, tons dw na, measurements na, cyl na, diesel, bhp na, knots na.

VOLGA MARU. *Japanese*. Ore/oil carrier. Built by Mitsubishi HI Ltd, Yokohama, for Sanko KKK. 45,234 tons gross, 76,400 tons dw, measurements na, cyl na, make na, bhp na, knots na.

VOLGOBALT NOS 20, 21, 22, 35, 36, 37, 38, 39, 40, 45. *Russian*. Cargo. Builder na, for USSR. 2,178 tons gross, 1,240 tons dw, measurements na, cyl na, diesel, bhp na, knots na.

VOLGONEFT NOS 30, 44, 45, 47, 52, 53, 54, 55, 56, 57, 64, 65, 66. *Russian*. Tankers, Built in Russia 1968-69, No 45 Volgograd Shipyard, Volgograd, No 48 G. Dimitrov Shipyard, Varna, for USSR. 3,519 tons gross, 4,987 tons dw, measurements na, cyl na, diesel, bhp na, knots na.

VOLNAY. *British*. Bulk carrier. Built by Upper Clyde Shipbuilders (Clydebank) Ltd, for Harrisons (Clyde) Ltd, Glasgow. 22,189 tons gross, 37,500 tons dw, 633·5ft loa (incl bb) × 90·18ft breadth × 36·9ft draught, 6-cyl John Brown-Sulzer diesel, 13,800bhp, 15·5 knots.

VOO SHEE. *Chinese (Taiwan)*. Tanker. Built by Ishikawajima HI, Aioi, for Chinese Petroleum Corpn, Kaohsiung. 52,440 tons gross, 99,157 tons dw, 830·18ft loa (incl bb) × 120·92ft breadth × 47·92ft draught, 9-cyl IHI-Sulzer diesel, 20,700bhp, 16·5 knots.

VOREDA. *British*. Cargo. Built by Schps Gebr van Diepen, Waterhuizen, for Harrisons (Clyde) Ltd (Ch Salvesen [Management] Mgrs), Glasgow. 695/1,437 tons gross, 1,600/2,575 tons dw, 253·18ft loa × 39ft breadth × 14·33/18·84ft draught 8-cyl, Atlas-MaK diesel, 1,500bhp, 11·5 knots.

VORTIGERN. *British*. Pass/car/rail ferry. Built by Swan Hunter Shpyds Ltd, Wallsend & Neptune Shipyards, Wallsend, for British Railways Board, London. 4,850 tons gross, tons dw na, 376·92ft loa × 63ft breadth × 13·5ft draught, two 16-cyl tw sc Crossley-Pielstick diesel, 14,560bhp, 19·5 knots.

VYTEGRA. *Russian*. Cargo. Built by A. Zdhanov, Leningrad, 1967, for USSR. 4,676 tons gross, 6,357 tons dw, 400·09ft loa × 54·92ft breadth × 22·2ft draught, 9-cyl Bryansk-B & W diesel, bhp na, knots na.

Vortigern. *With this ship British Rail appear to be returning to the more pleasant names of earlier days. Perhaps it would not be expecting too much for that fine ship* Holyhead Ferry No 1 *to be renamed with a suitable Irish Sea name, instead of a catalogue number for a title?*

The Vortigern *cost about £2,500,000 to build, and is the first of a new class of all-purpose ships, ie, passengers, cars, lorries, buses, railway freight wagons and sleeping cars. During the summer she runs on the Dover-Boulogne service, but during the winter is employed between Dover and Dunkerque mainly as a train and commercial ferry. As a train ferry her deadweight is 1,200 tons, and as a car ferry, 900 tons. She is a 1 class passenger ship, accommodating up to 1,000 passengers, of whom 48 are in cabins. Crew personnel number 63. Vehicle capacity varies according to the type of unit, but roughly as follows: garage, 40 cars, gallery decks, 80 cars, main deck, 120 cars, main decks with galleries raised, 40×30ft lorries, or 35 railway freight wagons or 10 sleeping carriages and 11×35ft wagons, or 24×40ft wagons. The ship has both bow and stern doors. Accommodation includes 2 bars (verandah and smoke room) a self service restaurant seating 140 persons, a nursing room for mothers and small children, several lounges with both armchairs and reclining chairs, and a light refreshment and tea room in the forward lounge. She is propelled by 2 Crossley-Pielstick 16 PC2V 450 diesel engines driving twin controllable pitch propellers through gearboxes. Each engine has a maximum output of 7,280bhp, and the service speeds are 19½ knots as a car ferry, and 15½ as a train ferry. Bridge control of the engines is provided, and there are twin spade rudders aft, with a bow thrust unit forward, with fin type stabilizers for comfort.*

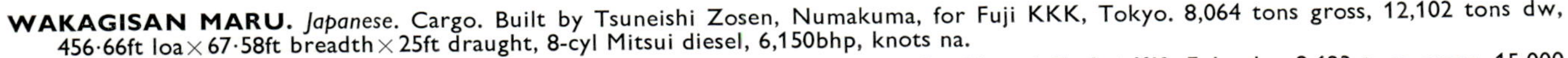

WAKAGISAN MARU. *Japanese*. Cargo. Built by Tsuneishi Zosen, Numakuma, for Fuji KKK, Tokyo. 8,064 tons gross, 12,102 tons dw, 456·66ft loa×67·58ft breadth×25ft draught, 8-cyl Mitsui diesel, 6,150bhp, knots na.

WAKASUGISAN MARU. *Japanese*. Cargo. Built by Mitsui Zosen, Fujinagata, for Maruni Shokai KK, Fukuoka. 9,623 tons gross, 15,000 tons dw, 452·84ft lbp×72·25ft breadth×28·25ft draught, 7-cyl Mitsui-B & W diesel, 8,400bhp knots na.

WAKATERU MARU. *Japanese*. Cargo. Built by Imabari Zosen, Imabari, for Soki KKK, Imabari. 2,996 tons gross, 6,097 tons dw, 334·58ft loa×53·66ft breadth×22·03ft draught, 6-cyl Hanshin diesel, 3,500bhp, knots na.

WAKAURA MARU. *Japanese*. Cargo. Built by Namura Zosensho, Osaka, for Nippon Yusen Kaisha, Tokyo. 7,673 tons gross, 11,600 tons dw, 454·41ft loa×61·92ft breadth×28·92ft draught 6-cyl, Hitachi-B & W diesel, 6,600bhp, knots na.

WEIPA MARU. *Japanese*. Bulk carrier (for Australia-Japan bauxite trade). Built by Uraga HI Ltd, Yokosuka, for Daiichi Chuo KK, Tokyo. 14,044 tons gross, 23,594 tons dw, 544·66ft loa (incl bb)×78·84ft breadth×30·92ft draught, 6-cyl Uraga-Sulzer diesel, cpp, 9,600bhp, 14·5 knots.

WILLI REITH (Sis META REITH). *German*. Container ship OSD/CSD, 8 pass 250×20ft containers incl 106 on deck. Built by Schiffb Unterweser, Bremerhaven, for 'ORION' Schiffs-Gesell Reith & Co, Hamburg. 2,881/5,478 tons gross, 5,370/7,315 tons dw, 408·41ft loa×58ft breadth×20·66/24·27ft draught, 16-cyl Deutz diesel, 6,400bhp, 18 knots.

WINHA (Sis PURHA). *Finnish*. Tanker. Built by Cons Nav & Ind de la Mediteranee, CNIM, La Syene, for Suomen Tankkilaiva O/Y, Helsinki. 17,350 tons gross, 25,000 tons dw, 619ft loa×72·33ft breadth×32·84ft draught, 7-cyl Gotaverken diesel, 9,250bhp, 14·5 knots.

WIRTA. *Finnish*. Cargo OSD/CSD, Built by Rauma-Repola O/Y, Rauma, for Suomen Tankkilaiva, Helsinki. 6,971/9,729 tons gross, 11,652/14,675 tons dw, 496·33ft loa×68·92ft breadth×28·09/31·64ft draught, 6-cyl Gotaverken diesel, 10,350bhp, 18 knots.

WISMAR. *East German*. Cargo, ref, OSD/CSD, 12 pass. Built by Mathias-Thesen-Werft, Wismar, 1968, for Deutsche Seereederei, Rostock. 3,918/5,969 tons gross, 5,428/6,840 tons dw, 424·41ft loa×56·84ft breadth×22·1/24·93ft draught, 7-cyl Halberstadt-MAN diesel, 7,000bhp, 16 knots.

Wayway. *This photograph of the log/bulk carrier* Wayway *is interesting as showing all the deck cargo equipment in place for deck cargo of timber This ship was completed late in 1968 (register Vol XVII). She has 5 holds with top side ballast tanks and a bottom side hopper construction. 5 sets of Hitachi type 15-ton derricks are fitted, with very wide hatches. She is sufficiently stiffened for carrying timber on deck, and is of Hitachi's Economy type. The main engine is a Hitachi-B & W 762VT2BF140 with a maximum continuous output of 8,400bhp giving a trial speed of 16·935 knots. Her owners are the Windsor Shipping Co Ltd, and her deadweight is 23,950 tons.*

WITTENBURG. *East German.* Cargo, ref, OSD/CSD, 12 pass. Built by Mathias-Thesen-Werft, Wismar, for Deutsche Seereederei, Rostock. 3,918/5,969 tons gross, 5,428/6,840 tons dw, 424·41ft loa × 56·84ft breadth × 22·11/24·93ft draught, 7-cyl Halberstadt-MAN diesel, 7,000bhp, 16 knots.

WOERMANN UBANGI. *German.* Bulk carrier. Built by Hitachi Zosen, Innoshima, for Deutsche-African Linien GmbH & Co, Hamburg, 11,976 tons gross, 18,170 tons dw, 511·92ft loa × 74·18ft m breadth × 30·18ft draught, 7-cyl Hitachi-B & W diesel, bhp na, knots na.

WORLD CHAMPION. *Liberian.* Bulk carrier. Built by Hitachi Zosen, Mukaishima, for Liberian Stamina Transport, Monrovia (World Wide Co, Hong Kong). 11,430 tons gross, 18,000 tons dw, 511·84ft loa × 74·25ft breadth × 30·09ft draught, 7-cyl Hitachi-B & W diesel, 8,400bhp, knots na.

Wilmington. *This vessel is understood to be the largest vessel yet built at Aberdeen. She has 4 large clear holds, fitted with Macgregor power operated hatch covers, automatically controlled, helping to cut down her port time, and the engine room is designed to operate for periods of 16 hours, unmanned. There is a high degree of automation installed, with a Vickers bow thrust unit. Exceptionally good accommodation is provided for all on board.*

WORLD CHIEF. *Liberian.* Tanker. Built by Kawasaki Dkyd Co Ltd, Kobe, for World Wide Shipping Ltd, Monrovia. 98,481 tons gross, 178,300 tons dw, 1,081·09ft loa (incl bb)×158·25ft breadth×54·25ft draught, Kawasaki turbs, 33,000shp, 16 knots.

WORLD DIANA. *Liberian.* Bulk carrier. Built by Osaka Zosensho, Osaka, 1968, for Liberian Integrity Transports SA, Monrovia (World Wide Co, Hong Kong). 11,846 tons gross, 20,028 tons dw, 513·25ft loa×74·25ft breadth×32·14ft draught, 7-cyl Mitsui-B & W diesel, 8,400bhp, 14·75 knots.

WORLD HONG KONG. *British.* Bulk carrier. Built by Scotts SB & E Co Ltd, Greenock, for Marine Navigation Co Ltd, London (World Wide Co, London and Hong Kong). 12,341 tons gross, 19,150 tons dw, 520ft loa (incl bb)×72·09ft breadth×30·25ft draught, 7-cyl Scott-Sulzer diesel, 8,700bhp, 14·75 knots.

WORLD KINDNESS. *Liberian.* Tanker. Built by Mitsui Zosen, Tamano, 1968, for Drummond SS Co, Monrovia (S. Niarchos). 41,477 tons gross, 87,771 tons dw, 844·75ft loa (incl bb)×122·18ft breadth×43·88ft draught, 9-cyl Mitsui-B & W diesel, 20,700bhp, 17 knots.

Woermann Ubangi. *This is the 12th ship in Hitachi Zosen's standard 18,000 ton deadweight bulk carrier, which will be employed on the line's services between Germany and East Africa. The main engine is a Hitachi-B & W 762VT-2BF-140 type giving 8,400bhp at 139rpm. Trial trip speed was 17·25 knots. Her keel was laid at Innoshima on May 15th, 1969 and she was completed on October 30th, 1969, and delivered.*

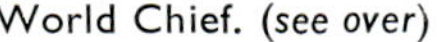

World Chief. (*see over*)

World Chief *is the latest very large crude oil carrier (VLCC) in the ever expanding fleet of the associated companies forming the World Wide (Shipping) Ltd group of Hong Kong. This 219,259 ton dw turbine tanker was built at Sakkaide (Kawasaki Dockyard Co) for Liberian Express Transports Inc, on behalf of World Maritime Bahamas Ltd. Four 220,000 ton VLCCs are on order for the group.*

WORLD KNOWLEDGE. *Liberian.* Tanker. Built by Mitsui Zosen, Tamano, for Langham Shpg Co, Monrovia (S. Niarchos). 41,477 tons gross, 87,780 tons dw, 844·75ft loa (incl bb) × 122·18ft breadth × 43·88ft draught, 9-cyl Mitsui-B & W diesel, 20,700bhp, 17 knots.

WORLD PELAGIC. *Liberian.* Bulk carrier. Built by Ishikawajima-Harima HI Ltd, Nagoya, for Liberian Virtue Transport Co, Monrovia (World Wide Co, Hong Kong). 9,854 tons gross, 16,734 tons dw, 477·84ft loa × 71·66ft breadth × 29·84ft draught, 6-cyl IHI-Sulzer diesel, 7,200bhp, 14 knots.

WORLD PRESIDENT. *British.* Bulk carrier. Built by Scotts SB & E Co Ltd, Greenock, for World Wide Shipping Co Ltd, London. 12,341 tons gross, 19,170 tons dw, 520ft loa (incl bb) × 72·09ft breadth × 30·25ft draught, 7-cyl Clarke-Sulzer diesel, 9,700bhp, 14·75 knots.

WORLD PRIDE. *Liberian.* Bulk carrier. Built by Maizuru Jukogyo Ltd, Maizuru, for Liberian Silver Transports Inc, Monrovia (World Wide Co, New York and Hong Kong). 11,434 tons gross, 19,145 tons dw, 512·33ft loa × 74·25ft breadth × 31·29ft draught, 7-cyl Maizuru-B & W diesel, 8,400bhp, knots na.

WORLD VIRTUE. *Liberian.* Bulk carrier. Built by Osaka Zosensho, Osaka, for Liberian Valiant Transport Inc, Monrovia (World Wide Co, Hong Kong). 11,800 tons gross, 19,600 tons dw, 513·09ft loa × 74·25ft breadth × 31·9ft draught, 7-cyl Mitsui-B & W diesel, 8,400bhp, knots na.

WYOMING. *USA.* Cargo (216 × 20ft containers). Built by Avondale Shipyards Inc, Avondale, for States Steamship Co, San Francisco. 9,493/13,053 tons gross, —/14,150 tons dw, 579ft loa (incl bb) × 82·18ft breadth × 32·07/—ft draught, GEC turbs, 24,000shp, 23 knots.

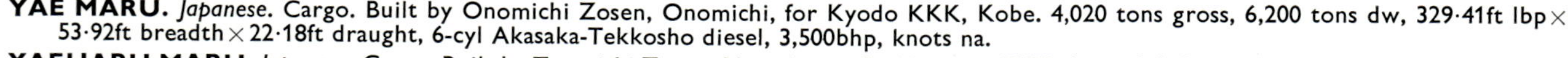

Y

YAE MARU. *Japanese.* Cargo. Built by Onomichi Zosen, Onomichi, for Kyodo KKK, Kobe. 4,020 tons gross, 6,200 tons dw, 329·41ft lbp × 53·92ft breadth × 22·18ft draught, 6-cyl Akasaka-Tekkosho diesel, 3,500bhp, knots na.

YAEHARU MARU. *Japanese.* Cargo. Built by Tsuneishi Zosen, Numakuma, for Yaegawa KKK, Anan. 2,999 tons gross, 5,108 tons dw, 334·75ft loa × 49·33ft breadth × 20·84ft draught, 6-cyl Akasaka-Tekkosho diesel, 3,200bhp, knots na.

YAMABISHI MARU. *Japanese.* Tanker. Built by Mitsubishi HI Ltd, Nagasaki, for Yamashita-Shinnihon KKK, Tokyo. 99,200 tons gross, 179,600 tons dw, 987·66ft loa (incl bb) × 158·33ft breadth × 59·09ft draught, Mitsubishi turbs, 30,000shp, knots na.

YAMAFUJI MARU. *Japanese.* Bulk carrier. Built by Koyo Dock, Mihara, 1968, for Sato KKK & Sanei Sempaku KK, Numakuma. 8,999 tons gross, 14,056 tons dw, 488·84ft loa × 70·33ft breadth × 26·41ft draught, 6-cyl Mitsui-B & W diesel, 7,200bhp, 14·25 knots.

YAMAFUKU MARU. *Japanese.* Cargo. Built by Imai Zosen, Kochi, for Kajiyama KKK, Hojyo. 2,520 tons gross, 4,200 tons dw, 278·84ft lbp × 47·33ft breadth × 19·66ft draught, 6-cyl Hanshin diesel, 2,800bhp, knots na.

YAMASHIN MARU. *Japanese.* Cargo. Built by Imai Zosen, Kochi, for Kajiyama KKK, Hojyo. 2,999 tons gross, 5,000 tons dw, 308·41ft lbp × 51ft breadth × 26·25ft draught, 6-cyl Hanshin diesel, 3,500bhp, knots na.

YAMATO MARU. *Japanese.* Cargo. Built by Kurushima Dock Co Ltd, Imabari, for Kinkai Yusen KK, Tokyo. 3,990 tons gross, 6,200 tons dw, 331·41ft lbp × 53·25ft breadth × 21·92ft draught, 6-cyl Mitsubishi-Sulzer diesel, 2,500bhp, 14·25 knots.

YAMAYOSHI MARU. *Japanese.* Cargo. Built by Honda Zosen, Saiki, for Tensho KKK, Shimonoseki. 963 tons gross, 1,432 tons dw, 224·18ft loa × 32·92ft breadth × 14·58ft draught, 6-cyl Hanshin diesel, 2,100bhp, knots na.

YANAGI MARU. *Japanese.* Cargo. Built by Kurushima Dock Co Ltd, Imabari, 1968, for Mitsui Bussan KK, Tokyo. 4,429 tons gross, 7,200 tons dw, 377·33ft lbp × 57·5ft breadth × 22·41ft draught, 6-cyl Mitsubishi-Sulzer diesel, 4,600bhp, 14 knots.

YGUAZU. *Liberian.* Cargo. Built by Mitsubishi HI, Shimonoseki, for Manora Corpn, Monrovia (Suisse Atlantique, Lausanne). 10,344 tons gross, 14,425 tons dw, 496·18ft loa × 69·66ft breadth × 30·96ft draught, 6-cyl Mitsubishi-Sulzer diesel, 7,200bhp, knots na.

YOSEI MARU. *Japanese.* Cargo. Built by Kanazashi Zosensho, Shimizu, for C. Itoh KK, Osaka. 4,038 tons gross, 6,183 tons dw, 361·35ft loa × 53·25ft breadth × 21·75ft draught, 8-cyl IHI-Pielstick diesel, 3,520bhp, knots na.

YOSHIDA MARU. *Japanese.* Tanker. Built by Kawasaki Dockyard Co Ltd, Kobe, for Terukuni KKK, Tokyo. 44,898 tons gross, 75,800 tons dw, 806·9ft loa (incl bb) × 125·84ft breadth × 42·41ft draught, 9-cyl Kawasaki-MAN diesel, 20,700bhp, 16·5 knots.

YOSHIN MARU. *Japanese.* Tanker. Built by Watanabe Zosensho, Nagasaki, for Yamato KKK, Hakata. 1,125 tons gross, tons dw na, 214·66ft lr × 34·25ft breadth × draught na, two 6-cyl s sc Daihatsu diesel, 750bhp, knots na.

YOUNGGLY. *Liberian.* Bulk carrier. Built by Mitsubishi HI Ltd, Hiroshima, 1968, for National Maritime Corpn Ltd, Monrovia (First SS Co, Taipeh). 23,750 tons gross, 42,838 tons dw, 638·18ft loa × 93·25ft breadth × 37·91ft draught, 7-cyl Mitsubishi-Sulzer diesel, 11,200bhp, 16·75 knots.

YOZAN MARU. *Japanese.* Bulk carrier. Built by Sasebo HI Ltd, Sasebo, for Shinwa KKK & Harumi Sempaku KK, Tokyo. 12,360 tons gross, 19,500 tons dw, 511·84ft loa × 76·92ft breadth × 30·62ft draught, 7-cyl Mitsubishi-Sulzer diesel, 8,500bhp, 14·25 knots.

YUHO MARU. *Japanese.* Cargo. Built by Kurushima Dock Co Ltd, Imabari, for Arimura Sangyo KK, Naha. 2,999 tons gross, 5,450 tons dw. 301·84ft lbp × 52·58ft breadth × 21·5ft draught, 6-cyl Hatsudoki diesel, 3,500bhp, 12·5 knots.

YUKAZE MARU. *Japanese.* Tanker. Built by Geibi Zosen Kogyo, Kure, for Osaka Keijo Unyo KK, Osaka. 781 tons gross, 1,484 tons dw, 213·5ft loa × 31·5ft breadth × 15·09ft draught, 6-cyl Akasaka-Tekkosho diesel, 1,250bhp, 14 knots.

YUKI MARU. *Japanese.* Cargo. Built by Koyo Dock, Mihara, for Geishu KKK, Kurahashi. 2,996 tons gross, 5,440 tons dw, 330·84ft loa × 51·58ft breadth × 21·33ft draught, 6-cyl Ito-Tekkosho diesel, 3,500bhp, knots na.

YURI KOSTIKOV. *Russian.* Stern trawler, fish factory, ref (B26 class). Built by Stocznia Gdanska, Gdansk, 1968, for USSR. 2,944 tons gross, 1,338 tons dw, 272·66ft loa × 45·41ft breadth × 18·18ft draught, 8-cyl Jugoturbina-Sulzer diesel, 2,400bhp, 13 knots.

YUSHO MARU. *Japanese.* Cargo. Built by Nippon Kokan, Shimizu, for Showa KKK, Tokyo. 7,900 tons gross, 11,400 tons dw, 446·25ft loa × 65·09ft breadth × 27·92ft draught, 6-cyl Sumitomo-Sulzer diesel, 7,000bhp, knots na.

YUSHO MARU. *Japanese.* Cargo. Built by Kanazashi Zosensho, Shimizu, for Dowa KKK, Tokyo. 3,996 tons gross, 6,187 tons dw, 361·33ft loa × 53·25ft breadth × 21·84ft draught, 6-cyl Hatsudoki diesel, 3,500bhp, knots na.

YUYO MARU. *Japanese.* Tanker. Built by Koyo Dock, Mihara, for Takebayashi KKK, Yuasa. 2,550 tons gross, 4,000 tons dw, 304·84ft loa × 44ft breadth × 19·84ft draught, 6-cyl Akasaka-Tekkosho diesel, 2,600bhp, knots na.

YUZUI MARU. *Japanese.* Vehicle carrier. Built by Hashihama Zosen, Imabari, for Nakano KKK, Tokyo. 2,000 tons gross, 1,400 tons dw, 314·92ft lbp × 47·33ft breadth × 14·18ft draught, 8-cyl IHI-Sulzer diesel, 3,720bhp, 14·25 knots.

Z

ZAANSTROOM (launched as ROSITA MARIA). *German*. Cargo (63×20ft containers). Built by J. J. Sietas Schiffsw, Hamburg, for Otto Nagel, Lubeck. 500 tons gross, 1,230 tons dw, 242·33ft loa×35·41ft breadth×13ft draught, 8-cyl Deutz diesel, 1,320bhp, 12·5 knots.

ZABAYKALSK. *Russian*. Cargo. Built by Stocznia Gdanska, Gdansk, 1967, for USSR. 4,682 tons gross, 6,132 tons dw, 406·25ft loa×54·7ft breadth×22·37ft draught, 5-cyl Cegielski-B & W diesel, 5,450bhp, 17 knots.

ZABRZE. *Polish*. Cargo, ref. Built by Stocznia Szczecinska, Szczecin, for Polish Ocean Lines. 6,576 tons gross, tons dw na, 444·25ft loa×58·25ft breadth×25·11ft draught, 6-cyl Cegielski-Sulzer diesel, bhp na, knots na.

ZAKARPATIE. *Russian*. Bulk carrier. Built by Stocznia im Komuny Parysitiej, Gdynia, for USSR. 16,331 tons gross, 22,885 tons dw, 614·18ft loa×75·33ft breadth×30·84ft draught, 6-cyl Cegielski-Sulzer diesel, 9,600bhp, 15·5 knots.

ZAMOSC. *Polish*.. Cargo, ref, OSD/CSD (BH46-1 class). Built by Stocznia Szczecinska, Szczecin, for Polish Ocean Lines, Gdynia. 4,183/6,581 tons gross, 5,708/7,234 tons dw, 443·58ft loa×58·25ft breadth×—/25·1ft draught, 6-cyl Cegielski-Sulzer diesel, 7,200bhp, 17·5 knots.

ZAPOROZHYJE. *Russian*. Bulk carrier (B470-1 class). Built by Stocznia im Komuny Paryskiej, Gdynia, 1968,-for USSR. 16,331 tons gross 22,896 tons dw, 614·18ft loa×75·33ft breadth×30·84ft draught, 6-cyl Cegielski-Sulzer diesel, 9,600bhp, 15·5 knots.

ZARECHENSK. *Russian*. Bulk carrier. Built by Stocznia im Komuny Paryskiej, Gydnia, 1968, for USSR. 16,331 tons gross, 22,885 tons dw, 614·18ft loa×75·33ft breadth×30·84ft draught, 6-cyl Cegielski-Sulzer diesel, 9,600bhp, 15·5 knots.

ZELZATE. *Belgian*. Bulk carrier. Built by N. V. Boelwerf SA, Tamise, for N. V. Ubem SA, Antwerp. 12,850 tons gross, 20,000 tons dw, 524·92ft loa×75·25ft breadth×32·47ft draught, 6-cyl ACEC-MAN diesel, 8,400bhp, 15·5 knots.

ZENKOREN MARU No 2. *Japanese*. Bulk carrier. Built by Uraga HI Ltd, Yokosuka, for Mitsui-OSK Lines KK & Sawayama KK, Kobe. 30,601 tons gross, 50,050 tons dw, 675·92ft loa (incl bb)×105·84ft breadth×38·92ft draught, 8-cyl Uraga-Sulzer diesel, 12,800bhp, knots na.

ZENKOREN MARU No 3. *Japanese*. Bulk carrier. Built by Ishikawajima-Harima HI, Aioi, for Taiyo KKK, Kobe. 31,853 tons gross, 47,600 tons dw, 682·33ft loa (incl bb)×105·84ft breadth×37·09ft draught, 8-cyl IHI-Sulzer diesel, 12,800bhp, 14·5 knots.

ZIEMIA KIELECKA. *Polish*. Bulk carrier. Built by Italcantieri SpA, Castellamare di Stabia, for Polish SS Co, Szczecin. 15,744 tons gross, 26,083 tons dw, 642·92ft loa (incl bb)×75ft breadth×34·73ft draught, 8-cyl CRDA-Fiat diesel, 11,200bhp, 16 knots.

ZLATNI PIASATZI. *Bulgarian*. Fish carrier, ref. Built by Nosenko Shipyard, Nikolaev, 1968, for Okeansky Ribolov, Bourgas. 5,942 tons gross, 5,170 tons dw, 426·5ft loa×55·18ft breadth×23·62ft draught, four 10-cyl tw sc diesel electric, bhp na, 16·5 knots.

ZLATOUST. *Russian*. Bulk carrier. Built by Stocznia im Komuny Paryskiej, Gdynia, for USSR. 16,332 tons gross, 22,896 tons dw, 614·18ft loa×75·33ft breadth×30·84ft draught, 6-cyl Cegielski-Sulzer diesel, 9,600bhp, 15·5 knots.

ZNA. *Russian*. Cable ship. Built by O/Y Wartsila A/B, Abo, 1968, for USSR. 5,600 tons gross, 3,245 tons dw, 427·84ft loa×52·66ft breadth×17ft draught, five 6-cyl tw sc Wartsila diesel electric, 4,950bhp, 14 knots.

ZVENIGORD. *Russian*. Bulk carrier. Built by Stocznia im Komuny Daryskiej, Gdynia, 1967, for USSR. 16,331 tons gross, 22,896 tons dw, 614·18ft loa×75·33ft breadth×30·84ft draught, 6-cyl Cegielski-Sulzer diesel, 9,600bhp, 15·5 knots.

Acadia Forest

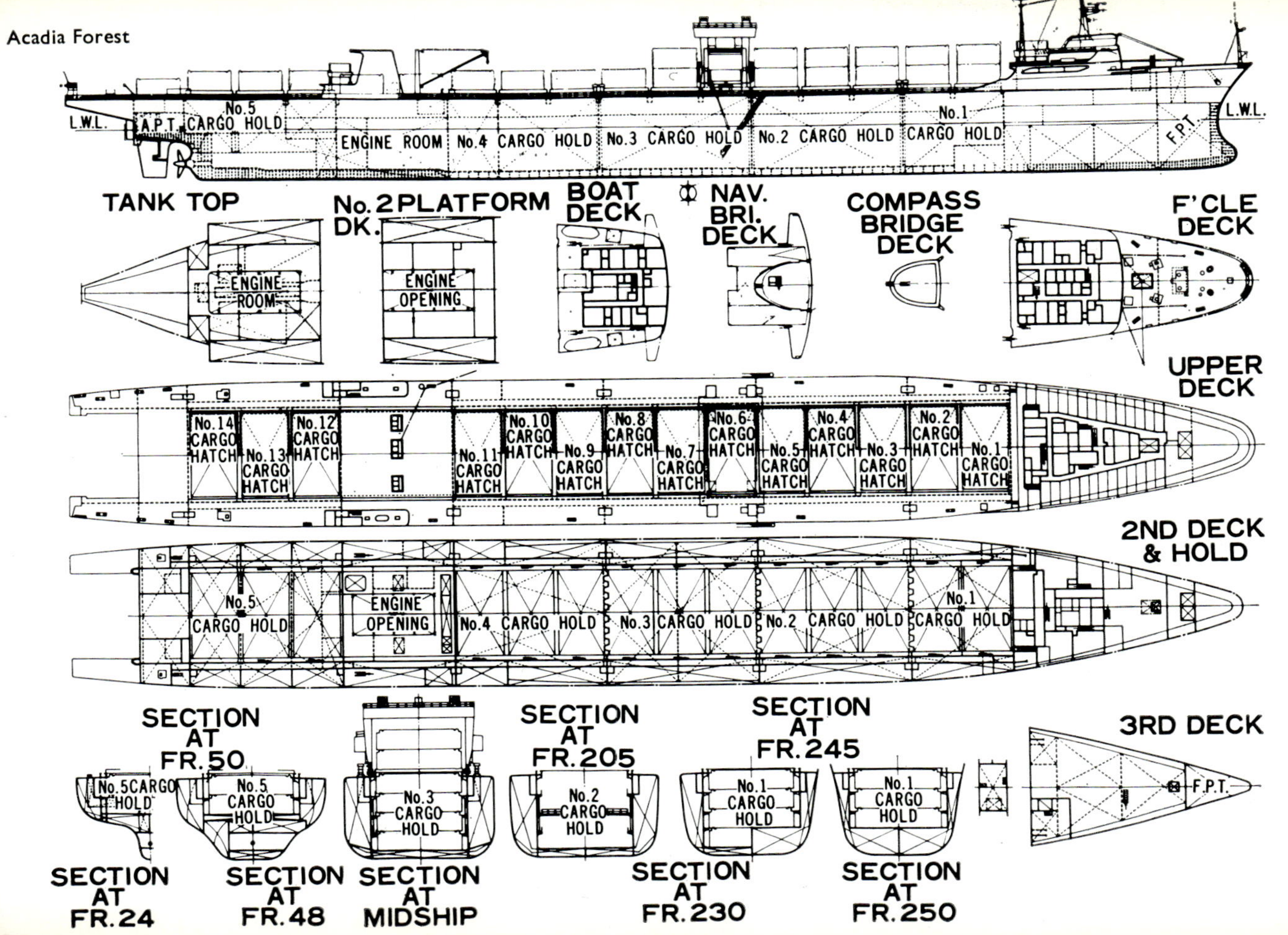

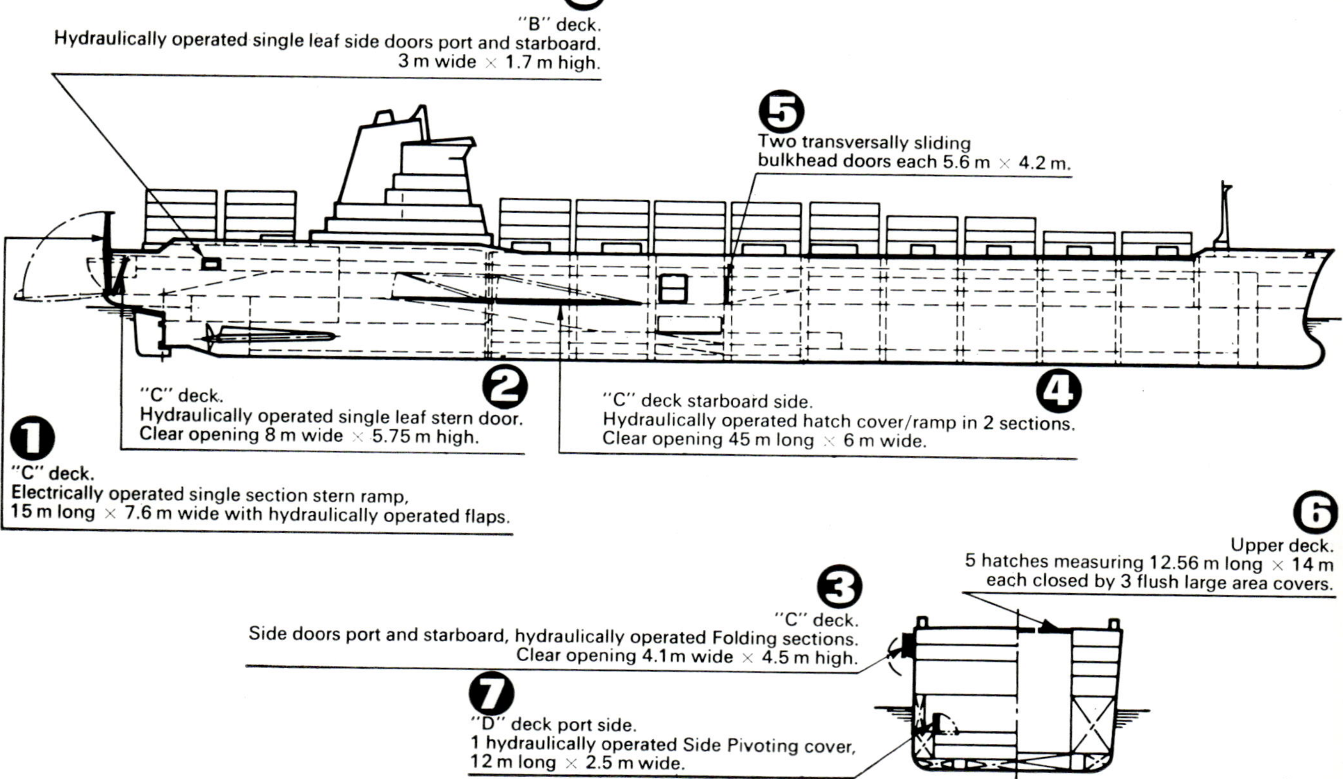
8
"B" deck.
Hydraulically operated single leaf side doors port and starboard.
3 m wide × 1.7 m high.
5
Two transversally sliding
bulkhead doors each 5.6 m × 4.2 m.
2
"C" deck.
Hydraulically operated single leaf stern door.
Clear opening 8 m wide × 5.75 m high.
4
"C" deck starboard side.
Hydraulically operated hatch cover/ramp in 2 sections.
Clear opening 45 m long × 6 m wide.
1
"C" deck.
Electrically operated single section stern ramp,
15 m long × 7.6 m wide with hydraulically operated flaps.
6
Upper deck.
5 hatches measuring 12.56 m long × 14 m
each closed by 3 flush large area covers.
3
"C" deck.
Side doors port and starboard, hydraulically operated Folding sections.
Clear opening 4.1 m wide × 4.5 m high.
7
"D" deck port side.
1 hydraulically operated Side Pivoting cover,
12 m long × 2.5 m wide.

Atlantic Causeway

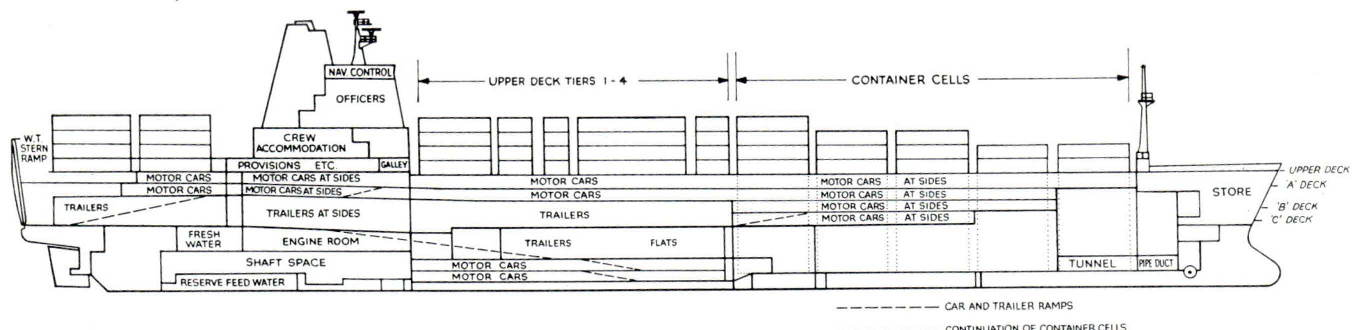

Encounter Bay

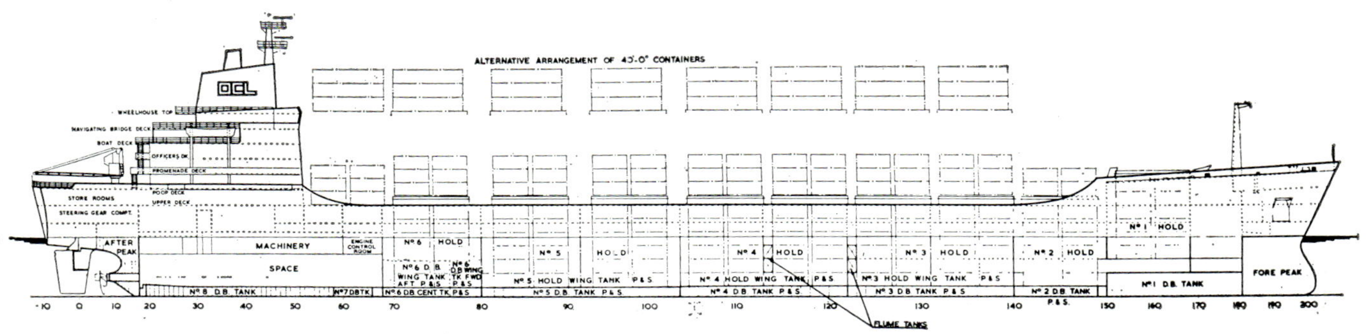

Maasdam

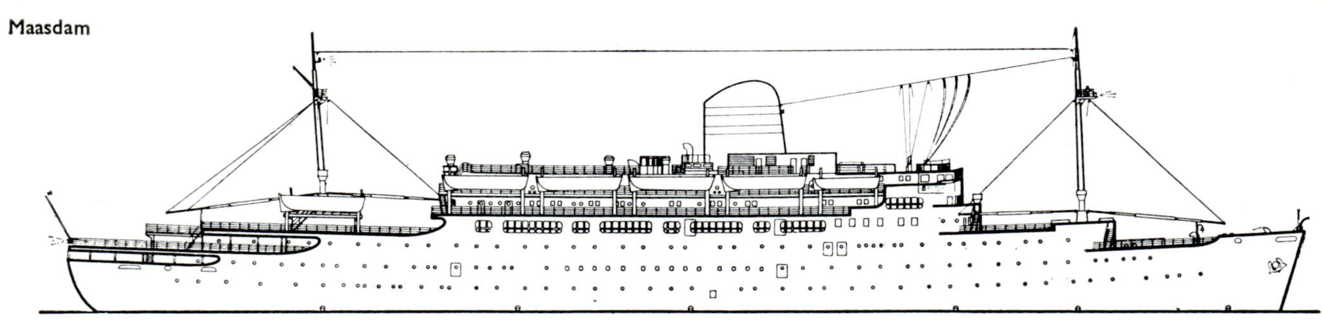

Stefan Batory

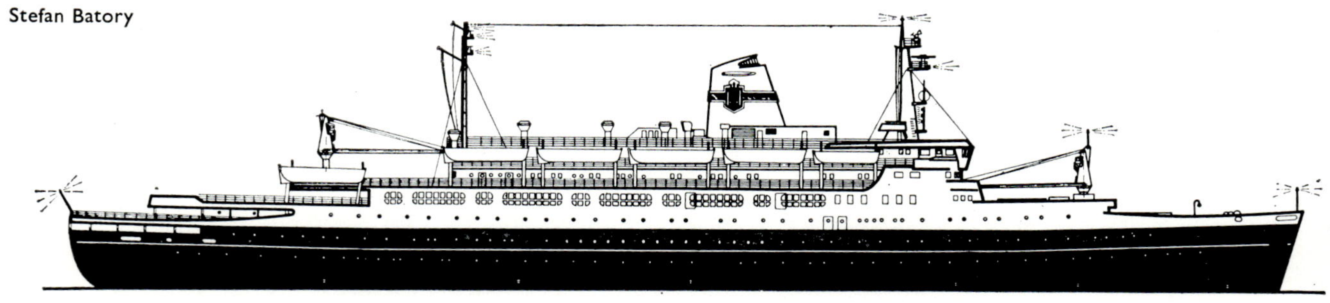

Stefan Batory. *In 1968 the Polish Ocean Lines purchased the Holland-America liner* Maasdam, *built in 1952, as a replacement for their famous but elderly* Batory. *She was sent into Gdansk for modernization. The changes in silhouette are clearly seen in the diagrams. Inside the ship the grand lounge on the promenade deck has been rebuilt and modernized, additional shelter provided on the promenade deck by adding a physical training hall with adjacent rooms and a nursery. On D deck, the former deep tanks were replaced by a cinema cum theatre, convertible into a chapel when required. Considerable replacements of wood by steel were made in order to comply with the latest SOLAS requirements for fire precautions, and numerous fireproof covers to manholes and fireproof insulation in various areas. She now carries 39 first class and 780 tourist. The crew numbers 337.*

Texaco Hamburg

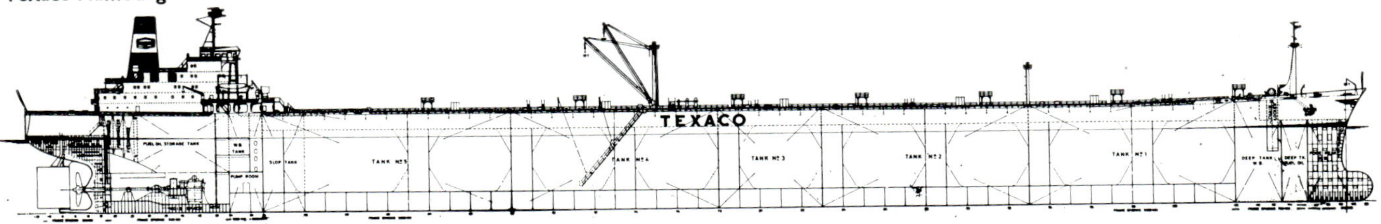

S.S. "TEXACO HAMBURG"

Preview of the most powerful tug to be built for British owners. United Towing Co. Tug, 14,000bhp, building by Robb-Caledon SB Ltd at Leith, which will be capable of towing a 300,000 tanker at 7 knots. Length 263ft, speed (light) 19 knots.

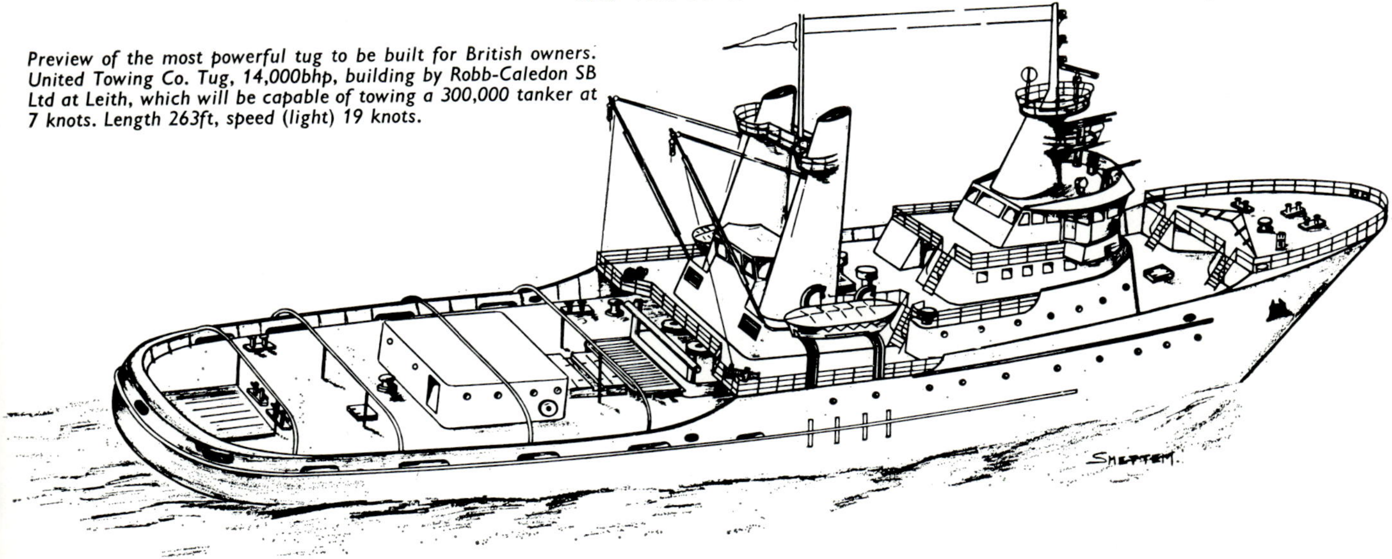

Merchant Ships Launched during 1969*

(Ships of 100 tons gross and upwards excluding wood and non-propelled craft.)

SUMMARY OF WORLD OUTPUT

At 19,315,290 tons gross, the total tonnage launched in the world during 1969 was 2,407,547 tons more than in 1968. As was then the case, no returns are available for the People's Republic of China and Russia (U.S.S.R.).

This figure is an all-time record for the fourth year in succession, with Japan continuing to lead the rest of the shipbuilding nations with another outstanding performance (9·3 million tons), representing 48·2 per cent of the world total. West Germany retains second place with 8·3 per cent with Sweden third (6·7 per cent) and Great Britain & Northern Ireland fourth with 5·4 per cent. France with 4·1 per cent regains fifth position closely followed by Norway. Next in order come Denmark, Netherlands, Spain, Italy and Yugoslavia.

With the increase in output of very large tankers, record tonnage figures are becoming almost commonplace and West Germany, France, Norway, Denmark, Spain, Yugoslavia, East Germany, Finland and Brazil each record their best individual output.

Gross tonnage launched in 1969 as compared with 1968:

	Tons	Tons
Japan	9,303,453	(+720,483)
Germany (West)	1,608,545	(+256,717)
Sweden	1,292,884	(+180,293)
Great Britain & N. Ireland ...	1,039,516	(+141,357)
France	791,193	(+300,822)
Norway	711,938	(+216,717)
Denmark	600,285	(+117,703)
Netherlands	595,661	(+292,352)
Spain	559,694	(+ 53,307)
Italy	463,529	(− 42,585)
Yugoslavia	410,116	(+120,562)
U.S.A.	399,884	(− 41,241)
Poland	364,226	(− 60,251)
Germany (East)	298,441	(+ 17,964)
Finland	227,094	(+ 54,071)
Belgium	130,635	(+ 22,269)

* Reproduced from *Lloyd's Register Annual Summary of Merchant Ships Launched during 1969.*

Some notes concerning the individual countries may be of interest.

JAPAN

Output of 9,303,453 tons is 720,483 tons more than in 1968, and is the country's tenth successive increase. It includes 20 of the 42 ships launched in the world over 100,000 tons gross.

Oil tankers total 4,516,996 tons, and bulk carriers 3,114,409 tons including 1,345,719 tons of the combined bulk/oil type.

General cargo ships total 1,314,364 tons and include 50,463 tons of specialized container ships.

Fishing craft total 73,512 tons and other important specialized ships include a lighter carrier of 36,862 tons and liquefied gas carrier tonnage totalling 48,592 tons.

Of 5,626,086 tons (60 per cent) built for export, 2,577,544 tons are for registration in Liberia, 1,045,655 tons for Great Britain & N. Ireland and 722,626 tons for Greece.

GERMANY (WEST)

West Germany retains the second position it regained last year with a record output of 1,608,545 tons which is 256,717 tons more than in 1968.

The total includes 771,756 tons of oil tankers and 211,291 tons of bulk carriers.

General cargo tonnage amounts to 508,505 tons of which 110,053 tons is specialized container ships. Also launched was a passenger ship of 16,254 tons.

Of 1,046,124 tons (65 per cent) built for export, 497,097 tons are for Great Britain & N. Ireland.

SWEDEN

Sweden's output of 1,292,884 tons is 180,293 tons more than last year and is only marginally short of 1967's record figure for this country.

Oil tankers total 936,501 tons and bulk carriers 209,669 tons, including 103,135 tons of the bulk/oil type.

Six general cargo ships were launched during the year.

Fishing craft, all carriers, totalled 48,975 tons. Also launched was a large liquefied gas carrier of 44,088 tons.

Of 1,010,217 tons (78 per cent) launched for registration in other countries, 393,149 tons are for Norway and 339,935 tons are for Liberia.

GREAT BRITAIN & NORTHERN IRELAND

Great Britain & N. Ireland's output of 1,039,516 tons is 141,357 tons more than last year.

Oil tankers total 272,186 tons, and bulk carriers 448,630 tons. General cargo tonnage amounts to 251,196 tons and includes nine ships between 10,000 and 15,000 tons.

The total for export is 384,646 tons (37 per cent).

The amount of tonnage imported (2,142,680 tons) is the highest ever recorded.

FRANCE

France's output of 791,193 tons is 300,822 tons more than in 1968 and is a record for this country.

Oil tankers total 512,843 tons, 65 per cent of the total tonnage launched.

General cargo tonnage totalled 132,200 and that of fishing craft (45,177 tons) included 47 ships for Kuwait. Other specialized ships included liquefied gas carriers totalling 67,757 tons.

Tonnage for export amounts to 172,797 tons.

NORWAY

Output of 711,938 tons is 216,717 tons more than last year and is a record for this country.

Oil tankers total 382,807 tons, and bulk carriers 225,642 tons.

Only thirteen per cent of all tonnage is for export.

The amount of tonnage imported is 1,057,762 tons.

DENMARK

Output of 600,285 tons is 117,703 tons more than last year and is a record for this country.

Oil tankers total 457,288 tons, three of which are over 100,000 tons.

Seventy per cent of the total (419,288 tons) is for export.

NETHERLANDS

Netherlands' output of 595,661 tons is 292,352 tons more than in 1968 and is the highest figure since 1959.

The total includes 471,543 tons of oil tankers, 79 per cent of the total tonnage launched.

Seventy per cent of the total is for export including 274,166 tons for Great Britain & N. Ireland.

SPAIN

In spite of its seventh successive year of record output Spain has dropped to ninth position among the world's leading shipbuilding nations. The total of 559,694 tons includes 272,994 tons of oil tankers and 149,530 tons of general cargo tonnage.

Fishing craft total 35,038 tons.

Tonnage for export amounts to 187,352 tons.

ITALY

Italy's output of 463,529 tons is its lowest for three years.

Oil tankers total 195,959 tons, and bulk carriers 117,046 tons.

Also launched were two liquefied gas carriers each of 30,445 tons.

YUGOSLAVIA

With a total of 410,116 tons, output is a record figure for this country. It includes 155,711 tons of oil tankers and 169,598 tons of bulk carriers.

The entire output is for export and includes 166,015 tons for India.

UNITED STATES OF AMERICA

Output of 399,884 tons is 41,241 tons less than in 1968.

Oil tankers total 231,698 tons and general cargo ships 125,341 tons including 56,876 tons of specialized container ships.

POLAND

Output from Poland (364,226 tons) shows a decrease for the first time since 1963.

Oil tankers total 56,812 tons and general cargo ships total 180,086 tons including twelve, each of just over 10,000 tons.

Output of fishing craft (104,712 tons) is the highest in the world and includes four fish factories, each of 13,572 tons.

Of the total 88 per cent is for export, mostly for Russia.

GERMANY (EAST)

Output of 298,441 tons is a record for this country. A continued feature is the absence of oil tankers and bulk carriers. General cargo ships total 196,078 tons and fishing craft 91,296 tons.

Ninety-two per cent of the total is for export, 201,063 tons of which is for Russia.

FINLAND

Output of 227,094 tons is a record for this country.

Oil tankers total 32,192 tons and general cargo ships 160,895 tons, including 48,854 tons of specialized container ships.

Also launched was a passenger ship of 17,500 tons.

Eighty-six per cent of the total is for export and includes 97,252 tons for Russia.

BELGIUM

Output of 130,635 tons is the highest since 1959.

General cargo ships total nine ships of 96,325 tons, all of between 9,000 and 13,000 tons.

Fifty-four per cent of the total is for export.

WORLD SUMMARY

Size and Type. The largest ships launched in the world during 1969 were:

	Tons	Launched in
*s.s. *Universe Iran*	149,623	Japan
*s.s. *Universe Korea* ...	149,623	Japan
*s.s. *Esso Cambria*	127,158	Netherlands
*s.s. *Esso Nederland* ...	127,158	Netherlands
*s.s. *Esso Scotia*	127,158	West Germany
*s.s. *Esso Northumbria* ...	126,543	United Kingdom
*s.s. *Ardshiel*	119,678	Japan
*s.s. *Ardlui*	119,678	Japan
*s.s. *Japan Marguerite* ...	117,404	Japan
*s.s. *Keiyo Maru*	116,458	Japan
*s.s. *Japan Canna*	116,457	Japan
*s.s. *Caterina M*	114,270	Italy
*s.s. *Esso Copenhagen* ...	113,760	Denmark
*s.s. *Esso Europa*	113,759	West Germany
*s.s. *Thorshammer*	113,656	Sweden
*s.s. *Alva Star*	113,532	Sweden
*s.s. *Veni*	113,532	Sweden
*s.s. *Mobil Pegasus*	112,657	Japan
*s.s. *Kaien Maru*	111,500	Japan

* Oil Tanker

Oil Tankers. Compared with 1968, the tonnage of oil tankers launched during 1969 shows an increase of 2,713,080 tons to a record figure of 9,325,810 tons. More than half of this total was made up of tankers of over 100,000 tons gross.

As a percentage of all ships launched, this represents an increase from 39·1 to 48·3 per cent. In 1967 it was 31·6 per cent.

All of the 42 ships over 100,000 tons are oil tankers.

Leading countries of build in tons gross as compared with 1968:

	Tons	Tons
Japan	4,516,996	(+544,125)
Sweden	936,501	(+545,980)
Germany (West)	771,756	(+263,553)
France	512,843	(+162,352)
Netherlands	471,543	(+315,299)
Denmark	457,288	(+100,163)
Norway	382,807	(+201,121)

Bulk Carriers. Output of bulk carrier tonnage has fallen by 815,684 tons from 5,638,733 tons last year to 4,823,049 tons which represents 25·0 per cent of the total launched.

Included in this total is 1,520,854 tons of the combined bulk/oil type.

Leading countries of build in tons gross as compared with 1968:

	Tons	Tons
Japan	3,114,409	(− 51,894)
Great Britain & N. Ireland ...	448,630	(−103,215)
Norway	225,642	(+ 40,977)
Germany (West)	211,291	(− 66,300)
Sweden	209,669	(−399,393)

General Cargo. Output of general cargo ships in 1969 was 3,599,613 tons which is 453,375 tons more than in 1968 and represents 18·6 per cent of the total launched. One hundred and four ships of between 10,000 and 15,000 tons were launched as compared with 95 in 1968. Thirteen ships were between 15,000 and 20,000 tons and six were between 20,000 and 27,000 tons.

Leading countries of build in tons gross compared with 1968:

	Tons	Tons
Japan	1,314,364	(+191,232)
Germany (West)	508,505	(+ 93,170)
Great Britain & N. Ireland ...	251,196	(+ 69,843)
Germany (East)	196,078	(+ 12,836)
Poland	180,086	(+ 22,191)

General cargo output includes 320,827 tons of specialized container ships of which 110,053 tons was launched in West Germany.

For the purpose of these returns, figures shown of general cargo ships are for ships of 2,000 tons gross and over.

Fishing. Output of fishing craft of all types has fallen from 526,878 tons in 1968 to 519,005 tons in 1969 and includes eight fish factories totalling 76,349 tons.

Leading countries of build in tons gross as compared with 1968:

	Tons	Tons
Poland	104,712	(− 21,851)
Germany (East)	91,296	(+ 2,208)
Japan	73,512	(− 26,248)

Registration. Tonnage intended for registration elsewhere than in country of build amounts to 10,750,857 tons, which is 55·7 per cent of the total output. Figures for 1968 were 9,562,290 tons (56·6 per cent).

The following analysis shows which countries contributed most to export, and lists the net increase to existing fleets:

	('000 tons gross)			
	Launched in country	—Export	+Import	Net increase
Japan	9,303	5,626	—	3,677
Liberia	—	—	3,235	3,235
Great Britain & N. Ireland ...	1,040	385	2,143	2,798
Norway	712	97	1,058	1,673
Greece	49	37	859	872
Russia (U.S.S.R.)	—	—	752	752
Germany (West)	1,609	1,046	150	712
France	791	173	24	643
Italy	464	35	—	429
Panama	—	—	409	409
U.S.A.	400	5	2	397
Spain	560	187	—	372
Brazil	105	—	260	365
Sweden	1,293	1,010	79	362
Netherlands	596	416	136	316
Denmark	600	419	122	303
Finland	227	196	220	251
Kuwait	—	—	233	233
India	24	—	188	212

TO CLASS WITH LLOYD'S REGISTER

Of the steamships and motorships launched in the world during the year 5,534,560 tons (28·7 per cent) are to be classed with Lloyd's Register.

Of this total 801,247 tons were from yards in Great Britain and Northern Ireland and represent 77·1 per cent of tonnage launched there.